of

;

ıP

In The Frame

Memory in Society
1910–2010

Dai Smith

Parthian
The Old Surgery
Napier Street
Cardigan
SA43 1ED

www.parthianbooks.co.uk

First published in 2010
Reprinted in 2011
© Dai Smith 2010
All Rights Reserved

ISBN 978-1-906998-22-6

Editor: Penny Thomas

Cover design by Marc Jennings
Typeset by books@lloydrobson.com
Printed and bound by Dinefwr Press, Llandybïe, Wales
Cover photo: Striking miners waiting to go into a mass
meeting at the Empire Theatre, Tonypandy, Wednesday 2
November, 1910. © National Museum of Wales.

The publisher acknowledges the financial support of the
Welsh Books Council.

British Library Cataloguing in Publication Data

A cataloguing record for this book is available from the
British Library

Contents

'*...our fate [in 1946], for better or worse, is political. It is therefore not a happy fate, even if it has an heroic sound... and the only possibility of enduring it is to force into our own definition of politics every human activity and every subtlety of every human activity... unless we insist that politics is imagination and mind, we will learn that imagination and mind are politics, and of a kind that we will not like.*'

Lionel Trilling in *The Liberal Imagination* (1951)

Memory in Society

This book is an alternative history of the past century in Wales. It is not counter-factual history, nor revisionist history, just alternative. The viewpoint I use to recapture some of this unfolded history – almost two-thirds of which I have now lived through – is resolutely my own, and so it is necessarily askance, central, tangential, even close-up-and-personal, because squinting myopically can sometimes bring up the telling detail which is lost in a panoramic view. My intention is by no means to dismiss the educational utility of the summary narratives in catch-all textbook surveys. They are invaluable as accounting tools, bottom-line summations of the monographs that categorise and analyse in the discourse of academia. And both types are innately superior to the vapours of sentimental gush which still strive to overcome cool heads in decidedly un-cool Cymru. So alternative here means extra, additional, and, hopefully, distinctive. In any case its concentration on details observed and things felt as much as experienced is a plea against the imposed homogenising of lives that follows on from any flattening of active memory, public and private, in society. Memory is the citizen's defence against the tyranny of what the writer John Berger once called the fiction of a 'perpetual present'. Memory informs us of our Future.

The alternative perspective which follows will take the reader into a territory – a mythical and veritable Dai Country – in which my own life-of-the-mind was touched upon and formed by the writers and painters, boxers and historians, friends and relatives, critics and photographers, rioters and correspondents, who are to be variously encountered in these pages. If it is a mosaic I hope it will also be seen, at its end, as one with more than a random pattern. If it has autobiographical overtones, its undertone is that of a collective biography. My true subject, objectively drawn I would contend, is consciousness, and the actions which consciousness caused the people of this Welsh world to take. That consciousness might have been the decision, not the impulse, to wreck the commercial life of Tonypandy in 1910 or the instinctive need to chase after world boxing championships across the Atlantic. It is a consciousness of experience which was articulated in histories, novels, letters and conversations. It can be plumbed in the significant forms of painting and the stunning imagery of photographic arts. It is there in gestures and in acting, in sport and in jokes, and in the understated cultural value system of the working-class triumph that was South Wales at its collective peak and moral best. That is my view anyway, and the book is my argument for its validity, made by showing rather than telling.

The individual chapters line up with chronological starting points, but they range, disconcertingly I hope, widely to-and-fro across the passing memory-tides of the past one hundred years. There is, however, a constant which has made this book a hybrid in form and in style, a cultural history which is also a misplaced memoir whereby, along with the people, places and events I conjure up, I have put myself firmly in the frame. Perhaps this came about as a happenstance of age. The accumulated years enforce a recognition that the writer has accrued acquaintance with experience that is not, even for the dispassionate craft of an historian, quite separate any more from those acts of witness and testimony which elsewhere, once turned cold, serve others as the gravitas of historical evidence. Yet if this then serves as a type of confessional vade mecum it is one (mostly) drained of the colour of private life since I have only centred on personal involvement where it directly impinged on the professional work I have undertaken for more than forty years – as historian, as academic, as broadcaster, as writer.

Undertaking: a word with heavyweight connotations, all too akin to an undertaker's work of tidying up. But you don't go to funerals, whether real or conceptual, by chance. Bodies and societies both hook you for life, and disappear. Looking back, I can cough up, as a pro, that not only am I in the frame with the pictures of the disappeared, I have been, as much as them, well and truly 'framed'. The question is: by whom? by what? and why? What follows is, I hope, a partial answer to those questions since this book darts in, around and out of the native places, people and matters which mark out any life, but it also proposes a solution to a larger mystery, one that is still too often dismissed as the inflated braggadocio of South Wales' history. I submit, once again, that it is, on the contrary, plain, not luxuriant, unvarnished, not embellished, Fact. Or, as I prefer to put it, with Fact in mind, it is the created Fiction of South Wales.

This is a book of epiphanies then. They remain, even amongst the contemporary mish-mash of newly built Cardiff Bay where our crystalline Senedd has found such an unlikely site. On windy street corners Bute Street, the shrivelled jugular vein of Imperial South Wales, is still sectioned by the pillared-and-porticoed bulk of its late Victorian grandeur. The mercantile houses and banks of the global coal trade can still be seen. That unashamed carbon footprint of the 1885 Coal Exchange in Mount Stuart Square, broad-shouldering the timid out of its Capitalist stride, still commands awe. And you can still look up, here and there, and sense Wall Street on the Taff and sniff on the wind the Welsh Chicago which Cardiff was christened in 1905. Evidence then, albeit brief and, after 1918, fleeting. Here is a small section of the Wales Trade Directory for 1922:

Consuls

Argentine Republic, E. De Loqui, 75 St Mary Street
Belgium and Netherlands, Edward L. Downing, 53 Bute Street
Bolivia, John Bovey, 32 Mountstuart Square
Brazil, D. O. Alves, 53 Bute Street
Chile, J. Lorrain, 116 Bute Street
Colombia and Venezuela, A. Aldana, St Mary Street
Denmark, A. Thomas, 9 Mountstuart Square

Dominican Republic, Will Jones, 1 Dock Chambers, Bute Street
Ecuador, A. Aldana, St Mary Street
France, R. Monnet, 4 Dock Chambers, Bute Street
Greece, N. Stephenatos, Pierhead Chambers, Bute Street
Italy, V. A. Tattara, 112 Bute Street
Norway, E. Dahl, Post Office Chambers, Bute Street
Russia, P. Gorianow, Consulate Chambers, 53 Bute Street
Spain, Rafael Triana, 10 Custom House Street
Sweden, A. A. Dooley, Merchants' Exchange, Bute Street
United States of America, L. A. Lathorp, Bute Crescent
Uruguay, G. E. Petty, 106 Bute Street

If there was a presiding Deity over all this it might have been a crossed-fingers type of God, like Oneiros the Ancient Greek God of Dreams, whose name echoes all too clearly our own dreamy doer: Aneurin. Dreams and deeds should not be as incompatible as some latter-day saints in the Church of Pragmatism would have us believe. Inter-war Wales scared its experience and its image on subsequent generations but, as I argued in *Aneurin Bevan and the World of South Wales* in 1994, the experiencing generation had a previous touchstone to its identity – one that was aspirational, dynamic, even futuristic. And, of course, lost.

The most remarkable summation of the Lost World of South Wales' El Dorado, and, crucially, of how to capture the fiction-in-fact, was written under another god-like pseudonym – Mulciber – in 1939. When I first read it, in Gwyn Jones' *Welsh Review* at the time I was beginning my own historical research into South Wales, it stopped me dead for a while, and it has haunted me ever since. The author was probably the magazine's editor, the scholar and novelist, the Anglo-Welsh Colossus himself and, more or less, the inventor of the self-same term: Professor Gwyn Jones, born in Blackwood in 1907, so in 1939 just into his prime years. The name chosen by the anonymous critic, Mulciber, is an alternate for Vulcan, god of fire and metalworking, and, maybe more to this point, a fallen angel in Milton's *Paradise Lost* who was architect of a Demon City. Mulciber, at the fag-end of the ashen, interwar years and on the eve of the Second World War which would usher in a new Old South Wales, here contemplated the need for a work of fiction that could be both real, or true to specifics, and universal, or essential, in its reach outwards:

How? you may ask. In part, by choice of subject. We must get away from the family – the unit so far. More accurately, though we keep the family, we must extend our circle of interest. There are the workers in our chosen industry, there are the employers, there are the links between them, and there are the womenfolk dependent upon them. There are the tradesmen who supply them, the shareholders living on their backs, the teachers and preachers. We must write about their fun, their follies, their vices, their hobbies, as well as their jobs. The complete picture. And this not for a couple of years. One such subject is the history of the South Wales coalfield. Now, when this is handled as an epic (and it is an epic, second to none!) we must start with the coming of the Iron masters, the blasting of the valleys, the eruption of townships like wens on the green hills, the pollution of the rivers; then comes the change to Steel, and then to Coal, with its Barons squeezing the land like an orange, its importations of labour; its industrial and political vicissitudes – lock-outs, strikes, the truck-system, the soldiers called in, the unions, agitations, violence, treachery, victories and defeats. The national question, too – the change of culture, the strangling of a language, the coming of a mongrel race, the evolution of Shoni. And we must have the railways and canals, the great export trades that sent the ships of the world on Welsh coal to the farthest corners of the earth... We must have the strength of nonconformity, the power of the pub, the birth of a University, the growth of a city on the flat palm into which the valley-fingers run. This is a subject... it presents colossal difficulties: the striking of a balance between the individual and society, between society and industry.... The treatment obviously must be realistic, even naturalistic, but it must be humane. There must be documentation, both by way of naked statement, and as a basis for statement. There will be no room for inessentials – human activities must be seen in perspective. There must be action. There must be tremendous vitality and strength to sustain such a work... there must be trial and error. The pioneers may do little more than show what is possible, and better men will drive them to oblivion. The length of the novel at first sound is alarming. The epic of the South Wales coalfield might well need a quarter of a million words. It must be one book, not a trilogy, though this particular novel might well be in three sections: iron, steel, coal... an epic scope, a magnitude of conception and treatment so far unattempted.... Books like this must be written in no partisan spirit. The communist bludgeon for Lib-Lab heads won't serve here, and the Lib-Lab hood of wool for Communists will be equally out of place.... There must be the consciousness of progress, the amelioration of conditions above and underground... the world's debt to the old liberalism, to radicalism, to the newer creeds. The book must be its own lesson. It must overcome the difficulties of the proletarian novel in general as well as the specialised difficulties of the industrial epic. Who has not deplored these: clogging detail, clumsy writing, the awkward progression of narrative, typification of characters, rigidity of outlook?

Candidates to that point – from Jack Jones' *Black Parade* of 1935 to Gwyn Jones' own *Times Like These* in 1936, via Rhys Davies' *Jubilee Blues* (1937), on to Lewis Jones' epics *Cwmardy* (1937) and *We Live* (1939), were clearly not considered the answer, any more to be sure than Richard Llewellyn's seductive and egregious *How Green Was My Valley* published in the same month as Mulciber's critique, October 1939. Nor could I quite see, some three decades later, the fiction which might have gone on to address Mulciber's purpose. I now think I was probably looking in the wrong place. The argument has been too much about genre, about style, about fictional meanings and theoretical disquisitions, when the stuff itself was its own expression. By which I mean that awareness of the structure of feelings with which the inhabitants or citizens of South Wales were, in varying degrees, imbued. The proper question to be put was not about how the detail of their lives could be re-presented but how the sense of material disappearance, shiveringly there decade by decade from the 1920s on, could be articulated as an existing cultural consciousness which, in turn, also shaped material existence. They had experienced the fluidity of great social potential embedded in inchoate economic energy and they sought cultural channels for it thereafter.

Not entirely, of course. But sufficiently so for successive generations to find themselves living in a South Wales that was always conjugating its meaning in the past tense. Sometimes, as for Gwyn Thomas who got the joke and said so, the only privilege accorded those conscious of their predicament was, as the rebel leader Jeremy Longridge affirms in Gwyn's 1949 novel *All Things Betray Thee*, in 'adjusting the key of the scream we utter'. Elsewhere, in the same novel, written at the apex of South Wales' significance as an aspirational community, he suggests that to see, to wonder and to protest is enough. The look is a backward one.

Patently he assumed a future society as intellectually replete with ambition as it would be materially enriched. He would be disappointed, and say so. No less loudly than the generation represented by Ron Berry and Alun Richards, though for them the obverse of the society they hated to see depicted in a sentimental fashion was the sense of more grounded, yet fractured, lives and communities, rather than the vision beyond the present for which Gwyn Thomas yearned. The tango between improbable Future and unrepeatable Past was a step sequence all our better fiction writers essayed. There is now a deep-felt present desire to stop the dance, to go solo, to break the ties. Yet even the breakdance routines of our latest fictional voices cannot quite leave the reflected audience behind. The honest dedication of a writer intent on the contemporary moment, like Rachel Trezise, can shun the demanding ghosts shut in the shadows by the neon light of her prose, but their absence is still a haunting wail in the surviving lives of her socially truncated characters.

Culture is indeed how we change, not just who we once were. But it is also, if it is to peer into every revealing corner, about being responsive to all the things that shape memory in society. History is as inescapable as it is strictly irretrievable. It only becomes a deadweight on creativity in the here-and-now when it is dressed up in the garb of maudlin nostalgia or stripped bare of all its once-sentient possibilities. Too much of our recent 'History for the Public' in Wales has avoided the responsibility of meaning in favour of the indulgence of empathy. On television especially, in recent years, our actual past has been made over into a mortician's simulacrum of life in which 'ordinary' housemates play at 'what it was really like' in a grotesque 'celebrity' displacement where exit doors are always conveniently available into a 'real' present. Too much of the recent historiography emerging from the laboratories of academe has willingly exchanged the dangerous advantages of vivisection for the cold analysis of dissection. For if it is indeed the case that much of the 'new' history being written about South Wales in the 1970s and 1980s was too close to the contemporary society in which it was composed to be completely free of the charges of special pleading, ideological commitment and personal passion, it is unfortunate that the theoretical disquisition and number-crunching of the past decade or so has yielded up a revisionist historiography so bloodless that its only connection to our current society is that of a hospital drip to a terminal corpse.

We are coming, then, to the central human issue of values. Can they be transmitted from generation to generation when so much of their innate validity for individuals is circumscribed by the condition of their birth within particular societies? For a classic 'collective' society such as the World of South Wales once was, the question is a transcendent one. It is what leads to the mangled debate about its perpetual re-invention as a socially attached, and therefore progressive, force which the Labour Party, aka Movement-as-was, tries to have with itself as it twitches on the mortuary slab reserved for the pre-deceased. It is the retrospective DNA of the cart-before-the-horse variety, which allows us to argue, in the face of a great deal of evidence, that a nation's solemn attempt to preserve and disseminate its heritage is of paramount interest to a future creativity. Yet without untrammelled creativity there is not, will not be, and never has been anything worth inheriting. It is a lingering reference back to that dark philosophy we once imbibed with our post-war condensed milk to the burping effect that economies and markets, global or otherwise, are to be organised for the public weal rather more than for private squealers. And the list could, of course, go on to embrace the built environment, educational provision, familial and class privileges, whether by wealth or location, identity that is not stamped out on some identikit template for nationality, and the truly pathetic marketing ploys for Team Wales, Brand Wales and, worse, Wales plc. These are the brain-dead mantras of institutional gurus who have convinced themselves that for commercial purposes a fragmented society can be repackaged and sold to their punters as if it is the brand which makes a nation, rather than the nation which has created the makings of whatever 'brands' they are being, as with professional and regional rugby in our national game, made to suffer. Consider the Millennium Stadium full of families, from grandparents to children, arrayed in the supportive red of their national team and that team playing in the banana yellow jerseys designed for a brand of golden beer. Everything has a price until all is devalued.

Societies of purpose, as ours once decidedly was, are not reducible to markets and profit margins. Social values, widely shared and deeply understood, are the markers of coherent and viable societies in the past, and surely will be so into any desirable future. It is not then nostalgic or historical wish-fulfilment to work, culturally and socially across all our institutions, to retrieve and take forward the values, not the actual circumstances, of what was worthwhile in past lives that particularly speak to us, connect with us, represent us still in their own finished individual lives. Quite dramatically, almost sensationally until both the parallel similarities and differences hit home, the Canadian moral philosopher Charles Taylor, reviewing a subtle ethnographical exploration of the all-but-vanished Crow nation in nineteenth-century America, took an obliquely sympathetic glance at our own plight. He compared the lost system of tribal values by which the Crow lived with the entrenched, stubborn and equally lost communal values of the twentieth-century coal-mining society of South Wales. We had, it seemed, passed into history, or, worse, out of it in our irrelevance to the new century in which we are so evidently adrift. This was not just an anthropological claim, it was an ethical lament made all the more poignant for holding together in one insight vanquished Crow Indians and a vanished South Wales:

> The development of the modern capitalist economy has long been imposing less drastic versions of this kind of culture death on mining villages in Wales and West Virginia... the emergence of a world civilisation, highly unified economically, politically and in communications, has exacted, and will go on exacting, a tremendous human cost in the death or near death of cultures. And this will be made worse because those who dominate modern civilisation have trouble grasping what the costs involve... but human beings can find the resources to come back from a virtual death and invent a new way of life in some creative continuity with the one that has been condemned....
>
> The hope is 'radical' because it is virtually impossible to say beforehand what the shape of this new kind of life will be. This has to emerge in specific new forms, drawing on the particular cultural resources of each society.

The book Taylor reviewed was Jonathan Lear's *Radical*

Hope: Ethics in the Face of Cultural Devastation, a work that centres not on the actual, and almost complete, disappearance of the Crows in the wake of the wars of aggression amounting to genocide against Native Americans in the late nineteenth century, but on the courage required, and evinced, by Plenty Coups and other Crow chiefs who decided to adapt rather than, as with their contemporary the Sioux Oglala warrior Crazy Horse, to die heroically, and leave no trace. The key is an adaptation that is not supine and imitative, but active and creative. When a meaningful way of life, or history, is exhausted, so that in Plenty Coups' words, 'After this, nothing happened', then, in Lear's words:

> What would be required... would be a new Crow poet: one who could take up the Crow past and – rather than use it for nostalgic or ersatz mimesis – project it into vibrant new ways for the Crow to live and be [and]... 'poet' [means] the broadest sense of a creative maker of meaningful space. The possibility for such a poet is precisely the possibility for the creation of a new field of possibilities. No one is in a position to rule out that possibility.
>
> ...Plenty Coups' gesture [of committing his life story to print through telling it to a white American friend]... witnessing the death of the Crow... [is]... in order to clear the ground for a rebirth. For if the death is not acknowledged there will most likely be all sorts of empty ways of going on 'as a Crow'. Only if one acknowledges that there is no longer a genuine way of going on *like that* might there arise new genuine ways of going on *like that*.

...[When] The entire culture is in the process of being forgotten... the only hope is to write it down in the hope that a future generation may bring 'it' back to life.

Plenty Coups was a witness to the collapse of the Crows' future: he witnessed a time [after the buffalo] in which 'nothing happened'. Such a witness manifests a new and intensified form of Crow subjectivity: he takes on the responsibility of declaring whether the ideals around which he has shaped his life are any longer viable. That is, he is willing to speak for the health and viability of the old ways of constituting oneself as a subject. But this can be done in the hope of clearing the ground for the creation of new forms of Crow subjectivity. There is reason to think that Plenty Coups told his story to preserve it; and he did so in the hope of a future in which things – Crow things – might start to happen again.

The intentional paradox of this present book, then, by its contemporary delving into the issues, struggles and expressions of a society decidedly past, is that only in this confrontational way can a future of value be derived from the world to which many of us belong by choice and all of us belong by an inescapable compound of geography, history and culture. If we act on this as well as merely acknowledging it then, in dream and in deed, things, our things, 'might start to happen again'.

In The Frame

Frame

Memory in Society
1910–2010

No Through Route

I had seen the photograph many times over the years. It always astonished me. It is a witness before the event. And the event would be one of the most significant upheavals in the social history of Wales, leaving a wake of change. The photographer was Levi Ladd from Ladd's of Tonypandy, mid-Rhondda. He must have elevated himself and his tripod to the right of this subject, looking across the main road, Dunraven Street, at the mouth of the hill that switchbacked up from the valley bottom. The hill cuts its undulating line across the horizontal streets: Eleanor, Primrose, Kenry and topmost Ely, before the railway line – built to take coal from the Cambrian Combine pits to Barry Docks – marked the start of the mountain which led over moorland to Gilfach Goch. To the right of the massed men, barely in shot, is the Cross Keys public house to which many of them will, no doubt, shortly go. On their left is the side entrance, for musicians and artistes, of the Empire Theatre of Varieties, a red-brick palace of entertainment – for drama as well as music hall – built in late 1909 for this synthetic township and its divergent population. It is the first week of November, 1910.

The men, and it is only men we see, arc dai-capped and mufflered against a damp cold, and they are mostly young; bowler hats were the headgear of choice for the old-fashioned. There were almost twelve thousand men employed by the Cambrian Combine in the immediate vicinity of Tonypandy, and they had all come out on strike from 1 November in solidarity with the workmen of the Ely pit in the Naval Colliery who had already been locked out in a dispute over wages and working conditions for two months. They had, on this day, all just drawn the last pay they would receive for almost a full year. Now, on Wednesday 2 November, they will shortly resolve not to allow any men or officials to do any work at the collieries or even enter the colliery yards. At the start of the following week they will assemble for a mass meeting in the Athletic Ground, or Track, at the top of the hill below Gelli farm and parallel with Ely Street, where they will listen in silence both to their own conciliatory leaders and to the chiding Stipendiary Magistrate, Daniel Lleufer Thomas, who will inform them that Winston Churchill, the Liberal Home Secretary, had halted the movement of troops dispatched to the strike area but had authorised the coming of a force of 170 mounted police and 200 Metropolitan police on foot to quell, by their active presence, any intimidation, by violence, of any colliery officials, as well as any direct threat to colliery property at the scattered pits of the Combine.

What we see in the photograph is the body of men visible up to the first of the streets which slash across the

2

terraced ascent to the Athletic Ground. An Edwardian army of immigrant labour, largely pulled into the Rhondda in the decade that has just reached its climax in 1910, is cascading down the hill to face Levi Ladd's camera, the first rows halting for the picture to be taken, with thousands upon thousands backing up behind them. Faces at the rear strain upwards to catch the focusing lens of the camera. Behind them the further white blobs grow indistinct in Ladd's glass plate. The rims of caps are endless black discs above the typically pallid faces of the colliers. The bulky, time-delaying photographic process has stopped the human flood for an instant, for a flash. When this communal mug-shot is completed for the archive the unsmiling faces will crack open again and the tumult of noise, a rumbling cacophony of Welsh and English, will fill the vacuum of silence. Within the week this human tsunami will have fought and defeated the local constabulary, quickly besieged and helpless to intervene, positioned on duty in the Glamorgan Colliery in Llwynypia, to the north of Tonypandy. They will then have systematically wrecked the shops and commercial life of mid-Rhondda. They, or most of them, will become Tonypandy rioters and not only the political but soon the social and cultural life of twentieth-century Wales will be altered by their decisive hand. The moment is that momentous.

Any historian of these events, as I became in the late 1970s, would move an eye over the perpetrators, more in mutual acknowledgement of being in the frame together, than in a quest for deeper clues. But I had looked, from time to time, with different, personal intent. My grandfather, himself an immigrant from the slate

3

quarries of Blaenau Ffestiniog in 1908, was living in lodgings in Williamstown, above Penygraig to the south of Tonypandy. He was then working at the coalface in the Naval Colliery. He would be on strike all through that seismic year 1910-11. He often talked to me about it, or rather at me, a bored child, listening at his fireside. He died in 1965. Much later, when I saw this photograph, I wondered if he was a part of the crowd and scanned the grainy newspaper reproductions in vain. He had been a gentle and noticeably cultured man, an early stalwart of Eglwys Dewi Sant, the Welsh-language Anglican church with a predominantly North Walian congregation, just across the street from the men in the photograph. Perhaps he had gone home in despair at this turn of fortune in the new El Dorado to which he had brought his Ffestiniog sweetheart of Welsh and Basque antecedence, Maria Roberts. There were no children in the marriage yet; perhaps he thought this collective endeavour, its rights and its dangers, was not for him. Yet he did not, and would not, as numbers of others soon did, 'leave the district' in the dismissive newspaper phrase of the day.

When, in 2008, the *Welsh Encyclopaedia*, factual Bible for the twenty-first century's Welsh cultural needs, finally dropped its bulky testament onto my desk, I was not surprised to see the picture used once more to illustrate the Tonypandy disturbances that gave my hometown the contemporary sobriquet of Tonypandemonium and its legendary status in our more sober lives. But I was soon startled by it again. This time the photograph was reproduced in a sharp print with its size reduction on the page actually clarifying features. Still, there were thousands of faces, and Dai Owen would only have been

21, years away from the man in his sixties whom I first remember. Yet the detective-historian's typical doggedness in the quest for misplaced evidence made me stop and examine each face more slowly, line by line, moving on from the impossible to the might have beens that were not until, half hidden in the squash, his dark cap pulled down over his forehead, were the unmistakeable hooded eyes and slashed upper lip of my grandfather. I stared for a long time. Not to be sure, for I was that immediately, but because he looked so much older than his years and as if all that was to follow was already upon him. After all, he was about to intervene in History.

*

The memories that precede us define us. The stories around us confine us. Exits can be hard won. Entrances are never unattended. Mine came on a snowy winter night. A caped policeman hammered on the brass knocker on the front door of our mid-terrace, bay-fronted house in Ely Street. There were no telephones in any house in the street then so the hospital in Llwynypia had phoned the police station in Dunraven Street, a very steep hill and a ten-minute upward trudge away. The war had not yet ended and the constable must have grumbled or cursed his way through the pitch-black night and the snow flurries now blowing hard into his face. The snow was sweeping down on the ranks of serried streets from the mountain clumped above our topmost terrace. He would have stamped the snow off his boots in our porch, which was set a few steps above the street and our tiny gesture of a garden. Perhaps his torch picked out the typical brown and green ceramic panels – ours were of tweed-suited fishermen, gents clearly, angling at a river bank – before finding our number, 59.

My grandfather, Dafydd Humphrey Owen, aged 56 and working at this time as a fireman in the Cambrian colliery itself, across the tip and up the cwm in flanking Clydach Vale, opened the door and spoke to the policeman. It was two in the morning of 11 February. He hurried to call my father, aged 31 and invalided out of the army with a collapsed lung that never fully recovered, to tell him that I had been born and that his wife, my mother, was haemorrhaging. There was no hope she would live. He must go at once.

The house is all awake now. My grandmother, Maria, or MamMam, bedridden in the bay-windowed front room with the cancer that will kill her before I can remember her, begins to weep. She is held close by my mother's sister, Morfydd Esther, who turns to send my five-year-old cousin, Robin Owen, back upstairs to their eiderdown-covered bed in the icy back room where the washstand holds a pink-and-white china pitcher and bowl for washing and a framed photograph of his Royal Marine father, Bill. My own English father, Burt Smith, dresses and stumbles out into the muffled street, advice and urging in muttered Welsh and enunciated English swirling unheeded around him. His walking stick is no use to him in this weather, he runs and falls and runs and slips and rests and runs up the street, over waste ground, down hills, to the main road and three miles up the snow-filling valley to the wood-framed cottage hospital. Or so I was often told. My mother, Enid Wyn, surprised everyone by living. In retrospect I would be singled out by the ambient circumstances of my birth for life. By the place, Tonypandy, and maybe even more so by the year, 1945.

South Wales, more widely even than its throbbing central vein, the Rhondda, was a place of pregnant promise in the mid-1940s; of promises long made and, it seemed, promises soon to be kept. There is no overstating this. It was not only the end of the war in Europe which would be celebrated in March; in July came the astounding election victory which brought in a majority Labour Government for the first time. The reforms now envisaged were root-and-branch and were intended to end, or so it was hoped, any lingering backward glances at a burdensome past that, as late as 1939, seemed almost insupportable in its referential dead weight of milestone dates.

1910: the year-long fuse of the Cambrian Combine Strike with its attached and indistinguishable firework of riot which made the names of Churchill and Tonypandy forever synonymous, and, more importantly, presaged the minimum wage.

1926: another year-long travail and the definitive defeat of the post-war miners' army which had fought nationwide campaigns to secure economic and social justice, and the nationalisation of the coal mines, dangled and removed by government in 1919 and 1921. Aneurin Bevan would refer to the General Strike and lock-out of 1926 as a re-run film spooling to an end he had already experienced for real.

The 1930s: a decade in which much of Bevan's acute sense of featuring helplessly in someone else's filmed scenario seemed to affect a whole population condemned to see their own jerky, documented and grimed images made available on screen for the use of others in newsreels and romance.

1945: for South Wales this was a salvation year that was, more than anything, replete in its own moment. It was now a geographical locus that held on to an entrancing cultural vibrancy which had proved to be almost fatally gripping despite the actual poverty and migration which had accompanied it.

All that is why, intemperately kicking down the worthy chronological signposts, the schoolteacher poet Idris Davies, then resident in the Rhondda, wrote, in 1945 'A Carol for the Coalfield'. It is a hymn which fastidiously measures or weighs a contemporary mood he did not entirely trust but, nonetheless, weary of back-lit projections and the exhortation to Forward Marches, ends with a defiantly humane reminder to live in the here and the now: a frisson or sentiment that is necessarily more private than public.

A Carol for the Coalfield

From the moors of Blaen Rhymni down to the leaning wall
Of Caerphilly Castle you shall hear the same accents
Of sorrow and mirth and pride, and a vague belief
That the future shall be greater than the past.

The man in the Rhondda Valley and the man in Abertillery
Have shared the same years, the same days of hope and desolation,
And in Ogmore Vale and in Ammanford both old and young dream
That the future shall be greater than the past.

On the ragged hills and by the shallow polluted rivers,
The pious young man and the old rascal of many sins,
The idealists and the waster, all sometimes believe and say
That the future shall be greater than the past.

Mothers praying for sons away in the wars, and mothers waiting
On doorsteps and by firesides for men coming home from the pits,
And the old folk bent and scarred with years of toil, all some-
                                                    times hope
That the future shall be greater than the past.

Last night the moon was full above the slag heaps and the grave-
                                                    yards
And the towns among the hills, and a man arose from his dream
And cried out: Let this day be sufficient, and worthy of my people
And let the night winds go on wailing of the future and the past.

This was not an imperative which the coalfield was slow in obeying. For a decade and more, legendary, almost mythical South Wales was as quick to slough off its valley vestments as the population had once been eager to trans-migrate to Slough. These particular Welsh voices and faces were never again so audible and visible beyond Chepstow. In the 1940s, South Wales was as much a cultural driver of the palpable unities of British social history as, in the 1990s, Wales would signify – if less dramatically than Scotland – an end to the ease of such assumptions. Yet from 1945 the stuttering narrative of the history of working-class Wales suddenly found, in political and cultural terms, a claim on England that led to a burst of forceful pressing, and a connected eloquence for its case.

Those shape-shifting Labour governments from 1945

to 1951 had, in their ministerial ranks from the Cabinet down, six former officials of the South Wales Miners' Federation, including a former President and Vice-President of that influential union. In James Griffiths at Industrial Insurance and then as Colonial Secretary and, of course, in Aneurin Bevan at Health and then Housing, we see figures, and let there be no mistaken academic hesitation here, intent on transforming British society without heed or let. By 1951 the intention had certainly penetrated the radar screens of those who thought it malign and Bevan a 'disreputable demagogue'.

The historian Hugh Trevor-Roper, Oxford don of exquisite literary sensibility and a matching snobbish toadiness, wrote to the art critic, his friend Bernard Berenson, in Italy, four days after Bevan had resigned from the Cabinet in April 1951, to rejoice that Bevan was now cast into outer darkness, or, at the least, back to Wales 'where may he long remain, preaching non-conformity to the barbarian inhabitants'.

Bevan in particular was seen to be imbued not only with the determination to establish security against future deprivation, as a 1930s mantra of reformist Labour would have it, but also with the determination to see a participatory democracy, as vividly imagined well before 1926 in that vital pre-Depression Wales, made into an expansive cultural process beyond the vagaries of any electoral cycle. This was the insupportable arrogance of the Welshman. It was why it was Nye Bevan that Richard Jenkins (Burton), indissolubly wedded to Pontrhydyfen in spirit wherever his talent took him in body, wished to portray as an emblem of those South Wales miners whom the actor forever acknowledged as the 'finest men' he had

10

known. The resonance was all too apparent, and for many in 1950s Britain it was unwelcome dissonance.

In 1955 Woodrow Wyatt, then a flamboyant Labour MP and tabloid newspaper columnist, effortlessly made the linkage he, and many others, saw not as a garland of honour but as a choking chain of infamy when he wrote 'Bevanism must be relegated to the past, together with Tonypandy and the nineteen-thirties'. Well, we in Tonypandy were quite happy to relinquish the decade but we rather cherished the other implications behind our notorious place name. And if it was only in recalling the power of those names at that time that we could marry the rhetoric of argument and counter-argument to the residuum of evidence, then it would be sufficient to interleave the idealism behind a socialist Britain with a molten Welsh core. But there is, of course, more.

Richard Burton personified a bravura compound of bruised masculinity and touchy sensibility in a manner that invigorated a fey and somewhat arch post-war British theatre. His rapid, and essentially irreversible, slide to the more dangerously tawdry craft of the cinema was quite predictable. His South Wales was by now well accustomed to seeing itself imaged on the screen, in earnest documentary and sympathetic news montage, and imagined in photo plays constructed to warm hearts and drill minds: all Kitchen and Kitsch, no Intellect and Institutes. To watch Irish-American John Ford's sieve and filter of the coalfield's history in his 1941 Welsh-Hollywood Frontier drama, *How Green Was My Valley*, in, say, Aberdare's plush new cinema, The Rex, opened in 1939, was to undergo a cultural trepanning through the bore-hole of cinematic lobotomy. The process would have been literally mind-blowing if absorbed as straight as Llewelleyn's equally distorted novel of 1939 had been elsewhere. Audiences in places like The Rex had long been inoculated against such surrealism by the hypereality of their own experiences. Perhaps in an area suffused with picture palaces, flea-pits and am dram halls for more than forty years before the Second World War, this is not entirely unexpected in the performance society that was South Wales then.

It was a pullulating world, village by village and township to township, still rocked by the fervour of a gymanfa ganu, by singing festivals both sacred and secular, musical communion ranging from oratorio to music hall, from eisteddfodau to musicals, from street carnival to annual jamboree to brass bands and operetta. A larger stage constantly beckoned. The Welsh National Opera coalesced its lesser ambitions in 1949 to seek a more resonant articulation of its then quasi-professional standards. The West End was a known destination. No stage for any dramatic performance was, however, bigger than that of the cinema. Working-class audiences, far more so than the more socially restrained and culturally hamstrung middle classes, adored the Pictures. They were rocket ships out of the Valleys that could beam their lucky passengers back to friends and family.

We certainly knew our own, and we also knew we were known elsewhere. Stanley Baker would tell a fellow tough in *Hell Drivers* in 1957 that he was from 'Blaenllechau', and spit out the sibilants defiantly to our delight. Later, in 1961, in *The Guns of Navarone*, he would be the knife-wielding Brown who had earned himself the nickname of the 'Butcher of Barcelona' in an earlier war. In mid-Rhondda it was clear which throats he had been slitting. Closer to home Alan Ladd, fresh from *Shane* (1954), starred in *The Black Knight* in Castell Coch just down the Taff on the train ride to Cardiff; and in our very own Tonypandy and Trealaw railway station, one of our own generation, after auditions in all the local primary schools, bought a ticket in Norman Wisdom's 1953 *Trouble in Store*. I can only say that we never felt remote from whatever the action was in post-war Britain. We were making it, from Merthyr's Eddie Thomas and his British and Empire titles as a welterweight and Abercynon's Dai Dower and his flyweight titles a little later, to Rhondda's own rugby greats (especially against New Zealand in 1953) Cliff Morgan and Gareth Griffiths. We touched our heroes then. Roy Paul from Ystrad won the FA Cup with Manchester City in 1956 and paraded it up and down Rhondda's streets, and it was Rhondda's Jimmy Murphy who would guide the post-Munich Manchester United team to another cup final in 1958, and Wales to the World Cup quarter finals in Sweden.

The 1940s and 1950s witnessed starbursts from South Wales. In the Rhondda Fawr alone we were well aware that the Garrick Players, trainers of actors and producers of plays for local consumption, from their base in the Engine House of Llwynypia Colliery, had sent Clydach Vale's Houston brothers, Donald and Glyn, on their way as, respectively, leading man and character actor. A contemporary of theirs in the adjacent Rhondda Fach would be even more startlingly catapulted from sullen schoolboy to teenage film actor and would, by the end of his short life at 48 in 1976, be widely seen as the template for the next generation of working-class actors to storm British and world cinema. Stanley Baker, more than his friend and fellow-meteorite Burton, was readily understood as a singular portent of wider things to come: authentic, at ease with himself, ambitious to succeed and confident to be, always, one of our own.

Our literary shooting star – in prose rather than poetry – was a Thomas who, albeit briefly, threatened to vie for transatlantic fame with his western namesake, Rhondda's Gwyn to Swansea's Dylan. By 1953 when Dylan was dead, Gwyn's early searchlight illumination of the South Wales of his first forty years – 'Whatever a man does after the age of forty should be forgotten because in nine cases out of ten he is utterly worn out by what has gone before' – exchanged its unremitting beam for the delights of *son et lumière*. Before that, however, it was not only in Britain that Gwyn Thomas' *Folk Tales from the Modern Welsh* – his tongue-in-cheek sub-title for his first book in 1946 and, in essence, the work he did to the early 1950s – were extravagantly praised. In the Truman years in the USA a thirties liberal sensibility was not yet stifled by the creeping conformity of Eisenhower's America, and, there too, the young Welsh novelist, as Studs Terkel told me face-to-face in Chicago in 1994, was widely known and discussed. He was championed by left-wing populists like Howard Fast, future author of *Spartacus*, but read more delicately perhaps by the poet Norman Rosten, intimate of Arthur Miller and in the late 1940s a room-mate in a writers' rented studio of Norman Mailer. Louis 'Studs' Terkel, weathervane of genius long before he became conduit of the voices of the many in his Oral Histories,

14

remembered how the intellectual and dissident denizens of the Windy City, such as the novelist Nelson Algren, had no trouble seeing Thomas' 'scarecrows' – a *New York Times* description – as their own fellow citizens. Indeed, when Gwyn Thomas' great historical allegory, *All Things Betray Thee*, was published in 1949 in the USA under the title *Leaves in the Wind*, the *New York Times* said that what 'one encounters here are reality and the tragic elements of dream'; whilst the *Pittsburgh Press*, even quicker in tracking the writer's unfettered appeal, was specifically reassuring to any potential transatlantic readers: 'A book that tells of a Welsh mining village in 1835 – but if the author had been writing about a Pennsylvanian mining village in 1935 he couldn't have written a truer picture'.

The significance that was sensed elsewhere, then, from all this projection outwards from the bastion of South Wales, was that talent of great expressive ability had somehow been nurtured and sustained here. And this in a region which was, by the post-war period, recognised beyond these shores as comparable to any working-class communities of power and desperation created into and out of the interwar Depression. Yet, for those prepared to look and listen more closely and more intently, this perceived cultural significance was inseparable from the constancy of the insistent message being transmitted. In sum, that neither pity nor sentiment was adequate or wanted. Instead, our writers and performers centred on the desire for and necessity of hope, twinned by the fear of disappointment and the resignation of the stoic. At least this was how, in the early 1950s, it, and we, appeared to the best outside eyes we attracted.

15

No more discerning eyes than those of the great documentary photographers, W. Eugene Smith and Robert Frank, looked through the lens to the core of the twentieth century. Smith came to South Wales in the winter of 1950 and Frank followed in the early spring of 1953. The similarities are striking, the contrast in what they chose to see, or perhaps what chose their seeing, is even more so. Their witness appears to hold in its gaze a truth that is almost irreducible by the very nature of the medium. Not so much that the camera never lies as we once might, with literalness in mind, have said and meant, more that the truth their cameras found, posed, adjusted and cropped from moments of visual discovery to the black arts of the dark rooms, is a truth of undeniable recognition because, as with a poem or a story or a drama, it speaks of a hinterland of validation. Yet, too, their witness was only a fleeting one, and one that tells of their singular frozen framing as much as of our more jumbled framework of existence whose lines stretched in and out of a past and present not really stilled by the moment of capture.

Eugene Smith's brief foray into South Wales had its own back story. The great American photographer of the war with Japan was 31 years old in early 1950. He was, along with Robert Capa, who had himself visited the South Wales Valleys in the war years, one of *Life* magazine's stellar forces. Smith's forte had become the 'photographic essay' or assemblage of pictures, mostly with people involved, which told an emotionally charged story. Before he arrived he had made for *Life* in 1947 the masterly narrative 'Country Doctor', and when he left Britain he would follow it up with his stunning 'Spanish Village' in 1951. The coalfield of South Wales did not yield a published essay of images. But we can now see, from fragments of his notes and from his unpublished contact sheets, that it almost gave him another such masterpiece. If it had happened it would have been through the chance of his coming and by the magnetic nature of what he saw beyond the purpose of his British assignment. This was, strictly, to cover the British General election of February 1950 from a Labour Party perspective, though not necessarily sympathetically since Henry Luce, *Life*'s irascible proprietor, had made it plain that he wanted his reader in America to see, graphically, how 'Socialist' Britain was holding back the economic progress that only came with the modernity of market capitalism. For *Life* it was not a question of party politics, as their editorial of 20 February 1950, three days before polling, made clear:

We hope that the Socialists lose, their defeat would be a good thing for Britain and a good thing for the US. Our opinion has little or nothing to do with the merits of British Conservatives as compared to British Socialists. The primary American concern is not with who governs Britain but with the British people and their state of mind. Socialism is, among other things, the symptom of an unhealthy and underproductive state of mind. In Britain this state of mind is best summed up in that seductive Socialist phrase, 'fair shares for all', which has been proved to mean full shares for none and full effort from almost none. When and if the British people shake themselves out of this state of mind they will be of a mind to... be on the road to the recovery of fiscal independence that they so far have failed to attain.

Smith, at some level of professional obedience, duly obliged. A part of his photo spread showed a cement lorry bearing on a board the slogan: 'Under Free Enterprise British Cement is Cheapest in the World'. The vehicle is being held up in an idyllic country lane by a farmer and his herd of obstructive cows. The lane was in the Vale of Glamorgan. Gene Smith had hired, and choreographed, truck, driver, farmer and cows for eight pounds. Victorian antique inefficiency was Luce's shorthand for the Britain that was allegedly impeding the industrial future. Smith would repeat the motif, albeit more lyrically, in Tredegar where a horse-drawn milk cart at dawn straddles, and contradicts, tram lines, tarmac road and a lone motor car.

When he left Wales, after almost a fortnight, to photograph election night in London, and especially Clement Attlee, Labour's Prime Minister, in his constituency in Walthamstow, Gene Smith had had his radical roots – he had wanted to cover the Spanish Civil War on the Loyalist side but was too young – utterly revived. In London, having followed Attlee around that wintry February, he knew fully which side he was on. Nonetheless the shot he took of Attlee, seated and overcoated against the cold, even indoors in that underheated Britain, was of the pained and creased face of a manager who has just been told of a devastating run on his bank. On 6 March 1950, *Life* headlined it as 'Attlee Surveys the Ruins of Victory'.

Inasmuch as Labour's overwhelming parliamentary majority of 1945 had been slashed to five by a combination of electoral factors, not least Tory recovery in rural areas of England and Scotland (though not Wales), the portrait was an eloquent reveal. *Life* could only register surprise: 'The theory that queue-weary city wives would march on their fallen arches against Labor was not confirmed. The fact is that Labor won its biggest votes where the queues were, in the cities. Despite its loss in Parliament, Labor won nearly a million more popular votes than the Tories and actually increased its poll over 1945.' If it had been a Presidential contest it was, as Smith could readily see, 'No contest'. He had also come to understand why that was so. And South Wales had been the focus of his viewfinder.

He had arrived in England on 3 January 1950. With his American assistant, Ted Castle, he travelled to South Wales in the noticeably big 'American Car' that had been shipped over already filled with the equipment he needed; rations as well as cameras and film. On 15 January, a Sunday, they were in Cardiff and soon reconnoitring the decidedly non industrial Vale of Glamorgan. Here he took his picture of the obstructive cows on 19 January. It was a contrived composition but one politically acceptable to *Life*. He told his wife, by letter the next day, that it was the only 'good' thing he had so far accomplished in Wales. The day before, on Wednesday 18 January, he had visited for what he called 'lunch', and we then still called 'dinner', a local and well-connected miners' leader in Rhondda: Ben Harcombe, who lived in Kenry Street, Tonypandy.

The dates are important because they indicate a formal pattern that was not yet being discovered instinctively, more that it was being explained to him what he should note with the didactic insistence that had become second nature to South Walian informants. He had a number of these contacts as his sketchy note memo tells us and he did, as he sought them out, imbibe their rhetoric and the well-rehearsed platform maxims which he duly wrote down:

'Nationalisation is a means to an end.'
'Coal Board taken place of Coal owners as enemies.'
'Society bound together by Rights and Duties.'
(Such as Army)

We can see exactly who fed him the lines if we note the contact addresses he kept. One was scribbled as 'Archie Lush, Political Sec for Bevan, 5 Gladstone Place, Tredegar' and, sure enough, there is the diminutive Lush, Aneurin Bevan's electoral if not political begetter, wagging his finger over hot coffee in one of Tredegar's Italian cafés to his fellow conspirators and *consiglieri*, the eponymous Dark Philosophers about whom Gwyn Thomas had already written. Eugene Smith would meet these practical dreamers on Saturday 21 January when he went to Tredegar for what he noted as 'Labour Men Supper'. Bevan himself was absent all this time, campaigning in areas of weaker Labour support in England, so his person, other than in the shape of a bust in the Tredegar Workmen's Library and Institute, escaped Smith, but his effect permeates the images of Tredegar that Smith took under the guidance of the 'Labour men'.

Notably, in the birthplace of the founder of the National Health Service, itself scarcely two years old in 1950, these were of the Tredegar Medical Aid Society, the voluntary forerunner of the NHS, and of the medical staff and patients at its Park Place Surgery and Dispensary, a building of cinematic opulence in Tredegar's otherwise mean streets. In the Institute the photographer neglected neither the books on the walls of the library nor the prints of paintings in the reading room nor the posters on street corners, set above carefully gathered ragamuffin kids proclaiming a future through steel production by them and for them. It was as if he were defiantly proclaiming it all, this socialist modernity, to Henry Luce, who never saw the photographs, as '*Life* magazine eat your heart out'. Smith then returned to the Rhondda for his last look at the South Wales Valleys – he had already talked in Cardiff with both Alf Davies, who had succeeded his fellow Communist Arthur Horner as President of the South Wales Miners' Federation in 1946, and Cliff Protheroe, the Labour Party's Secretary in Wales – and to take evocative, moody photographs of men coming off a bus from the Remploy Factories which the Labour Government had set up after 1945 to re-train disabled miners for alternative work. He had thought it through: 'In South Wales', he wrote later, 'there was little physical evidence of a grimly-fought election... I decided... to try photographic symbolism of Labor party claims and promises and through these show the basis of their strength.'

When he recalled the pain he had observed on the Prime Minister's face on election night, Smith thought Attlee was reflecting on the burden of a constructive future, not on the shards of defeat: 'I watched this man of heart, this Prime Minister, and how confidence of victory had its effect on him. Each mounting vote of majority seemed to sink him further into contemplation of the future.... It seemed now, as victory appeared more secure with each new count, that this hard road, these obligations were a cross of great weight for him to bear. His face took on the quality of a man almost spiritual,

21

with the haunting burdens of millions upon his shoulders... I photographed not with a camera, I forgot it was there, I photographed with my heart, and I was trying to capture his soul upon film.'

That window into a man's soul had opened for Smith almost a month earlier and it was this aperture which had allowed him to see Tredegar's intellect, Rhondda's re-construction and a Prime Minister's responsibility all in the light of revelation. It really clicked for him when Smith, both his own Vale of Glamorgan trickery and the rhetorical flights of his instructors behind him, had 'left the main caravan for part of a day, photographing where I would, and anything I felt could be tied to the election.' The 'main caravan' was both the *Life* assignment and the local guides to potential journey direction. He, on the other hand, had needed to find a deeper, more instinctive inspiration. And so he did: 'It was a day in which my seeing seemed boundless, and though mostly unprinted, it was perhaps the most creative day of my life.' He discovered the core of his creativity by leaving through the back door, and literally so.

For a stranger, the usual route in or out of the Rhondda in 1950 would have been through Pontypridd and on up through Porth to find the still densely packed terraces and frequent collieries of post-war full employment. Smith could not have failed to see a society, from township to township, thrumming with a communal and commercial life that was everywhere teetering on the brink of material and cultural change. It was neither tense with politics nor readily reduced to symbols.

Tredegar and Tonypandy, and their connected siblings,

were perhaps too complex a compound for the element of direct, unmediated seeing for which Smith hankered. He needed an object to which he could give undistracted and unremitting attention if his empathetic psychology – his camera from the heart – was to be engaged. Too many maxims, too many slogans, too much baggage for his mind had perhaps obstructed his view. Then there was the happenstance. In his second week, probably on Monday 23 January initially, Smith fell lucky at last. His large American car set out for the Rhondda but took the route through the Vale of Glamorgan which led into the Ely Valley to the south of the Rhondda proper and where, fifty years on, Rhondda Fawr's western bypass from Talbot Green and Llantrisant upwards now begins. Only in 1950 you bypassed nothing and the first coal settlement you would come across would be the stark, small and isolated pit village of Coedely, just before the larger communities of Thomastown and Tonyrefail begin to hint at the Rhondda itself.

The colliery development was a late one, almost an afterthought where the seams of the coalfield stretched out and ended. It was sunk between 1906 and 1910, with the settlement of the village as abrupt and contiguous, from 1908 to 1912. Thereafter there was little change for half a century to the eighty terraced houses thrown up opposite the colliery on the north-eastern side of the Ely river. Four streets, one at the bottom, one at the top, two as vertical as a funicular, an elementary school, a chapel and the basic amenities of butcher, baker, cobbler, ironmonger and front-room grocer with the familiar coalfield itinerants making infrequent rounds – one-legged Harry Penny selling cockles from his flat cart pulled up and down the Valleys by his struggling pony; Lipman the Jewish vendor carrying plate glass on his back like a vitreous turtle and, later, a 'Shoni Onion' man from Brittany, pushing a bike festooned with onions. For anything else you couldn't grow in an allotment or rear in a coop, you left Coedely.

Eugene Smith stopped at Coedely. It was the first, complete in itself pit village, as opposed to Rhondda's sequential townships, which he had seen. It overwhelmed him in its brute togetherness: houses, works, slag, people. The relationship stripped to an essence. This would be his day of 'endless seeing'. The car would have stopped on the main road which was flanked on its eastern side by Collwyn Street from which, at almost perpendicular angles the others, a few red-bricked houses, shot off to be capped by the top Terrace. The homes and faces in his photographs are readily identifiable. At this point he is seeing women and children because the men are in work or asleep after their shift. It is Monday, and because that is traditionally wash day, clothes are being hung out on back-garden washing lines. He climbs beyond the top-terraced street to take panoramic views of the colliery, the coke works, the mountain, the streets, the coal tip. He had begun collecting the elements of a unique Eugene Smith photographic essay, one which was never printed up.

What he saw largely remains on the contact sheets now kept in the archive of the University of Arizona in Tucson. They would have served as the narrative thread of that never-to-be-made essay of images of the South Wales he had fallen upon in Coedely. Its separate elements were back kitchens, tin baths, neighbours on doorsteps, tired, grey, empty clothes on a line, shy children, dirt-encrusted men dredging filter ponds for wet slurry, smoke from the coke-oven chimneys drifting into a grey sky, the pyramid of slag, the terraced barracks, a spatial unity of disparate things that coalesced because of the coal that was worked.

The editorial layout he would now imagine required one central image that could encapsulate that catalyst of work. Towards the end of the afternoon of a creative day like no other he had ever had, he stumbled across it, or at least the elements of it. When he had left and reflected, it was on 'a spread on Labor in mind, with certain photographs specifically... three miners... a strong symbol of men born into poverty or near poverty in this long-depressed area of antiquated mines.' The most specific of those pictures he made is the single best evocation of the spirit he had sensed and to which he subscribed as he worked on it, cropping background, foreshortening and playing with light and dark until the effect was brought to a pitch-perfect tonality. A week after the first image had been captured he wrote: 'Their faces speak volumes of history, present and past, and what injustice can do... the photograph... goes way up to the top of the heap for it crackles with power.'

It is by no means a simple picture. The way he marked his contact sheets, the multiple takes of that shot, shows clearly how he altered the men's positions inch-by-inch and how the background was lost or shaded to foreground them. Yet also there was something beyond a trinity of ages that he had instantly understood, and, miraculously, caught. These men were indeed about power as surely as Bevan had been when he set out to pursue it from miners' lodge to council chamber to Parliament and to government itself. They were, by dint of who they were, self-assured and self-empowered. They were, because of when and where they were, men waiting in expectation. The picture is timeless now as a symbol but its greater magnitude lies in the poignancy of its evanescence. When it appeared in *Life* magazine in February 1950 it was captioned 'Labor's Backbone', and serves that wider, passing purpose. What pulls the viewer in beyond any awareness of the connection to a caption-writer's journalese is the way in which, as a grouping and as individuals, the men seem to look beyond the instrumental camera in an intrinsic assertion of themselves that is intense, alienating and, indeed, powerful. Smith's final published print was cropped in his studio to ensure the effect. It is a work of art.

Since the 1930s Welsh miners had figured before the camera in a chorus line of contextualised poses: quickstepping across slush-covered wasteland, trudging disconsolately home, emerging shoulder-to-shoulder from the pit cage and, invariably when taken straight on, whether for the soft focus of Edith Tudor Hart or the gritty filter of Bill Brandt, grinning toothily in blackface. Their work and their hardened or worn-out physical attributes were generally far removed from the condition of the ideal and sympathetic viewer. The camera's intent was always, hitherto, to create a bond. But not here. Not now. Not Eugene Smith's trio in 1950 in Coedely. They do not offer themselves up for individual sympathy or public redemption. They are self-contained almost to the point of insolent threat. That is their power.

As Smith walked about Coedely, talking and taking photographs into the early afternoon, he had wandered downhill and across the road towards the filter ponds of the coke works where drams were being filled with the slurry. Then he would have seen the afternoon shift walk past him at two o'clock on their way to work and the coking plant men and surface workers going the other way, home, at two thirty. Finally, the miners themselves leaving the colliery around three o'clock. Among the last of these were the three men he transfixed as one of the outstanding images of the last century. We now know their names: Ossie Watkins, the oldest, on the left; Vernon Harding, the youngest, on the right, and his uncle Willy Griffiths in the centre. In 2008 Vernon Harding wrote in reply to one of my many queries:

> My feeling about the photograph is this. It shows three miners, their faces black, obviously on their way home at the end of their shift, in the background can be seen a small mining village with rows of terraced houses climbing up the slope at the foot of the hillside, the three miners are all looking backwards in the same direction, their attention fixed on something behind them... it's implicit in the photograph that they are looking back at the Colliery, and by Colliery I mean the Winding Gear, the steel gantries and the wheels spinning round on top raising the cage, with the full drams of coal being moved along the rails by the surface workers. I believe that is what Eugene Smith envisaged when he took the photograph. What we are actually looking at is Eugene Smith taking the photograph, and behind him the gates of the Railway Crossing and a line of full coal trucks on the Coal Sidings. I have enclosed a photograph of the area marking where we were with an X.

He had been watching us walking down the sidings and then crossing the Railway. Because we were colliers and among the last to make our way home, we would have been almost the last to pass him... I believe he knew exactly what he wanted and how to achieve it.

I would not say we were surprised by his presence or request, he was a stranger to us and, though I do not remember his words, I am sure he introduced himself and explained what he was doing there and that he wanted to take some photographs. Regarding our attitude to spending ten minutes or so with him, it was no trouble. Ossie suffered with a lame leg, so he was glad of a little breather before we climbed the gradient to our homes.

They were tired after the shift, but patient and polite. Smith clicked and clicked again. The light of the day was beginning to fade. He positioned the three men precisely, drawing their bodies closer yet gapped, as in a generational transition, from left lower to right upper. 'I do not remember,' Vernon Harding recalled, 'him giving any request regarding our expressions, only our positions as slightly sideways and glancing back.' Their look is, therefore, askance. Smith said, at a later time, that it was why they seemed quizzical. Quizzing yes, puzzled no. The expressions move from a resigned geniality to a distancing acknowledgement to what is not quite, but almost, a challenge. The eyes, coal-rimmed and in unison, are not friendly. They pose but are not submissive. It is a look held in common and without fear, one directed at whatever they may be asked to look upon. They have the stance of men left standing, of men who know that they are the lookers not the observed. Where they have immediately come from is marked on their faces, on their clothes and in their bearing. It crackles, as Smith instinctively knew, with power. He had found his subject and it, in a more lasting manner, had found him.

Margaret Thatcher would have shuddered at its implications. She certainly saw it in *Life*'s February issue of 1950 since her own photograph, a head-and-shoulders portrait, was part of a photo gallery of parliamentary candidates on the counter page: 'Youngest Woman Candidate is the Tories' Margaret Roberts 23, for Dartford'. Her 'enemy within' was still in charge in 1950. She would not enter Parliament until 1959. Coedely Colliery finally closed in 1985, in the wake of the year-long miners' strike of 1984-85 which her government engineered and won, snapping 'Labor's backbone' in the process.

Eugene Smith had teased out the underlying hubris of modest men. Over the page had shone the anticipatory visage of their distant nemesis. Or not so distant if the shutter fast-forwards fractionally to October 1951 and Labour's third general election since 1945, one in which, in another incredibly high turn-out of almost 83 per cent, Labour polled nearly 14 million votes, the highest poll and the largest vote ever won by any British political party. However, with the Liberal Party in collapse, Labour lost its parliamentary majority to the Conservatives who would now be in power until 1964. The moment had passed. Perhaps it is this which makes Robert Frank's completed photographic essay of 1953 so very different in tone and expectation even though he had been influenced by Smith's pictures and corresponded with him. The proximity in time and place indicates a promisingly useful comparison but it is, in fact, the contrast between the two photographers' seeing in Wales which has become more telling.

Robert Frank's Welsh album was assembled just before his return to the United States and the creation of his breakthrough work that would be, when published in 1958, the studiously unstudied *The Americans*. It prefigures the emotive fuzziness with which Frank will move beyond the journalism of the photo-essay but that mode is still rooted in the Welsh studies and in the preceding work he had made in London. The capital emerges through a Victorian smokescreen to reveal top-hatted, frock-coated bankers gliding about their murky business in the City within a city, while coal merchants hump their lump-filled hessian sacks off the back of lorries and into the cellars that fuel the heating of what was then the world's finance centre. But if this is where the energy ends in combustive heat, where does it come from? Frank himself had come to London from Paris in the winter of 1951-2. What he saw in its fog-shrouded streets were sharp-edged apparitions of the British class divide. The comparative class stance is implicit in the positioning of figures in the London pictures, and then, when Frank exhibited them directly alongside his Welsh ones in New York in the summer of 1953, given an objective differentiation. In the story of Ben James, miner – his work and his family – Frank seems to move the time frame back towards the despair of the 1930s even as his smeary technique often appears to prefigure the coming triumph of expressionism in the art of photography. Smith's wider contextualisation is replaced by both a quest for a more realistic psychological insight and an almost romanticised subjective isolationism.

Confronted by the depth of insight in Frank's moody imagery it comes as a shudder to realise how much he had been impelled to travel to the iconic British coalfield because he had read that farrago of universalised symbolism that was, and is, *How Green Was My Valley*. In London he had also 'met a man from Wales talking about the Mines' and he resolved to go on the journey which 'became my only try to make a "Story"'. His contact was not with the Miners' Union, as Smith's had been, but with the National Coal Board, founded just six years previously in 1947. Frank's request was for a compact, self-contained pit village, and the one to which he travelled in March 1953 was precisely that, even more so than Smith's splintered fragment of the Rhondda at Coedely. The official escorted Frank up the Llynfi Valley to the north-west of Bridgend, on the fringe of the Vale of Glamorgan, through the mining township of Maesteg to its satellite, Caerau. He could not have been further from any residual trace of greenery. Caerau, its streets slung together around the eponymous colliery of 1889, was high and bleak, with only the elevated triangle of its coal tip and the sweep of the mountain's plateau above its basic settlement. The pit workforce, at around 500 men, was at a quarter of its employed heyday of 1918, but with no other employment in 1953 and, as yet, no pithead baths, the sights and the smells of Caerau above ground were those contracted underground. There was no relieving factor other than the road out. A generation was shifting. Frank duly took a family portrait of Ben James in his Sunday best, Mrs James with her potted plants and their well-dressed son, studying geology at Swansea University.

Robert Frank stayed in Caerau on two occasions that March, bringing his wife and son with him the second time, and his affection and sympathy for the place and people amongst whom he had parachuted remains tangible in any viewing of the 'story' he snapped rather than constructed. He had, in one sense, inherited a narrative to allow him to do that. In another, more disturbing way, it is as if the political and social militancy for which Caerau was renowned, and of which there is no trace in his tale, has been reduced to a weary despair – in eyes, on faces, through slouched-over bodies – lived out in shuttered terraced houses set down amongst the wasteland of spoil and slag which, with the deepest irony imaginable, has here become the playground of their children. The only joy in these photographs is lit up when the miners queue for their pay or when scruffy kids scramble in whirling snow on the lower slopes of a coal tip; in the distance the colliery waits for their growing-up and across the bottom of the frame a black dog pads his way in front of them. His wife, Mary, wrote from Caerau to Frank's parents in New York: 'The children are very rough and Pablo likes them a lot.'

When I look at those kids I can see myself, doing exactly the same thing at exactly the same age, just a mountain or two to the east. So, it is not as if, even at this extremely subjective level, Frank is distorting anything in what he found around him. It is more that we are reduced, again, to possessing hope only in a future generation whilst the present time continues to suffer and wait and it is as if Idris Davies had sung his carol for his coalfield in 1945 in vain. There are no generational unities in Frank's pictures, only the separations effected by age and education. It was the way South Wales, too, and in spite of its best hopes held in common, would go within a generation. The Americans, Smith and Frank, had penetrated to related, yet distinct, truths about our general conditions of life in the first decade after the Second World War had ended. No fault of theirs, then, to add that they had not penetrated to the lived experience of that general condition.

I had felt this very strongly when I looked intently at their work following the book and exhibition at Tate Modern, *Robert Frank London/Wales* (2003), and then when, in making a film for BBC4, *The Lost Pictures of Eugene Smith* (2006), I flew to Tucson to visit the Center for Creative Photography of the University of Arizona to research Eugene Smith's 'unprinted' Welsh images. What was nagging at me was an innate inkling that something needed to be said about what they had not seen. And, suddenly, using a loupe, or jeweller's magnifying lens, at a desk in Tucson I recognised something I had not expected to see, a steep hill, a precipitous mountain, a shop doorway and the hinted presence of my own father.

This time Eugene Smith had positioned himself almost at the top of a nigh on perpendicular hill, looking down to a valley bottom. On the right of the frame is a horse drawn milk cart so I assumed at first that this was another shot of Trevor Jones the Milk of Tredegar who featured in the published and famous pictures in *Life* magazine. Then I shivered. This was not flat, head-of-the-Sirhowy Valley Tredegar, it was switchback mid-Rhondda with Trealaw mountain looming in the background over Dunraven Street, the commercial artery of Tonypandy. This was Gilfach hill that led up to all the higher terraced streets, a vertical road parallel with and a half a mile away from the twinned hill that climbed from the Empire Theatre where my grandfather had gathered with thousands of others in 1910. When Smith looked down Gilfach hill I was almost five years old. I could have been in the picture. I wasn't, but the door and shop front windows of Morgan's wet fish shop, perched just above the site of the old fulling mill or Pandy, were open as usual and there inside, for sure, was the outline of its white-aproned manager, my father. We can ascertain from Smith's diary note that on Wednesday 19 January 1950, he had first made it to the Rhondda to meet for lunch with Ben Harcombe, a union official at the Cambrian Combine Colliery – now 'owned' by 'the people' – who lived in Kenry Street, two-thirds of the way up and just across at its furthest end from Gilfach hill. Smith had presumably wandered out onto the hill to see what vistas could be seen. The take is atmospheric enough, but no more than that. It held no significance for Eugene Smith.

After the eerie sense, for me, of having touched the shade of my father, the contact sheet began to suggest a great deal more. It was not just his presence, that was also absent in any completed manner in Smith's final product, it was all of the rest of a place and a childhood that remained unseen. And unheard. And not smelled. And somehow static, not swift with the changes we were all feeling almost daily in how we ate, how we dressed, how we holidayed, how we dreamed. The latter not because everyone now left annually, in the autumn, for a week in Blackpool to see the Illuminations, so redolent of light and joyous wastefulness after the darkness of the War years – my family, for one, could not afford to do so – but because there were, suddenly, more and more rail and petrol-fuelled trips to the nearby seaside, and into our lives came denim jeans and sloppy-joes, as we then knew T-shirts, and, from 1953, no more ration coupons for sweets, and the appearance of the grittiest, grainiest, fruitiest ice lollies which a back shop could sell to compete with the nirvana of smooth and commercial Koola Frutas in the picture houses: the Plaza, the Picturedome and the Empire alone in Tonypandy itself. This is not a litany to a consumer-fest because, then and there, it was both feeble and fragmentary. It is more the contrast between image and experience with which memory, richer and deeper, instructs the evidence of History.

The wonderful evocations of Smith and Frank are like still but deep pools to my overflowing, even shallow, childhood streams. Admittedly, they photographed in the dank light of winter and early spring, when snow was in the air and only the grey-white pall of steam and smoke seemed to brighten the smudged faces of men and the dirt encrustation of their shapeless clothes. In Robert Frank we see no lightness of being at all, not in their demeanour or in the unbearable heaviness of their unrelieved industrialised hellscape. But, in precisely those very winters, my recall is of streets bright for hours on end after dusk with frequently spaced iron-stalked gas lamps around which families, not only children, grouped to talk, and, for us, to play. Inside our houses coal fires made with the best granulated steam coal, that broke in shining fissures, would blaze without let or care and, by the mid 1950s, we had electric light bulbs instead of the dim and foetid splutter of gas, and electricity, too, for washing machines, vacuum cleaners and soon television sets. Our eyes were brimming with colour – the synthetic but enticing gloss of the cinematic palette, from Eastman Color to Technicolor, of course – and vividly so in the springs and summers we lived through, but they did not photograph. Again, contrast is the key chromatic element.

That contrast is most readily shared by looking at both the contemporary and later memory paintings of a dazzlingly talented trio of Rhondda painters who were then, as two of them continued to do, transforming the clichéd visual concept of the Rhondda. In the early works of Treherbert's Charles Burton (b.1929), Ystrad's Ernest Zobole (1927-1999) and Pontypridd's Glyn Morgan (b.1926), we comprehend the subtlety of shade in sunny streets and how the shapes of hills and the pine-ends of houses interlock, where lines of sight and lines of force intersect. How, in short, a jumble of material and man-made landscape becomes a mindscape whose form and colour can be, in its very distinctiveness, wild to the point of juddering off the expected chromatic scale in a riotous cacophony of tints.

I cannot say I knew any of that at the time. But clearly the painters did and, equally clearly, 1945 and all that moment meant was central to their vision of painting the Rhondda as if, in formal terms, they were painting any-where else. The Rhondda, or rather the suggestive meaning of the Rhondda, was definitely their subject and their objective was to use their formal training, or what they found to hand in the work and example of artists such as Cedric Morris and Heinz Koppel who had come to visit and to see from the 1930s to the 1950s. The new, native born generation was soon re-arranging the visual furniture in the way that Gwyn Thomas had already re-ordered the accepted contours of working class depiction in prose. Their purpose was the same: to escape the confines of what was literal in representation because what was then otherwise unseen, as they well knew, was what shaped their society, its landscape and mindscape both. The processes of cultural desire and social change infiltrated their formal apprehension of the tasks they set themselves.

An early picture of Glyn Morgan's shows the view to the north of Pontypridd: colliery winding gear at Hopkinstown and the coal trucks of the Barry Sidings strung across the pitted hillside below the trademark coal tip, with the cleft between overlapping bluffs hinting at the hidden industrial Shangri-La to the north. It is 1947. The coal industry has just been nationalised and disillusion is still at a distance. The sky swirling about the foreground of bracken browns and the smudge of tarry greens is a translucent pink. The whole composition is carefully understated as if the dawn is less assured than the days that have already coloured the picture. Within four years, by the time he paints the picture he calls 'Tonypandy' in 1951, the customary components of pit, river, tips and terraces have been deconstructed in his mind (though it is still clearly identifiable as the Naval Colliery where the Combine Strike of 1910-11 had its origins). The earlier representational fidelity has succumbed to a tilting turntable which slides oblongs into triangles and vibrates with startling colour clashes. The canvas is a riot. The pigment is off the scale expected of the content: burnt orange against egg-yolk yellow and blues from purple to night to azure, counterposed by solid chunks of crimson block and washed-out pink. The painter had written to his potential patron, the collector Winifred Coombe Tennant, in the autumn of 1950:

> ...the mountains are so beautiful that they take one's breath away... all that mystery and dignity... I should like to have a large studio on wheels, thousands of canvases, and two lifetimes to paint the Rhondda valley.

The two painters who did, one way or the other, spend their lifetimes doing just that are the two who have consequently done the most to remove the cultivated cataracts of visual cliché from our eyes. Their achievements, different and yet complementary, are, as we can see clearly now, hard won and deeply resonant. Of his great friend, and fellow conspirator, Ernie Zobole, Charlie Burton has perceptively said that the whole work was 'an autobiography in paint'. Certainly Zobole's presence in his own framing grew more and more insistent as he witnessed the withering of collective social ambitions outside the frame and his own increasing spiritual isolation from the society which he could never relinquish in either person or paint. In the 1950s and 1960s the painter peopled his streets and hills with their still connected inhabitants. The pictures of his last two decades have the flattened conceptual perspective of a medieval map-maker whose world is marked off by sea and sky, while inside the vortex looping strings of cars, their lights blindly groping a path up and down illuminated bracelets of go-nowhere roads, are observed by the sole and desperately solitary figure in his doorway or from his studio. Finally, this corpus of obsessive refiguring and configuring became a social history of indictment as much as a personal *via dolorosa* to the grave.

This same brave and gimlet-eyed stare at their native place was held steady over the years by Charles Burton, undoubtedly the most formally talented and intellectually driven of his generation of painters. For him there could be no question but that the act of painting was, first and last, about the art of painting, its formal properties and its projections as well as precedents. It remains important to him that the tag of 'Rhondda' painter carries with it no sense of a reduction in formal reach or diminution of painterly intent. Burton's extensive output, particularly the long mid-career work that had no overt reference to those Welsh places, is testament enough to his stunning virtuosity. Nonetheless, the paintings of the young Burton – whose *Coming Home from the Club* famously won the Gold Medal at the 1954 National Eisteddfod – are a meticulous, almost architectonic, placing of brilliantly evoked cameo figures set in a Rhondda landscape. They are modulated with a subtlety at once emotional and cerebral, from a hilly pre-industrial echo that was then still to be seen and heard, to the warm huddle of gathered streets and the cooler promise of the civic signalling of public buildings. Somehow, by dint of technical composing, he holds that poised mid-century world in the palm of a hand offering up these pictures of quiet and deceiving simplicity.

Suddenly, in the 1990s, the impulse came to Burton to revisit the literal scene again through the medium of paint. What had been seen before as contrasts – of black present and green past, of steam railway and immemorial mountainside, of individual vivacity and honeycombed humanity – became an abyss of perception. The divide in the work is of Jekyll and Hyde proportions. There are memory pictures of the street life and social practice of the pre-war years that exude charm without the sugar dust of sentiment, more dreamy stage-sets of snow-blanketed or tree-whirling otherworlds where nature transfigures the dreary, and then contemporary views, tactile capture of wall and road and house and garden and the finite play of light on these things which time will, one day, also crumble. And, set against all that, there are large-scale works that comfort nothing other than the need for unremittingly honest reflection.

Such pictures present apocalyptic, de-peopled visions in which the detritus of the past seems to have expelled the better memories. Two paintings in particular are the antithesis of both colour and hope. The first, finished in the mid-1990s but conjuring up the shapes of the bustling mid-1940s, is a mix of muted blueish grey and blanched green. We see the township from on high as if it is conceived by a draughtsman working on his architectural blueprint in 3D. The eerie townscape is devoid, other than through its roads and buildings, of any human presence. It is as if some mysterious blast has taken away any trace of human life, or the activities of that life, and yet left their habitation intact, a site for the archaeological musing of others later, an urban Marie Celeste, a Pompeii without the explanation of natural catastrophe. Uncannily, pains-takingly accurate in its small-town detail, it is a drama about to, or which perhaps never did, happen. Not only no human actors, no cats or dogs or carts and horses or buses and cars or, more sinister yet, only closed doors and blank windows and smokeless chimneys. Nothing. *Nada*. Yet this void is not just an oblique commentary on what actually once was, and did not stay. It is also a footnote for this present and future time, a reminder of the messiness and vitality of community and of how it can be wiped away by neglect or forgetfulness or expunged through the deliberate use of such passive traits by the active and wilful, for whom the values of History are mutated, as if by the valuation of the estate agents of a philistine polity, into a perpetual and therefore socially lobotomised present.

Equally intense in its bleakness, but now more emotionally suffused with a contemptuous anger, is Charles Burton's masterpiece of 2007. It is a picture whose power derives from its ability to penetrate to the belly of the beast: no camaraderie underground, no communal succour, no humanity – other than the unseen slavery, above and below, that is directed to patterns of toil and concomitant ugliness by the underlying threnody of Rhondda's counterpointed human buzz. The pit. Here is the hated Hook and Eye colliery, wonderfully so labelled by its workers, of the upper Rhondda. The pit, or rather its inhuman manifestations, colours and designs the picture. Its waste spoil creates gashes of black veins riven into mountain slopes. Its progeny are the spawned and eyeless grey barracks of its worker-servants. Its systemic support systems are the slashes of macadamed roads and rail lines that feed in and extract out, and the concrete grey feeder containers for water to produce steam, and so power. The picture is filthy, a sour vomit of dirty ochre and the muckiness of off-white. In both of these late-career masterworks there is only a hint of relief in a

41

glimpse of sun seen through a race of clouds shadowing the dented mountains.

From the new century, looking back on the whole gamut of work from these two exceptional painters, Zobole and Burton, from the 1950s on, we can only be chastened by their constant refusal to depict their polychromatically changing society in the black-and-white conceptualism of one-dimensional assumption which is the more usual fate visited upon working-class societies of this complexity and intellect. Perhaps this is why they were self-consciously 'painters', not 'artists'. If their work had been widely known from the beginning in their own place, we would, at the very least, have recognised there was formal proof that in that cusp post-war decade we were not measuring out our lives in monochrome.

What I can say, too, is that colour bled into our lives in the early 1950s in quite explicit if informal ways, from cinema to clothing, but most noticeably for the young in the comic or illustrated books we read and swapped avidly. In post-war Britain the black, white and grey blocked-out drawings of comics had seeped into the pink and fawns of the Classic Illustrated Novels with their fuller-colour shiny front covers, but the real efflorescence came with the parcels of American comic books shipped over to 'starved' Britain from numerous American and Canadian relatives. Here, with a printed-paper smell so pungent as we hungrily sniffed it that the very colours seemed like exotic chemical flowers, were sharply acid yellows, a spectrum of green from moss to lime to woodland, zingy vermillion reds and shimmering blues you could swim in or float through. Gifted by the consumption of all this techno-aestheticism to imagine ourselves in full colour we could, and did, take to the hills and mountains and red cinder tips behind and above our terraced streets. They did, and do, bear a comfortingly near resemblance to the parched hills and clattering canyons through which others, for our delight, rode elsewhere. It all seemed to come together.

If Eugene Smith had walked down Gilfach hill in 1950 and turned right, he would have walked into a public world that was only slightly less frenetic on a daily and nightly basis than in its Edwardian turn-of-the-century heyday. The walk, the 'Tonypandy Parade', could be for groceries or goods or clothes and stretched from one end of Tonypandy Square down De Winton Street to Dunraven Street and into the precincts of Penygraig and the Co-operative Wholesale Society; so past Jones the Fruiterers, two of them, a Home and Colonial, a Pegler's grocer, Thomas the Drapers, Leslie Stores and Twissler's for china, or into the Penny-Bazaar and the grander Woolworth's with a reminder of harder days in the existence of Barney Isaac's three-balled pawnbrokers. You could still have a studio portrait taken in Ladd's, perhaps after a haircut in Salter's or Diamond's, crammed into a shirt whose collars and cuffs had been boiled and ironed to stiff perfection in Wong's Chinese Laundry.

Refreshment was constant, and available every few steps you took, whether coffee or hot fruit cordials in Julio Bracchi's eponymous Italian café, or any other 'Bracchi', whether Colombotti's, the Empire or Pino's, with the best fish and chips in Hathaway's opposite the Methodist Central Hall. In this hall William Joyce, Lord Haw Haw, had promised to have the Luftwaffe bomb for us, and they never did. Stronger drink was wherever you liked, all in

43

the same two mile stretch, from the De Winton Hotel, the Pandy Hotel, The White Hart, the British Legion, the Affiliated and District Club, the Dunraven Arms or the Cross Keys. After a double bill of pictures in the Plaza my father would visit one or other, and my mother and I would slowly walk home in a drifting cloud of others, eating our chips from vinegar-sodden newspaper and gazing at the mannequins who were modishly displayed behind the plate-glass windows of superior Theophilus and daringly named Nanette's.

In 1955, I was aged ten and master of all the topo-graphical intricacies of this small world: its unpaved back lanes, its hidden alleyways, its scrumpable vicarage apple trees, its disused quarries, its rhubarb and blackcurrant back-garden feasts, its brilliantine black river, its abandoned colliery buildings and bile-green feeder dams, its street games, its illegal open-air card schools, its mountain dens and all the intimate places a child can relish and know against the encroaching and official adult world. I was also old enough already to feel myself bumping up against that public life in the narrowing tubes of exams and schooling. The parallel lines converged that year, 1955, when the old Rhondda Urban District Council, its gold-stamped capitals RUDC embossed on the deep-red municipal buses, became a borough council and was to be granted its incorporation by no less a personage than the Duke of Edinburgh, or Prince Philip as we whispered in the schoolyard, as if he were the veritable Prisoner of Zenda come amongst us to make flesh our confected view of the strange otherness of whatever royalty was.

44

It was a Saturday morning. By some pre-arranged or maybe just instinctive childhood means we had left our blanketed and rumpled nests early, slid across cold linoleum floors, our passage rippling the surface of the unemptied chamberpots beneath parental beds, and met in the street. Then, from Ely Street and the Athletic Ground down, in unknowing parody of our grandfathers' route we cascaded; down the Empire hill, flattening and slowing on the intersecting streets to gather speed and force again as we hastened to pay homage to royalty. Or perhaps just to gawp. At the bottom of the hill we duly lined up outside the shops our grandparents and their friends had wrecked a mere forty-five years earlier. We saw the long black sleek cars if not much more than the hand of the sleeker royal sat within. It passed us quickly. And then there must have been a sort of herd impulse by which a score or more of us, not a word exchanged, ran and ran after the motor procession up and through Tonypandy, past the Square, our normal, self-imposed boundary limit on foot, re-tracing at similar speed but backwards the track of the rioters in November 1910. The Square, a simple crossroads in truth, was now left behind us as we kept running up the valley, a route we usually reserved for convoy riding by bus into alien territory, on beyond Partridge Square and Llwynypia Hospital where I, and so many of us, had been born, to Gelligaled Park whose open-air thirties' swimming baths were our summery haven and where I, and a hundred other transfixed males, had seen, the year before, our first bikini, green with red polka dots, on a slim brunette who is probably still honoured in many Rhondda dreams.

We scrambled off the road through bushes to the open

field where the Prince was reviewing a Guard of Honour before the ceremony. Back in the bewilderingly named Tonypandy Mixed Infants the next week we had to fill in our diaries in soft green-covered RUDC (no longer) exercise books. It seems that what impressed, and horrified, most was the command to the honour guard of soldiers to fix bayonets and the bright spurt of blood that suddenly appeared on the sliced thumb of one young squaddie who, to our fascination, wobbled and seemed about to faint. A regimental sergeant major, inches away from us and not without a hint of tenderness, said, loudly enough, 'Steady, boy, steady'. And he was. I think we cheered then. We should have.

The motto of the newly incorporated Rhondda Borough Council was 'Hwy Clod Na Golud: Fame Outlasts Wealth'. What a burdensome legend to have to bear. It may not have seemed quite that in 1955, in the continuing flush of welfare socialism and rising material living standards, but it glinted before us like an aristocratic boast that was bound to mock whatever was to come with the provenance of its historical lineage. Perhaps this, leaving aside our heedless helter-skelter enjoyment of post-war life at home, and the boastful projection of our collective skills and talents abroad, was what Robert Frank had depicted with a doleful irony as the heroic survival yet required by such as us, to allow future exit routes for individuals. Perhaps this was also what Eugene Smith had, earlier and an aeon away, shown as a valiant unity: individuals entwined with their society, one that offered, at least voluntarily, no surrender to circumstance. Certainly, the motto's lapidary observation, and the lingering truthful insights of both photographers, have held more lasting sway as fame than the flitter and glitter of wealth, whether in the Rhondda or across South Wales. So much so that it cradles, rightly I would argue, the significance of our indisputably achieved but sharply circumscribed history – cradles, but does not necessarily, or always, reveal what lies behind the selected image or the constructed narrative.

*

The Vernon Harding I met in 2005 to discuss his chance, and now celebrated, encounter with the artist-photographer Eugene Smith seemed immediately to be the man-in-the-photograph. His own personal back story was what lit up those eyes in 1950. He had grown up in the Depression and through the war. His mother had died when he was seven, leaving two boys in the care of their father. Vernon himself had been born in 1928 in Coedely and went to work down the pit with his widowed father in 1942 when he was fourteen. By the time Smith met him eight years later in 1950 he was twenty-two and a tough, seasoned collier. He sat down in 2001 to write, in a spare and telling prose that has no rival for its knowledge of the detail of work, a fragment of reminiscence of his early life. The year is 1943:

> Age 15, grandfather clock chiming 5:30 downstairs, Father calling time to get up for work, listen to front door open and close and the sound of Father's hob nailed boots on the stone-flagged pavement outside, receding and fading as he reached the end of the terraced street. Jumping out of bed clad in only an

old shirt leaving 13-year-old brother still sleeping, run down lino-covered stairs and into back-kitchen, switch on electric light, blackout curtains still drawn over the kitchen window, working clothes on guard in front of the fire place, the mantelpiece above holding the tea caddy, the two brass ornaments each side, and the brass rail hanging below. The black leaded grate, the hob one side, the oven with the little latched door on the other and in the centre the fire gleaming, warming, cheery, the flames flickering and dancing. I stand on the patchwork mat in front, on with singlet and shirt, moleskin trousers, held up by wide leather belt. Sit down on wooden chair by fireside, on with stockings and hobnail boots, tie up leather laces and then open back door to bailey to wash under cold water tap over outside sink. A quick visit to the outside lavatory situated at the top end of the garden. Still dark outside as I swill out my three-pint tin jack and then fill it, tapping in the cork attached to the handle by a thin metal chain. Inside to eat a piece of toast browned in front of the fire on the two prongs of wire-twisted toasting fork. On with my coat and scarf hanging on back door, daicap on, pulled down over right ear, jack placed in patch pocket sewn on coat on left and tommy box in pocket on right, tam in inside pocket. The six-o-clock hooter from the colliery and the grandfather clock chiming in the middle kitchen tell me it's time to leave for work. Switch off the light to save the bob in the meter and out the front door leaving it unlocked behind me.

Down the street my boots ringing on the pavement, past the air raid shelter at the bottom of the street, along the main road then down the narrow road leading to the railway sidings and Coke Works. Half light of dawn, the stars above glistening and shining in a clear sky, cold, the frost gleaming in the fields on my right and the railway sleepers forming the bridge over the river Ely. I shiver as I hear the water burbling under the bridge and flowing on down the valley...

The Colliery lying dormant, waiting, ready to burst into vibrant life, when each interlocking operation would wake and greet a new day. The Blacksmith's shop, the Sawmill, Brickworks, Coke Works, the full drams rising, tipped at the screens and circling round empty to be sent down again, the journeys of slag being hauled to the Tip, and the men, the essential ingredient, making each operation a part of the whole. I reach the lamp room, call out my number '539' to the lamp man through one of the small windows along the side and place my lamp check inside as I receive the lamp in return. I walk to No2, the Upshaft, the section around the shaft is all boxed in, to control the flow of air, and join the small group of five or six at the Pit top. We are the early ones who catch the 6:30 bond. Only men are raised until 7 last bond which is always full. My Father goes down at 6, he will be in the face by now. The banksman searches our pockets for cigarettes or matches before we step inside and he closes the gate. He signals the winding man and the cage rises slightly as he pulls back the lever controlling the flanges. The cage drops, the doors slam close. Slowly at first, then gathering speed, the shoes clanging

49

against the guides, the air fusty and warm; clearing my throat as my ears pop during the descent, thinking about the hole below and us hanging on the end of a 2in wire rope. The cage slows, lands gently at pit bottom and the hitcher opens the gate. The Fireman is standing by the hitcher's manhole to test our lamps before we set out on our mile-long walk to the coalface. We leave the well-lit double parting at Pit bottom and continue along the main heading, the dust cushioning our steps, the roof, supported by either steel rings or double timber, varying in height above our heads. The steel pipes conveying the compressed air that drives the blast engines and supplies the coalfaces, running along the sides of the heading. We reach the road leading off to Jeff district. The others turn off here, opening and closing the brattice-covered door that controls the flow of air, and I carry on alone. I change my 14lb lamp to my right hand and adjust the water jack in my pocket. As I enter our heading I see the yellow glow of my Father's oil lamp down at the face. I stop at the manhole where we keep our tools and strip off, hanging my coat, shirt and daicap on a cramp driven into the road post. I put on my tam, take my pick and water jack and join my Father at the face.

The seam we are working is called the No3 and varies in thickness between 15ins and 2ft 3ins. It has a rock top and softer rock floor. We drive a heading, turning stalls to the right. This involves working the seam over a width of 10 yards as we move forward. The 8 yards on the left are worked within the confines of the seam, the remaining 2 yards are worked as part of the road. The furthest section of the 8 yards is where we cut the 'Rib', where we advance leaving the remaining pillar of coal behind. The seam is worked by laying on the rock floor and using a pick to cut a 2-3in gap between the floor and the bottom of the coal to a depth of 6-8ins over the width of the face, this is called holing and working the coal. A mandrel is then used to peel off the 6-8 layer. Curling boxes, with a capacity of about a hundredweight, are used to load the cut coal, the box is pushed into the coal and then filled by the hands and forearms gathering it in. It's then dragged or slid to the road to be placed in the dram. The large lumps are saved, a level-bedded dram weighs about a ton, but by using the large lumps as racing around the sides and infilling the middle with small coal the weight can be increased by another 6-10cwt. As we are paid on tonnage and the time between changing drams, 'hitching' varies, this method is used to make our tonnage as high as possible. The seam is advanced 2-3 yards using wooden props to support the roof and double timber for the roadway. The height and width required for the road and dram to advance 2-3 yards involves blowing out a section of the bottom rock, approximately 6ft wide and 5ft deep. Using a boring machine driven by compressed air two 6ft holes are drilled 3ft deep and two 6ft holes at 5ft. These are called the first and second lifts and are fired by the Shotsman on the night shift. Clearing the blown rock is known as 'on the muck'. My Father using shovel, pick and sledge throws the broken rock up into the recently cut areas of the seam, which is now called 'the gob.' I lay midway in the seam using the larger stone to build a wall to contain the smaller rubble and a shovel to 'double handle' the muck and fill the furthest area of the seam, removing the wooden props as the work proceeds. My Father like most colliers chewed 'Plover' twist, which he kept in a small brass box in his trouser pocket breaking off a screw periodically and spitting indiscriminately anywhere and everywhere. Before throwing the larger stones he shouts 'fingers' and unless I am quick I am nursing skinned knuckles or maybe another black nail. On top of that I get the dubious pleasure of handling stones covered with tobacco spittle fragrant to the touch. Sometimes while handling the broken stone I stop and gaze in wonder at the delicate tracery of the fragile fronds of the green fern, captured and imprisoned, etched forever between the layers of the riven rock, and I marvel at the sight.

When the muck is cleared, which takes most of the shift, we erect a pair of double timbers to support the roof. This involves using the hatchet to cut a V notch on the top of two 6ft posts and placing them parallel to each other on opposite sides of the heading. These are called the arms. The distance between the notches on the top of the posts is determined by using a 5ft measuring rod and hand spans if required. Drove notches are cut in the cross member timber, called the 'collar', the required distance apart, the timber lifted and the notches fitted together. Wooden wedges are then driven between the 'collar' and the rock roof to secure it. Great pride is taken in ensuring that the fit of the notches is perfect the first time of erection. When turning a stall or constructing a double parting the length of a cross member can be between 8-12ft with a diameter to suit and requires 2-3 men to assist in lifting and securing it. You can imagine the gentle words of dismay that are uttered if the fit is awry and the timber has to be taken down and the notches adjusted. Time is money, asking for help is accepted but if it exceeds the required time because of bad workmanship the whole district will know before the end of the shift.

There is a hierarchy involved in the running of a Colliery. At the top, the Manager, responsible for the overall safety, organisation and profitability of the Colliery. The Under Manager with delegated powers. On the surface, the Engineer, overseeing the electrical side, the Head splicer, the wire pit ropes, journey ropes, cage and guidon, the Winders in their pristine engine houses where no unauthorised person was allowed to enter. The Head lampman, the Tip foreman, the Screens foreman. The Blacksmiths who made the rail partings, repaired the shackles, sharpened the tools and found time to make the iron contraption with the pronged forks, that sat over the bars of the grate and supported the bucket on the fire, which was used in most miners' houses. The tapered iron poker and small, L-shaped poker for raking out the ashes. The Sawyers who cut the timber, sleepers and planks, and made the pastry boards and rolling pins that were used by the

53

women of the village to roll out the pastry for the pies, tarts and Welsh cakes, and maybe to threaten an errant or malingering husband. The shunters, spraggers and riders. The Banksmen, with the power to stop any offenders from entering the cage. Underground the Overman, the Firemen and the Shotsman. The Hitcher and the spragman at pit bottom, the engine drivers and riders, who moved the journeys. The Gaffer haulier, in charge of the hauliers and pit ponies who changed the drams at the coalface. The repairers, mostly working on the night shift, who maintained the roads, cutting pokings, or renewing double timber, broken by the 'squeeze' of the rock above. At the coalface, at the cutting edge, the colliers with the skills of a fitter, a railwayman, and a carpenter, using basic tools, working with inadequate lighting, poor ventilation and breathing the killer dust. And always the rock overhead, forbidding, brooding, waiting. We normally fill 5-6 drams during the shift, producing about 8-9 tons. We eat our 'snap' around 10:30 or when there is a break in the hitch. My tommy box mostly contains cheese sandwiches with maybe a Welsh cake for afters. The piece of dirty sandwich I held in my fingers I throw in the gob. Our time at the face normally ends about 2 and we carry our tools back to the 'bar'. This is a 3/8inch rod of steel about 1ft long with a larger diameter section on one end and a slotted section on the other. The mandrels, picks, hatchet, sledge and various other tools are threaded on the bar through holes drilled in the shaft, a small metal 'cotrell' is placed through the slot and locked, making the tools secure.

We dress and walk up the heading, meeting the men and boys from the neighbouring stalls, talking quietly until we reach the first double parting. The hauliers and pit ponies are just leaving. We trail behind breathing in the dust kicked up by their hooves until they turn off for the stables. Reaching Pit bottom we fall in the 'gwt', resting against the empty drams. 2:30, the hitcher counts the first 30 men into the cage and signals them away We catch the second bond, the cage rising, slowing as we near the top, lifting the doors as we reach the surface, the banksman lifting the gate, warm rays of sunlight glancing through the struts of the overhead gantry as we cross the yard making our way to the lamproom ... then down the banking and along the sidings towards home.

Eugene Smith might well have had an intuition of that; a regime for a boy which is strictly unimaginable even in South Wales in this new century. He may even have sensed or seen some of the artisan and craftsmen skills the collier required. But I suspect there was no way in which Smith could have imagined the immediate balance available after work, in living, which the young Vernon found ready for him in that society, to take such an arduous life forward with such intent.

Vernon was a part of a wider culture in his South Wales, from playing Saturday football to going to the latest 'pictures' in Tonyrefail to see a double bill, and hiss a war-time Prime Minister on Gaumont British News 'bringing the latest pictures of our forces on land, sea, and in the air' because 'my father told me he's the one who sent the troops to the Rhondda during the strike and the Pandy riots'. But the culture was participatory and aspirational as much as it was directed and consumerist. After work and household duties Vernon invariably visited his uncle Evan Griffith, Willy's older brother and Treasurer of the Coedely Lodge, in the top terraced street:

> He opened the glass-fronted cabinet that housed his little library, special offers from the *Reader's Digest* [and] turning around, he left me alone. I knelt down and placed the [borrowed] book on the shelf inside, then ran my gaze along the slim volumes, reading the gold lettering on the spines. 'Alexander Dumas, Robert Louis Stevenson, Sir Walter Scott, Mark Twain, Victor Hugo, R. M. Ballantyne.' Which to choose, which to choose. Right, this one: J. Fenimore Cooper, *The Last of the Mohicans*, was it there that I acquired my love of books that would last all my life? I closed the cabinet, showed my uncle my choice and thanked him, then back home.

Vernon Harding left the colliery in 1959 when he was thirty-one years old and spent the two decades after that in civil engineering, housing and road construction, joining the Land Reclamation Unit in 1979 as on-site Clerk of Works, heavily involved in the tip stabilisation process that had followed on the appalling, and preventable, tragedy of the tip slide in Aberfan in 1966. He was brought back from a temporary retirement in 1993 to be involved, until his final retirement in 1998 aged 70, with the reclamation of the Coedely Colliery and

Coke Ovens site – 'They were sure that I would like to be involved with that scheme to ensure that the work was done correctly.' They were right. It was, and it was also, in a sense, part of Vernon Harding's legacy to the people of the place where he still lives.

Eugene Smith left his own lingering legacy. Vernon Harding, when he was finally able to view and contemplate the full extent of Smith's work in South Wales, told me:

> ...I always suspected that he had taken more than one photograph in Coedely. I find it strange to discover that he had spent the whole day in Coedely, wandering around, talking to friends and neighbours and yet all of us ignorant of our participation in his pictorial recording of that time... and afterwards, when I looked at it again, Eugene Smith became very real to me. I began to look at those photographs through his eyes and... as you mentioned in the [BBC4] film, when looking at the photographs in the [Tredegar] Miners' Institute: 'It must have blown his mind.'
>
> He must have talked with some of those men, men with forthright views and the ability to express them. In his journeys around South Wales taking those photographs, he must have spoken to a great number of people, absorbing some of their philosophy, their attitudes and it [must have] left a lasting impression on him.

Eugene Smith's view of his subject matter had been sharpened and deepened in South Wales. Inevitably it remained partial, not quite attuned to a more complex past nor to the flux of that present time. I would argue that adding what we know outside the frame of Smith's picture of three Coedely miners does not completely change its contemporary force and passing meaning but perhaps it helps to complete it in then unforeseen ways. Certainly any simple separation of ways of knowing and ways of seeing should be sidelined by any society not content with being be-dazed by its own mirrored image.

*

In 1978, as a young social historian more concerned with proclaiming the neglected importance of Welsh working-class history in its political and institutional form than with its diurnal detail, even though the latter held a guilty fascination for me, I agreed to give a lecture on the riots in Tonypandy. At that time I thought them lesser, from the secondary sources I had read, than the Cambrian Combine strike that both preceded and followed them, and which I glibly assumed to be their cause. But I began to see, from the circumstance of birthplace and its accompanying local geographical knowledge, that the accepted narrative of triumphant police and cowed strikers did not fit the stop-start chronology unfolding around the November siege of blackleg labour in the Glamorgan Colliery, Llwynypia. And only then did I realise that the shops in Tonypandy were smashed not by a retreating mob but by a coldly enraged and knowledgeable crowd intent, by their own action, on exposing the social pathology of their forming society. The detail of home ownership and rentals by a shopocracy, of the strikers' emblematic disdain for authority, of both medical profiteers and capitalist coal owners, and of the impulse behind a Carnival of Disorder, then all became not incidental but piece by piece revelations of what was thought in silence and acted upon with eloquence. In short, they were defining their community against the definition of others. They were interventionists intent on innovation.

At least that is what they were when, here and elsewhere, they acted in concert. If I look again at that young man, my grandfather, swept up in an irresistible collectivity at the bottom of the Empire Hill in 1910, I am still not sure I would see, without knowing, the face of a participant in the Tonypandy riots. Then I look at him in another group photograph, this time of the one-hundred-strong Williamstown Male Voice Choir, formed in 1911 during the year-long Cambrian Combine Strike. It is now 1918, that hopeful summer three months before the end of the most terrible war. He is now 29 years old and the father of Morfydd, born in 1914, with Enid to come in the last days of the year. For her it will be a childhood of national strikes, in 1919 and 1921 and 1926, and almost two decades of seemingly immovable unemployment. The family will consider migration to London and to Kent. Instead they will stay. Almost a century later, looking at this picture of a lost world, of those improbably dress-suited miners, the thronged choristers who had won the National Eisteddfod contest in Neath that August of 1918, I see that the community is indeed already defined and I know that the singer will not be separated from the song which, in this book, I try to sing again.

The Killer

Snapshots of Gwyn Thomas from the early 1930s, after he had gone from the Rhondda to Oxford University aged 18, until the mid-1940s, when he published his first fiction aged 33, show a sunken-eyed, hollow-cheeked and almost cadaverous man. They were, he recalled, 'a tribute to emaciation and gloom'. The student of Spain has an Iberian cast of features in these photographs and a jutting lower lip beneath a firmly shut, unsmiling mouth that hints at the later smoulder of a young Richard Burton. By the time Gwyn's thyroid condition had been controlled and regular rations ushered in by full-time teaching and a careful wife, the writer had taken on the heavy-set look which carried the epithets of jowly and burly with it. In 1953 he sent his friend, the poet Glyn Jones, a studio portrait of himself in lieu of a Christmas card. On the inside cover of its paper frame, opposite the toothy, smiling jester he had become, Gwyn wrote: 'See what a gross thing the thin, unhappy poet has become.... In grinning place of holly.'

Features can deceive. The Judge who was the ascetic beneath the skin had become the Joker who, through the 1950s and 1960s, dominated the airwaves, sometimes uncomfortably so, as the quipping humourist from the apparently now good-natured post-war Valleys. One image at least. The novels had become increasingly wordy and farcical until their abrupt end in 1958 with one, *The Love Man*, that was neither. His own verdict was: 'The novel is not dead, only the novelist.' The regular columns in *Punch* occasionally strained for the belly laugh the younger and gifted clown had known effortlessly how to cause: a nervy rumble in the pit of the stomach. Yet as Gwyn turned to writing stage plays and from the deadly *The Keep* of 1960 onwards, with school teaching soon left behind, the moralist's scalpel was never out of reach. The Joker's mask could slip readily, and had done so even in the becalmed 1950s, to reveal the sardonic and acerbic Wit for whom human grace in the collective was, to reverse the accepted order, all too often betrayed by human folly in the singular. In school we knew him as Killer and for once maybe the nickname of schoolboys may have penetrated deeper beneath the skin than we could have imagined.

He killed us constantly with his classroom jokes. We died daily with laughter. He involved us in his conspiracy against school authority. He taught us to stifle our pleasure with silence. We learned to grin with an inane knowingness that was insufferable to headmasters. When he finally abandoned the teaching profession to which he had clung for security for twenty years, we could feel ourselves the audience on which the great dissembler had first played out his trickery. He left with the abruptness of a broken love affair. He returned at the end of the school year with the grateful penance of the forgiven to make a speech to the whole school: masters and boys. The latter were treated to a world-turned-upside-down for the hour in which it lasted as the school and all its ways, its secrets and its name calling, was given its real life, our experience of it, through his fictional telling. The authority of the school, especially those of his colleagues who were unloved by him, and their name was legion, was mocked, flayed and dissected for its pretension and its occasional sadistic brutality (this was a Boys' Grammar School with internal public school trappings behind its external Victorian red-brick facade, set on one of the many hills in the railway and docks town of Barry). He talked of 'leaving in the night like a Bedouin packing up his tent', of how one master had 'political views to the right of the Pharoahs' and that to 'get lower' than another, in the general judging sense we instinctively shared at our relatively uncorrupted age, 'you would, boys, have to get under the linoleum!' Then, the Killer was gone.

I had encountered him when I arrived in the summer of 1957 at Barry Grammar School where he had taught since 1942. He did not teach me directly until 1959 when I joined his pre-sixth form Spanish class for two years. But I had been put in his way slightly earlier as a 'new boy' from the Rhondda. I was introduced, so to speak, to Rhondda's most famous writer by a colleague who understood Gwyn's benevolent interest and sensed my own detached sense of not quite belonging. And then there was *The Barrian*, the school magazine which they made the published writer edit. Gwyn Thomas was thus the first to accept anything of mine for publication: me and scores of others of course.

His presence in the school loomed large whether you were taught by him or not. In part, because he, and he alone, was on the Welsh Home Service with his evocative-of-us drama documentary radio plays, and then on *The Brains Trust*, on the common culture that was then nightly BBC television. In part, because he drank with some of our fathers – 'soaks his feet in it', they said – in *The Park* or the RAFA Club – 'pissed over my shoes, talking so much in the Gents!' – and his views were sought by the local newspapers (there were two) and even the *South Wales Echo*. Mostly it was because he was talked about by other boys who could not quite believe, and so repeated and embellished, what he had said in the shared imprisonment of the classroom. Or in the school library, used for small-group teaching purposes, whose coal-fire grate shared the chimney piece of the back-to-back care-taker's house and through which embrasure, one day, came the red hot poker of an over-enthusiastic Mr Moody, hence impaling, in Gwyn's retelling, a boy dozing in the heat until wakened by a 'flaming assegai not used so effectively since the last Zulu conflagration. So avoid falling asleep before the fire, boys, if you hear Mr Moody at work in his kitchen.' Or, best of all, when Gwyn was the master in charge of dining room service in the clattering tin-roofed canteen. The custom was, once all the trestle tables had been served from the hatch by junior boys, for the supervising schoolmaster to say a thankful grace for the eyes-closed, heads-down boys. Usually a teacher who inspired tranquillity by a threatening presence and a known reputation had no need to do more than intone the first words to see silence settle like a pall over the flock about to eat. Only in Gwyn's case there was no threat, no presence and a reputation for a hair-trigger temper that was rendered harmless by his inclination to burst into self-deflating guffaws at the peak of any tirade of anger. This day, I remember, we talked and chatted and threw pieces of bread as Gwyn's serving spoon banged down over and over on a central table until, at very long last, in concentric circles of complicit communication, we did get the message as our cold dinners congealed in their slide of gravy grease. To our surprise, the silence imposed with such difficulty was now extended. Not a masterly word was spoken. The silence deepened all around us. It began to worry us. Eyes peeped open. Then, Gwyn's voice, as always a combination of staccato bark and throaty invitation.

Boys. Boys. If you're as slow getting down to grace tomorrow as you've been today, it won't be a master they'll be sending... it'll be a missionary!

Uproar. Gwyn chortling, and that expertly placed 'they' distinguishing us, and him, from 'Them'.

I think few of us read any of his books when we were at school though, in Gollancz's yellow-jacketed, red-covered hardbacks, they filled the shelves of the town library. Certainly I only began to read him in any depth when I came across his early novels arranged in sequence in their American editions on the subterranean shelves of Columbia University's Low Library in New York in the late 1960s. I entombed myself amongst the stacks, crouched over a dimly lit table, for days on end. They proved to be more than a whiff of home. They offered me an intellectual pathway back to a half-buried historical experience.

65

Shortly before he died in 1981, I went to visit Gwyn in his house in Peterston-super-Ely, in the Vale of Glamorgan, within a twitch and a shout of his two previously long-inhabited spiritual homes. He lived between the Rhondda where he was born in 1913 in Cymmer, Porth, into a large and exuberantly boisterous family and Barry, that unlikely Tonypandy-by-Sea, where he had taught Spanish in the Grammar School from 1942 until he decamped to the life of a freelance writer and broadcaster in 1962. Lyn, his wife and amanuensis since 1937 – she had enlarged knuckles on her small hands from type-thumping out Gwyn's almost indecipherable handwriting on an ancient green monster of a machine – had warned me that he was decidedly unwell. Diabetes and a long-time general aversion to taking care of himself had ruined his kidneys and made a man for whom personal mobility was akin to unnecessary actuarial risk even more static than his usual rooted self. Forewarned, I entered the living room cautiously to find Gwyn, seated and beaming, sipping a large dry martini and offering me one as compensation for his not being able to make it to the pub. In the hour or so that followed Gwyn was only confined in body for his mind soared and his wit darted as delightfully and as bewilderingly as ever, and I was as bewitched by it and him as much as I had been as a dazzled schoolboy, an amused TV viewer or, later, a deeply admiring reader of his work.

Gwyn's own maladies were turned to the comic uses he employed for society at large. His diabetic condition had triggered a host of ailments and caused lengthy hospitalisation, with blood samples taken so regularly 'that I have to be shaken three times a day'. I told him that he seemed better than when I had visited him in hospital. He grimaced: 'Ah, yes. But it's the eye, you know, this eye. The left. Can't see much with it now.' I peered closer. 'Oh. It looks all right,' I muttered. 'I know, I know,' he said: 'the bugger should win an Oscar for simulation.'

Gwyn's barrage of wisecracks, quips and anecdotes, however well recalled as conversation, were, strictly speaking, the scaffolding of an inimitable act, a performance that can be remembered but not repeated or fully revealed in print. In part that was what made him so special. He needed an audience before whom he could parade his wit and, in turn grateful for that presence, he did not stint on the entertainment factor. When I was made sufficiently helpless with laughter he struggled out of his chair to pour another large gin and vermouth. He swallowed some diuretic pills with it, claiming both tablets and liquid as a medical prescription. Then he apologised for having to go to the bathroom, with a parting shot:

These things have made me big in the water business. I'm passing so much of the stuff Birmingham Corporation have made a bid for me.

I wrote the evening up, inadequately, but in a rage to place him in the consciousness of a generation already leaving him behind, in a profile piece for *Arcade*. This Wales fortnightly had been created by John Osmond to help mend the divisive culture fracture that had been signalled

67

in Wales by the 1979 referendum on devolution. I had voted 'Yes'. Gwyn certainly would have voted 'No'. But that was irrelevant in 1981 in the early years of Thatcher's Britain. This is what I scribbled then in my attempt to enfold his humour and his humanity within the thrust, and demise, of South Wales' history.

What gave his early writing such intensity and gives his voice in conversation, the raised finger calling attention to his seriousness, such thrilling passion, is his intellectuality. And it is precisely because he has written and talked of working-class life in Wales with such verve and humour that this most obvious fact about a most cerebral writer has been largely missed.

The irony is not lost on *him*. What is more galling is the wilful blindness this shows towards the minds of the people among whom he grew up. It is not community warmth, or sentimental hearts, or family sacrifice, or even the heroic submission to a manual labour that killed you bit by bit, so that you live piece by piece, that he celebrates. His writing, and the history of South Wales, would be so much more conveniently dismissible if it were. He remembers a review in the *New York Times* that said he wrote of 'scarecrows on a refuse tip'. The grimness of the image was all right, yet it, too, failed to see the wonder of what these modern rag-pickers had discovered: Gwyn Thomas' subject was the 'underlying threnody – the intellectual climate discovered by them'.

A world had been thrust into a white-hot blast

furnace of modernity, turned to molten steel and then, via war and depression, made stiff and unyielding to reason after a cold water plunge. But reason they did: 'Minds were pitched high on thoughtful protest, and stayed there.'

The great lock-outs of 1921 and 1926 transformed grassy hillocks into open-air universities. The mornings were given to cutting coal in the levels opened into the hillsides, the afternoons to talk. Games were played with the same zest, 'little Olympics' built around 'Catty and Dog': a workers' croquet – miners, with great skill, competing in teams to hit a sharpened wooden stick with an idle mandrel shaft, out of the circle and away, up and across hills and tips. He feels he 'assimilated their experience into mine'.

And at home brothers and sisters would rush into the kitchen like messengers from some classical Greek play bringing the news of the outside world in. His father planted flowers in the narrow front abutting onto Cymmer High Street: A.J. Cook, then catching fire from Rhondda militancy as Somerset Salvationism was sloughed off, would use the Thomases' slightly higher stoop as a vantage point for demagoguery, and Gwyn's father was alienated from the left wing by this constant trampling down of his blooms.

Intellectual excitement, not horticultural care, was the order of the day. Men and women came, in his view, to a profundity of understanding via these cultural shifts and economic disasters, that led them to recognise that 20 years before, as the new century dawned, they had been 'speaking and thinking gibberish'. Some of them went, literally, mad through this abrupt passage of time – 'When the bottom fell out of your trousers, the bottom fell out of religion.'

From this bewilderment came an analysis of the nature of its absurdity. South Wales made, for the first time ever in Wales on a large scale, new, vital assertions about human society. Unlike other industrial areas in Britain the divisions of craft mentality were almost completely transcended. The class struggle signified the march of humanity and it was thought, not emotion, that was the explosive in the mind. It had to be placed carefully. The unemployed, after 1926, 'were not always in the mood for big propositions after a week eking out existence on the dole', so men like Lewis Jones, unemployed leader of the unemployed, would waken them with a wit that could convulse an audience, before leading them to more serious pastures. In a working class possessed of high literacy the 'cult of the word' was nurtured by 'high priests of self-expression'. Lewis Jones, a man he thinks the most gifted of all those richly-endowed leaders, and hauntingly poignant for choosing to stay away from 'velvet summits', was 'constantly hinting at the need to deepen our wisdom, our sophistication. That we must cease to be simple.'

Gwyn Thomas, held spellbound in the enormous community demonstrations against the Means Test in 1935, wrote a naturalistic novel called *Sorrow For*

Thy Sons. The style was very different from the one he later forged.

He remembers watching the thousands upon thousands who marched down from Penrhys mountain and the Rhondda Fach into Mid-Rhondda to merge with the crowd, and the oceanic sense of being a part of it that he had.

A man near Lewis Jones, grasping for some appropriate rhetoric, intoned – 'Multitudes. Multitudes. Coming to the Valley of Decision.'

Lewis Jones told him sharply – 'They're just coming together so get rid of your bloody Bible.'

Gollancz liked Gwyn Thomas' first book but felt a bit scorched by it. The subsequent oblique style was a way of reaching out without deafening the audience. The material he had to convey was so overwhelming that it could lead to simple-witted melodrama. 'Protest inhibits humour.' And humour is, above all other things, the mark of a self-conscious humanity. Gwyn Thomas thrived on the badinage of the Marx Brothers and the tennis-game repartee of American big-city writers. His characters talked the way they did because 'only the very best language was good enough for the people I was writing about'.

Their language proclaimed their humanity when so much else denied it. Their humour shouted out, and sometimes whispered, their defiance. 'Somebody ought to analyse my humour. One thing it proves is that the South Welsh did enlarge understanding. I was only a clue to the great thing that was being achieved – a mountain of achievement that has crumbled away. I think my humour shows the way in which the intellect of the Welsh working-class might have developed their world.'

Those incredible novels and stories of the late forties and fifties tried to help carry that culture over. South Wales had not yet become a 'Turkish brothel' (a theme of his 1962 musical play *Loud Organs*), the Labour Party and the Communist Party not yet become either silent or corrupt, the 'phylloxera of nationalism' not yet at work in the vineyard. In the 1950s Gwyn Thomas gave a new dimension to radio drama and documentaries in Wales with a series of highly popular plays. For a time he thought there was a chance of an Abbey Theatre in the wake of Synge and O'Casey, in South Welsh terms, but that did not survive the stultification of the Welsh media.

And South Wales itself? The centre did not hold. No focus emerged after the optimism of the late 1940s; the energy was diffused; the disjunction between its being and its potential was shadowed by false, fleeting prosperity – 'the refulgent dreams of my dark philosophers would turn out to be nothing'.

He thought himself to be, in the title of one of his essays, The Judge as Joker. And, from the start, he was as merciless as he was funny. This is the hapless Omri in his 1951 masterpiece *The World Cannot Hear You*:

Whatever calamity dealt Omri a clip, there was no answering anger; only a slight shrug and a message to the calamity that he, Omri, after a good deal of futile standing up and catching it from a wide range of missiles was now ready to lie down, be still and have done with all protest and strife. We, his friends, took the view that life, while often stupid and churlish, would sweeten its mood after a few decades of attention and protest from voters like ourselves who were doing spells of duty in the compost, and we denounced Omri as being socially a nuisance in this taste for complacence and inertia.

Not even when he closed up his home after his broken marriage and had gone back to live with his brother Bodvan had he improved much. Bodvan was the opposite of Omri. He was smaller again than Omri but he was a walking glow of energy, the nearest we will ever come to Napoleon in this essentially modest strip of the Celtic fringe where the rates are so high they make everybody look short. Bodvan had the kind of appetite for owner-ship and power which would have allowed him to pick up the world and suck it dry of juice like an orange if he had the opportunity and time to get a grip. In all man's experience of seeing property cornered never had the corners been more sharply defined and defended than in Meadow Prospect. Pits, two iron works, shops, houses had been assigned their pockets as rigidly as the stars their constellations and the owners had no wish to be rearranging the heavens, not even for such an eager voter as Bodvan. He overdid eagerness. Any man who goes about with a light in his eye clearly telling life that he expects much from it is asking for trouble. Life, which nourishes itself on darkness, and hates to have the shaking flare of torches thrown on its threadbare years, will notice the light in the voter's eye and will take pleasure in dowsing it. We warned Bodvan about this, reminded him that we had formally moved and got it passed in the Library and Institute that from what we had seen there is no mountain higher, no ocean deeper than the frustration of man. But he did not listen. When he had come down from the North with Omri in a peasant's cart he had got no work more profitable than hauling in the pit. He had tried hard to please. When Bodvan smiled at an official it was a major movement and every other light below ground could be snuffed out. But every official in whose face he was beginning to see the portals of preferment would move off to another area or drop down dead during one of the wilder hymns before Bodvan got his fingers around the door knob. We told Bodvan that his oriental manner of bowing and scraping was too rich for the blood of these dour voters and whenever he tried to capture their hearts he used too strong a grip and guaranteed a seizure.

When the slump moved in among us and the years of the skeleton came, Omri agreed with us that the world's worst winter was at hand and he decided to settle into his warren, attend the Discussion Group at the Institute and read the thicker books, existing generally as a root of unprotesting coma until the more watchful voters, sensing a return of light and warmth, would shout down to warn him that Spring was back again. Also, a month before Omri had finished work he had had

all his teeth out and when he moved on to the
Insurance he had to cancel an order he had put in
for dentures and he passed on to the dentist the
verdict of Eddie Wedlock that by the time he would
be in a position to pay for them his gums would be
so shrunken he would need to call in a miniaturist to
work on the ivories. Omri's toothless gums made
him look a lot smaller and his face more resigned,
and there is no doubt that he found the world and
man's whole dilemma almost enjoyable as he sat
there in the reading room of the Institute sucking his
gums and wondering how the people in the Tatler
ever get to look so confident on such a planet.

In his early fiction, essentially the short stories and novels
of the 1940s, the savagery was only just about sweetened
by the wit. He perfectly well understood the umbilical
cord that held the two together and why. Reflecting on it
as early as 1952 at the end of a great creative spell and
what he called 'the last gasp of the first violent mood' in
which he had been writing, he said:

> What I write is tied umbilically to the astonishing
> Rhondda Valley where I was born and brought up. It
> is a great sprawling mining community hemmed
> between high, close hills. In the course of my child-
> hood and youth this rapidly assembled and matured
> community of 200,000 people was shrunken and
> twisted under the impact of long strikes and a bitter
> depression. The people, largely of Celtic stock,
> already plagued by a vague 'mystique' of racial
> defeat   and   a   passionately   lyrico-religious

temperament, found their life-view darkening as their economic and spiritual underpins were sent spinning... I was... never free from the fierce conviction that the essence of their strange wild humour could and should be communicated, making audible every tone of their bawled comment on a pitiless and crumbling environment. Into that humour went a comradeship in multiple discomfort and mutilated longings, the pervasive memory of a half-buried, brooding, bardic culture, tales of immemorial grief set to the sweep of harps; and to frame man at his daftest, nature, in the shape of hills of a mould superbly smooth, and insistent rain mist edging down towards the valley bed...

Take, then, the three novellas of his first violent mood with its 'hints of the most extreme savagery'. First published in 1946, they were reissued in the Library of Wales series in 2005, under the overall title of *The Dark Philosophers*. In the title story the self-same dark philosophers so hound the Reverend Emmanuel Prees with their scornful opinions and unforgiving wit that he has an induced heart attack and dies. He is a man who, in their view, betrayed his calling to witness for the downtrodden and instead accepted the comforts of rich benefactors. And, like Simeon in the shortest story, he is a sexual predator, as is Oscar, who is also, in the darkest novella, a Welshman who owns a mountain on whose slag heap the unemployed scavenge for coal. Oscar, too, has to go. He is a Welshman who goes up a mountain slowly but comes down quickly when an apprentice dark philosopher pushes him off its edge. Murder is a metaphor for impotence in these tragedies of fictional vengeance. The impotence is shared out, collectively, by his dark philosophers – of whom Gwyn often said he was himself the darkest – who speak, wonderfully and uniquely, of 'what they have seen of human desire and social waste. Or rather they sing like a displaced operatic chorus, not quite believing the absurd plot of life into which they, and their kind, have been unfortunate enough to stray.

Marvellously, the cover photograph of the Library of Wales edition of *The Dark Philosophers* seems to represent them – Ben, Willie, Walter, Arthur and the collective and narrative 'We' – perfectly, as from the life, or rather from *Life*. It was taken in 1950, during the General Election of that year which confirmed the widespread desire for a socialist Britain, and was taken in an Italian café in Aneurin Bevan's Tredegar. It shows a small group of earnest men in dark overcoats talking and plotting over their white china coffee cups. The photographer was, of course, Eugene Smith.

He could not have known, other than instinctively, how close he came in this particular photograph to capturing the essence of mind, the consciousness, of those industrial valleys at their political and moral peak. Here were the dark philosophers, momentarily, in triumphant action. And they are listening to the bespectacled plotter-in-chief, the man who had schemed – and then some! – to have Nye Bevan nominated for Parliament in 1929 and who had sustained him, with fellow members of The Query Club, ever since – forever quizzing and chivvying the assumed authority of others. It is none other than Archie Lush, Bevan's diminutive friend and political agent, another representative, as Gwyn Thomas thought Bevan was supremely so, of that South Welsh praxis of thought and action which had come to a head in the late 1930s and 1940s.

What is transparently clear is that Gwyn Thomas was a key cultural part of that society – both as a product and as a maker. He wrote a stage play *and* a television play about the meaning of Aneurin Bevan within that whole social and historical context of South Wales in the first half of the past century. Mere details, the dates of things, the names of places, the facts about elections or strikes or whatever made up the fabric of that readily clichéd time, did not interest him. He was concerned with knowledge and with the action that should, or might, follow in its path. In 1962 he told an interested, and similarly connected, Richard Burton what he was trying to say about the recently dead Bevan:

> I want the piece in no way to be a chronicle of things that pushed a dead man towards his end. I want to go right into the hinterland beyond Nye; all the voices in the valleys that were faintly heard but never truly sounded.
>
> I would like to express the valour, wisdom, laughter of all the men and women in our part of Wales who thrust Aneurin like a lance at the spiteful boobs at Westminster who regarded us in their innermost thoughts as a kind of intolerable dirt. A thundering vindication [then] of us and our kind.

That was his key theme – in novels, stories, plays and essays – and a chorus of humour was his chosen means.

Plural in voice because their singular story was about the many, and with sardonic amusement because laughter was the proof, beyond all others, of their consciousness of themselves as a higher part of humanity no matter what their miserable material circumstance. Briefly, it did all seem to hold together.

So there he was, in the very early 1950s, at the height of his first fame, hailed in America as well as in Britain as one of the most brilliant voices of his time, and, for a brief period, confident that his writing fitted perfectly into the culture and politics of that post-war world. He had created a style to suit his subject and his purpose. His output was prodigious – seven novels, in addition to two collections of stories, between 1946 and 1956, publication in the States, and translations into Russian, Norwegian, Swedish and Dutch. By the end of the 1950s he wrote no more novels but a new tack as a playwright and a librettist, drama *and* musicals, had opened up and shorter fiction and prose works of an autobiographical nature never ceased. This range and volume of work is part of the reason for the later obscurity of his fame and the lasting refulgence of his talent. There was so much in so many modes that slower-footed critics just could not, still cannot, keep up. We will be measuring him in our universities and coming to grips with him as readers for a long time to come.

Yet there are other ongoing reasons for the divisions of opinion around Gwyn Thomas. He himself used to say that a fortune-teller in Ponty market in the 1930s once had a sign outside her tent that read 'The Future Told: Cautiously', but he, himself, always threw caution to the winds. When the Wales that might have strode on in the footprints of Bevan faltered and stumbled into self-satisfaction and self-congratulation as the 1950s became the 1960s it was Gwyn, on television and radio or in print, who could be relied on to say how diminished society's aspirations had become. When he said publicly that Ebbw Vale, then mightily prosperous as a steel-working town, was 'less than beautiful', Labour councillors berated him and one told him if Nye could return he would spit in his face. Gwyn just expressed amazement that Bevan's own message was being so swiftly forgotten in a silt of sentimentality and parochialism – of how he [Bevan] had taken 'the image... of the valleys into which he was born and presented it, its imperfection, its struggles, its humour, as a challenge to those parts of Britain that have never been scarred by poverty or the monstrous toll that heavy industry exacts from beauty'. For Gwyn, to look at *that* landscape – the Central Wound as he called the Rhondda – is to 'catch the echoes of that half-impish, half-angry, irony that ran through the thought and speeches of Bevan'.

To turn his own half-angry irony onto the Welsh language was to put Gwyn even further beyond some people's pale. But, of course, he never spoke against the Welsh language as such, how could he – humanist and linguist – possibly have done so? His ire was directed instead against what he regarded as at best the sanctimonious maundering of an irrelevant petit bourgeoisie of shopkeepers, teachers and preachers attracted to the self-interested kraal of protective nationalism and, at its worst, a self-willed loss of the wider potential which South Wales' lived experience had revealed. For him, no one deserved it more in the neck than the saintly Gwynfor Evans, progeny of Barry, that railway and docks town which had given birth to the politician in 1913, the year of Gwyn's own birth in the directly connected Rhondda.

The two men would regard the town to which Gwyn would go in the Second World War to teach in the Grammar School from where Gwynfor had gone, via Aberystwyth, to Oxford in 1934, the same year his Rhondda contemporary had eagerly left that university, with markedly different outlooks. The Barry-born contemplative saw his native place as without any roots or traditions in Welsh. A culture that only had depth in the north and the west from which the Evans family had originally come. It was a vulgar place in the precise sense of the epithet's embrace of a raucous population and a working-class base. This was why Gwyn Thomas warmed to its bubbling irreverent humanity.

Gwynfor Evans' grandfather, Ben, tried to offer a different kind of leadership from his key position as minister to Barry's small but influential Welsh-speaking middle class from the town-centre bastion of Tabernacl. When the town council's education committee agreed to support the local Catholic school, catering for the increasing numbers of Barry's immigrant families as the town mushroomed in size from some 400 in the 1880s to almost 40,000 in the early 1900s, it was the Liberal nonconformist elite spearheaded by minister Ben Evans who vociferously opposed it to the extent of non-payment of his rates. He went on to election to the council itself and to hold the chair of the education committee, soon purged of all elements not in keeping with the principles of Welsh dissent and democracy. Rates, religion and righteousness would be, as a Trinity, an Evans family obsession after Dan Evans, the entrepreneurial son who had come with his father from the slightly more comforting confines of Llanelli, opened up in 1905 his ironmonger's shop, close commercial neighbour to the spirituality of his father's chapel. They thrived together, with Dan travelling the Vale of Glamorgan to put his fine baritone voice to good effect, for no fee, 'but if you want to show your appreciation, I've opened in Holton Road, Barry, and you'll find a shop there you'll appreciate'. They did, and branches of Dan Evans soon dominated the town. Trade, and extensive money-making, was all important. In 1926, with General Strike and miners' lock-out shaping Welsh historical experience on the ground for generations, Dan Evans from Barry's Chamber of Trade congratulated the town's shopocracy 'for the grand way in which they had supported the [National] government in the very disastrous period they had just passed through'.

More disastrous for some, of course, than others. It was learning later of all this from within the intimacies of the town's life and its simmering resentment that would cause Gwyn to splutter in 1980 at the news that the former Plaid Cymru leader was threatening to starve himself to death, surrounded by books on Gandhi, if a Welsh-language television channel was not granted by the Thatcher government.

How many people did Gandhi lead? And to talk of 'a fast unto death' (who used that one last?) in what was once one of the Capitals of world hunger!

Gwyn Thomas was reviled for this. But he had made similar connections, and been similarly reviled, before. Once, on a live television broadcast in the 1960s, a kind of dinner-party format for debate, he had been asked to reflect on the apparently rising fortunes of Plaid Cymru and its then leading light, Gwynfor Evans. He was brusquely dismissive. And then this:

> Gwynfor Evans, of course, comes from Barry. A town I know well. His father, Dan, opened a store in the town, having travelled from the west. And made his fortune selling work implements and moleskin trousers to the town's dock workers and Rhondda miners. In the Second World War, Gwynfor, a pacifist, retreated to the family farm in Llangadog that had been bought with the money of those dockers, and there he settled to grow tomatoes on his tomato plantation. And there he remains, far from the Barry which nurtured him and made his family's fortune, up to his arse to this day in fascism and ketchup.

For Gwyn Thomas there was no brooking the argument that it was in the English language that the secular and radical civilisation of South Wales had been culturally significant. It was for this reason, along, we should recall, with some prominent Welsh-language educationalists and advocates, that he deplored in the last decade of his own life the growth of separate linguistic streams in the world of education. And his reasons were social and considered, not knee jerk or dismissive, whatever the consensus of our contrary contemporary judgement or perspective might be:

This is the worst wound you can inflict on a community. Welsh patriots have often boasted that with landed gentry so thin on the Jacobinical Welsh ground, we would never commit the sin of snobbish separatism implicit in the English Public School system. Yet a growing and muttering multitude see in the Welsh Schools simulations of Eton and Harrow. A Welsh Lord Rosebery, totally insulated from the anglophone proles, is being concocted at this moment along the banks of the Taff. God help us. The Valleys of south-east Wales had, by the beginning of World War Two, gone over totally to the English-speaking world. The attempt to degrade and replace English in the schools of those areas will do nothing but mischief in minds already plagued by every neurosis that comes with insecurity. Bilingualism, pushed to the ultimate, will complete the work of spoliation and ruin begun by the coal-owners, and the collapse into dereliction of their weird kingdom.

The passionate social and academic drives of the valleys in their prime will be lost in places slumped between the stools of two imperfectly mastered tongues. The society that produced a small army of Aneurin Bevans will be lucky to come up with one darts champion and a few penillion groups of second rank.

We should not underestimate the depth of his despair by the 1970s at the atrophying of a whole society's potential for fulfilment. For that is what he believed had happened to industrial working-class South Wales as it settled into the slough of reformism and the sloth of stasis. It would be wrong, however, to assume that Gwyn was in any way averse to the social and economic changes that brought in wall-to-wall carpeting instead of stone-cold linoleum or indoor lavatories instead of top-of-the-garden outhouses or washing machines instead of all-day Monday rub-a-dub-dub. That, and any temporary pleasures of music, drink or flesh to be garnered in, were all welcome. In a nutshell, that was why he so adored Barry Island, his Kingdom of the Chip, where generations of day trippers had found the pleasure principle made close-up and personal in that Proletarian Pleasure Dome by the sea.

Barry Island has been the jewelled eye in the childhood summers of millions of us, and from its docks has poured a quantity of coal large enough to have left at least three mountains to the north of the county quite hollow. There are few South Walians for whom Whitmore Bay... has not furnished some hook of memory on which to hang a pleasant, evening thought.

Barry is, of course, a Jekyll and Hyde town. It developed rapidly into one of the finest Welsh ports, and it also had a stretch of sand that gave it the glamour of Bali for the herded troglodytes dreaming of the sea in the austere terraces of the valleys to the north. Now [1960s] the docks have passed their zenith of wealth and power. The amount of coal passing through the dock gates would just about keep a vestry warm.

For Gwyn, this enjoyment, and more, should have come alongside the deeper enlightenment which he felt had once been more than glimpsed. His own humour grew to be more benign and sad, when it was not becoming slapstick and farcical, to accommodate the retreat.

I walked, at dusk, along the beach. I passed the very spot where in 1923 I almost drowned when serving as a short recruit in a human chain organised to stand in the sea and dredge with our toes for the teeth of the Sunday School superintendent who had swum right out of his loose, hired costume, and had shot his dentures in an explosion of shame.

Whitmore Bay has a warm loveliness. Trample such a place as you may, beauty continues to have the tough persistence of the lugworm. As I stood there a cloud of children squealed in the last mad ecstasy of a long day's freedom. A circle of gulls waited patiently to re-inherit the silent beach and a few of them squawked about the day's litter. The fairground still hummed to staunch those very real hungers felt in lives that have been pressed squat by an excess of disciplined labour and social dreariness.

If all that was release, it was no longer liberation of the kind once promised and endlessly discussed in the Workmen's Libraries and Institutes across the coalfield. These were the brains of the coalfield's body. Their books were prized and their guardians respected as dispensers of the available wisdom. Gwyn did not think they were there in place of a more rowdy and undisciplined humanity but he did see them as places that could serve as laboratories of the spirit. By the 1960s they, too, had palpably withered and were soon to disappear. His lament was no less heartfelt for being gentle:

There was a time when the Birchtown Institute was a very considerable place. The walls were distempered to match the prevailing shades of philosophic determinism. Acid overtones of radical dissent had eaten into the dark didactic murals. In the draughts room there was a plaque over the spot where Ramsay Macdonald had sat to play a game after being driven in by a cloudburst that had dispersed the open-air meeting he was holding in 1911. On the top of the main staircase was the photograph of a man who had shaken the hand of Gandhi.

At one time the lecture hall had boomed with orators, and thousands of members had developed a sort of eye trouble known as 'magic lantern blink', brought on by too violently adjusting the eyeballs on hearing any sound similar to the rap of the pointer that introduced a change of slide. And Birchtown always seemed full of that type of sound. The smaller rooms of the Institute had been full of tight, intense classes of adult thinkers that had been going on for anything up to twenty years on topics ranging from the Seven Qualities of Godhead to the Fourteen Points of Wilson.

Now the lecture room was silent and some climax of tedium and shabbiness had caused the last of the disputatious students to creep away from the smaller rooms. The rot had started with the anthropology class, the deepest-rooted comb in the whole thinking hive. One Thursday night they had suddenly stopped in mid-concept, feeling as old as the material they had been handling. And they had walked forth from the Institute renouncing all interest in man's beginnings. Their faces were blank, their eyes emptied of all the lighted curiosity of yesterday and their arms were anthropoidally adroop. Two of them had taken to Dadaism and the rest to drink.

Some wrestling bouts had been tentatively arranged in the lecture room, but they had drawn on tiny audiences, and the heavier falls of the fighters had caused bits of ceiling to land on the head of the librarian who was already dazed by the swift eclipse of literacy in the Institute, and who was in no mood to put up with any more.

A residual life went on in the draughts-and-chess rooms, but the players sat for so long in a state of querulous stillness that it seemed they were merely trying to fox death. The snooker room was the one section that still buzzed and glowed a little, but the clients there were torpid and thoughtless and when the door of the snooker room was left open the eyebrows of the man who had shaken the hand of Gandhi were seen to grow lower and darker.

Close to Gwyn Thomas' death it was too easy to make the mistake of thinking that with the demise of the singer the song, that particular, haunting song of a world with only physical traces left, had died too. If we continue to think that, then we lose two more things – the universality of the values expressed in that song and the imperishable work of a writer who survives his world by enshrining it in words. He railed but he did not despair. In January 1981 he spoke fervently of the need to make an achieved culture available to the descendants of the world he had witnessed: 'That culture,' he said, 'through novels, poems, plays and history is open to them. It can carry them on.'

Gwyn Thomas, in full flight when he and the best of his world coincided, knew exactly what he was doing and why. In a rare response to the literal minded who were scared into thinking by his visceral tickle stick, he wrote this, in 1952:

> About that comic view of life – I have tried to sound the deeper, more subtle humour of the place into which I was born, the sheer expletive astonishment of a proud, intelligent people outraged by ugliness, poverty and neglect. A comic vision of the world – and that there may be some who do not consider my own vision at all comic does not stop my argument – is a commentary on the human situation and often the most poignant.

Paradoxically then, the almost untranslatable Welshness of his material, once stripped to the bone, to its human essence, is what made his words so very much translatable and transferable to the mind and experience of others. Paradoxically too, this has made him a discomforting figure for some in Wales to accommodate, let alone love.

For me, all this gives an extra frisson to the nickname we schoolboys gave him when he was a master at Barry Grammar School. We had indeed called him Killer. No one quite knew why. Perhaps it was for the irony of so calling a man whose explosive temper we knew to be harmless or for the cinematic allure of his fast-draw, quick-fire patter. Maybe it was the jowly resemblance to Edward G. Robinson's gangster persona and perhaps the customarily worn slouch hat whose snap brim he fingered, here in American Wales, to acknowledge, at a distance, the dai caps of all our pasts. Or, maybe, because at some level of adolescent instinct we knew him to be a killer of pretension, an assassin of hypocrisy, a murderer of tyranny, a knifer of snobbery, a strangler of cruelty, an implacable enemy of all who would repress or restrain, and a fighter, equipped with all the valour, wisdom and laughter of his own kind. He enlarged our understanding; and not just ours.

Boxing with Life

I first heard the name Hedley Thomas in 1966 in a booth in a back room of the West End Bar at 116th Street and Broadway, New York City. He was the uncle of my new friend from Aberdare, Viv Thomas, whom I'd met at Columbia University that fall. After Coleg Harlech and Cambridge, Viv was doing graduate work in economics. I was studying comparative literature after the confines of an Oxford history degree. Viv's stories of home were often of a larger-than-life character, and especially about his respectable father's handsome but ne'er-do-well younger brother who charmed and conned and connived his way through life without any great exertion of any other kind. Hedley had been born in the 1920s. He was, by his own twenties, flash by nature and Flash by name. By middle age he had dwindled in scale to minor acts of deceit and the perpetual non-payment of money borrowed or purloined from friends and family. Yet once, Viv had told me, Flash had plied his post-war trade in London and fallen out with some who did not easily let debts or favours slide. Hedley Thomas had returned to Aberdare when big city street conflict between members of the notorious Billy Hill and Jack Spot gangs saw him caught in a cross fire that was not conducive to his continuing good health. I first met Uncle Flash in the summer of 1968 in the bar of Aberdare's Victorian Market Tavern. He was in company and on form, and although at first Viv was wary and even somewhat disdainful of him, the laughter was soon as constant as the stream of stories of wickedness and mayhem with which Hedley 'Flash' Thomas plied us. He also sold us some tickets, or, at least, the promise of tickets.

The talk in the bar that warm night in Aberdare was not of the Prague Spring or of the events of May in Paris, it was mostly, as I remember, about boxing. The preliminary conversational bouts were reminiscences of Abercynon's Dai Dower, and of the smiling pluck with which the curly-haired flyweight had stormed through the 1950s as British and European champion, before, weary and dehydrated, his world ambitions met their match in 1957 in Buenos Aires, in the shape of Pascual Perez, Argentina's own exceptional world champion.

The melancholia of irretrievable defeats hung over the dark philosophers of Fistiana that night as the name of another South American, the most famous one in South Wales in the 1960s, spun us into the vortex of only-justs and what-ifs in which Welsh fighting prowess had seemed to swirl helplessly generation by generation. The name was Saldivar. Vicente Saldivar. Featherweight champion of the world since 1964. The following year he travelled to London for the first of his three intensely fought and

physically draining victories against the British, Common-
wealth and European featherweight maestro, Merthyr's
Howard Winstone. Saldivar was Mexican, or, more
precisely, an Indio from Mexico. Winstone was Welsh, or,
more accurately, of Irish and Jewish extraction allied to
Merthyr's Welsh mix.

They would fight twice more after 1965, each match
doing what only boxing can do as the dross of slugging
was somehow alchemised into a compound of skill and
heroism that was minted proof against any subsequent
debasement. There was nothing that could be said to be
base about these fighters.

In June 1967 Saldivar once more put his crown at risk,
this time at Ninian Park in Cardiff, again over 15 rounds.
They ended up toe-to-toe and blow-for-blow after
Winstone had dominated the fight with his unbelievable
ring craft and boxing technique. Unbelievable but not,
that night, unbeatable as a controversial decision allowed
Saldivar to remain undefeated by the narrowest points
margin possible. Not only Winstone was devastated by
that night. Nor would three tries for a Welshman prove to
be a prophetically lucky saying for Howard. In Mexico
City in October 1967 Saldivar retired the Welsh boxer, his
toughest opponent, in twelve rounds of the scheduled
fifteen when Eddie Thomas, Winstone's guide and mentor,
threw in the towel to save his fighter from further
punishment. So exhausted was Vicente Saldivar, however,
that he promptly retired altogether. And that was our
own comeback moment. Winstone, the Howard we all
possessed as familiarly as if personal acquaintance was
only a formality to be secured later, had decidedly not
retired. His dream had survived the carnage of Saldivar.

In January 1968 Howard Winstone fought the formidable Japanese opponent, Mitsunori Seki, in London and at last became the world champion he thoroughly deserved to be.

Until that point, all the odds had been stacked against him. An accident in Merthyr's Tri-ang toy factory, itself a by-product of the Labour Government's post-war industrial transference policy in the 1940s, took the tips off three of his fingers and so nullified the punching power of his right hand. Then there was the fact that Saldivar, his triple nemesis, was a punching southpaw which had reduced the effectiveness of the Winstone-Thomas strategy of jab-and-move, using his piston-like left hand. And now, aged 29 in 1968, there was the constant struggle to make the nine-stone limit for a featherweight. Yet, somehow, the bet had come up trumps. Now, with Howard finally the world champion, we could savour the defence of his world title, scheduled for July 1968 in an open-air setting in Coney Beach, Porthcawl, against the Cuban boxer based in Spain, Jose Legra, an opponent whom Howard had already defeated twice previously.

There was a buzz about the whole business, as if Merthyr's self-proclaimed centrality to the sport was to be justified at last. I had grown up hearing about it, and after my father had gone to work as the manager of a fishmonger's in Merthyr's High Street in 1953 I came to feel and see it. My father had talked often of Eddie Thomas, whose welterweight victories and singing bravado on the wireless as British champion from 1949 to 1951 had lit up our lives. Now he talked daily with the great man, and of how everyone knew that Wally Thom who took away Eddie's titles in October 1951 was not fit to lace the great, and unfortunate, man's oversize boots. Thom, whisper it loudly forever, would later be the referee who gave Saldivar victory by half-a-point in Cardiff in 1967. Hard luck stories, or worse than that, were the real staple of our lives in boxing: from Farr's stand-up fifteen rounds against Joe Louis in 1937 in New York to Jimmy Wilde's punch-fest beating by the Philippine Pancho Villa in that same city in 1923, when the incomparable Wilde finally relinquished the world's flyweight title he originally won in 1916.

It was the year after Wilde's triumph that Pontypridd's Freddie Welsh, Wilde's great idol and the world light-weight champion since 1914, had conceded defeat to Benny Leonard in New York.

Many years later Eddie Thomas told me that he thought, from what he had read and heard, that Welsh was, of all of them, the master craftsman in the completeness of his ring armoury. Greater even than that dazzling stylist from Cardiff's Irish Newtown, Jim Driscoll, who gained the epithet 'Peerless' to add to his given name, when he became the unofficial world featherweight champion in New York in 1909. Eddie grudgingly conceded Driscoll his deserved fame but he never forgave him for ending the career of Merthyr man Billy Eynon, with whom my father was working in mid-century Merthyr, and who would often hunker down on the coconut matting of our kitchen to teach me to duck, feint, parry and hit.

Billy Eynon, congenial and bespectacled, did not have far to squat to square up to an eight-year-old boy. He was not much over five foot himself and, in his prime, an eight-stone bantamweight, that weight division poised between Driscoll's feather above and Wilde's flyweight below. Billy Eynon sparred with both of those older men. It is said that he gave Wilde such a tough session that he was avoided thereafter. Jimmy Wilde, Quaker's Yard born in 1892 but Rhondda bred, was just a year older than Billy Eynon, born in Treharris in 1893 and Merthyr trained. A year before Wilde became a world champion in December 1916 (by beating Young Zulu Kid in London), Eynon fought for the Army Featherweight Championship in a ring erected in the centre of an open bowl of a landscape in Salonika. On the slopes of the surrounding hills were more than two hundred thousand servicemen sent to Greece to open up the front against pro-German Bulgaria. They never did. But Billy won his battle. Billy carried the photograph to prove it throughout his life. 'They got the idea of Wembley from there,' he would say with a smile that dared you to question the conceptual provenance of architect Owen Williams' 1922 stadium in north London.

After the Great War, working in the pits seemed even less of a calling to a man able to command the sizeable purses of £40 and £50 a time. But it was harder and harder to make the bantamweight at which he fought Jim Higgins for the British and Empire titles in London in 1921. In Billy's view the Turkish bath sweating he had to do, not once but twice, on the day of the fight was like going twenty rounds before he began the real thing. Yet in the scale of things he won that fight in the eyes of spectators, both the disinterested and partisan. Only the referee disagreed. Billy Eynon never had another chance. A year later, whilst waiting for a rematch against Higgins, one several times postponed, he stepped into the ring for an exhibition bout with the forty-two-year-old, retired and irascible, Peerless Jim Discoll. Some say it was an accident which caused a thumb, the digit scarcely covered by the thin four-ounce gloves then commonly worn, to enter his eye and end his career. When I knew him he was sporting a glass eye behind the National Health spectacles. There was nothing one-eyed, however, in the admiration and love felt for this man in Merthyr and beyond.

Easy to see how for many, inside and outside the close circles of boxing, Howard Winstone, gifted and hamstrung, idolised and bereft, was the latest reincarnation of South Wales' fascination with itself and its representative boxers. Tickets to see Winstone fight, and surely beat, Legra in Porthcawl's Coney Beach, with a crowd banked up on wooden seating, were too good to miss. We gave Flash Thomas our money and he told us that he would soon confirm where and when we should meet up for tickets and transportation to and from the fight night.

On the afternoon of 27 July 1968 I caught the bus from the centre of Cardiff – Lord Beeching had thoughtfully axed the trains to Aberdare long since – to meet Viv, and our destiny as the latest spectators of Welsh boxing glory. He had learned from Flash that we were to rendezvous with some others in a pub in Cwmbach, have a pint or two, relax and await transport. We were in place by early afternoon. By mid afternoon the bar had filled with more than thirty men, most much older than us, who, it quickly became apparent as the joshing and drinking increased, were also waiting under Flash's orders. Counting heads, one of our number gave his opinion that Flash must have commandeered a bus, possibly even a charabanc, or, as more joined us, maybe two. At three o'clock the pub was full and rocking with anticipation. Only Flash had not yet arrived. He was not there at four either and Viv began to make the point, forcibly, that he was not really, in fact, related in any way, shape or form to Hedley Thomas.

At four-thirty, with the boxing due to begin on the undercard in the early evening, anxiety had begun to sour the beer. Anger was not far below the surface of what had so far been good-natured froth. Then the small mullioned windows of the stone-built pub grew dark, their light blocked by the side and size of the vehicle we all heard grinding its gears as it pulled up outside. At last. The pub emptied as we poured onto the pavement. Silence was followed by exasperated swearing and then by slightly hysterical laughter. We were looking at an old-fashioned, high-sided, furniture removal van and a driver busily and nonchalantly dropping down the ramp at the back end. Our transport had arrived.

And there was a message with the driver, who was narrowly escaping the usual fate of messengers who were themselves the bad news by bearing at least some that was good. Flash was waiting for us in Porthcawl with tickets. The grumble subsided. There seemed to be no alternative. The forty or so of us who had given Flash our ten pounds – 'A bargain, boy, a bargain. Special rates!' – walked into the body of the van and sat on the thoughtfully provided packing cases or stood clinging to the hessian straps that dropped down the sides of the van to restrain the goods to be transported. In this case, ourselves.

If we had not, sloshing with an afternoon's intake of

bitter ale, felt sick to the stomach before we arrived in sandy Porthcawl we did by the time we had jerked and rolled to our sporting destination. We were met in the failing light of day, an hour and a half later, not by Flash who had, it seems, been called urgently away to the sick bed of his ailing mother in Aberdare, but by an associate no one knew but who did indeed have tickets. Twenty of them. He did a quick head count. They were divided amongst us with the advice that at the back of the make-shift arena, a fretwork jumble of green wooden seats and stacked benches, there were gaps where, as some gave up their tickets at the gate, others might, unseen, sneak in. It was then a matter of squashing up as best as could be managed.

As for the big fight, for which we did arrive in time, Howard was knocked down early on, his eye soon swelled up to dangerous proportions and he retired from the fight in the fifth round and, thereafter, from the ring, permanently. We read all that in the papers the next day. We didn't actually see anything more than two tiny figures flailing at each other in the gloaming, almost as minuscule as in Billy Eynon's photograph of Salonika, because we were, at a conservative estimate, about half a mile from the action and, replenished in Porthcawl, now blind drunk. Before the van came to pick us up to take us back to Cwmbach at midnight, a line of us Sports could be seen puking quietly and tidily into the grey, persistent and floppy waves of the sad summer sea.

Sober, and possibly a little wiser, I went back to my diurnal stint on the high leather-covered stools of Cardiff's

Central Library in whose reference section I was spending years turning the yellowing pages of South Wales' bound newspapers for my research work on the profound and significant history of the South Wales miners. It would no more have occurred to me that you could try to write profoundly and significantly about South Wales boxers than it would have done to trust Hedley 'Flash' Thomas with another penny, nickel, dime or red cent. How wrong I was.

I came to a deeper understanding, beyond events and episodes, when, with my great friend from Barry schooldays, Gareth Williams, we began in the late 1970s to consider exactly how, by its style as much as by its content, a history of rugby football in Wales could be used to reveal its social significance. The result was *Fields of Praise: The Official History of the Welsh Rugby Union* in 1980. My push towards writing about boxing as, perhaps, a pastime even more revelatory of its formative society came more slowly for there was less, at first sight, to work on in that more bleakly isolated sporting world. How wrong I was. In the late 1980s I wrote 'Focal Heroes', an essay which I intended to do for boxing within Welsh historiography what *Fields of Praise* had attempted to do for rugby: to consider the public nurture and reception of the boxing world in industrial Wales by attending to its intrinsic qualities. I had begun to research by having in mind the defeat of Farr as an epiphanic moment in the Welsh psyche – that if Tommy had not lost we would have needed, after all, to invent the heroic failure – but what startled me in the course of that initial research was the greater discovery of a social dynamic revealed through boxing. This neglected catalytic tone in Welsh social history and popular culture centred on the figures of Farr's predecessors, of Wilde, Driscoll and Welsh.

After the essay was published I spoke a great deal about its own inner, literary dynamic – for I was already dissatisfied with its too-easily-won conclusion – with the Pontypridd-born novelist Alun Richards who was, by blood and even more by imagination, related to Freddie Welsh. I felt, more and more as the years went by, that whichever mode of historical narration was employed, this boxer, emblematic of the aspiration of others but also of their ambitious and ruthless society, slipped away from the knock-out blow as effortlessly as he did in the ring. The master craftsman on whom the journeyman historian of boxing could not lay a glove, or a mark with a pen. For a decade I tried, privately, in writing that was intentionally fictive and dramatised to get closer. But my problem, in seeking another genre by which to box Freddie in, was always in admitting that the insight of characterisation or of psychological probing that could be represented in fiction was never enough for my bigger ambition, which was – the art of the historian as vital to me as evidence itself – to unite man and society in a form that would be enlightening about both because separate about neither.

The unity is only feasible if we take on the imaginative challenge of finding a style, different from but akin to that of the novelist, which is neither fact-bound nor fiction-free but makes no pretence that its evidence, however scrupulously marshalled, can make complete sense without a literary structure, one that history rarely seeks to accommodate: and in my view now, very much to its detriment. My following attempt to find a way of framing

101

the 'Life and Lies of Freddie Welsh, Welsh American', is a gesture towards a cultural history of Wales which understands that style is itself a component of intellectual understanding.

Freddie Welsh is our contemporary in a way no other boxer from the past century still manages to be. More than any other Welsh sportsman, ever, his career in and out of the ring oozes the essence of postmodernism: iconic, playful, enigmatic, open to endless interpretation, an artefact that questions the virtual presence of what passes for reality and exposes the drear actuality of what we compress and represent as History. In this last respect he offers up, too, a possible route to a new and richer historiography of sport. As an intellectual discipline, the latter is scarcely more than a quarter century old, and especially so in Wales, but it is already mired in a dutiful trudge from happening to emblem or from economic accountancy to audience assessment within a framework of sociological analysis, social history and journalistic mirroring of the great deeds of the Hero. It can be very entertaining but it is too often no more enlightening than the narrative format of a Boys' Own Adventure Story when what is required is the skeletal X-ray of a *Lord of the Flies*. Boxing history has encouraged, all too readily, a transmission of the chronological, the biographical and the episodic with an occasional nod to the climax of events that are loaded with the symbolism of catharsis through confrontation. It is as if we observe a dormant light bulb and then one that sheds light but make no enquiry about the process of electricity, or the hand that reaches for the switch.

Freddie Welsh's life and career belie such simplicities and mock any hero-worshipping piety. He was as complex and contradictory as the society which heedlessly nurtured him and as tragic as the culture he consciously helped to create with humanity's star-crossed needs in mind. To his story we need to restore the twined agencies of intent and of circumstance. His sporting life needs viewing in the context of his forming social identity and his own desired relationship to the future society whose ideal lineaments he craved and described. The culture which we then deconstruct from the one that was being materially constructed should reveal its tensile filaments as much as its rigidities of structure. We should see the dream-like aspirations which carried the individual actions forward, as much as the limitations which would prove to be its collective destruction. And beyond all this, in truly listening to the teller of the tale we cannot neglect the signs the teller may have ignored or never seen, or created to deceive.

The writer of history and the writer of fiction tell different truths in related ways but only now, perhaps, is Welsh cultural historiography beginning to reach the point from which the writer of fiction – which Freddie Welsh in graphic mode most certainly was – always jumps off. Freddie Welsh is, I believe, a clue to a greater mystery we will not solve if we do not bravely allow opposites to remain in suspension, as he most certainly did. He was boxing with life.

*

Consider then, Frederick Hall Thomas. He was born in 1886, the son of John Thomas, a Pontypridd auctioneer or buyer and seller of property, a man of wit and means, and of Elizabeth Hall, the daughter of a Merthyr hotelier when that iron town was still Wales' most populous centre. The family was, in terms of the overwhelmingly proletarian coalfield, middle class, prosperous and professional. Soon Elizabeth ran her own hotel in Pontypridd, her first-born and eldest son went to local nursery and boarding schools. After his father's early death and mother's remarriage, he was sent across the Severn to Long Ashton Public School, W.G. Grace's very own alma mater, in Bristol. Freddie rebelled against any academic or, rather, pedagogic discipline and even against a subsequent apprenticeship to a Rhondda boilermaker's firm as an engineer. In 1903, aged sixteen, with two friends of similar background and disposition, he swallowed the Canadian Pacific Railway's inducements to the Empire's youth to emigrate and sailed for Montreal. He went courtesy of the money supplied by his mother. Most of his Pontypridd and Rhondda contemporaries and future supporters, including Jimmy Wilde and later Tommy Farr, were only destined to migrate underground. Within a year he was back home but, restless and again bankrolled by his mother, he took off again, this time for three years, from Liverpool to New York City in 1904.

The legend, and its embellishments away from actual witness, would grow thick and fast in later years as Freddie learned to feed newspaper copy to the media which would tell his tale and sell his tickets: how, impoverished and desperate for a crust, he had stumbled into a department store position as a physical instructor and had become, by chance, good at it, quickly graduating to prize-fighting in the numerous small venues and shabby halls of the eastern seaboard of the United States. He takes the name Freddie Welsh in case his mother hears of his deeds. Maybe. What is for sure is that he rode the rails as a hobo and toughened up enough to work for a fellow Welshman, another Thomas, as a strikebreaker for five dollars a day, three times the wages of Chicago's regular meat packers who were locked out, twenty thousand of them, for wanting more than twenty cents an hour and less than an unremitting pace of work in the city's huge stockyards. Freddie, and two thousand other blacklegs, housed in the empty sheds now conveniently used as barracks, were protected by armed police and the private, ruthless Pinkertons. Bombs, gunshots, cracked heads and the occasional outright murder were indicative of the turbulent labour troubles of turn-of-the-century America, and close enough to what was happening in South Wales. The links would bring Big Bill Haywood, the syndicalist leader of the Industrial Workers of the World, from the States to greet the striking and rioting miners of Tonypandy in 1910. Frederick Hall Thomas could feel, almost, right at home.

When he returned home again to South Wales in 1907 Freddie had a fiancée, the New Yorker Fanny Weston née Weinstein, whose subsequent marriage to Freddie would stay under wraps for a number of years to ensure his ascetic image – physical training and non-indulgence in the 'vices' – would stay Baden Powell-pure for the Empire's press, even as, in private, he lit up a cigarette and frequently relaxed by being 'lit up' himself.

Disconcertingly he now had an American style, of dress and accent, and notably of fighting – a defensive crouch rather than the classic upright stance of, say, Jim Driscoll – which did not endear him to the public, even a Welsh one, until he proceeded to knock out all and sundry and, with one rare loss of concentration, sweep away all before him as the lightweight champion – 9 stone 9 pounds – of Britain and the Empire. He was a constant transatlantic fighter until 1914, in pursuit of the world crown squirrelled away by successive American champions who largely learned to evade the canny Welshman.

One who did not, on his native patch in Cardiff, in December 1910 was Peerless Jim Driscoll, acknowledged as the unofficial featherweight champion – 9 stone dead – of the world after he had comprehensively out-boxed Abe Attell in New York earlier that year. Freddie weighed in, practically naked, at 9 stone 6 pounds and Driscoll, in sweater, trousers and boots, tipped the scales accordingly. But that was at 2pm in the afternoon and they fought late in the winter's night. Freddie's tactics, of holding, boring with his head, clinching to kidney punch and non-stop verbal taunting, finally enraged the classic stylist who headbutted Freddie across the ring in a street brawl that promptly disqualified him.

Gamesmanship, though, was always Freddie's game. It was why the dress-suited gentlemen of London's National Sporting Club only grudgingly admired him, and returned the same measure of resentment with which they adored gallant Jim Driscoll.

Looking back from the 1940s the British boxing scribe Norman Hurst, who knew both fighters well and thought Driscoll to be 'one of the greatest boxers and ring tacticians the world has ever known... fit model for an artist', sourly recalled Freddie as 'a ferret where business was concerned... Business man first, Fighter second, Business man third. That summed up the late Frederic [*sic*] Hall Thomas, known to fight followers the world over as Freddy [*sic*] Welsh. As a young man [he] had visions of making good as a big business man. America was forever luring him to her shores. In America he thought he could build up a fortune.'

Freddie Welsh was a hustler. He organised a 'South Wales syndicate' which put up the purses and picked up the expenses – expecting a profit of course – for his local contests and marketed 'their' fighter further afield. The coalfield society of the professional class from which he came was, after all, rich and thriving in the Edwardian era. Freddie staged ticketed open-air training events, to which women in particular were, and unusually so, made welcome; and he made them free since it was publicity and advertising and public clamour which he wished to encourage. It was the long-term pound not the short-term penny which lay at the heart of his business plan. The population of South Wales saw its biggest decennial increase, largely through inmigration, from 1900 and Freddie cashed in by buying and renting out houses, all in his mother's name. He cultivated his public appearances outside the ring· a smile to flash his gold teeth from a railway carriage, a wave of his jewel-beringed hand, the glint of a diamond stick-pin. He mixed in the most affluent of companies, attracting in particular the support of D.A. Thomas, the millionaire owner of the Cambrian Combine in mid-Rhondda, future Lord Rhondda and former

Cambridge boxing half-blue. That tycoon – alongside other coal and land barons of the Welsh aristocracy of Capitalism, and attended by the incipient Welsh bourgeoisie of doctors, lawyers, dentists, mine managers, engineers and shopkeepers – was at ringside in Olympia, London on 7 July 1914, the night Freddie became the first Welshman to become a world champion when he defeated the American Willie Ritchie over twenty rounds. The declaration of war with Germany early in the next month was almost an anticlimax after all that. It certainly was for Freddie. He had chased and cajoled Ritchie for a title fight across three years and two continents, and he had not been in it for the glory. To avoid the war and clean up as champ he had to return to America to undertake the series of 'no decision' contests in which he fought, with mind numbing regularity, every conceivable challenger over ten rounds. Under the moralistic boxing laws of most states in America only a knock out could deprive the champion of his title, and no one was better equipped to fight stalemates than the boxer who now openly declared his loathing of the so-called sport in which he had long invested his human capital.

Freddie Welsh remained world lightweight champion until Benny Leonard, aka Benjamin Leiner, draped him over the ropes of the Manhattan Athletic Club, aka Casino, in May 1917. By then it was Freddie who was loathed. At home, occasional letters to the press accused him of being 'a slacker' as the slaughter on the western front bedecked the coalfield with black ribbons. In non-belligerent America he was increasingly depicted as the greatest pacifist ever to move backwards in the ring: cartoons drew him as a granddaddy with safety in mind, but for three years as the champion he was gambling on his superior skill and filling, as the *National Police Gazette* put it, 'his coffers with gold'. For some Americans, bemused by the social circles he now sought to move in – politicians, bankers, industrialists, writers and theatrical producers – it was, patently, a case of the biter bit. Donald O'Brien of the *Los Angeles Times* choked with indignation even before 1914 was out:

Freddie Welsh is a young person who feels himself to be superior to his job. His manager... thoroughly despises boxing as a business. The result of which combination is that Mr Welsh is the worst failure of a lightweight champion who ever held the title.

Flattered by the society and companionship of these men [the rich and powerful] Freddie has but one idea, to be one of them. The world's championship means to him only the money and the increased glitter of fame that will make his position the surer among the men into whose circle of life he hopes to scramble.

In a few months, Freddie will make a face at the championship; poke his money in his pocket and the name of Fred Hall Thomas will go on the lists of some club and Freddie will begin the real fight of his life – to 'break in'.

In fact Freddie fought fifty-three times between reaching his sporting summit in the summer of 1914 and falling off it in the summer of 1917. His last real triumph was in 1916 when, against all the odds and in the second of their three encounters, he somehow rejuvenated himself to bring ringcraft to his aid in utterly outboxing the younger, faster and all-American favourite Benny Leonard, his personal nemesis within a year. Yet for Freddie, the truth of his own views was now more important than the formerly circumspect notion of avoiding rubbing salt in the wounds of the boosters of the 'noble art', the 'sweet science' of fisticuffs.

> With me fighting is a business, not a game: and certainly not a pleasure. I have forgotten the days when the glory of the title and the publicity it brought would have set my head swimming. Every businessman aspires to be the head of his particular business and it is the same in the prize fighting art. I have craven the championship because it is the highest pinnacle of the business in which I was engaged. And now that I am there it is my business to stay there and make as much out of it as possible.

He was thirty one-when the 'staying there' stopped and he was down-and-out and dead a decade later aged forty-one. He had, once again, been netted by circumstances. America's entry into the war in 1917 saw him, now an American citizen, enlist as a lieutenant in the US Army, based in Washington, to help retain and rehabilitate soldiers and then, with age no longer his ally, missing out, despite a flurry of forlorn comebacks, on the post-war boxing boom that threw the sport, and the prize money, wide open and catapulted fighters, like his close friend Jack Dempsey, to the heights of Roaring Twenties celebrity and wealth.

Freddie would never be quite American enough. His American Dream had only one chance of staying afloat but it was a major chance, or so it seemed, to those who attended the opening of his sumptuous health farm at Long Hill, near Summit, New Jersey in 1917. This was his major investment: a plutocratic mansion on a hill, surrounded by fields, a river for fishing, a golf course, woods, orchards and sunken gardens, equipped with a gymnasium, squash court and two swimming pools, one outside and one inside, and where two dozen rooms were panelled in hard wood and an automobile could take you to New York City within an hour. Or you could stay indoors and read your way through Frederick Hall Thomas' well-stocked library. Or maybe work your way through his well-stocked booze supply. For you could come here to train or to party. He had sunk the fortune earned in the ring in this venture.

It was too grandiose, too intermittently used, too expensive to maintain and a victim of the early Prohibition era that followed on the passage of the Volstead Act by Congress in 1919. When he finally could not keep up the payments and had to sell in 1926, he had already spiralled downwards into drink and depression. He died, away from his family, in a seedy New York hotel in the sweltering heatwave of July 1927. The doctor said it was cardiovascular disease, maybe aggravated by a beating he had recently taken in a speakeasy; the sceptical thought it was suicide from despair; the romantic that he had died from a broken heart; the historian might consider that they found the body of Frederick Hall Thomas but that Freddie Welsh had long departed.

Frederick Hall Thomas was born in Morgan Street, Pontypridd, just across the Taff over the famous single-span bridge that was, in 1886, exactly one hundred and thirty years old and flanked since 1857 by the parallel road bridge which effectively marked the end of any lingering sense of the market town as a mere confluence, signalling instead its full-blooded emergence by the 1880s as the urban gateway to the central valleys of the modern coalfield.

The boy's roots were in its earlier and even rougher origins: his paternal grandfather was Morgan Thomas, a monoglot Welshman and a champion bare-knuckle bruiser with plenty of backers to follow him, personally and financially, from one 'bloody spot' on the mountains to another for illegal fight-till-you-drop contests. His father, John, wore a new-found respectability along with his three-piece suits and watch fob but he too was a 'sporting man', albeit confining himself to side bets and heavy wagers on anything from footracing to the fights in the itinerant boxing booths or behind the public houses he frequented and ran.

In the first decade of his life young Fred lived in a town whose population quadrupled in size to over 30,000, and within a wider industrial cauldron which, from the Rhondda Valleys down, positively exploded in numbers to almost 200,000. There was a social riot of homebuilding, chaotic street layout, a pulsating migrant influx, entertainment in music halls and cinemas, colliery development, breweries and manufacture of goods, shops and markets, schools and chapels, pubs and accompanying police stations to allow a measure of control over a rowdy, young, largely male workforce who played as hard as they worked and drank to match. He would have seen an overflowing, changing Welsh world where English was, especially in Pontypridd, soon spoken more freely on the streets than Welsh. The newspapers, harbingers of aspiration as in the American frontier West and purveyors of sensation as in any big city, groaned gratefully with accounts of the drunk and disorderly, the vicious and the murdered, of sexual assaults, both individual and collective, and simultaneously and smugly informed their readers of the worthies trying to stem the Gadarene tide with appeals to pride, of the local, civic kind, and to a wider patriotic fervour, both Welsh and Imperial. When he looked for a boxing soubriquet for himself, in New York, he first chose Fred Cymry or, in other words, we, us, ourselves, the tribe. Welsh was just a convenient and pronounceable translation.

He was sent away to public school because it could be afforded but also because he was showing signs of a lack of decorum as marked as that of his grandfather. He scrapped in all the schools he attended, bringing to the disciplinarian traditions of Long Ashton the fist-fighting ferocity and bloody-minded rebelliousness he had discovered on the slopes of the Graig and in the stone-covered back lanes of his home town. Living near the old Bridge in the Bridge House hotel and then at the Bunch of Grapes on the other side of the river, he joined the 'Bridge Gang', young ruffians intent on defending their patch from any one of the other 'Gangs of Pontypridd', a collectivity to place in the roll call of Victorian street armies from London's East End to the Gangs of New York themselves.

113

On his return as a professional fighter from America in 1907 and with a quick series of sensational victories to back up his claimed prowess, Freddie began the process that was his cultural destiny: to unite in himself the raw outlaw society of proletarian sport and the self-improving world of professional middle-class Wales. He became, literally, a bridge. He claimed to have studied the 'science' of physical culture and the 'art' of boxing but he allied this to the school of hard knocks and brutal experience he had found on both sides of the Atlantic before he was twenty.

In an extraordinary way he personified unity within a South Wales that was riven, and would soon be so marked for half a century, by irrepressible class division and social tension. He claimed that boxing – the padded gloves, the laws, the improved decorum – was fast establishing itself as a respectable pursuit and he posed for photographs in evening dress on a bardic chair or in the country tweeds of an Edwardian gent. But he entered the boxing ring stripped for the primeval act of conflict in a sport that was no such thing, a tribal warrior for sure but one with an ambivalent identity and an ambiguous purpose.

If Freddie had ever been born anew it was when, as a boy, he plunged into the Taff to rescue a drowning man, probably a worse-for-wear collier who had slipped from the bank into the fast waters of the Berw Pool, just above the old bridge and his mother's hotel. Freddie was a Local Hero at the age of twelve and a class act all his life but it was the duality of his upbringing and of his personality which sealed his representative status for his pendulum society. There was never any doubt about where he had come from or for whom, beyond himself, he fought in the ring.

Before the Driscoll fight in 1910 he had trained in the Clarence Theatre in the centre of Pontypridd and had charged a small fee for entrance to the always packed-out sessions. He donated the money to the new Pontypridd Cottage Hospital. A third of the eight thousand tickets for the fight, with the Cambrian Combine strike entering its third month, were reduced in price to accommodate some of his supporters. The cheap seats, two thousand of them at five shillings a head, which he forced on the promoters of his 1914 world championship win at Olympia, guaranteed train loads of 'Welsh toilers' disembarking at Paddington.

...I have always had a soft place in my heart for the Welsh colliers, who have followed my career in all parts of the world, and have stuck true to me through thick and thin. I am very anxious to see a great crowd of my friends from the 'hills' at the fight at Olympia, and suggested to the promoters that they should provide an unusual number of low-priced seats in order to enable my collier friends to be present. The syndicate would not hear of my suggestion at the outset but I pegged at them and would not budge an inch, with the result that I won [otherwise]... it was not possible for my Welsh workingmen friends who would... have to pay their railway fares as well if they wanted to see me fight.

Their voices dominated the arena when Freddie entered the ring late that night: 'Hen Wlad Fy Nhadau', in the full and choral repetitive version with a blast of 'Sospan Fach' to keep the whole thing boiling. These were the men who booed D.A. Thomas, and his friends in their dinner jackets, after the victory, thinking them to be Willie Ritchie's American backers. One shouted, 'What do you American millionaires think of it now?' The reply was, apparently, 'Cymru am Byth' but, just perhaps, the jeerers were more astute than it may seem. After all it was Thomas Jones, the quintessential professional Welshman of his day, who also thought that if 'Lloyd George is a Welshman, Lord Rhondda is an American'.

Now champion of the world – 'I was fighting for the honour of Wales' – the man who had become the great Freddie Welsh by beating an American champion returned home to lead one long triumphal procession in an open car from Cardiff up to Pontypridd, its streets thronged with admirers, and on, via the Bunch of Grapes, past the old bridge to the Taff's headwaters at Merthyr, his mother's home town, where he boxed exhibition rounds for the crowd. This Wales was, with coal as its global fuel, already a world-renowned dynamo of modernity. Freddie Welsh was, by name and fame, proclaiming it so and thereby imprinting Wales itself on a popular culture of sport that was worldwide beyond the rugby football that had, in exactly the same span of time as his own life, become the Welsh 'National Game'.

Frederick Hall Thomas emblazoned a red dragon on his silk dressing robe and took it off in the ring to reveal a sash around his trunks that was stitched with leeks and dragons. He had no qualms about the Union Jack on his regalia either but it was Wales he proclaimed to all who could hear from Pontypridd to America across an ocean one contemporary economist, surveying the argosies of coal-laden ships from Cardiff and Barry Docks, would soon astonishingly refer to as Wales' Atlantic lake. And here, in similar mode, is Freddie himself in 1914, two weeks before the First World War ended all this cultural hubris:

> When I think of the size of... our little country, and then think again how small that portion of it is that we call South Wales, I am... filled with pride at the recollection of the things that have been done by the men of our race.
>
> ...A country where men can play rugby football as Welshmen play it – men who have beaten the best that the world can send against us – can, I am sure, produce boxers with the same qualities of handiwork and skill and courage which have made her rugby footballers famous and feared the world over...
>
> I am looking forward to the time when we shall hold a straight flush from fly to heavy of British boxing championships. Even then the limits of ambition will not have been reached for there will be the world's titles to strive for.

Or, in his case, to flaunt and retain. That latter aim would soon sour his reputation in the America he adopted, but in his particular Wales his popularity never really waned no matter what his tactics or his hard-headedness. Winning and surviving were indistinguishable in the ring for him as they were, in life, for his working-class followers. Freddie did not play by the rules if he could break them. And, in a displaced sense, neither did they if the rule of law was both oppressive and repressive. When he had faced up to the aesthetic superiority of Driscoll, the darling of the National Sporting Club, at Cardiff's American roller rink in 1910, it was only just over a month since crowds of miners and their womenfolk, thousands strong, had confronted mounted hussars and metropolitan police on the streets of Aberaman and Tonypandy. Their cries of rage were Freddie's ringside jibes; their stone-throwing was Freddie's illegal kidney punching; their un-British behaviour was his American-style fighting. Of course the fight ended in a brawl outside the Queensberry rules and naturally it cascaded into a free-for-all between the boxers' rival seconds and supporters and then on through the crowd onto Cardiff's streets.

For the striking miners who had another twelve months of struggle to survive but who did win a minimum wage settlement in 1912, Freddie Welsh was one of them that night and no matter who his opponent was, even the likeable Driscoll, he won for them. In the ring, in Britain at this time, Freddie Welsh was a revolutionary. That night he de-constructed the '*beau ideal*' of British boxing. He had discarded the straight left and side-on posture of the classicist for a ducking, weaving, crouching, infuriating, ugly stance of a fighter who was not there to be hit but would suddenly unleash punches from every angle and at bewildering speed. He was coiled until his opponent's impatience served to become self-defeating.

Newspaperman James Butler saw and reported on the fight as being the only time Driscoll, in a brilliant career, had ever resorted to questionable tactics. This is how Butler remembered it:

This grim struggle took place... five days before Christmas of 1910. It captured the imagination of Wales. The Irish population of Cardiff was behind Driscoll, the rest rooted 100 per cent for Welsh, who although born at Pontypridd, had begun his fighting in Philadelphia.

Welsh and Driscoll had never liked each other. As soon as Freddy ducked under the ropes he cast a contemptuous glance at his lighter opponent. It was deliberate tactics to rouse the Driscoll temper, because Welsh, a strong two-fisted American-styled battler, realised he could not match the featherweight in skill, but in a rough-house scrap Welsh had few masters.

For four rounds it was all Driscoll. He gave the Pontypridd battler a lesson with his left hand, but Welsh was determined to get aside, and when he succeeded he opened up a vicious kidney attack which he learned in America... and also roused Driscoll's ire further by bringing up his head sharply in the clinches.

Peerless Jim completely lost his head. He allowed Welsh to dictate the way the fight should be fought. It was the only time I saw Driscoll not in control of himself in the ring... So bitter was the hatred by the tenth round that the finest boxer this country has ever produced was rushing in red-eyed like a man gone berserk.

...It was now a street-corner fight, and not a pretty sight to watch, both men butting whenever the opportunity came. 'Peggy' Bettinson [the referee seated at ringside] was to blame. He had allowed

Welsh to get away with 'murder' and the struggle had got out of his grip now.... The infuriated Driscoll pulled his head back and, with a sickening thud, butted Welsh under the chin, and flung him halfway across the ring.

Freddy staggered and Driscoll, completely mad with temper now, went in for the kill, but the referee was roused at last, and climbed into the ring and dragged the crazy pair of combatants apart. He motioned Driscoll back to his corner, and awarded the decision to Welsh. But that was only a start. A more bitter fight than ever was now raging.

And that, of course, is the revolutionary's unconfinable intent. You do not play the game – you subvert it if you can. If you are Jack Dempsey slugging the giant Jess Willard into the canvas with loaded gloves in 1919. Or Cassius Clay suckering Sonny Liston into defeat by psychological trepidation. Or Muhammad Ali absorbing and timing the power of George Foreman back against himself. Or Freddie Welsh spoiling Jim Driscoll's party piece and self-discipline at the end of riotous 1910.

Trickery was an admirable trait in the minds of sports fanatics in South Wales. They applauded the feints and deceptions, all barely within the laws of a rugby football game, originally intended to define a middle-class, English public-school pursuit, which were elaborated by Dickie Owen at the base of working-class Welsh scrums. They delighted in the on-field circus japes of the halfback brothers, the Jameses of Swansea, who soon travelled north to play professional rugby, and in the wage demands made on behalf of professional football players by soccer supremo and strike leader Billy Meredith of Chirk, Manchester United and Manchester City. They saw nothing amiss in professional powderhall racing and in the ruses used – lead in the shoes, to be removed in later races – to obtain the best betting odds on their favourites. The burgeoning middle classes in Welsh rugby administration may have moved to ban Aberdare RFC in 1908 for the systematic bribery of opponents which allowed them to win the Glamorgan League but the lifetime dismissal of Dai 'Tarw' Jones, the Rhondda rock of Welsh packs, including that of 1905, which defeated the All Blacks, would win him nothing but sympathy and no disgrace for the monetary offence. Freddie Welsh was a part of this Welsh mosaic too, and not only in his legitimate endeavour to make money from his business as a boxer.

The question that hovers over his career is the biggest of them all: was the victory over Ritchie in 1914 'a fix'? And if so, by whom? What is, generally, not thought to be in doubt is the superior boxing, overall, of Welsh against Ritchie. However the American had only consented to the bout at all because, without precedent, Freddie was fighting for nothing. The entire purse, a twenty-five thousand dollar guarantee, was to go to the champion, win or lose, with Welsh to receive half of any gate receipts left after all expenses were met. There were none. What is known is that the challenger had no such funds to guarantee Ritchie's prize money. Or funds immediately to hand to pay back the guarantee. What is known, too, is that over half a million pounds in bets changed hands after the fight and that the rumours were of syndicates trying to get 'the fix' in, one way or the other. Freddie Welsh's explanation of how the fight came about at long last took refuge in the tribal lore with which he was selling his story to the world:

> It's natural with us Welshmen to sit the thing out. I'll never forget watching the men of my race squatting around, smoking their pipes. They're all miners. They're used to squatting down in the coalmines for hours at a time, with hardly room to move, picking away at the coal with short little backs. Then when they come up out of the mines after the day's work and want to rest they will sit quietly... I inherit that spirit and it was that alone that gave me the courage to wait patiently for my whirl as a world's champion.

Patience and, perhaps, the backing of a notorious New York gambler, Arnold Rothstein, who by 1912 was the 29-year-old multi-millionaire kingpin of organised crime, later seen as the guiding intelligence behind the crime syndicates of the 1920s, as Jewish advisory brain to the Italian Mafia. Rothstein, whose biggest coup was his involvement, or virtual involvement, with the fixing of the 1919 baseball World Series and consequent immortality as Meyer Wolfsheim in F. Scott Fitzgerald's 1925 master-piece, *The Great Gatsby*, was gunned down, aged 46, in a New York hotel room in 1928. He worked the race track and politicians and the boxing game, all to his advantage of course. He was, like Freddie, articulate and well read. No thug, just a businessman making money out of illegal activity. And employing armies of thugs – in loan sharking and labour racketeering as well as bootlegging and drugs – to allow him to do so. There is no doubt that he would know of, and maybe even personally know, the Welsh fighter as he would later know, certainly personally, his New York Jewish compatriot, Benny Leonard. It was Arnold Rothstein, owner of judges and banker to politicians, who had arranged a boxing licence to allow Billy Gibson of the Bronx to promote fights in New York City. The grateful manager promptly assigned to Rothstein ten per cent of his fighter Benny Leonard's ring-earnings for life. Rothstein, in that sense, owned Leonard too and bet on him, before and after he took the Welshman's championship. Nor did it stop there with Rothstein.

In 1922 Benny Leonard, challenging for the welter-weight crown, deliberately threw the fight, on a foul, in order to be disqualified despite the fact that he had just been fouled himself. A.R., the 'Big Bankroll', cleaned up. Billy Gibson, notoriously shady in all his dealings, became the handler of another boxer from New York's East Side, the future heavyweight champion Gene Tunney, who overturned all the odds to outpoint Jack Dempsey in Philadelphia in 1926. That was in Maxie 'Boo Boo' Hoff's Philadelphia where the Jewish mobster's writ ran. Arnold Rothstein had rung his friend and accomplice to ensure it did. Hoff first paid off all Tunney's debts – 20,000 dollars worth – and then claimed, in turn, twenty per cent of Tunney's future ring earnings. Gibson was certainly party to this even if Tunney proved evasive later. Considering that Tunney went on to beat the infamous 'long count' against Dempsey in Al Capone's Chicago in 1927, those earnings, and hence those potential percentages, were considerable. Arnold Rothstein bet heavily on Gene

Tunney both times. Arnold Rothstein claimed that he never 'bet on boxing'. Arnold Rothstein lied.

But back in 1914 Benny Leonard was just an 18 year old starting out, and the big money was required elsewhere. According to Rothstein's latest biographer, the twenty-five thousand dollar guarantee plus expenses that Willie Ritchie demanded to fight Freddie Welsh, and which was deposited in advance in a New York bank account, came courtesy of Arnold Rothstein. Did A.R. believe the betting odds against Ritchie would return his money if Welsh could be persuaded to throw that fight – as Freddie claimed a few years later he had been, lucratively, asked to do – or was the loan attached to Ritchie's future prospects? That seems most unlikely since the fight was in London and Freddie the odds-on favourite. Besides, the money went to Ritchie only via Freddie and his backers so it was, given the win, Freddie Welsh who was beholden. To someone for sure. If to Arnold Rothstein then, one way or the other, the gambler who never knowingly laid out money that would not come back would, one day, recoup. Perhaps that day came in the Manhattan Casino in the summer of 1917 when a champion who was not counted out, merely retired by the referee, handed over the crown, and the percentage earnings that went with it. There are no ledgers to check, no accounts to be verified, no witnesses to call to the bar of history. Except maybe for 'The Little Hebe', Abe Attell, featherweight champion of the world from 1901 to 1912 – with an unofficial loss to Driscoll in New York in 1909 and a loss to the heavier Welsh in 1908 – and Rothstein's 'bodyguard' and bagman on retirement.

Abe Attell was always Rothstein's inside man in the boxing game; he was the layer of bets and doublecrosses for A.R. at the 1919 World Series; he co-ordinated and sat in on the meetings with Gibson, Tunney and 'Boo Boo' Hoff prior to Tunney's 1926 triumph; his memory of the two biggest gates in boxing history to that point (and until the 1960s) did not mention the fighters Jack Dempsey and Gene Tunney, only the outside-the-ring gang lords of Philly and Chi: 'What you had was this: It was the Italians against the Jews. The Jews won!'

Billy Gibson, Leonard and Tunney's so-called manager, was the 'William Gibson... of Fifth Avenue' who was named after Rothstein's murder as one of the gangster's closest and most trusted associates. So trusted he was a proxy for some of Rothstein's assets. And Freddie Welsh died in the Hotel Sidney, at 59 West 65th Street, a drinking joint and gambling den, or 'policy bank', where bets were cleared or, more to the point, cash was collected from 'number runners' who worked the streets for criminals and gamblers like Arnold Rothstein who held daily court, and dispensed personal loans at very high interest rates, from his Broadway restaurant HQ, Lindy's, on 50th Street, just a few blocks and a lifetime away.

Newspaperman Damon Runyon immortalised the eating place in his Broadway vignettes as Mindy's and A.R. as 'The Brain'. This, too, was Freddie Welsh's world as sports columnist and short story writer Ring Lardner, from personal knowledge, knew and Scott Fitzgerald, from genius, intuited. What we can say, at the very least, is that if Freddie Welsh, in his American persona, really does seem, in part anyway, to be the literal model for Fitzgerald's Jay Gatsby as Rothstein was for his Meyer

Wolfsheim then, equally, we can imaginatively assume that by placing both of his fictional creations, Gatsby and Wolfsheim, in one telling frame he gives us another kind of fix on Freddie Welsh and Arnold Rothstein and the world championship of 1914.

The rite of passage towards becoming an American had, one way or the other, been completed by then. In a sense his significant story was over because both his twinned worlds, countries and identities, were about to diverge, even if it took a little while longer for him personally. In another sense such connection, real or imagined, as Freddie Welsh had seemingly forged brought him a different kind of longevity, a cultural role that American writers, though not Welsh or British ones, mined for creative insight. Before Dempsey lit up the minds of American poets and painters and writers, Freddie Welsh was moved centre stage as a magnet to appreciation in Ring Lardner's stories. And if Ring Lardner's great friend F. Scott Fitzgerald, who allegedly boxed a few rounds with the retired Freddie, did indeed catch the traits of Freddie's re-made, dream-like life in the eponymous hero of *The Great Gatsby* then the case for his emblematic importance in the tableau of modern life that sport was revealing is crystalline. Even more so than in the telling detail of a washed-up fighter who owns a health farm, which Hemingway brilliantly evokes in his boxing scam story *Fifty Grand*. This story reverses the Leonard fix of 1922 and adds a heavy dose of anti-Semitic rant to clinch its outrage.

But all that is literary history, the sucking out of the bone marrow, those vital juices which novelists need in place to enliven their fables with the meaning of individual lives. Cultural historians still need to see the panoramic picture of time as well as space and so to exchange the camera's flashlight bulb for its wide-focus lens. Those great and insightful American writers, after all, knew the import of Freddie Welsh but little of Frederick Hall Thomas or of the society that requires him to have, then and now, meaning in and for itself.

*

We return then to the dilemma of our enigma. Freddie failed to become an American success and he died alone in a New York apartment. He only came back to South Wales once after 1914 and that was briefly, in the doleful year of 1923. He could not but have sensed the failure that was building at home: economic distress, social decline, political struggle, cultural despair. Within five years of his death another great Pontypridd boxer, Frank Moody, returned from a successful stint in America and was boxing for nothing to raise funds for Pontypridd's bereft Cottage Hospital. Freddie Welsh was from this world but, in all ways, no longer of it. And yet in the pomp of his lifetime he had consciously sought a different outcome for both it and himself.

If the First World War had not broken out in August 1914 there is little doubt that the world's champion would have lived in Wales as well as in America. Before the 1914 fight he said: 'I shall make my permanent home at Cardiff, where the people have been so good and true to me, and probably also take a flat in London. You see, I am now rearing a family, and must become a householder.' And after it, to cheers, he declared: 'I am very glad to have brought the title back to Wales. If you are proud of me, I am much prouder of my countrymen. Winning a championship is not an easy matter, it takes years of hard work and disappointment... I hope to defend the title for two years, and to retire undefeated.'

After that statement of intent, made to an admiring crowd in Merthyr Tydfil, he and his young family had gone to Paris for a holiday.

He had actually, at this very time, compared France to Wales as two parts of the world where boxing had made such 'a rapid advance'. If an assassin's bullet in Sarajevo had not triggered the declaration of war that so rapidly followed, it is not inconceivable that Freddie would have cashed in across the Channel as well as across the Atlantic. Jack Johnson, the world's black heavyweight champion, then in enforced exile, was already a French idol as the light heavyweight, Georges Carpentier, from the northern coalfield around Lens, would soon be. If post-war American writers would move sport, as a harbinger of popular culture, centre stage, European painters and poets – Picasso, Braque, Appollinaire – were already, pre-war, fascinated by both ring mechanics and the populist cultural penumbra emanating from the limelight of boxing halls. Primitivism, whether taken from the African dance masks on which Picasso outrageously modelled the faces of his whores in the 1907 masterpiece *Les Demoiselles d'Avignon* or transmuted into the precision and brutalism of the prize ring itself, was the imaginative catalyst such pre-war modernists seized on to see beneath the skin of their civilisation right down to its cultural bone. Boxers, like bullfighters, seemed to be at the emotional limits of an intelligence that was as frightening as it was irrational. Cubist experimentation and the passion of its practitioners for boxing, one that was being engendered in Paris at precisely this time, were at the intersection of the discovery of modern life in artistic expression.

Freddie Welsh would seem to have been destined to take his trade and his country into the vortex of a modernism that was spinning out of the French capital city. He was in the advance column of progressive thinking already as a faddist of habits both protean and well publicised – a vegetarian, a teetotaller, a yogi, a non-smoker, a water drinker, a naturist. He was a follower of the creed of individualism and universalism, of the integrated here-and-now which the American communitarian sage Elbert Hubbard preached, and whose credo proclaimed, amongst other paeans of exhortation to bodily and spiritual perfection, that: 'I believe in salvation through economic, social and spiritual freedom. I believe John Ruskin, William Morris, Henry Thoreau, Walt Whitman and Leo Tolstoy to be Prophets of God.'

Freddie, for good measure, subscribed to Hubbard's bold 'I believe in the Motherhood of God' and he backed it up, in the here and now, by publicly advocating female suffrage. Unlike James Gatz who, as Jay Gatsby, stocked his library with real but uncut and unread volumes, Frederick Hall Thomas read voraciously and, as Freddie Welsh, quoted his favourites to the world's press. He took his library with him in his cabin trunks wherever he went. The construct, complex and contradictory, that was

Freddie Welsh is unimaginable in any other fragment of space and time. His sporting prowess was a means to an end, but that end was only in incidental terms a material outcome. He had a vision of himself that was a cultural dream and one which might, through individual attainment, translate a rooted and collective social being into an evolved and changeably flexible modern way of living. His Wales could then flourish as an America: his America could be infused with what had been the values of Wales.

War and Depression were the nightmare into which the dream turned. In America his lonely, impoverished death in 1927 anticipated, for millions, the Wall Street Crash of 1929. In Wales the great strikes of 1919 and 1921 heralded the collective defeat of his 'collier friends' in the travail of 1926 and in the social pit of the 1930s into which a generation fell. The latter knew that in 1937 in New York, Tonypandy's Tommy Farr was now, in truth, a cracked grace note to the echo of the music Freddie Welsh had made for them as he crouched like a collier and battled like a street fighter. There was no way in which they would not have remembered how it was and how it had not, in the end, become. For if it was never, entirely, Freddie Welsh's Pontypridd he was, by virtue of the historical slipstream in which he had first found and then defined himself, abidingly, Pontypridd's Freddie Welsh.

The View from
Dowlais Top

It is invariably easy to spot giants in Wales though rarely
do they come in twos. Mine were barely five foot tall in
their stockinged feet. They were both also Merthyr men,
or rather they were Dowlais boys, and between them they
helped shape the written history of Wales in the second
half of the past century, to lasting effect. One was, of
course, Glanmor Williams (1920-2005) and the other
Gwyn A. Williams (1925-1995), historians profoundly
different in temperament, personality and style, often
wary of one another to the point of near hostility, and
scarcely in agreement about the history of the country
they both served so well. Yet, possibly to their perpetual
surprise, they were yoked together as much by their
origins as by their profession.

I turned up in Swansea in 1967 to begin a PhD in the
History Department which Glanmor Williams had created
and directed since he had been given a Chair at the early

age of 37 in 1957. What had attracted me from across the Atlantic was the emphasis on industrial and urban Wales that I could see, at second-hand reading from a distance, he had been inspiring since the early 1960s. Glan was a genial, piping-voiced, benevolent dictator whose influence and bounty was both channelled and selective. I was one among many fortunate recipients. On our first meeting, he suggested that 'his best friend', Ieuan Gwynedd Jones, then Senior Lecturer in Swansea, become my supervisor and, in a sense, my institutional life as an historian was under way.

I was introduced to Gwyn Alf by Glan when the former arrived as External Examiner at Swansea in 1969. My own time there was about to end temporarily since I had been appointed to a lectureship at Lancaster, from where Glan would bring me back in 1971 to a comparable post in Swansea until my decampment five years later.

'Lancaster?' Gwyn had queried at that drinks party in 1969. 'Lancaster? You should've c... c... come to York, b... b... boy. [Pause for effect]. My c... c... colleagues are a-f... f... flame with inertia!' Was I captivated then? By the dramatic delivery, the stammer wielded with Bevanite precision like a stiletto or by the artfully reused quotation from Disraeli about Gladstone's front bench (a typical Gwyn Alf 'steal')? Or was it the implication that I could have gone to York if only I had not applied to the wrong rose county? Maybe it was just the sheer fizzy and captivating persona of this chain-smoking (unfiltered Gauloises), bouffant-haired (white with a nicotine-yellow streak from back to front) pocket battleship. He dominated the room, attractive to men and women alike (other than to those in both sexes who detested him), loud in laughter, switching in mid-speech from the bonhomie of agreement to fiercely disputatious argument or even personal denunciation. He seemed alive in every pore of his combative body. His tongue licked its way over words as if they were flames that could burn it or engulf his listeners. He seemed, indeed, mad, bad and dangerous to know (to use a Byronic 'steal' he would like said of himself). I had never met anyone like him. And I wanted to know him a great deal more. I was to have my wish. Glan would understand why but he always felt that it had been a mistake, and he was right to think that Gwyn, for all his huff and puff, would never build at Cardiff the kind of institutional powerhouse for Welsh history that was Glan's core purpose, and great achievement, at Swansea. But then I, too, was more of a maverick in my own way than Glan might, from the guild vantage point he espoused all his professional life, have been able to approve of as the decades passed.

Style was at the heart of it. For Glan style, especially in writing, was an affectation, even an encumbrance, if it was not in the service of the lucid. Elegance was to be found in simplicity. Communication needed to be direct. Historians, in particular, should eschew the adjectives that had penny-coloured the narratives of belletrist chroniclers and ration the adverbs that might slow the wheels of the driving verbs. I saw, and see, his point. And you could never write the sweeping line of a textbook narrative or the generalising survey of centuries without such a close literary discipline. All of which may be one reason why I never wished to do so, and never did.

Gwyn certainly had that ambition, a key to recognition of gravitas within the profession, eating away at him. He thought that not being in those stakes was one of the reasons why he was not, in his pomp in the 1960s and 1970s, given the same heavyweight accolade as other 'British Marxist historians', and was instead relegated to the margins of also-rans besides the magisterial syntheses of an Eric Hobsbawm, a Christopher Hill, or even an E.P. Thompson, with whom he competed in other ways. The latter, all passionate rhetoric and layered metaphors, was certainly a better model as polemicist and historian for Gwyn, whose admiration for Thompson's 1963 firework *The Making of the English Working Class* was boundless. Yet Gwyn also sensed that a large part of the academic marginality which this lover of the centre stage indeed resented was to be endured because of the Welsh dimension which Glan had imbibed and championed long before him as being at the core of their generation's necessary work as historians. Gwyn scattered evocative nouns and epithets for spices, oils, dyes, wines and perfumes through the drier pages of his solid study of *Medieval London* (1965) because he could not resist the trickery of historical synaesthesia even in the mercantile listings of an economic and social treatise. His later style, even in the volume on Gramsci, *Proletarian Order* (1975), and most dramatically in his headlong romp *When Was Wales?* (1985), was a breathless laying-out of a magpie's treasures in an intellectual souk that reverberated with stylistic tics.

In other places, generally the less declamatory pages of quieter academic journals, Gwyn's gift for historical enquiry and scholarly marshalling of cautious evidence

Ely Street, Tonypandy, 1910: postcard

Striking miners waiting to go into a mass meeting at the Empire
Theatre, Tonypandy, Wednesday 2 November 1910. (Dai Smith's
grandfather is highlighted.) © National Museum of Wales

The Williamstown Male Voice Party, winners: Male Voice Contest,
Neath Royal National Eisteddfod, August 1918

'Three Generations of Miners'. W. Eugene Smith,
Wales 1950. © Magnum photos

Coed Ely 1950. X marks the spot where
W. Eugene Smith's 'Three Generations of Miners'
was photographed

'Tymawr Colliery, Pontypridd', Glyn Morgan 1947.
Oil on Canvas

'Tonypandy', Glyn Morgan, 1951. Oil on canvas,
© Glyn Morgan, with kind permission of Peter Lord

'Ton Pentre and Landscapes Beyond', Charles Burton, 1994.
Oil on canvas © Charles Burton, with kind
permission of BBC Wales

'Glenrhondda', oil on canvas, Charles Burton 2008,
© Charles Burton with thanks to the Martin Tinney Gallery

Ernie Zobole, 'The painter and his landscape', 1960s

Ernie Zobole, 'The painter and his landscape', 1990s

Sept. 16th 1936

Total. Takings. Less. Tax. £ 106 - 6 - 0.

Expenditure. Rent of Hall. Bills. Rosin. Tickers. Garage. 3 - 19 - 6.

Tommy Farr. 15rh — 41 - 11 - 7.
Charlie Bundy. 15rh — 27 - 14 - 5.
Billy. Jones. 10rh — 2 - 2 - 6
Idris. Morgan. 10rh — 2 - 8 - 0
Jacki Hellier. 6rh — 12 - 6
Dai. Vickery. 6rh — 12 - 6
Enspector. — 16 - 0
Referee. 3 - 3 - 0
Timekeeper. 2 - 6
M.C. and Staff 2 - 0 - 0

Total. Expenditure — £ 84 - 14 - 6
Balance £. 21 - 11 - 6

27 OCT 1938   27 OCT 1938   27 OCT 1938

Total. Takings. Less. Tax. £34 - 1 - 2.

Expenditure.

Rent of Hall. Garage. and. Bills £ 3 - 3 - 0
Billy Thomas. 10rh 1 - 10 - 6
Oliver Cullen. 10rh 1 - 10 - 0
Tom. Enoch. 6rh 10 - 9
Idris Morgan 6rh 11 - 0
Tommy Kid Farr 15rh 8 - 11 - 3
Ex. Seaman. Harvey. 15rh 11 - 19 - 6
Referee 1 - 15 - 0
Timekeeper. 2 - 6
Vince Hughes mc. 5 - 0
Tom. Patridge 7 - 6
Bert. Leach. 3 - 6
Leo Isaacs. 3 - 6
Rue. Isaacs 5 - 0

Total. Expenditure. £ 30 - 15 - 0
Balance. 3 - 6 - 2

List of fights, Tommy Farr

Tommy Farr

Alun Richards in conversation with Dai Smith

Freddie Welsh

Ron Berry and Dai Smith, in conversation.

Vernon Harding and Dai Smith at the National Musuem of
Wales's exhibition of Eugene Smith's photographs, Cardiff 2010.

could shine through, but he had decided to be Carlyle's historical 'remembrancer' for Wales and, on a platform or on the air, no one did it with such showmanlike panache. To see Gwyn in full flow before a large audience – as on the History Workshop weekends in Ruskin College from the late 1960s – was to witness declarative genius at work, an amalgamation of learning and wit, of electrifying delivery and compelling speech, of oratorical brilliance and forensic argument, a crackling firestorm that swept on and on until, in its crescendo of effect, Gwyn would appear consumed by himself. It was magnificent. It was unique. It was Dickensian. Its very Welshness was what, quite unfairly, caused it, and him, to be all too often admired and dismissed as just an act, when it was the citizen-historian as activist-intellectual that we were in fact seeing.

Amongst the many tributes paid to Gwyn after his death, aged 70, was an address by Glan given two years later in their old school in Cyfarthfa Castle, Merthyr. It is a tribute whose praise is as heartfelt and sincere as it is sensible and measured. Those in the audience, and any readers thereafter, could be in no doubt how highly Glan rated Gwyn as a member of the guild. However, for those of us in that audience in April 1997, the tone and the nuance of Glan's voice and gesture also left no doubt of the conviction of the older man that his younger schoolmate – Glan in Form VI in 1937, Gwyn in Form III – had, from a combination of inner angst and outward chutzpah, not entirely fulfilled a narrower promise by straying so widely and erratically from the marked path:

Much as Gwyn accomplished he didn't really pull off what he'd had in mind... he didn't carry all his colleagues in Cardiff [in the distinctively anti-Welsh History Department] with him [in the 1970s]... I... wonder whether or not we as Welsh historians else-where gave him all the support we might have done.

...Was I the only one who had derived the impression that in his latest [years of work] he preferred television to books? A stuffed shirt historian – me, for instance – might be tempted to argue that television has its limitations and deficiencies... entertainment tends to take priority over information...

I can readily believe... that his rural retirement [to west Wales in the late 1980s] eased that tension which at times threatened to become unbearable between his devotion to left-wing sympathies and his commitment to nationalism. I used on occasion to fear that he was in danger of splitting up the middle.

Perhaps the split was more amoeba-like than that. Between Glan's cool dissection and balanced appraisal – in politics as well as in History – and Gwyn's effervescent commitment to a History written with the barricades in mind, was a common ground where they fought, the Labour stalwart and the renegade communist-cum-nationalist, in a common cause where neither doubted the other's good will or doughtiness in the intellectual endeavour both had espoused. In a Wales whose defining geographical and social edges were being blurred from the 1970s as surely as the available means to communicate such change were being scrambled by technological advance and a deep-seated, anti-intellectual populism, they were united in their attempt to retrieve the past in order to inform the present of a future that might not be fully available unless it was made so. For both these great historians their differences, and their links, were rooted and forged in a very particular place at a deeply significant time: interwar Dowlais and Merthyr.

> Each of us [Glan had begun in his address in Cyfartha], in the opening words of the familiar old rhyme, was a 'bachgen bach o Ddowlais'...
> Both of us were born and bred in the town. Neither of us could have got it out of his system, or ever wanted to.

*

Made in Dowlais. The legend on the iron rails that once went out from there to girdle the globe. Made in Dowlais. The last three words, Gwyn would delight in bragging, that Anna Karenina would have seen in 1876 as she plunged to her death on that Moscow railway line. And 'Made in Dowlais' Glan and Gwyn certainly were. Yet the making, a convergence of time and place, does not quite encompass their full, complex and divergent meaning. Their deepening sense of their upbringing not only infused their lifelong progressive sympathies, it grew increasingly rich as both, at the end of their lives, placed themselves as figures in a wider social and cultural landscape. Their last writings were in different ways autobiographical in root but they were also, I believe, both stretching to find forms of writing beyond the historical convention to which they, of course, also subscribed, in order to probe for a translation of the meaning of Glamorgan's broader history in their own lives, and, by extension, its significance in ours.

Naturally this does not gainsay the straightforward manner in which Glan's deep empathy with those who had suffered in their lifetimes through material poverty, and subsequently from their relative neglect by academic scholarship in Wales, had led him to write so sensitively in the 1970s about the 'general and common sort of people' in sixteenth and seventeenth-century Glamorgan: his chapter on Glamorgan Society (in Vol. IV of the County History he edited) was a fine work of both historical imagination and scrupulous scholarly reconstruction. Nor, at an inevitably obliquer remove, can we be in any doubt that when Gwyn wrote the following in his daring *Goya and the Impossible Revolution* (1976) – in those same 1970s that saw Wales bookended by the last successful miners' strikes of 1972 and 1974, only to be confounded in 1979 by the vote against Devolution – it was not just Bourbon Spain and its legacy which was stirring him to an intellectual and personal fever:

The shuffle towards modernisation begun in the 18th Century did not reach its destination... the cycle which opened [then] proved to be, in terms of objective historical process, a cycle of frustration... For reasons rooted in the history of Spain, that species of revolution [modernisation anointed with bourgeois revolution], proved to be as impossible as it was necessary. Spain... turned itself into a living folk museum of contradictory politics, with its half-formed and unarticulated 'classes' inhabiting different historic time scales.

Spain then. And Wales? And Glamorgan? And Merthyr? And Dowlais? I'm tempted to say, too, 'and the Rhondda?' Because Welsh literary scholars, unlike historians, have not been slow to transfer their biographical and contextual studies of imaginative writers onto historians through biography, treating them as being writers as much as they are scholars. In the last volume of Glanmor Williams' County History in 1988 (Vol. VI, *Glamorgan Society* 1780-1980), M. Wynn Thomas wrote an enlightening chapter on 'Literature in English' which compares the early nineteenth-century growth of Merthyr and Dowlais around iron, with the late Victorian explosion of Rhondda's coal society. And then he comments on Jack Jones' Merthyr novel of 1935, *Black Parade*, and its hero, Harry, as he pauses in some trepidation at the prospect of crossing the mountains from Merthyr to Rhondda, and thereby:

> the great divide – between the two neighbouring industrial conurbations that are nevertheless so culturally and historically *out of step*.... It is the, partly literal, foreignness of the Rhondda that Harry, brought up in a distinctively Welsh, and even Welsh-speaking, industrial society jibs at. Merthyr writers themselves have therefore tended to present their relationship to the pre-industrial Welsh past rather differently, emphasising the continuities as well as the discontinuities that constituted change in their

case. (Compare the contemporary cases of the Merthyr historian, Gwyn A. Williams and the Rhondda historian, Dai Smith.)

It is true that Gwyn, when irate with me, as he was more than once in those quarrelsome 1980s, did call me, just the once, 'a fucking Rhondda Englishman', but I take comfort in the manner in which Gwyn, in truth, emphasised 'fractures' more than threads in the history of Wales; although, to turn and turn about, he did, of course, retire to the west Wales of his distant forebears and did learn to speak the Welsh he decidedly did not speak as his native tongue in the Merthyr of his youth and early manhood. Glan, perhaps a little waspishly, and certainly conscious of both his own childhood and his own superb command of spoken and written Welsh, recalled in his memorial address for Gwyn how he had been intrigued by 'Gwyn's love affair with the Welsh language' which, despite some foundations, was, he averred, 'pretty scrappy' until 'his struggle to master it' late in life:

> He didn't wholly succeed, but he did astonishingly well... [then] I saw almost nothing of him after he'd plunged into the depths of 'pura Wallia'... and so I never got the chance to quiz him about the way he was making out.

There are, I suppose, ways of looking forward as well as looking back which are not necessarily dependent upon generation, language, geographical location or even biographical data. They might, indeed, be ways induced by choice: by ideology or intellect, morality or ethics, hopefulness or despair. Dowlais was a catalyst for these two great historians in more ways than one, even the most obvious one. Idris Davies wrote his remarkable and prescient poem of 1945, 'Marx and Heine and Dowlais', precisely with that title because of the concatenation of meanings the place had already come to signify.

I used to go to St John's Wood
On Saturday evenings in summer
To look on London behind the dusty garden trees,
And argue pleasantly and bitterly
About Marx and Heine, the iron brain and the laughing
sword;
And the ghost of Keats would sit in a corner
Smiling slowly behind a summer of wine,
Sadly smiling at the fires of the future.
And late in the summer night
I heard the tall Victorian critics snapping
Grim grey fingers at London Transport,
And sober, solemn students of James Joyce,
Dawdling and hissing into Camden Town.

But now in the winter dusk
I go to Dowlais Top
And stand by the railway bridge
Which joins the bleak brown hills,
And gaze at the streets of Dowlais
Lopsided on the steep dark slope,
A battered bucket on a broken hill,
And see the rigid phrases of Marx
Bold and black against the steel-grey west,
Riveted along the sullen skies.

And as for Heine, I look on the rough
Bleak, colourless hills around,
Naked and hard as flint,
Romance in a rough chemise.

Throughout life Dowlais invoked memories in both Glan and Gwyn. It also evoked consciousness: historical as well as personal. Dowlais, deep in them, underlined for both how history may be comprehended but not necessarily how it was felt. I believe that in their autobiographical musings they may have pointed us towards the validity of one of their last lessons for historians of regions like Glamorgan and places like Dowlais: that forms of study can grow conventional and stale even to the point of misapprehending the cultural dynamism of such societies as theirs which, in its original essence, encompassed and dictated both change and innovation. Effective re-presentation of the intrinsic nature of the society might therefore require shape-shifting within a given narrative structure, even for the objective historian who may be also intent on rekindling the silent experiences, inward and reflective, which are usually left to the novelist or the remembrancer.

Their Dowlais lives overlapped, these 'bechgyn bach o Ddowlais' being born there within five years of each other: Glan in 1920, Gwyn in 1925. Near to their deaths both Gwyn and later Glan told us, but in such contrasting styles, of the detail of their upbringing. There was the sober chronicle of Glan in *A Life* (2002), and the filigree take of Gwyn in *Fishers of Men* (1996). But we, like them in their own practice of the historical craft, must not mistake the placement of witness for the weight of evidence or the flash of memory for the light of meaning. There are then, first, the clues they scattered late, and then there are the lives we can trace separately amongst social patterns already set for them. The view from Dowlais Top was always subject to a Janus-like glance. Clues, nonetheless, there are.

Glan wrote a measured autobiography as a series of gathered-together episodes. Towards its end, frankly, it becomes something of a chronicle; but then there were so many good deeds and matters to record from his remarkably productive life, so many bouquets, typically, to hand out. But in its opening chapters it is fresh and astute beyond mere convention. Not least because in his maturity he strives to remember accurately the contrast between what he came to know subsequently of the society of his youth, and what he felt about it at the time:

> Looking back on what life was like in the Dowlais of the 1920s and 1930s I am struck by the extraordinary paradoxes that characterised it then. At the time, of course, those contradictions did not strike me at all. Like most other youngsters, I just enjoyed life and lived it unthinkingly. The existence I knew was the only one I had experienced; I took it all as part of the natural order of things. Indeed, I suppose I assumed that most people lived a similar sort of life. But with the passing of the years those paradoxes have come to stand out more plainly...

He goes on to identify five such paradoxes and they relate to social and cultural differentials as well as to the economic whirligig of the time. We will return to them. But first I want to pick out a paradox he scarcely notes: his father was first a collier, until badly injured, then an insurance agent and later a factory worker. Throughout the interwar years, though earning a pittance, he was never out of work. Glan's working-class childhood in the Pant, above Dowlais, was not only firmly attached to an earlier, Welsh-speaking, literate and nonconformist world (he was an ardent Baptist at Calfaria), it was relatively protected, if not quite as much so as that of his near contemporary, the railway signalman's son, Raymond Williams, born in 1921 in Pandy, just over the mountains at Abergavenny and directly linked to Dowlais by rail. Both of them only children, they passed and went to their respective grammar schools when most of their 1920s playmates, boys and especially girls, did not. By the time he was a teenager in a vibrant sixth form, Glan was, and remained, conscious of the material and spiritual plight of his fellow men and women. But he did not, in Britain's second worst unemployment black spot, the first being Jarrow in the north-east of England, ever experience such direct misery personally. However, such proximity without tangibility can, as in those who survive wars, be even more telling in subsequent life.

If we turn to Gwyn the contrast is even sharper, and because of his later über-identification with a proletarian world of incipient revolution which was to be highlighted wherever he found it, in Turin or Tonypandy, it was felt as a personal paradox even more acutely. Indeed I believe it is a profound indicator of his lifelong unease. For Gwyn was of course the son of a schoolmaster whose wife, too, had been a teacher. He was the firstborn of two boys

144

whose father was almost at the pinnacle of local society when he became a headmaster:

> We all met in *our* kitchen. I realise now [he wrote in *Fishers of Men* in the 1990s] that it was because we had more room and our family lived on the princely five-pounds-a-week teachers' salary.

Gwyn's boyhood home was set amidst the grime and clangour of Dowlais but it was a double-fronted, terraced house in Lower Row, Penywern, which looked down from its slight elevation onto the more packed housing below in the meaner streets such as the one across the railway line, Francis Street, where Glan himself grew up.

And when adolescent consciousness of the world in those turbulent years from the late 1930s onwards (he was 15 in 1940) came to Gwyn, it was to wider horizons which he looked:

> I devoured [my father's] books... followed up by total immersion of a Baptist intensity in Dowlais Library with its books and newspaper section and even, twice, daring raids into Alien Territory in Merthyr Library! I took all the gang with me. Our heads were forever buried in books and journals. All around us Dowlais was wrestling with the Depression and the long hopeless queues of the unemployed. We, locked into a kind of dream, hardly saw them.
>
> We burned and bled with our comrades in Spain, with our people in the shelled Vienna flats. We became experts in the horrors of darkest Hungary,

the agonies of Jugoslavia, the stifled hopes of Czechoslovakia. We relived the struggles – and the controversies – of the German Socialists and Communists, worshipped Rosa Luxemburg; we cheered on Leon Blum and the Popular Front in France – and everywhere. We even started on the Chinese and their Long March.

Gwernllwyn Chapel Gang became, almost overnight, an extra mural branch of the Third International. In my case the conversion was permanent.

Never was identification by displacement put more vividly. Gwyn, hilariously in those 'Stories Towards An Autobiography', then recounts how marching groups of youthful Christian redeemers overnight became gangs of anti-fascist guerrillas on the heights of their stricken town, on the pinnacle of Dowlais Top itself. This is Gwyn as a Welsh Tom Sawyer not yet made sober enough by his profession or by his maturity to distinguish play-acting from the rigours of performance. That would come, but only after the army in late 1943, Normandy, Germany, and then post-war in Aberystwyth, where Glan had preceded him in 1937.

Aberystwyth, the University as Mecca, was the most uncompromisingly Welsh *difference* either had encountered in their Dowlais-bound lives. Glan, who recounts how predominantly English speaking Dowlais had become by the 1920s, discovered here in Aber a peer generation who spoke Welsh to each other, and promptly improved his own. Gwyn's parents were both Welsh speaking and believed that their infant son would absorb the language by osmosis. Despite the hearth, chapel and school, he did not:

> Our language was English... Welsh became to us a Chapel tongue, a sacerdotal language. War and the threat of war dominated our English speaking adolescence.

Yet, he also says:

> ...though difficult to recall how I actually felt at the time.... We felt superior to the generality certainly and with reason. Valleys culture was international and rich. But we in no sense felt that Welsh was inferior. If anything it enjoyed some sense of moral worth.... Certainly, having spoken English only since I was six, I felt guilt over not being fluent in Welsh...
>
> Aberystwyth was a legend of my youth. The Peoples' College, 'built on the pennies of the poor', as they said, the College which was the theme of innumerable University Sundays in our Chapel. The College of my grandmother's inexorable 'Higherr and Aberr... doctorr, preacherr or teacherr!'
>
> 'That's where I'm going,' I declared. I did too.

The view from Dowlais Top stretched, for these two young men, to an immediate future that was to the north and west. Glan had actually been told by his headmaster that he was to follow in the footsteps of the gifted economist and future Tory Minister, Aubrey Jones, and go to the LSE after studying Economics and German in school. He boldly demurred: he stuck to Welsh and History, to our benefit, though he occasionally wondered if it was to his own. Aberystwyth eventually turned out Glan as an early modern historian and Gwyn as a medievalist. Yet the view from Dowlais Top was also to the east and the south and the memory of it and its subsequent revelations would inflect their written history as it continued to haunt their lives. It is time to turn to what exactly lay *below* Dowlais Top.

The myth of former glories was close enough to what had actually existed, and they would have learned this, at least, by rote. The Dowlais Ironworks, established in 1759, principally caused Merthyr to become the iron-making metropolis of the world by 1830, and the biggest town in Wales for well over the first half of the nineteenth century. Dowlais had on its steep slopes fourteen blast furnaces in just one site and employed over 7,000 men. It was the largest ironworks in South Wales and turned readily to steel making from the late 1850s. It was Capitalism and the attraction of Waged Work writ large. When Glan was born just after the end of the First World War this prosperity, and its attendant gaggle of chapels and clusters of pubs and raucous music halls and glamorous cinemas, was the common memory and, even as it faded in the 1930s, Dowlais remained the receptacle of the paradoxes to which he had referred in his memoir: massive industry on the edge of rural Breconshire; Welsh cultural mores and language intermingled with Irish, Spanish and English migrants; religious observance tinged with radicalism, shaded into secularism and irreligion; even, scandalously, the wild and antisocial behaviour of drinkers, boxers, choristers and the irredeemably feckless. It was the complex, variegated social creation of the iron and coal industries, not some monocultural entity stamped out of a sociological pattern book. But it was, too, monolithic, as Glan brilliantly depicted it.

> [Dowlais] was virtually the creation of a single family – the Guests.... [and they have] left [their] mark everywhere in the town: in the great iron-works; the endless lines of trucks bearing the sacred initials GKN; even the names of the streets – Guest Cottages, Ivor Street, Charlotte Street, and so on... commemorated them. The unmistakable stamp of the family could also be seen on all the biggest and grandest buildings in the town: Dowlais House, parish churches, the Guest Memorial Library, Dowlais School and the Dowlais Stables, which provided better accommodation for horses than human beings.... All were monumentally built on classical lines with massive dressed stone... like Dowlais Market.
>
> [And] when the huge furnaces were working, the lurid glare from them turned night into day in a sort of pseudo sunset that lit up the sky and could be seen for miles around.

'I stood,' wrote Idris Davies in the mid-1930s, 'in the ruins of Dowlais, And sighed for the lovers destroyed, And the landscape of Gwalia stained for all time, By the bloody hands of progress.' How terrible was the fate of Dowlais in the eyes of those who had known its glory; in the eyes of those like Idris Davies, born in 1905 in Rhymney and so, as an adult, fully aware of the boyhood home of these two historians; or in the view of Rhondda's Will Paynter, born in 1903:

The year 1934 was one of intense activity for me. I was a leading communist in the Rhondda, but... involved in meetings and discussions throughout South Wales. The Rhondda was a pretty grim place with heavy unemployment, and although many pits were still working, the wages were low and there was plenty of visual evidence of the poverty and drabness of life...

But if the visual evidence of poverty was apparent in the Rhondda, it was ten times more so then in the places I was now visiting for the first time, places at the top of the valleys; Merthyr and Dowlais, once with as great a concentration of industry as any in South Wales but now derelict... Nantyglo and Blaina, ghost villages filled with workless people. I had not imagined that such poverty-stricken places existed.... The ruins of the old blast furnaces and early pits remained, together with the housing conditions of a century earlier... and it is not surprising that they were the centres of opposition to the means test.

Gwyn was ten when the Unemployment Assistance Board Offices in Merthyr were invaded by a crowd of men and women from Dowlais, led by Dowlais' Communist militant, Jack 'Bolshi' Williams. Files and records were ripped up and strewn over the streets. It was a set piece he recounted in many ways, many times. He had no memory of it, of course, as he confessed to me when he read about it in *The Fed* in 1980. It was a relic he had snatched from a later historiography in order to burnish the public remembrance of the significance of Dowlais as the mature historian now conceived of it in the 1980s. That irruption was in 1935. Dowlais had been finally knocked flat just five years before. Paynter remembered how when he got there to agitate for action, he saw men picking up cigarette ends from the gutter and smoking them by passing them around on the tip of a pin and how, even more hidden and silent still in Glamorgan's history, behind some of those boarded-up shopfronts in Dowlais High Street you could buy a girl for an hour for sixpence.

What had happened, beyond the general precipitous decline in coalmining employment after 1926, was the closure of the main section of the Dowlais steelworks in 1930, with the loss of 3,000 jobs – complete closure followed in 1936 – and the reduction of the local mining workforce from some 16,000 men to 4,000 and shrinking. Merthyr Tydfil's general population had reached a peak of 80,000 in 1921; by the late 1930s it was down to 60,000 and only just levelling off thereafter. Average male unemployment was the same in 1935 as it was in 1931: 12,000 people or 70 per cent of the insured population, whilst 90 per cent of the total number of unemployed coalminers in the Merthyr District were registered in Merthyr and Dowlais.

Unemployment figures overall for Dowlais were still above 73 per cent in 1939, which is when the think-tank Political and Economic Planning seriously proposed following through on the government's 1935 Enquiry into Merthyr Tydfil – which had found over half the male population to be 'surplus to requirements' for any foreseeable future – by closing the entire borough down and transferring what was left of its population to a new location on the Usk.

Amongst schoolchildren, according to the Medical Officer of Health in 1935, diseases ranging from tuberculosis to scarlet fever and the general condition of bone deficiency or rickets arising from malnutrition were rife. An employed collier could expect wages of around £2 a week; those on the dole not much more than half that sum. In the 1930s families in Dowlais lived in Victorian cellar dwellings fitfully lit by naked gas jets, their living and sleeping quarters infested with bugs and seeping water, their low-ceilinged, dark rooms heated sporadically by waste coal scratched by the unemployed from the slag heaps of Dowlais Top. This is from the *Sunday Express*, 22 November 1936:

> Joe got home at half past four this morning. He had been on a night shift at the Patches. For three years he and four pals have been working their own hand-made pits on the Patches [of Dowlais Top]. So have 600 other Merthyr and Dowlais unemployed. They take their coal home, dragging it perhaps four or five miles, and then their homes are sure of a fire whether there is food or not. Some of it they sell at 1s. 7d. a sack and some is given away to the elderly and widows.

Statistical revisionism has more recently inoculated us, with its gradient slopes of relative measure, against the almost unbearable force of this melodrama of misery; or else we could also legitimately acknowledge the soulsaving work in house building undertaken by the local Quaker settlement, and the deeper visions of the WEA and their Arts Settlements in Dowlais, and, of course, the domestic resilience of those who stayed and did not succumb to despair. Yet too much elision becomes someone else's swerving evasion. Eighty years on, as BBC Wales' execrable anthropological series *Coal House* made all too clear, there is a preference in contemporary South Wales for the clichéd pap of reality television as opposed to the brutalism visited upon a whole society. The washed hands of the evaders high-five reality away across the decades. Even in the interwar years Dowlais had its very own Dr Pangloss in the shape of Councillor Isaac Edwards, JP, who addressed the Dowlais Chamber of Trade and Commerce in 1934 on life in Dowlais, then and fifty years previously. His conclusion was that in public adminis-tration, public squalor and public morality all had improved – drunkenness was down, windows were larger, Dowlais' record on drainage was unsurpassed and its list of great men from preachers to choral conductors to engineers a shining example on which to build. And, in 1934, as for 'Prosperity', it meant, said Isaac Edwards in words recorded by the *Merthyr Express* for a gape-mouthed Dowlais readership, to 'some people… merely material possessions, measured in terms of money. Others identified the word with Happiness [akin to]… the mind of a pig resting on a dung heap after having its fill, suggesting in so many words happiness meant merely "a full belly and a warm soft bed".' He would put forward the thought of 'General Well Being' as applying to man's physical, mental and moral nature, and, with this interpretation, he ventured to say that Dowlais was far more prosperous today [in 1934!] than it was 50 years ago. The statistics he had given were an indication of the change that had happened in the meantime... above all, what a boon today, in our prolonged idleness, was 'Unemployment Pay'.

Someone should have shown him the triumphant Coal Arch of Dowlais and its flanking miners on the royal visit of 1911 and how their equivalents sat on the upturned metal wreckage, that 'battered bucket on a broken hill', of the blast furnaces when Edward VIII dropped in on Dowlais in 1936. Some Pigs. Some dung heap. Some Well Being. Industrial Wales, encapsulated by Dowlais, came across her true remembrancers not in boosted Prosperity but in actual Destitution. Intellectual consciousness matured to encompass the challenge of inescapable experience. In 1963 Glan told readers of a fiftieth anniversary booklet for Cyfarthfa Castle Grammar School:

Encouraged [in the sixth form from that same 1934] by skilful teaching to read and think increasingly for ourselves, we taught each other almost as much in discussion outside the classroom as our teachers taught us inside. Living in Merthyr in those days there could be no question of our confining ourselves to academic issues and ignoring the desperate political and social problems of our time.... Few of us went on to University; times were hard and scholarships few... [but school]... had already taught us the essentials of that free, humane, and independent enquiry which is the breath of life in all higher education.

S.O. Davies, Merthyr's left-wing Labour MP, was warning the House of Commons in 1934 that further misery would entail revolution not the reconstruction which Labour had wanted. But S.O. also firmly opposed the riotous sacking of the Unemployment Assistance Board in 1935, the local event so cherished by Gwyn, ever alert for the Impossible Revolution that never came. Glan, indeed, also recognised the attraction of utopian ideals beyond the pragmatic and acknowledged the pull, for some, of communism; but he was equally sure that it was the older traditions of liberalism in Merthyr, from Henry Richards in 1868 on, that had cemented the politics of democratic socialism to which he clearly subscribed over his lifetime. Dowlais tinged both historians with a progressive hue in politics and in their broader human sympathies.

In Glan this could be seen personally in the things he made *happen* even more than in what he wrote specifically about Merthyr and Dowlais. His interest in history-from-below was quite evident from the powerful address he delivered in 1948 to the Council of Social Service for Wales on the theme of Local History. He was unequivocally for it. And particularly for Glamorgan, since 'there is no major facet of human history in Britain which is not represented in Glamorgan'. The Glamorgan Local History Society duly followed, with 'the mass of unwritten social history' as its driver within a year and, of course, *Morgannwg*, its journal edited by Glan and Gwynedd O. Pierce, began its illustrious career in 1957. It was his home patch which led him on to the revolution in Welsh historiography he, more than anyone, effected. The emphases and help he gave to others as he moved the historiography of Wales in the 1950s to its first real encounter with the history of his own people was undeniably revolutionary. We may readily recall the superb essays, or lectures, organised by the WEA – and notably by its tutor organiser, one Rhodri Morgan – on Merthyr Politics which were delivered in Merthyr in the winter of 1964-65. And we know, of course, that it was Glan who edited the subsequent book of 1966 under the same heading but with the subtitle 'The Making of a Working Class Tradition', an ambitious heraldic note, a hopeful clarion call, and one that consciously echoed E.P. Thompson's classic *The Making of the English Working Class* of 1963. But Glan's challenge, and even his boast in his editor's foreword, has been forgotten in our more consensual times:

> One of the most potent and enduring myths of Welsh historiography is that the Welsh radical political tradition derives mainly from the rural areas. The virile and fecund political consciousness of the industrial valleys has... had far less than its due... and in this process of reconsideration the place of Merthyr is a crucial one. It, more than any other Welsh town, has been the crucible and matrix of working-class political tradition. Here the old crust of custom was melted down and fused with new aspirations flowing from volcanic social and economic change, to be remoulded and hardened into a new political democracy...
>
> Like every man born in the Merthyr district, I take a proper pride in the tale [here] unfolded.

Even more potently he took a pride in the application in the book of essays of what he called new historical 'techniques' and 'conclusions' by younger historians, including the 40-year-old Professor from York, himself 'a Dowlais man', Gwyn A. Williams. A number of us who were deeply interested in the application of those new 'techniques' of social history to Wales, and in the disturbing 'conclusions' that could be drawn, responded as a generation to that book, whose immaculate conception, if not its actual procreation, was undeniably located in the Dowlais of the 1930s. A new history of Wales was born in Merthyr. The true begetters were Glanmor Williams and Gwyn A. Williams. In ways that are more apparent now than in their lifetimes, they also truly complemented each other.

If Glan, by dint of personal psychology, familial upbringing and, perhaps, being slightly earlier in his generational affiliation, was a rock of good sense and humanism, with Dowlais stamped through him, Gwyn, as Glan willingly conceded, was a thousand brilliant lights flashing and flickering on and off, not a barometer of the general climate but a spinning weathervane alert to and sometimes disorientated by the passing winds. It brought him great sensitivity as an historian ever-on-the-cusp of fashion, and considerable pain as one who longed for settlement, political and cultural – though strictly on his own terms of course. He could despair of Wales as well as be exhilarated by its intense version of the general human condition. This, too, was a personal conditioning from surreal, topsy-turvy, damned and delivered Dowlais. In the middle of his *When Was Wales?* in 1985 he presented us with this riff of a summation, with the defeats of 1979 very much in his mind:

> By 1983... Wales itself seemed once more to be dissolving into a congeries of disparate societies... whose very existence as coherent... societies was... problematical. We have run off our maps.
>
> This has happened within the space of a single lifetime. My parents, like many others, were schoolteachers from working-class families. Brothers, cousins, friends were colliers, often on the dole. The talk at the supper table of my childhood in Dowlais was of Labour and the ILP, what to do about the Communists, of my uncle's latest Welsh-language play on the Welsh radio, our local fascist Arthur Eyles and his rather more menacing colleagues abroad... of the ethics of canvassing for headships amongst an overpowering Labour council noted for both heroic service and unheroic nepotism and petty corruption, of TB (y dicai) and diphtheria (the Dip) which took away one of the children and nearly took both, of the noson lawens at the Chapel and the scholarship to Aberystwyth, of the fight with the fascists on the Bont and how difficult it was to discuss the performance of the Spitfire in Welsh.

If Gwyn had lived to 1997 and, for sure, to 2007, he might have found pleasure in the new institutions and the new politics that are emerging in a new, old Wales, or at least in quarrelling with them. Glan would certainly have welcomed both, particularly that old WEA tutor organiser at the helm for a crucial decade. What I am really sure of, however, is that in every sense that matters for historians still committed to the societies to whom they wish to tell their truths, Glan and Gwyn, our best exemplars in this, were moulded by Dowlais and that it was the view from Dowlais Top, backwards and forwards in time, and round the compass points, too, but mostly down the valley, that gave their history the taste of sincerity and the passion of poetry.

Into Dai Country

Neither man had ever chosen an easy route, and they were quick to let you know their opinion of those who had. To enter the face-to-face worlds of Ron Berry and Alun Richards was to be weighed, to be summed up, to be invited to take sides, to risk scorn and rejection, to be rewarded with guarded insights and, maybe, just maybe, to win the loyalty of abiding friendship. My own first, and separate, encounters with both of them were uneasy to the point of a measured hostility. Theirs, not mine. And yet I was from the very beginning drawn to both of them and to their work even if, salaried and pensionable and therefore compromised as I was, it was ever clear that, for them, the marks of experience they translated onto the page were shared stripes strictly unavailable to those whose backs were buffered by social and cultural support systems they scorned and mistrusted, and used as best they could.

*

As I learned later from reading their correspondence to each other, and then from both to myself – a brilliant and devastating commentary on writing, writers and their patch as much as a record of needed mutuality – to be pinned and even dissected was indeed, with an occasional dollop of praise, sometimes my fate too. Alun and Ron were the self-designated no-bullshit writers of post-war South Wales and, professional to their core, they took no prisoners on the page or in life, out of sentiment or pity. They judged. They valued. They affirmed the capacity of hard-won fiction to finger both the dissemblance of false witness and the resonance of whatever it was, word or deed or absence of both, which suggested another truth. Subsequently their novels and stories were, and are, difficult to stomach in a Wales either too intent on wallowing in maudlin populism about its past self or too narcissistic with self-promoting dismissiveness to acknowledge the history that infects all contemporary endeavour. In their lifetimes I found their indictment irresistible because, in different modes, they found the forms of representation which ensured that the significance of their best work would be more than local. All that was, of course, the reverse side of their celebration of and delight in the people who had, one way or the other, measured up.

For me, Alun came first. I had not read his first collection of short stories, *Dai Country*, when it appeared in 1973 and although we overlapped in Swansea when I lectured at the University from 1971 to 1976 and he lived in West

162

Cross, Mumbles after moving from Cardiff in 1967, we had no occasion or reason to meet. That changed in 1977 after I had taken a newly created post in Modern Welsh History at Cardiff University and began to construct courses – within a History Department since nothing so vulgar then sullied any major university English Department – which introduced students to writing in English about modern Wales. Alun's forensic probing of a stifled post-war society had, so far as I could see, no previous Welsh counterpart. He was also clearly replete with insider knowledge as his second triumphant collection *The Former Miss Merthyr Tydfil* displayed in 1976. There was though something else: a distancing that was, somehow, personal more than objective. I certainly did not rationalise it like that at the time but when I was asked by the *Times Literary Supplement* to write a full-page overview of the culture of contemporary Wales, with the first scudding clouds of devolutionary promise, or threat, in the air, I found myself, in a few brief lines, averring that the sharp and talented Alun Richards had the 'baleful eye of an outsider'. The piece appeared for St David's Day 1977 under the groaning title, not mine, of 'The Wherewithal of Welshness'.

At this time Alun used the research facilities of Swansea University – which he had attended in the early 1950s – and especially the bibliographical expertise of its librarian, the distinguished medievalist Dr Fred Cowley. It was Fred who alerted Alun to my reference to him in the *TLS* and, once read, Alun had both approved of its general thrust and fulminated against the insolence of this David Smith, from Cardiff University, with an 'outsider's' name if ever there was one. Fred Cowley explained that I had just transferred to Cardiff from Swansea and had just completed a PhD on the history of the South Wales miners. Alun fired off a letter, polite, if distant, praising the article by a tangential request for current books and articles to read in what was a burgeoning period of growth in Welsh historiography. I must have sent him the reams and reams of suggestions for further reading with which I was then burdening my undergraduate students. Another letter arrived, intrigued enough by my passing remark that I had been commissioned, along with my friend Gareth Williams who was then lecturing through the medium of Welsh at Aberystwyth, to write the 'official' centenary history of the Welsh Rugby Union. Alun had his own trenchant thoughts on writing about Welsh rugby, and indeed was an occasional rugby writer for the *Guardian* when his friend, the inestimable Carwyn James, was indisposed or indifferent to the deadline of a journalist. He suggested – a Richards ploy I would learn to recognise, and anticipate with a shiver for the adventure to come – that we might have a lunch together. The deal was struck. He would travel from Swansea to Cardiff to visit the Public Library in the Hayes from which he still borrowed most of his books, and by the bagful, and I would come by train that Saturday morning from his home town of Pontypridd where I had gone to live. We would meet outside the imposing late Victorian façade at High Noon.

I was slightly late and breathless. He was waiting at the top of the steps to the Old Library, flanked appropriately enough by two seated female figures, Study and Rhetoric. I, five foot and a squeak, looked up to see Alun, six foot plus and gleaming in a belted detective's off-white mackintosh, glaring down at me, a book-stuffed shopping bag in either hand, sunlight on his bottle-thick glasses deflecting my feeble smile. He knew me at once and let me know it: 'Whaddya mean, "outsider", you fuckin' Rhondda dwarf?' The growl caromed down the entrance as a direct hit, to be followed by his wide-mouthed grin and: 'Fancy a spot of lunch?'

The lunch – 'no tomatoes for Alun Richards, thank you very much' – went on for hours as he fascinated me with tales of his mulch-territory, Ponty, and quizzed me on the politics of union and labour history which then had me in its unrelenting grip. We were both obsessive about rugby and its social significance and would soon both be deeply involved in histories of the game – Alun via a film and book for BBC Wales, *Touch of Glory*, and me, with Gareth Williams, in delivering the centenary history *Fields of Praise* in 1980. Early on he had thought to ask me to help research his book but we had, in this at least, separate agendas. Beyond that, bit by bit as we exchanged information and then confidences, I came to know him as the most spectacular of friends, and my deepening admiration for his work never ceased. He died in 2004.

In the early stages of our acquaintance I was in awe of him for simpler reasons; that he was the funniest man, other than Gwyn Thomas, I had ever met and unlike Gwyn, though Alun's conjoined laughter and tear-making anecdotes were also polished for consumption, he could and would listen; that he was so attuned to the innovative pitch of trying to capture the South Wales which had formed, delighted, and angered him; and that, of course, he was already a highly successful writer for the page and for television by the late 1970s. It was because of this success that I met Ron Berry.

Alun, in one of the many conversations through which our friendship grew, had spoken of his unstinting admiration for the older writer. Ron Berry had been born in the upper Rhondda in 1920 and for Alun he always carried with him an air of unassailable prior experience, allied to rock-solid working-class bona fides of work as well as upbringing. Alun had grown up in his shopkeeping grandparents' comfortable house in Pontypridd after his father had abandoned his mother almost immediately upon his birth in 1929. That 'baleful eye', as his 1986 autobiography *Days of Absence* would reveal, was indeed that of a watching insider 'outsider', and closer to a psychological insight than I could ever have imagined when I wrote it. His full discovery of Ron Berry the writer had taken him on his motorbike in the early 1960s to meet, at Ron's suggestion, in The Red Cow in Treorchy. For Alun it meant a connection that promised support for his own rather isolated attempts to create a new texture for Welsh writing, one more grained and grounded than the myth and melodrama he felt had been served up to gagging excess. Alun's own novels had a crafted style, pellucid and restrained for effect, that was far removed from the pugnacious rodomontade with its parade of neologisms and riffing dialogue which Ron invented to cut through the noxious miasma of pretence which he detected all around, and sniffed out for fictive assassination.

They were immediate soulmates for that common reason and their purposefulness never wavered. Alun would, through scripting television and radio plays, go on to make a living from writing in a way the more ascetic and less yielding Ron would never really manage; but Ron underlined for Alun the manner in which real writing, writing that would echo and last, came out of living. Theirs was a mutual compact for life. For Alun Richards, reading Ron Berry in the early 1960s was a confirmation of what he knew for himself and a revelation in print for which he had already yearned publicly. In Keidrych Rhys' magazine *Wales* (founded in 1937), to which he had contributed his first stories in the late 1950s, he had written in October 1959 a combative screed entitled 'The Never-Never Land' to point to the fare on offer for voracious reader and tyro writer alike:

Consider the picture that the Joneses, the Davieses, the Thomases and Evanses have printed in their novels and short stories published before and after the war.

...One reads about this land in childhood and it is only a matter of time before one has the essential ingredients of an anthology-worthy-Welsh-short story at hand. A pony or trap, a wide-eyed boy in chapel, a mingy deacon, a potential suicide or ambitious footballer... and one has a representative picture of what apparently was wanted and accepted as part of the Welsh literary scene.

It is rather late now to ask, did all this really happen? Was Wales like this – ever? As a child one did not question it, but as far as Anglo-Welsh literature is concerned... [we] must do more than modify the views we already hold.

...Where, one wonders, are the stories about the ordinary un-poetic, irreligious non-chapel people that one sees now in their sixties and seventies?

Where in Anglo-Welsh fiction is the miner or steelworker portrayed with any accuracy, or discipline, or even the most haphazardous observation...? Can it be that... no one thought himself capable of portraying the elusive ordinariness of the everyday life of the voters?

...It is as if the writers here have regarded the poetry and the pity as being all that was required...

It is true perhaps the ablest of all the Welsh writers, Geraint Goodwin and Alun Lewis, never lived to prove themselves but this does not alter the general absurdity of the claims made for the [Anglo-Welsh] school. One only has to pause and wonder how Alun Lewis would have developed as a novelist if his critical interpretation of Army life had been repeated at home in post-war Wales. He was at least one writer who might have filled the void, and so far, there seems to be a void, not only where the working class is concerned, but no middle-class novelist has emerged either. Leaving out Emyr Humphreys who has ignored South Wales in his novels, the John O'Haras, the James Gould Cozzens, have not made their appearance to date. But the same conflicts for power, the movements between classes, the almost precisely similar social conditions have existed and do exist in Wales. Our ports are as cosmopolitan as any, our quota of immigrants not so small to be unnoticeable, and yet one looks in vain for a Welsh sea story comparable to any of James Hanley's. We have had Poles, Slavs and other refugees with us for many years, and yet scarcely a mention of them or their problems appear in print.

...Where, one might well ask further, can one get any true feeling of times past expressed eruditely and succinctly in Anglo-Welsh literature?

It was an agenda he had set out, in effect, for himself and one which, except for the very last part, he fulfilled. By the time 1979, and the savage rejection of the devolution package, which I supported and he disdained, arrived, he was in his successful pomp at fifty with the publication of a selection of the stories with which he had first broken the mould to be published by Penguin, along with the novel about the sea and seafarers, which he had adapted for the BBC. At the launch party for the novel and the stories in Cardiff I met Ron Berry, whose five novels were out of print. For the growing number of my students intent on adding literary study to their historical mix I had had photographed editions made and bound for the university library. All this, and my admiration for them, I told to the saturnine Ron, a figure of coiled menace, watchful and withdrawn, content in the reflected ebullience of the expansive Alun. I had become, as arts editor of *Arcade*, part of the disparate group assembled by the journalist John Osmond to create a new kind of journal determined to build towards a culture to counterbalance the negative debacle of the devolution referendum and I already had in mind a series of profiles of writers. I would do the interviewing and then the writing. I asked Ron if I could come to Treherbert to talk to him about his life and his work. I can only have imagined the icicle of silence that seemed to penetrate the bonhomie of wine and warmth but I did feel suddenly one-to-one and shivery with Ron as he put his weight on the stick that his arthritic knees needed and, without saying a yes or a no, muttered: 'Don't expect too much.'

What I had at his council house, with its steep but immaculately kempt back garden above Treherbert, was discreetly poached trout that he quickly pan-fried, and an afternoon of conversation that seared the mind. A deal of what I learned then about Ron had already been written by him as an autobiography which was rejected by successive publishers until, in a much edited form, it was published after his death in 1998 as *History Is What You Live*. Alun, who had worked hard with Ron to make this firework of a memoir publishable by some judicious editing, deeply respected the work-won expertise Ron carried with him as (reluctant) miner and (very reluctant) soldier. What was as much a clue to Ron's literary shaping of his direct working-class experience was, nonetheless, his aesthetic sensibility. He aimed for a modernist, even experimental, mode that ran across the grain of his subject matter. This was why, against Alun's more sceptical view of Gwyn's exaggerated grotesquerie, Ron thought Gwyn Thomas was the 'greatest aesthete' produced by the culture of all this gross materialism, the mythical Rhondda itself. But then Alun from urbane Pontypridd would never acknowledge, except in his ironic cups, that his own mundane town was indubitably Rhondda's metropolis. Indeed, when Alun and I unveiled a plaque for Ron in May 2004 on behalf of the Rhys Davies Trust, on the wall of his boyhood home in Blaencwm, the Pontypridd sophisticate confessed he had never been this far up into the blind end of Rhondda Fawr, with only the blocked-up tunnel of the old Rhondda to Swansea rail line once promising an exit.

They had grown up, less than nine years and twenty miles apart, but as different in upbringing and expectation as if they had come respectively from Surrey and Salford. Ron Berry had left his calling card early in the form of an 'Author's Note' he had supplied for his publisher in 1960. The blurb had, somewhat patronisingly, called him 'a phenomenon from the Welsh valleys... the son of a miner who still works underground, and once a miner himself'. A quoted friend, probably Mervyn Matthias, went somewhat better, with a lilting description of Ron as 'poet, reader, lover, scrapper, hunter, never a dancing man'. But Ron, square on and punching, had himself, physically and inwardly, spot on:

Ron Berry is 5ft 8ins, thick-set, pigeon-toed, peasant-fisted, and takes some living with some of the time. He was born in Glamorgan almost forty years ago, the eldest of five children. As a schoolboy he played rugby at fullback but 'miched' from a junior technical school to help out in a slaughter-house and roam the mountains. Later he played soccer as an amateur for Swansea Town. These were the days of his 'big-chested' prime. He boxed, swam, dived, cycled. He spent three seasons as assistant manager at a swimming pool; wintered in London factories and building sites, and lived marginally. He is still scrounging, with a wife, four children, a mocking National Assistance allowance, and a pair of legs pretty useless from arthritis and injury.

After completing a year in Coleg Harlech, Merioneth, he entered a teachers' training college, but was compelled to withdraw for financial reasons. Ron Berry says this episode deserves a book on the ethics of economics. Since then he has shaken hands with his destiny. *Hunters and Hunted* is his first token of faith.

When Alun Richards read Ron Berry's first published novel, *Hunters and Hunted*, in 1960 he felt that Ron's 'fuck-you, couldn't-care-less' colliers had finally struck a blow against the fey evasion of 'fucking-Meadow-Prospect', though Ron never quite subscribed to Alun's dismissal (sometimes) of Gwyn Thomas. Anyway, their decades of mutual admiration had truly begun with Ron's gob of a book. Alun revelled in Ron's stories of work underground and on the buildings, of absenting himself from the Army, of swanning around as a swimming pool attendant and becoming, by dint of willpower, a full-time writer. Alun, via national service in the Navy after teacher training in Caerleon, had manoeuvred himself around the Probation Service and survived serious tubercular illness to fetch up teaching in Cardiff, readying himself for his own breakout into the writing profession in the mid-1960s.

His Pontypridd was, however, cocooned from the everyday lives of most of that town's inhabitants in the 1930s and 1940s, and decidedly distinct from Ron Berry's proletarian Rhondda. Alun Richards was materially secure, in food and clothes and warmth, as he grew up, but, more, his was the world of a county schoolboy set amidst the middle-class streets and mores of a professional and shopkeeping elite. The gaps were enormous, and visible, even to the eye of a schoolboy, as he recalled in *Days of Absence* (1986):

In hospital I also thought about my schooldays and I would try to remember the names of the children who had sat next to me and the games we played in Infants' School... I see myself as a little cosseted pumpkin again, Grandma's boy still, standing at her side outside chapel... [and] when I went to school... There was also the embarrassing matter of my clothes since, by the bitter poverty-line standards of the 1930s we were well off and I had new shoes, a clean red jersey and short grey trousers from the town's largest emporium... the most obvious contrast was the condition of most of my school-mates... immediately noticeable in the newness of everything I wore and this became one of the first of the stigmas to mark me out from my fellows.

In later life Alun never forgot the false distinction that a white riding mac or a lemon-yellow pullover or a club tie or a cravat and blazer and cavalry-twill trousers with brown oxford shoes and paisley socks could bestow on the wearer and suggest to those who, in a ringing irony he used to love to use, 'did not have the clothes for the occasion'. The signals that Alun put on like new garments as he shed the attitudes that went with the outer clothes were, however, intended to align his chosen self with the dispossessed and spurned whose company he, thereafter, always willingly embraced and consciously sought The tall, handsome and self-confident naval officer was a hater of snobs and a rebel against social convention and educational narrowness. He was and remained in many ways apart from Ron Berry, but close in the anger and resentment the two shared against those who acted to widen social difference by clubby conformity rather than celebrate individual distinctiveness through social cohesion. Their whole dissection of their South Wales – its clear achievements, battered potential and deep, miserable betrayals – turned on that.

As the early letters between them reveal, they shared their sense of their destiny and of their work. Alun sought Ron's opinion of his 1963 manuscript, to become his first novel in that year, *The Elephant You Gave Me*, and he delighted in Ron's second novel, also that year, *Travelling Loaded*, with *The Full-time Amateur* and *Flame and Slag* to appear respectively in 1966 and 1968. Ron had seemed, to some, a Welsh equivalent of Alan Sillitoe, in the wake of that early 1960s vogue for down-and-dirty working-class experience, and the actor-director Bryan Forbes, later himself a writer, invited Ron to Pinewood to discuss film options. Perhaps the moguls stumbled over the originality of Rhondda intellect and society that, in Ron's prose style, was as contemptuous of the laconic as it was of the rhetorical. Either way Ron's commercial star waned almost as soon as it had waxed.

Alun, invariably a steadier craftsman, nurtured his own slow-burning success, and put away fictional forays like the picaresque social comedy 'Bear a Fair Presence' to find the income-bearing seams of radio, and then television. Canton, that preening patch of workaday Cardiff, had its bohemian corners and pubs even in the sixties, like the Robin Hood, where radio producers and documentary makers of influence and promise like Herbert Davies, the writer-turned-broadcaster Aled Vaughan and the poet and film-maker John Ormond met and drank. Alun was always uproarious in company and eager to introduce Ron and Ron's great friend, the collier boy turned painter Jim 'Chunks' Lewis, to this new world of Welsh professional broadcasting. Alun's stories were broadcast. Ron's play for voices, 'Everybody loves a Saturday night', was produced. Alun, tiring of the drudge of selling himself for a pittance in Wales, broke through with TV plays and adaptations for Granada Television. The famed TV Armchair Theatre of Sydney Newman from Manchester swept the timid and conventional aside. It was the decade of playwrights like Alun Owen and David Storey, and Richards and, by 1968, of Berry whom his younger friend was ever willing to promote and support. Alun, in particular, worked, wrote and networked tirelessly. Ron mostly wrote.

In 1967, with commissioned fees from Peter O'Toole secured for three years, Alun gave up teaching and the Richards family – Helen and their four children – left Cardiff for Swansea, for the sea and Mumbles to be exact. He published *The Home Patch* in 1966 and *A Woman of Experience* in 1969. His writing career was at full tilt. But *So Long, Hector Bebb* (1970), a multivocal masterwork on the rise and fall of the boxer Hector Bebb, would prove to be Ron's last published novel, at the age of fifty, for over a quarter of a century.

The letters which they exchanged never strayed far from this early established theme of the fate of a Welsh writer, rooted by place and ratcheted by ambition, and the cultural ambience of support for and suffocation of their work. In the 1970s they noted the arrival of *Planet* as a possible source of income (not much), as they would view *Arcade* in the early 1980s. Successive editors, from John

Osmond at *Arcade* to John Barnie, Ned Thomas' successor at *Planet*, and on to Robin Reeves, at *New Welsh Review* in the 1990s, were squinted at with suspicion, as was the Welsh writers' guild, Yr Academi (wrongly, and somehow knowingly, given the epithet 'Cymraeg' not 'Cymreig' by Alun, thereby emphasising the language attachment more than the national identity), and, of course, the Arts Council which helped both of them with bursaries and grants, but never by more than Alun felt they deserved.

Meanwhile, as Ron laboured on an autobiography, on nature writing and a novel, with only his stories now making regular public appearances, Alun prospered as TV adaptor, playwright and, crucially, in the early 1970s, one of the principal scriptwriters of the phenomenally success-ful Victorian sea saga, *The Onedin Line*, Sunday night's must-see on the BBC across the UK. He worked on the *Warship* series and on televised *Crown Court* dramas for the afternoons and, by the late 1970s, had his lifeboat novel, *Ennal's Point*, put on as a BBC2 series. As he told Ron at the start of the decade this meant putting aside a planned and started historical sea novel (*Barque Whisper* came out in 1979) but the labour was unremitting everywhere else, with award-winning story collections and the editing of major anthologies of Welsh short stories and sea stories for paperback giant Penguin. He was, himself, confidently astride a much-belittled Welsh literary scene, creative and critical, in which he felt confirmed in his dismissal of academics – especially the generation represented by his own 'Anglo-Welsh' bogeyman, the supreme man-of-letters, Professor Gwyn Jones (1907-99) – and of minor editorial figures like the feisty poet John Tripp (1927-86) to whom he remained antipathetic.

Whatever success came his way – and by the mid-1980s it had turned away – Alun invariably looked back and inwards to the South Wales that fascinated and repelled him. He was excited to meet, in my company, the outstandingly brilliant miners' leader and Rhondda communist Will Paynter (1903-84), and even more so to be able to introduce him to Carwyn James (1929-83), rugby genius and cultural nationalist whose biography Alun, somewhat unexpectedly to those who did not know how close they were, would write after Carwyn's death.

Ron was more sceptical about that history and its heroes, even about 'Janus-faced Bevan', but Alun was hooked, just as he had been by the intellectual capacity and social charm of Goronwy Rees (1909-79), who in 1957 had had to forsake the Principalship at Aberystwyth in the wake of his tabloid revelations about Burgess and McLean, and 1930s Oxbridge spy shenanigans in general. I used to tell Alun that Paynter had been a tough, maybe even ruthless, political commissar in the International Brigades in the Spanish Civil War. He would tell me how much I would have liked Goronwy Rees, a past disciple of the miners' cause and their Fed. I would wonder out loud about the chance of Rees being the fourth or fifth or sixth man in the lee of Philby. Alun would airily dismiss it all, as he would any innuendo, and angrily refute any 'nonsense' alleged about Carwyn's sexuality. There were, he would insist, 'standards'.

As the 1980s opened, despite the glamour of his Richard Burton narrated film on a century of Welsh rugby for the BBC, he could begin to bemoan the drying up of financially worthwhile work for the media. He had already seen, like Ron before him, the disinterest from

London publishers in self-proclaimed Welsh novels – his best novel, *Home to an Empty House*, had been published in 1973 by Gomer – and, besides, he began to feel his Welsh material was, temporarily, perhaps, mined out. Alun looked to the horizons. Conferences at universities in Australia, Canada and Japan in the early 1980s blossomed into almost a full year in Japan as a Japan Foundation Fellow in 1984-5, and then to Australia for six months at Performing Arts Academies in the universities of both Western and South Australia.

He mischievously considered the Down Under experience as akin to having to live in 'Rhydfelin' if you were really from Pontypridd, a town he increasingly considered central, in all its socio-cultural mores, both to his own philosophy and to the fractured state of contemporary Wales. Much of this bubbled up in him when he read my 1984 book *Wales! Wales?* in Tokyo. I think he saw the book, and the six BBC2 films with the same title which I had made in the preceding two years, as missiles from Ponty since we had settled there as a family, a blink of an eye from his own boyhood home, above the famed Tyfica Road whose 'Rhondda Baronial' mansions he ever considered the acme of whatever social grace money and snobbery had clumped together from the coal El Dorado that still haunted us all. The lore of Pontypridd's cultural mix of classes and aspirations transfixed by wars and education and doomed relationships in a swirl of locally transfigured history was never out of his sight now. Did I really know of 'Nifty' Neil and Dai Love and the Goodfield brothers? Did I realise how wonderful the Queens had been, all sunlight through stained glass pouring down a mahogany bar, before they (always 'they') pulled down the Arcade and left only the Llanover standing in a municipally induced bomb crater? And how was his great pal 'Slug' from Tel-el-Kebir Road in Hopkinstown? This was the original, and genuine, Tom Jones, a little older than Alun, who literally adored Tom for just being himself – a man-about-town (Ponty that is), one dressed to match his elegant demeanour, both gracious and ribald, replete with stories and slightly mysterious, this grammar school boy who played snooker like a pro, had trained for the Air Force in America and flown more bomber missions than was sensible or possible over Nazi Germany. Tom, in Alun's descriptive awe, was Gatsby come again. With Ron, whose acquaintances were as wide and whose own lore was as deep, Al could and did yarn for hours. His own physical absence abroad in the mid-1980s only made it all the more intense on the page.

When the *Oxford Companion to the Literatures of Wales*, edited by Meic Stephens, came out in 1986 and I sent him relevant photocopied extracts, it was on tales or lives that were winding down that Alun dwelt. The writer and broadcaster John Morgan (1929-88) – who had complained to me that he had been, inexcusably, omitted – was a meteorite that had, he felt, not quite flared enough for anyone's taste other than John's own. His work on Carwyn was 'ripped off', he felt, for a Welsh language television version. He had been working on a memoir, intending it to be two volumes but publishing it as a first instalment, *Days of Absence*, in 1986. It was, and is, a masterpiece. It took us from childhood to the first steps as a writer. Where it stopped, his life to that point in his mid-fifties had rolled on. It was a melancholy pause.

But Alun, no less than Ron, was resilient. He and Helen decided against exile – Australia and her native Ireland were considered – and Alun became a peripatetic Adult Education Tutor in Literature and Creative Writing ('Have Suzuki, Can Travel') for Swansea University's Lifelong Learning Department where Hywel Francis, my co-author on *The Fed* (1980), had become the Director. On his silver-gleaming beast of a bike, leather-clad Alun sought out Ron at midway points, notably the congenial Lamb and Flag in Glynneath which Ron reached splutteringly in his three-wheeled Reliant Robin. On Alun's sixtieth birthday – a surprise affair rigged up by Helen in a small waterfront hotel in the Mumbles from where he continued to launch his Onedin-named boat *Charlotte Rose* – the people of his life intertwined in the dark to wait for him. When the light switch was thrown he blinked at the upstanding gathering to take in three seated revellers – Jeffrey Iverson, a sharp-elbowed and percipient former TV producer for BBC Wales who suffered from a severe form of ocular tunnel vision; Ron Berry, whose knees no longer supported him without a stick; and the demonic actor Kenneth Griffith, who had been rechristened by Alun, for the intent in his looks and the provenance of his native town, 'The Tenby Poisoner'.

'Good God,' said Alun, his eyes sweeping over the three of them in their separate corner armchairs.

'Good God. They're all here.'

Then fixing, in turn, Jeff, Ron and Kenny: 'The Blind, the Crippled, and the Criminally Insane.'

It was around this time that I became more directly engaged – mostly by correspondence but also in writing about his novels and interviewing him for *First Hand*, the BBC Radio Wales Arts Programme which I presented from the late 1980s to 1993 – with Ron Berry. I had earlier championed his writing (and subsequent book) on peregrines for *Arcade* and was now, with Alun, striving to have Ron's memoirs published. John Ormond (1923-90), ever helpful and concerned, organised a number of us to make a (successful) plea for a Civil List pension for Ron And it was an even greater satisfaction, for him and his fans, when the last novel, for which I had proved to be an irate, enthusiastic and finally persuasive Arts Council reader, was published as *This Bygone* in 1996.

At this time, the mid-1990s, I was at midpoint in my own career change as Head of Programmes (English) at BBC Wales. I had, of course, long argued the case, in many spheres, for a fuller understanding and recognition of the vitality and richness of the English language literature of Wales. Indeed, 'Dementia' Griffith (1921-2006) and I now re-appeared on screen in Selwyn Roderick's great 1984 film on Idris Davies in what became a season of tributes to Ken Griffith late in the actor's life and, as a commissioner, I had a film made about Ron in the popular 'Read All About Us' series. On a wider front, on radio and television, the cultural hinterland of English-speaking Wales, in these years, was at last being fully explored. Not to Ron's surprise, of course, but maybe to those who had happily blinkered themselves against it, the flourishing intellectual life of 1940s and 1950s working-class South Wales was now made explicit.

As early as 1947 Alun Richards had heard talk of this upper Rhondda coterie of Bo-Pros (neologistic shorthand for Bohemian Proletarians of which the language-bending Ron Berry would have approved) and how they met together in pubs like the Red Cow in Treorchy before spilling disputatiously onto the street where, once, Bob Thomas put a brick through a plate-glass window in an artistic gesture more violently conceived than any of his subsequent sculptural statements. Aged eighteen and a newly enrolled student at Monmouthshire Training College for teachers in Caerleon, Alun mounted his push bike in Pontypridd, some sixteen winding, climbing miles away, and set out to find them. On that occasion, trawling from pub to pub in buzzing post-war Rhondda, he failed. He would only become first acolyte then friend to the older writer when their publications in the 1960s propelled them forward in tandem and tied them together for life as readers and critics of each other's work. Ron, in any case, back in the 1940s already had his own intellectual mentor and lodestar. This was Mervyn Matthias, talker and thinker, book buyer and lender, teacher and friend, who brought American and European writers into his orbit. Then there was the colliery electrician Bob Thomas (1926-99), who had made himself, with Rhondda river clay and a Royal College education, into Wales' principal figure sculptor. Ron's boyhood friend 'Chunks' Lewis was a watercolourist whom Alun and others readily collected and Charlie Burton (1929-) from Treherbert, no less than Ernie Zobole (1927-1995) from Ystrad, was a painter of European significance whose star had crossed Ron's own. But it would take decades more for recognition of Ron Berry's originality and the vibrancy of this world to be widely appreciated by university academics, though notably the critic John Pikoulis had no doubt of the lasting worth of Ron Berry's innovative rewriting of all this, and more. Ron and Alun consistently dissected, and with some gleeful disdain, the dessicated fare of most criticism. Ron could never quite shake off the feeling that even the poet and novelist 'nice' Glyn Jones (1905-95) had not quite approved of him, that he was, in fact, Ichabod, the man with no glory or honour, who had marked the visage of a more dignified Wales as a kind of graffiti-artist of the aesthetic, one sent to taunt instead of, as more customary in Anglo-Welsh lives, praise. Glyn Jones had given Ron a few paragraphs in his own memoir-cum-critical guide *The Dragon Has Two Tongues* in 1968, where Berry's prose is hailed as 'fresh' and 'buoyant', but the apparent anarchy and clowning of Ron's characters, 'besotted with language... abrupt, allusive, high-powered jabbering', was a worrisome condition for Glyn's sense of the Wales that had once been and the one which was, apparently, to come:

> He is the jesting chronicler... of a Rhondda in which coal, politics, religion and singing have lost their primacy. His hero in *The Full-time Amateur* is a portent perhaps, the prototype of the valley's man of the future, of a degutted South Wales without coal and without pits, whose people never meet together for political action, or singing, or worship, who are songless apart from their pop records and solitary apart from their strip-tease clubs and their bingo halls. 'Ichabod' is scrawled across the face of Ron Berry's Wales.

Glyn Jones might indeed as well have written 'Ach y fi' as 'Ichabod'. Either way Ron Berry would not have recognised the romance-tinged antecedents with which the poet wrapped the raucous, violent, poverty-infested Rhondda of Victorian and Edwardian times. He wore 'Ichabod', the biblical boy and warrior bereft of his father's brave inheritance, like a mark of pride, only he would not have acknowledged the occasion for pride in the arenas where Glyn Jones positioned it. Ron Berry found his exemplars of pride and honour elsewhere: in survival, in grit, in refusing to bend the knee or corrupt the mind, in stoic unblinking acceptance and, where possible, rebellion. 'History', for Ron, was all too often 'Shitstory'. To Alun he once wrote, dismissing some other know-all critics even more severely in passing so that I was actually let off lightly, that I too could all too easily be just a 'Pandy polymath'. And one inclined to the romantic, to boot. Guilty as charged. Even about Ron who, in his final years, delighted in the bravura heroics of hyper-romantic-realist Cormac McCarthy, another American writer against whom, he told Alun, Welsh writers simply did not measure up. Mind you, he went on to finger McCarthy's defects too.

Ron did not find it easy to acknowledge allies, let alone admirers. Yet he did, in the few years before his death in July 1997, really have a sense of how he was, at last, being valued. He delighted, too, in the late flowering success Alun had with radio and television plays, both of them clutching luck they knew was always all too transient. Rather like life itself they naturally thought, as their letters filled up with successive and successively serious aches, pains and systemic illness. Ron treated most of this with a grim askance glint at the poxy world; Alun with a spluttering amazement before grabbing at the next bit of passing pleasure. And they worked, on and on.

Alun had widened his fictional perspective to take on the bits of Wales – the urban middle classes, immigrants, children, the lonely – he saw as too readily excluded from the viewfinder. It connected him to younger writers he admired like Cardiff's Leonora Brito, and to Des Barry, from New York and Merthyr, whose novel of – and yet not of – Jesse James, *Chivalry of Crime* (2000), he prized for its bold telling. At home in Swansea Alun read in great gulping bursts. More and more he read history as much as fiction, and biographical studies more than anything. The detail of other peoples' lives was his own wide-eyed obsession, whether in Robert Caro's monster accounts of those real-life monsters Robert Moses, the New York master planner, and Lyndon Johnson, the Texan megalo-maniac turned President of the Great Society. When I started reading again the American novelist and short-story writer John O'Hara with renewed and deeper interest than in my twenties, Alun showered me with out-of-print copies and told me of his excitement in the 1940s on first reading O'Hara and that clumpy miracle-worker – narrative gold from the dross of his **prose** – Theodore Dreiser. Alun's last letters to me, almost right up to his death in June 2004, tied in, as he **had** often done in conversation, the writers he had learned from – Hemingway, Alun Lewis, Fitzgerald, Geraint Goodwin – and the nature of comparable societies and writers, from Pennsylvania or Indiana or South Wales. To have, as I did, Alun to pick up on my own ideas and speculations and better still to urge me on to finish my biography of

Raymond Williams was a boon almost as great and almost as appreciated as to have had his friendship for nearly three decades.

*

'The next time you see me,' he wrote to me in his letter of March 2004, 'I'll probably be tap-dancing.' The next time I saw him, on a cold late-spring day in that 2004, was the last time I saw him. He died suddenly of a heart attack at the end of June. Des Barry who, in 2009, wrote the Foreword to the Library of Wales' new edition of Alun's memoir and stories of Pontypridd and of its converging valleys, saw us together that day, and this is what he saw, with only one more afternoon and evening of food, drink, talk and laughter to follow this snapshot moment:

On 8 May 2004, a blue Saab 9.3 pulled to a stop on the lower end of Michael's Road in Blaencwm, and from the passenger-side door a tall man, a broad man, dressed in a dark suit and dark glasses, stepped out onto the road and waited for the other occupants to join him on the street. From the driver's side appeared a significantly shorter man, with close cropped grey hair and moustache, an equally dark suit and glasses; and their wives emerged, elegant in tight dresses, no less charismatic, the whole vision like a valleys version of the Corleones. The women walked beside their husbands up the road towards a small crowd gathered in front of a house; the terrace of which it was a part was framed by an arc of mountain, cliff and waterfall under bright blue late spring sky; a fusion of Rhondda and Hollywood, much like the prose – fiction and autobiography – of the taller of the two men, Alun Richards, writer and raconteur. He'd come to unveil a commemorative plaque to his friend, the Rhondda prose gangster, Ron Berry.

Letters from Dai Country

There are more than one hundred surviving letters between Ron and Alun, with others to me from both of them from the 1970s onwards. In the later decades, the correspondence grew in volume and length. As age increased and work diminished, though not entirely, they had become more epistolary the one to the other. All of Ron Berry's letters to Alun Richards were sent from Ael-y-Bryn, Treherbert, and were invariably handwritten in a sloping spidery fashion. The later ones to Alun, and to myself, were scrawled on a variety of coloured paper, anything from blue to purple to yellow to pink. Ron must have had an inexhaustible supply from an indeterminate source. Alun Richards' early letters to Ron Berry were from Sneyd Street in Cardiff until the family moved to West Cross, near Mumbles in Swansea, in 1967. They were either typed or, more often, handwritten with a fountain pen in Alun's bold and blocky manner. Neither writer always dated his letters and so I have surmised dates, sometimes approximate, by content or by stamp-dated envelopes where these survived. The reader will understand that where the letters are very intermittent the two were often in touch by phone or in person. Sometimes gaps were longer when Alun was in Australia, lecturing and visiting family, or in Japan on a fellowship or America on holiday. Ron stayed at, and responded from, home.

They knew what they had been about. They recognised what they had not done well or not done sufficiently. They constructed a rerun of their world which commented on that actuality. Their realism was tinged with idealism but never fabricated with illusion. They wrote to each other and met frequently from the 1960s. The selection I have made from their letters, with domestic trivia, gossip and the ephemera of passing news largely omitted, offers up a flashlight commentary on their literary practice, and that of others, and on their Wales. I have added, in square brackets, some information to elucidate only. From the 1970s I sometimes became a third leg substitute in this correspondence relay, and then a fuller one from the 1990s. Since I have left in their passing slaps at me I have compensated by keeping in the occasional praise which I deeply valued. Where either, or both, went savagely in private for the personalities or traits of others, some still living, I have omitted (with some reluctance) entire letters. I have excised the unkinder cuts and softened the thud of their more contemptuous thwacks. Enough remains, I believe, to allow us to see how seriously they took their craft and how profoundly they valued their calling.

The actual text of the letters selected and edited – split by decade from 1963 to 2004 – is, in this presentation, largely concerned with the writing profession, with Wales and with their own paths through the craft, but I have retained a personalised flavour, albeit short of full biographical and familial data – to let the reader feel the passion and the glee with which they regaled each other (and me) on the vitality of their work, the state of their health, and the failings of the Welsh world they have now, one way or the other, made alive forever.

*

1960s

9 Sneyd St
Canton
Cardiff

8 – 3 – 63

Dear Ron,

Thank you for your letter. I am glad you liked my MS (!) I always said the big disadvantage of every writer born north of Trehafod was that they knew nothing of the rich – or how inarticulate they were. But not to worry. Don't bother to return it until I see you. I'm going to get your book next week [*Travelling Loaded*] and look forward to reading it.

When I was in London, I asked Michael Bakewell, the Script Editor of Drama-Sound (BBC), to read it with a view to adapting it. If you don't hear anything in a *month*, I suggest you get your publisher agent to send him a copy and mention my name if necessary. They do some good things on the radio and he might adapt it himself if it's adq.

Am laid up with bronchitis and the wife is in Ireland where her father's very ill but otherwise I'm still counting the money with a sort of fascinated dread.

Come and see us if you're in Cardiff.

Ever
Alun

9 Sneyd St
Canton
Cardiff

29 – 3 – 63

Dear Ron,

Read your book – liked it, very funny and not at all beatnik – I think the whistler is a gem – and the whole book so different and good. Congratulations. I've scanned the papers for reviews but either I've missed them or they're doing you down, as they're very apt to do to anyone out of the swing in the gangs up there. I can't understand why it's supposed to be a beatnik book – it's much too warm, and very South Wales, I think – the real stuff and not fucking-meadow-prospect, if you get me. I'm sure you're right to go on and find your own shape, but listen to me talking like the old master.

Come and see us if you're down. Otherwise we'll come up and see you when the weather starts to hot up. Again, congratulations – if they haven't reviewed it, never mind

– in ten years time we'll be carving them up.
  All the best
  Alun

Radio Times 23 May 1966
Everybody Loves Saturday Night

Ron Berry introduces his new play for radio:

One sunny Sunday afternoon in Llandaff Fields I was introduced to Herbert Davies by that tall, combustive-hearted Cardiff writer, Alun Richards. I had two novels published and the Welsh Committee of the Arts Council had awarded me a few hundred pounds. A week later I sent Herbert Davies a synopsis of *Everybody Loves Saturday Night*; he commissioned the play and for the next few months I tried to make viable drama from the countless weekend pub concerts which were once – though not now – integral to all the mining villages of Wales.

If I have succeeded it is because the play has its roots in good pasture. I do not mean that Wales reverberates with superlative singing voices, but we are gutsy enough amateurs, singing for the love of it.

326 Mumbles Road,
West Cross,
Swansea,
Glam.

26 April, 1968

Dear Ron,

I think your book [*Flame and Slag*] is great. Much the best you've ever done and as I told you when I read half before, I think the journal is a marvellous device and the whole thing gutsy, ballsie, frying on the streets with pavement empathy. I haven't written before because I've pulled a muscle in my shoulder and have got eye-strain and am generally buggered, but this is to tell you how good it is, vintage stuff, the definitive book of S. Wales in my view and may it prosper.

I don't forgive you incidentally for pinching my sentence about the miners putting the Great into Great Britain, but no doubt you will give me a small royalty.

See you sometime. I've no news either. Again I like your cover. Four books now. Where will it end?

Congratulations and thanks.

Ever

Al

326 Mumbles Road
West Cross
Swansea

Dear Ron,

Marvellous news about the play – was that the one you sent to Harlech and the BBC. I hope so because all my first plays were rejected in Cardiff. I've been busy with the Director for my Somerset Maugham adaptation and busy with the D'annunzio. Otherwise, I've had back trouble too – a chill in the kidneys and in bed. No good news about the plays. Soon I will have three going the rounds from Michael White's top drawer to the bottom. The only thing to do is write a play about Michael White, but thank god I'm still getting research money from O'Toole until Xmas [1969]. But all in all I feel black, a small tortoise supporting this enormous shell.

Also there's been death about the place. The dog next door savaged five of the kids' rabbits in two goes and burying them, I keep feeling life is like this, in between the teeth all the time. Still, we don't do it for our health, do we?

I think your Hector Bebb is the best idea yet and will bet money on it, always have thought so. He's vintage S. Wales, through the particular to the universal etc, the real note, now dead. My guess too is that it's a cinch for the movies so I look forward to hearing about it. It's my favourite book and I look forward to reading it again.

Apropros, literary soirées. I did one and have never been asked again, which I hope happens to you! Remember to travel first class and get cracking at the stuffed olives.

We called in on Chunks [Jim Lewis, painter and Ron's boyhood friend] thinking to bring him back with us. An insane syphilitic answered the door, also a painter! He said, 'He's gone where I told him to go – with intelligent people.' He did a little dance in the doorway, offered to flog a painting, showed us a pile of income tax letters for Chunks before we bolted. I itched all the way home.

I'll come up and see you when my back is better – what a terrible sentence. I'm also deaf with phlegm. I'm thinking of getting a muffler and learning to squat with a solitary gob into the gutter every now and then.

See you the end of August here or there? We must have a good booze up before the winter. I'll write to Chunks.

There is no good news – ever. When you see the producer, express interest in his ideas, offer to rewrite anything, get the advance, then please yourself. I made the mistake of treating them all as idiots – and they still remember.

Chufti now

All the best

Al

1, Ael-y-Bryn
Treherbert

Thursday

Dear Alun,

Each time I began reading 'Bear a Fair Presence' critically, I reverted to enjoying it. The big imaginative shifts sent me every time. I like its wilfulness, a Jackie-jumper tamping all ways off the idiomatic dialogue. It's a gambol all the way, a holiday of icon toppling, a hitch-hike of the soul. But, as you already realise, who's going to publish it? You've knocked every sanctuary in this book (except religion), debunked power, the law, celtic culture, the throne, honourable toil, medicine and matrimony. You've gone in with a sledge and a cut-throat razor, and I'm sorry to have called it 'outlandish' in the Robin Hood to Herbert Davies. It's an upheaval, a volcanic gout upon the ordained poxes of Wales and Whitehall. Herbert'll have a double twitch. I think you'll have to lead him by the hand, and no doubt you can. But committee voices are bound to call for a softening process. It won't do just to be made Comic. Keep in the bland madness, the plain denial of order in human affairs. It's so South Walian, a kind of anti-bible concerning this place, these people, these times. Men like Trevelyan, for instance, don't know the *truth* let alone the way you undermine, turn it upside down, step on its clay feet, grist it down to Bear a Fair Presence – that title fits like a mouth.

I'd like to read it again, as a Reader, if you've no objection.

I've just learned my agent has failed to place the slice of autobiography with W. H. Allen and John Hale – two bloody books, the autobiography and *So Long, Hector Bebb*. I'm calling them in for rewriting. Which means I shan't sell anything next year [1970], unless something comes from Encounter or *Travelling Loaded* via Herbert. It's put me down this morning; I feel like cold chips from last night's bracchi shop. And I've been shaken to hear that the first girl I fell in love with has had one of her breasts removed due to cancer... if God was around I'd spit in his eye. The first love lasts; the shadow behind adulthood and decline. Like mothers and fathers, wives and children, these pendulums of love and hate which don't affect the automated sapiens.

Here's your quid – thanks.

So long for now

Ron

326 Mumbles Road

Westcross

Swansea

Monday

Dear Ron,

Now that you are famous and successful – do not abandon your old mates. How are you? In my travels to Manchester I have found evidences of your presence, a torn page of script here and there, news of vicious dogs. What are you up to, mush?

When is Hector Bebb coming out? [1970] I scan the pages for news. I've got David Davies in a play soon, saying the Lord's prayer in a pit fall. What casting!

I'm going to Manchester myself on Thurs but hope to be back in time to see your play but then I've got to go to London for the weekend starting Saturday to be back Wednesday so I don't suppose I'll see you this week.

Have you heard about *Planet*, this Welsh magazine? They're paying good money for stories but the Welsh ethos is thick in the air. Every bastard is an author according to the handout and the poets multiply. How about joining me in a Dial a Novel scheme, £14 a throw and the complete works are read sotto voce. I have heard nothing from you for so long that I suspect you are Chairman of the Arts Council by now.

Here's some good news. Nothing is going right but I have written a poem. Let's hear from you and try and fix something up in about a fortnight.

All the best
Al

1970s

326 Mumbles Rd
Swansea

Thursday

Dear Ron,

Your book [*So Long, Hector Bebb*] is a winner, anvil bent and vintage Berry through and through. I *like* Hector and Abe – what a pair – 'scale up the business-deal big'. I think it's the best thing you've done, but Christ it's hard as it has to be, the end, the awfulness of awful. Nobody else in the world could have written it. I've tried to say all this in reviewer's style and hope it will do it a lot of good in the Welsh Libraries who are probably the only important *Planet* readers, money wise. It's amazing that we can write at all, I think sometimes. One small point – what the hell is an Anglo-Welsh face, vide the one-arm veteran? I had a vision of Prof Gwyn Jones in running shorts and singlet – is it a sheep's face? I did laff at that. Great book anyway – *great*, and all the luck in the world to it.

Ultimately, books are the only things. I'm on one now – wearily. I would have written before but I've been down with bronchitis, flatlo, bronchial tubes going like a flute. Steve broke his arm, the schools are closed because of the caretakers' strike and nothing good is coming in from anywhere – nothing.

When I've finished, about Xmas maybe, I don't know what I'm going to do next. Have you had any news of anything? You ought to get publicity from Aled [Vaughan] and Co – but what the hell?

Congrats again.

Ever

Al

326 Mumbles Rd
Swansea
11 Nov 1972

Dear Ron,

Thanks for your letter. I have had two bouts of bronchitis so no fishing in October. Then the big ritzy sea novel of which I had done 20,000 words fell through and just when I was at the bottom, Michael Joseph decided to publish my short stories so I am back in business again.

It's been a bloody awful autumn though and only the

endless *Onedin Line* repeats abroad have brought joy. Now I'm doing something about the Navy for which I had to go back to a destroyer in Chatham for three days – all in the cause of breathless melodrama.

I wish I'd known Chunks was down. I'd have come up if you couldn't come down – but it might have been on one of my bad weeks – the fags suddenly got me and I was flat out, also corns appearing for the first time in my life. As far as I can see, the only future in television is in series in the cash sense, and the theatre has gone dead for me anyway. One just goes on, I suppose.

What has happened to the [auto]biography? You can't pack up after 200 pages. I take it, you're having a spell? I am making overtures with a view to selling my novel to a Welsh publisher in the hope that something might be done, but mostly I'm a frenzy trying to do these series – it's the agility of mind to get plots which titivate the fancy that is killing – getting the right bow for the chocolate box, all that. I can't bear talking about it, never mind doing it, but there it is.

One good thing, I was at Llanelli when they beat the All Blacks, a great ritual killing.

I'm going to be a fortnight on this Navy thing – hammer hammer, then I don't know. Is there any chance of you coming down for a bit at the end of November? What's the transport situation? I'll be away next weekend, the kids are swimming in Haverfordwest and we're going down, but hope to see you before Xmas. Will drop Chunks a line, but I expect he is in his ritual of spending and working.

Don't pack the [auto]biography up. Get on to the awfulness of *now*. What else is there to do?
See you
Ever
Al

326 Mumbles Road
Swansea

Friday

Dear Ron,

The books are nearly ready, *Dai Country* out on October 29 [1973] and *Home to an Empty House* on November 29. This last is dedicated to you and Chunks acting on the principle that the moment I dedicate a book to anybody, they get power mad and I never want to speak to them again?! Well, it happens.

I'll have the copies here for you in a week or so. I'll keep them so you can come down and read them aloud in front of me. I dedicated it to you both because somehow I don't see me doing another one for years, and we might all be dead, time's winged chariot arrived on my back with the plaster of paris – so I thought I'd better make it the two. It was the two I came up to see to the Red Cow in 1947 – Jesus.

Ever
Al

326 Mumbles Road
Swansea

20-12-73

Dear Ron,

Great news about your grant! I haven't written because I half expected to see you and Chunks who sent a card. Hope things will be better now.

The Penguin deal has come off – I've signed the contract – a half year to compile an anthology of stories but most of them have to be taken from published work over the last 50 years. I'm hoping to cram more contemporary work in however... There's a hell of a lot of stories written about school teachers and funerals and I want to get away from the Anglo-Welsh idea and into the world of work! It still has to sell to schools though.

Helen's home and the food is good if you want to come down this week?

Hope Renee's better

See you?

Al

326 Mumbles Road
West Cross
Swansea SA3 5AA

Sat

Dear Ron,

Here are your stories. I like them all but if I may I am going to pick 'Before Forever After' as 1st choice which is better from an anthology point of view since so few stories are concerned with the working world and so many Welsh SS are schoolroom bound and it's a strong and powerful antidote to the stories or some of them that will be on either side of it. I say I'm going to pick it but I expect I will have to submit the whole lot to another editor and maybe a committee so I am not telling anyone else anything until the thing is complete and they will deal with the money side in June/July [1974]. It's a shitty position to be in but I am playing it very cool until I get the volume done and confront them with it. Already I am getting unsolicited stuff and scraping letters which is a laugh – but I think your story is great, just what I want and they will leave it out over my dead body. My plan is to leave it until they have a printer's deadline, and then I will give them the goods – a bit of a Heycock [Llew Heycock was the effective, and notorious, Labour 'Boss' of Glamorgan County Council in the 1960s and 1970s] in me you will notice! But the money will be lousy, I warn you now!

Have had 2 good notices for Empty House [1973], then silence, but not to worry.

Hope Renee's better. All down with colds here.

See you sometime

Ever

Al

204

326 Mumbles Road
Swansea

Friday

Dear Ron,

Can't make Monday [March 1974] as I have to go to London for a radio broadcast. It's pissing down anyway and the cold snap has gone. We'll have a go before Easter if we can. I'll drop you a note.

The old Arts Council coughed again – John Ormond and myself with a prize and I've got the bursary. Literature is now being served! But my attitude like when I had TB is that it couldn't happen to a nicer chap! We soldier on.

Sorry about Monday. Will get in touch in about 10 days. There's nothing much to do this weather.

See you
Ever
Al

326 Mumbles Road
West Cross

Sunday [February 1976]

Dear Ron,

Sorry to hear about your teeth – that's to come after the flu – God, I've really been laid low. The penguin is out – have you received a copy yet – have you been paid – and how much did they pay you? I haven't a word about payment for my own story which is why I'm asking. Let me know – their correspondence system is terrible. Still, the volume looks good. Now for the Welsh knives.

Will try to make the play but I'm feeling about 200 and frightened of germs!

Let me know about Penguin. Look after yourself.

Ever

Al

326 Mumbles Rd

SWANSEA

11 May 1977

Dear Ron,

I've finished your book [unpublished novel in typescript] and liked it and recommended it to John Lewis of Gomer. It's a bad time for fiction but I hope he'll put it up for an arts council subsidy and then publish. I notice you used a lot of the biographical material, but the strange thing is, the public are more interested in biographies and books about things than novels. My own [*Ennal's Point*] isn't doing well at £4.25 despite reviews and the local bookseller put in an order for 100 when he heard it was all about the lifeboat, then changed it to 12 when he realised it was fiction! What a laugh!

I'm doing a Dick Whittington looking for work/commissions in London this week, but will be in touch end of the month.

All the best

Al

326 Mumbles Road
West Cross
Swansea
SA3 5AA

Thursday [13th May 1977]

Dear David Smith,

Thanks very much for your letter and suggestions. I shall have a good deal of reading to do! One of my projects in the next few years is a pictorial essay on the Welsh outside half with my own memories laced with photographs. I shall have funds to employ a researcher. I don't know if you'd be interested or could suggest anyone – a routine task turning up photographs and match reports. The whole thing, when I get down to it, will be very personal, not so much a history as a statement of prejudice! – but as I'm going to be busy on a novel, it occurred to me that the ball could be set rolling.

You mentioned your WRU History and it occurred to me that you might already have covered the ground and obviously know where things are. I've a few cards up my sleeve – but it might be too boring for you.

Anyway, I thought I'd mention it. If you're interested, perhaps we could have lunch some day. All this started after my speculative venture into sporting journalism – but they cut out all my remarks about Neath which I called 'the unreformed church of the day!'

Thanks again

Ever

Alun Richards

19th June, 1977

Dear Dai,

I enjoyed your stories, particularly the American one, 'Spilled Blood' [DS had sent a batch of stories in MS. None were ever sent for publication.] I'm sure John Tripp would publish it if you sent it to *Planet*, but as I told you when we met, articulacy and fluency in the manipulation of ideas, always seems to me to bode ill for the short-story writer. The whole point of being a writer is to move from ignorance into light, to discover something about oneself that one did not know before. It's like a journey and no point in making it if one knows the destination already. What I am trying to say is, if you write as fluently and intelligently as you do, the very fluency is a handicap to getting at the root of a situation or a character. You don't have to worry at it or your own ignorance like me, because you can explain it to yourself first.

I'm sure this isn't clear (!) but, to be brutal, I don't see the point of writing good stories when you could be a brilliant critic, cutting through the chaff that is so thick on the ground. Writers don't need critics, but readers do and I suspect you'll always be tempted to push ideas into stories, your own and not the character's and the short-story form won't hold anything extraneous. I liked your TLS piece so much, not only because I agreed with most of it, but because I couldn't have done it myself and don't know anyone else who could, and to be original in this way must be very satisfying, I should have thought.

Anyway, a good rule is never to listen to anybody and do what you want to do but I would like to see you blow up the Anglo Welsh for a start and if you want to write, a novel is much easier than short stories.

Let's have a chat about it. I shall be in Cardiff in the last week of June. The BBC are making a little film about me and I have un-Graigwened [Graigwen is the area of Pontypridd where AR had lived] myself into a visual old salt. Publicity rules the publishing houses and I'll have to come and dub it.

Will you be around. There is an ominous silence from you on the rugby score. Never mind. JBG [Thomas, Sports Editor, *Western Mail*] will spill all one day.

Let's hear from you. Sorry I've been so long replying.

Yours ever

Alun

326 Mumbles Rd
Swansea

16/1/78

Dear Ron,

It seems ages since I've seen you – aeons away, and I hoped you'd hear some good news about your novel but Gomer are up their usual jiggery-pokery. I've had my troubles with them and have more or less told them to get stuffed. They told me they were going to send your book to the Arts Council in the hope of getting a grant but Meic

Stephens [then Literature Director, Arts Council of Wales] told me they'd never received it in Cardiff and I haven't been able to get hold of them since I set up a nautical series for them which has sold out... The whole Welsh scene is the same – paranoid with gossip and nothing done at the end of the day.

I saw Aled [Vaughan] in John Ormond's for a brief shouting match – he's so arrogant and patronising it isn't true. I'm not going to bother again – they stimulate my rages to no point. Good news about your short story in London – it only goes to show, nobody changes here and they're such back-scratching amateurs, *Planet* and Co, bloody awful nationalist sociology all of which give me the Pip.

I'm working on an historical novel which gets worse with every page, anthologising as well, but without much enthusiasm – a long dead patch despite the Arts Council grant and I've either got to work on my hates with an ideas book, or do something else, I've decided. I'm in good biting mood tho.

I had a card from Chunks. Did he come down? I haven't heard any news of him for ages, you say you're on with your nature book – I hope it's going okay – they all tell me there's no dough in fiction! – and telly's gone dead on everyone.

D'you fancy a trip down sometime? I'm enjoying nothing except rugby and we could do a bit of pier fishing if you fancy it sometime. Drop us a line if you feel like it, only watch the snow. It must be ten years since I came off my bike on the Brenner pass up the Rhigos! – and I don't fancy long journeys these days. I was thinking about getting a 3 wheeler when someone told me the motorcycle licences don't apply any more – is this true? Can't be.

Anyway, hope to see you soon.

All the best

Al

326 Mumbles Rd
Swansea

Sunday

Dear Ron,

Sorry I've been so long replying to your letter. I've been head down on the yo-ho-ho, still slaving away on the new book. Still, I hope to be home and dry in a couple of months. How are you? How goes the nature book? I gave – lent! – all your books to Dai Smith who is preparing a lecture on the post-war stuff – he's a small bomb that guy and makes me laugh. His lecture on the Tonypandy riots [given at Swansea in 1978] ended with a paternity order against one of the Gloucester police – 2 hours summed up.

Let me know about coming down. I'm hoping to land some rugby film next year – anything but another book for a bit.

All go here. Hope to see you in a week or two.

All the best

Al

1980s

Monday 14th

Dear Ron,

Thanks for your letter. I've been in Australia for the last 6 weeks [1980] – jaunt arranged by Yr Academi Cymraeg [sic] – much competed for but fixed in the end because Qantas Airways offered to pay my fare if I'd write articles on *The Onedin Line* and sport – so much for the power of the literati. I had a great time on holiday, swimming and junketing in exchange for a few weeks lecturing and reading – swung myself a trip to Fiji and Singapore on the way home, old Ponty mates listening to Max Boyce – but for me a last swansong of middle age – what have I done with my life but stare at blank pieces of paper? I feel fit as a fiddle but put on a stone which only greying sideboards will disguise. A bit of luck, all this, which couldn't have happened to a nice-a-fella! Them's my sentiments.

I had a few pints with Will Paynter and Dai Smith yesterday – Dai's done a book on the Fed in the 20th century – a history. Both our rugby books come out at the same time – his [with Gareth Williams] serious, mine coffee table to coincide with the film in October. I got so shagged in the end, it's good pictures and tired journalism and now I have to write endless articles for Qantas

212

Airways Magazine to pay my debts – but no matter – the big relief in writing rubbish is that you know what it is from the start – and I hope to begin a big last novel soon – a burster. We shall see.

The WRU has given the least co-operation possible in the making of this film – a detestable bunch riding on the backs of glory-besotted youths – but I'm playing them cool until the book comes out. I had an offer of a 3 month job in Aussie next winter which I'll take if Helen's OK – I feel like wandering again and since Australia's like Rhydfelin it makes me feel a big noise. Let somebody worry about Richards is my motto. I fixed up for Chunks to do a book of Thames bridges but he never replied. Poor bugger is exhausted I expect. I know the feeling but am going to embark on a long grind now unless I get bloody sidetracked as I usually do. I met Chinese raving about R S Thomas in Adelaide and Gwyn they know and the only guy I met who read anything of mine was a night porter in Sydney who said I'd got my facts wrong – it was the 2ft 9 in the Victoria in Ponty, not the 2ft 6 [height of coal seams]!

Still, I had a ball and home to chaos but that's life. Would love to see you and Chunks anytime just give a ring. It seems ages since I saw you. Good luck with the novel. We'll have a jar soon I hope.

Ever,

Al

Dear Ron,

Thanks for your letter – I've been stomached myself, all aches and pains, but your arthritis sounds a bastard. Is heat any good? I get twinges in the shoulder and use a lamp which sometimes does a bit of good. Helen's been in hospital for a minor op and is dragging around – I suppose it's the age of infirmity; in my case added to by abuse.

I had a great chat with Will Paynter and Dai Francis [General Secretary of the NUM in South Wales] in a party to launch Dai Smith's book on THE FED [with Hywel Francis] – the party was better than the book which is very academic and nothing left out – a morass of unsiphoned details but Paynter is a character.

My own rugby offering will be out in September – a couple of good chapters and some fine fotos with a lot of waffle, a money-making exercise I hope. I'm trying to write an autobiographical novel – trying to start one, but the thing won't come – who wants to know what happened on a trip to Bristol Zoo in 1937? I can remember you telling me you were exhausted by *Flame and Slag* – was it? – and I don't get more than a couple of pages a day done and then sit around. We will all, I suppose, grind to a standstill and it's nice to do a bit of journalism. Did you know that Dai Smith is a power behind this new mag ARCADE? – with Ned Thomas. They are alleged to have money. I'm going to suggest that you do a fortnightly bit – if you're interested – 800 words on

214

a passion – birds/soccer etc? It should be fun to write, a bit of a change. I'm hoping to do rugby in the winter. I'm going to push for pros not academics and real cash if it can be got.

Sorry not to see you and Chunks – it doesn't look as if he'll ever do his Thames bridges and now they tell me that the cost of all these pretty books with pictures has escalated so much as to make them impossible. Hope you got the car fixed and that there's a chance of seeing you sometime. I'm going to London next week to correct the proofs and title the pictures of the rugby book, as it comes off the machine – there's so much competition from other books coming out at the same time that they're rushing and gambling a hell of a lot – I listen to them and nod – I don't understand.

All the best
Al

1 Ael-y-Bryn
Treherbert
Rhondda
Mid Glam

17th Nov '81

Dear Dai,

I haven't replied to your letter of 5th Nov. Because (two weekends gone by) I haven't heard from John Osmond [Editor of *Arcade*]. Since sending my *Peregrine* Ms to *Arcade*, I've heard some warming comments from strangers really, even been invited to read the MS as a kind of performance. Your letter though, confirms something else. It's what I've been smelling. I should have used a shit detector. That's it for sure, the old ty-bach metaphysic, the old druidically tinctured shit. Losers' shit since mistletoe worship. Since the stuff jewelled out as righteousness. As italicised gravitas. Zillions of Welshy cells zonking out the manurial author.

Dai, I don't know what else to say.

Look after yourself

Ron

326 Mumbles Road

Swansea

15 April 1982

Dear Ron,

Thanks a million for the book and the letter – something to browse over. Had a great session in Cardiff with John Ormond this week, but I'm paying for it now. John's doing a memorial to Gwyn Thomas in May – directing and compiling. He looks very frail and is about to retire, but otherwise thriving. We all said we'd go to the memorial night.

Am still screwing away, still not knowing whether it's going on or not. Half of me – anarchistic – hopes it's not. As you say, I've bled Mumbles!

It was great to see you. Let's have a few more meets this summer. As Lord Reith said, thinking no doubt of his limp Calvinist cock, 'Life is for Living'.

The boys are netting herring and bass on the foreshore. Sanity goes on somewhere.

All the best

Al

326 Mumbles Rd

Swansea

11/4/83

Dear Ron,

Glad you finished the novel. I haven't finished anything I've started in the last 12 months, a year of potching. However, letter from the *Western Mail* wanting me to do a column. Ugh. However, I'm hoping to get £40 a week until I go to Japan – it's not coming in from anywhere else and I suppose it's a chance to try and make it better. You say words are coming to seem like leather soles – obsolete – but there must always be beer money in journalism when you're 80. I used to get £40 a month for the *Radio Times*. I'd knock one off in a morning in the full knowledge that almost nobody ever read them. They didn't matter to me. Now it does, I suppose I'll be worse. Anyway, I'm going to have a crack and I'm going to praise all my mates. Strangely enough, a piece I did on Glyn Davies the [post-war Pontypridd and Wales] fly half, led to a year's work on the rugby film, so I might come up with another acorn. I met a jazz buff the other day whose article on an old negro trumpeter written in Mumbles was read out at the request of the widow at the memorial service in Harlem – a shy frail solicitor's office manager of 45, unmarried, whose aged parents bully him – the noise! Trouble is, you can't say that if it's real names, can't be anything but bland which cooks it from the start. Never mind.

Saw a pal from the BBC the other day. He's doing a film on Alun Owen [Welsh Liverpudlian playwright] who is disintegrating on the pop slowly. Says he's bent. I always think that to mean crooked, being a nice Ponty boy, but no, he says, 'when he meets George Melly, he kisses him on the mouth!' I think I'll start off my column with that. What I'm planning to do is a few portraits – I'm starting with the jazzman, and then I'm going to try and flog the pieces and myself as a researcher to make 10 films on the subject – this is my plan. The crazy thing is, the BBC brass and all the Machynlleths in S4C read and revere the *Western Mail* and the Welsh Edition of the *Radio Times* – it is prestige to them, a ticket to a Welsh eternity. Well, there should be something in it then...

I'm still waiting to hear from the Japs. I mean, how much they're going to come across with. Had a painted letter on a sheet of paper 2 yards long this week – like a poster – saying 'come to my house'. One thing, they don't have the Urdd out there.

See you

Al

Sat [November 1983]

Dear Ron,

I got up early – couldn't sleep – heard your letter come through the box. I've been meaning to ring you but have been going like a steam engine on the Carwyn book – just about finished – now collecting photographs. Welsh Wales penetrated, finding out things I don't want to find out. Best thing's an old photograph of him playing – a slender wraith that nobody could catch – and people's memories – of him side-stepping on his own shadow against Amman United, playing torero with his heels – and his brother remembering holding him upside down at 16 when he'd made a century for Tumble – £5 in silver falling out of his pockets, the colliers having made a collection 'for the schoolboy'! Perhaps these moments are the best – for sportsmen. Nothing matches them after perhaps. I've got a month to do a documentary script – whether they'll do it, I don't know. Then I go to Japan on the MV 'Thanus-Muru' from Southampton towards Tokyo on Jan 5th, a Jap container ship 55,000 tons, Jap food, down the Suez Canal – I'll bet Reagan is waiting. I'm half thrilled, half scared – there's a communal bathroom – all these little Japs and my 15½ stone and winter writer's gut. In all my dealings with them I behave like my old headmaster – I beg your pardon Richards San Velly Important man! It's a year's money guaranteed and God know what. I'm not supposed to work at anything but my anthology of sea stories of the Far East(!) when I'm out there, but I'm going to moonlight – that's why I'm going!

I'm having problems with the *Western Mail*, too busy to do it and very soon I'm off – but the Japs were very impressed with it. It makes me a COMMUNICATOR. Velly important. I couldn't get out of adjudicating that Xmas SS completely. Ugh.

I'm hoping to come up and see you before I go but I am getting a bit frightened of the bike and can't take the cold. Up to Ponty to see my old neighbour who is moving. Now an old woman. She remembered me arriving home, failed all my O Levels and my grandmother telling her 'They don't understand him in that school!'

My mind is going back all the time whereas I am going down the Suez Canal shortly. I've got to see you before I go – the obituary piece.

        << Pontypridd – Yokohama
         'He done his best'>>

I'll give your regards to the PLO. I'll bet the Japs will detach me first if there's trouble in the Gulf. Maybe they won't though – I'm going to 'help' with the centenary of the Mitsui OSK lines. I am going there as the Chairman of the Bench, I think. Councillor Richards.

'Ladies and gentlemen and what you brought with you … What a genuine plesh it is for me on this auspishus …'

I've gone for the 'Councils' in Carwyn's book

'S. Wales – the natural selection of the unfittest'

Best

Al

Tokyo. Japan

2-5-84

Dear Dai,

I have just cooked my last two eggs and the £2 rashers
– about the size of a biro, poured the last of the scotch
into the coffee, and finished your book [*Wales! Wales?*]
which Helen brought – I haven't been out for 2 days –
everybody in the bloody country is on holiday – nothing
is going right – the weather changes dramatically snow,
heat and now drizzle but I've finished your book and I
read it fascinated, learned things I didn't know and all in
all, it's the best I've read on the subject, certainly for my
life and times. Strangely, or is it, I thought the breakdown
of HOW GREEN the most interesting. You're a litterateur,
really you know – maybe you wouldn't have seen it that
way if you weren't a historian as well, but that I read and
re-read, learning things, his assumptions, I knew he got
most of it from an old Fleet Street journalist, that he was
crazy – my motorbike mechanic was his batman in the
Welsh Guards, but he still had the narrative skill that
carries the book along – no success is ever entirely
undeserved – but the falsifications were never as clear to
me until you made them. I thought that was brilliant –
and Tonypandy – and of course, the stand on *who we are
now* and an elbow into the pretensions of the Welsh-
speaking middle class. But you know all that, how we
agree. I thought the Bevan reference superb – you must do
the biog – and the sentence about Bevan being the eternal
gatecrasher who questioned the validity of the gates –
brilliant. I wish I'd written that. It's the key to the man,

as is Gwyn's unpublished novel – that quote – 'These people have no doubts – the serenity of the completeness of their armoury' – tells us more about what they – all of us – are up against than anything I've seen written. And that is so much more important than the Welsh language. If the Eng government can save the Welsh language it will, because it's not really important. I could go on, but I could have cheered to see you pinpoint this. The quotes are very good – I could have done with more – perhaps another time. Very flattering to see myself referred to, but thank God you understand what I'm getting at – I agree so much about the myth making – the quiescent Tourist Wales that is the future, if we don't break it, make new moulds. (Michael Joseph has asked if I were interested in a biog of Richard Llewellyn!). What knocked me – no, disturbed me, because, aware of it, I've never alluded to it – your own thoughts on P59. 'The density of relationships between place and people – the common fate of industrial leftovers everywhere' – 'to carry with you the unusable vigour of a textured life you know intimately, and uselessly – the shiver of unfullfilment – the evanescence.' I know this haunts me too – isn't it a tragic theme? – but you know, we would be different people without it, have different wives, relationships – we wouldn't be friends, and in ourselves, we haven't abandoned anything – and yet there's no going back, and it can't be reproduced. To me, this is the most profound sentence in the book – I'm not sure if I understand it right – of course I do! – but it's deep in its implications, isn't it? It's a huge theme. I want to talk more about this. There is a Greek myth that I can't bring to the front of my mind that is parallel to it – what is it? It's a binding thing – it

binds people. You're right, of course about Idris Davies –
but the relationship in *Travelling Loaded* is a part of your
centre statement above. This set my mind alight – one
more unintended accusation for the things I haven't done!
I'm going to read that again tonight.

All in all, a tremendous book – A country of the mind
– should have been the title, but the last sentence is a
knock-out. Carwyn used to say, it's England's turn next –
he was right, but they'll sell it and move to tax havens,
those who can! There are things I don't understand I'm
happy to talk to you about – and you've been very kind on
the whole – perhaps it's not an historian's job to go into
the incestuous hatreds and the kind of allegations
Goronwy [Rees] always made – the self-defeating
structures – like you, he adored the NUM – and I could do
with a bit more on the roots of Welsh inferiority! – but
maybe it needs someone from the other side to do that. I
only had one reservation – I'm not sure – so it's not a
criticism – in my own lifetime and those I grew up with,
the two wars, particularly the first, had a devastating
effect on people's lives and their thinking. It wasn't just
the missing faces – it was the crippling of the thought of
the returned generations. I don't know if that's the right
phrase, but of 1914-18 in particular I have always
wanted to know in general terms – as analysed by
somebody like you outside – what I know – have heard –
from individual experiences. There was an evanescence of
the spirit that blighted a generation and I would like to
know more about it from the point of view of its effects on
society. I can understand it in individual terms, that's all.
There's also the effect on the generations who just missed
the wars – Orwell is very good on this. Perhaps it's not the

historian's principal task – but it must be – it's so neglected – there's a huge gap in my understanding anyway. I would like to hear you on the subject.

I can't think the book will do you anything but good because as a whole it's so new and fresh, not the dead stuff, the usual regurgitations. The literary quotes are deadly. I wish I had read that book of Gwyn's [*The Dark Philosophers*] when he was alive. I don't quite agree with you on him. Maybe I'm deaf still. I think he gave up too early, but reading those quoted sentences, I'm ashamed of what I haven't done myself as a novelist – and you can't give a bloody academic more praise than that! So well done. I hope it got the reception it deserved.

As to what I'm doing here, I don't know. I live like a bug in a plastic box, terrified of spending. The money comes in every month. I go on voyages which are great – some fabulous early morning feelings at sea – but I'm having a hard time finding sea stories, my official task, although I'm going to write about the voyages for the Beeb or anybody. I do a bit myself and will do more. It's very lonely altho' I'm having fun watching the British at parties, and meeting Americans occasionally, getting the Vietnam story from the inside. I like the Japanese who have been great to me, but now that Helen's gone back, it's unsettling to be back on my own. I work mornings, prowl about the Press Club in the afternoons, bolt home at night except for an occasional piss up, usually with Brits. I think England is finished, a daily conviction when I see how prosperous people are here, apart from their houses which are terrible. It's like being inside a watch, every part working, but I haven't begun to understand the Japanese and while the Brits recount horror stories, I don't

224

really believe them. I spent 3 days on the pop with a commissioner of Police from NY – one of the best natural storytellers I ever heard – a Brooklyn cop – now he wants me to write his life story! I don't know. I shall be 55 in October and so much not done, but at least I'm having new experiences and meeting new people – I got really bogged down with lifeboats and village life and needed to get away after a bad year with no dough. The Carwyn Book is due out in 1st October and will cover the family costs so I'm free to stay here living like a student. I can't drink lying on the floor – after six pints, I had hot sake and was literally legless once – the hot and cold, the Japs reckon. They drink like hell, you see them, salarymen in suits and briefcases spewing all over the subway. I'm so big. I break room fittings, crush furniture – but they come up smiling. The efficiency of the ships is tremendous – they must be hiding something, but I can't find it. So I go on. I don't know how long I'll stay – as long as I can stand it for the money and I enjoy the voyages.

I'm reading a lot. Good American biogs in the Press Club. Jesus, Faulkner's drinking and Dreiser's women. I really congratulate you on the book. You must have the great feeling 'I bloody did it!' No one else has, or could. It'll be a long time before I have a similar salutation again. Now do the Bevan book. Put aside the temptations of telly and go on the wagon until I come home! Tell Slug [his friend Tom Jones] he owes me a letter. He can print it if he likes. Love to Norette and the kids.

Ever

Alun

31.10.84

Tokyo
Japan

Dear Ron,

How are you, my old mate? I have been in a state of limbo since Helen went back, deaf, anti-hystamine tablets reducing me to a somnambulistic state for about a month, living in a biscuit-box flat as big as a small garage, hiding from authority and waiting for the money to come in every month – just like laying low in the forces. Every now and again I make a voyage, then hide and live on yoghurt and prunes and Argentinean bully beef lifted from ships – and occasionally go on the pop with stray yanks who have been here since Vietnam and gone bamboo. I can't wait to get home for Xmas but before that I go to the Solomons, Iwo Jima and Saipan on a liner with a party of war widows! It sounds exotic and hilarious, but my bloody ear doubles up sounds and I get dizzy – I never thought that would be my affliction. Japan is – I dunno – OK for Japanese – no poor people in evidence, little unemployment, prosperous, a world of things, groups, rules – can't see the savagery there is at home from which all news seems dismal. How are you coping? You last wrote when the miners' strike started in March and you said it would be long and you were right. When not at sea, I spend days on my own brooding over things, wondering about everything. The heat here in the summer was terrible, and continued until mid October, now there are chill winds and typhoons coming up. I'm hungry for news, get very little… in my reverie I am frequently back in Ponty, not

Mumbles, isn't it strange? I saw a picture of a wolf in a deserted colliery winding room in a Jap magazine and went cold – but it was in the north of Japan – company went bankrupt after a big disaster and couldn't pay the compo. It made me feel cold. How are you, Renee, everybody? I hear occasionally from Dai Smith who has moved to Barry.

How is it, butt? Let's hear from you. Apologies for not writing. I'm getting to hate writing!

All the best

Al

c/o English Dept.

University of Western Australia

Monday 23/3/86

Dear Dai,

It's very kind of you to write and I very much appreciate all the enclosures from the Oxford Book etc. [*Companion to the Literatures of Wales*]. It's extraordinary to think of John Morgan fulminating about his absence – I can't understand it – it's such a small thing but I suppose he's reached a point when he wants to satisfy himself he's been. I don't know him well – I used to – but he was always such an urbane metropolitan big gun – on the way up, and a terrible name-dropper. He must be very lonely, counting his money. Also, fantastic to sit here thinking about Nifty Neil – your name dropping. I went to his wedding, the reception held in a pub in Treforest, I

227

think, crate after crate pulled out from under the table
and his lovely wife whom he kept examining with glassy
eyes as he got more and more drunk. He was a great guy
and Dai Love, heroes of my 17th year. I suspect they
pinched a good deal of my childhood stuff on Carwyn for
the Welsh film. I can't prove it, can't be bothered, but
they're all so greedy for status and want to prove only
they can do it themselves – the whole lot of them, all
cocooned on state money and they give me the willies. It's
a bit like it here, Western Australia being Wales and the
decisions made in Sydney or Melbourne. The real shock is
the heat – you can't do anything except stay in. Also, it's
very bourgeois, bland and university secure with gangs of
waspish queers and lesbians who I ran foul of describing
my eternal search for an amiable Filipino with an iron,
only to be told stiffly that some Australians buy Filipino
wives. They got really nasty at the odd loose word, and
the next minute I'm invited to dinner with the Lord Chief
Justice because he's wild about *The Onedin Line*! – All
polite again, naice society and it bores the pants off me.
It's actually very lonely, an air-conditioned flat and an air-
conditioned office, and air-conditioned minds – all the
dept hating each other, the prof – won't sit with the prof
of classics because he's a philanderer – and the gays
tweeting away, and sing song jollities at 6pm in the
University Club. Thimble brains earn fortunes and live in
palaces, but nobody bothers. Bland bland... I'm enjoying
teaching my workshop but an old lady of 70 comes to
both classes just to hear my voice because her father was
Welsh – won't do any work, just sits there. I had a night
out with Bryn Griffiths, disintegrating fast and being the
Welsh poet, a broth of a boy, but it sits on him hard now

and he's sad, getting regular dough from the Seamen's Union. Everybody seems to be fixed up here though and the other night, the President of the Welsh Society took me out for a slap-up meal with Lloyd George's granddaughter, over to lecture for Moral Rearmament – he jumped ship in Freemantle in 1947, his 17-stone wife (then thinner) waiting for him at the bottom of the gangway. The Moral Rearmers didn't drink so we got pissed – skinned out in Freo he was saying by the end of the evening. The Welsh connection haunts you – newspaper coverage of Welsh-speaking Japanese and Wynn Thomas courses advertised on the University noticeboard. It's all incredible and only a 2 [obit.] line notice about Tommy Farr. I think I told you about the boy I taught in Ely ringing me up after a radio broadcast. He was 39!

I am having awful trouble with my novel, stuck and can't get on and not making much headway with the money-making attempts outside the course here. I leave here at the end of April to go prospecting in Adelaide but I doubt if I shall stay long and plan to be home in July, with as much dough as I can save. The kids have been great, going home regularly and all being terrific correspondents. I don't know what the hell I'm going to do if I can't get on with this book – I shall get my honorary fellowship in July, then ask the Principal if there's anything going in security! I've never worked in a university dept before but I've become under-awed. There's so many wankers and you can't have a serious conversation, save for a few. All the Prof is concerned about is numbers – he's very impressed with these so I keep the Onedin fans on. There are other colleges, acclaimed institutions of education and academy of Performing Arts, and they all hate each other, all talking about standards. It's probably exactly the same in Swansea but here they have money. What is extraordinary is that there's a kind of universal unhappiness and dejection in all the sunlight. Nothing happens, everything is easy, there's no character. It's all so suburban and nice/nasty. I haven't ventured out alone, the pubs are terrible with solitary abos staring into dirty glasses, sawdust floors in one and then 10,000 young all healthy and dumb. It's made of sun-kissed plastic. The students are beginning to take me out but only to meet their parents! It's like that. I get to look older in the sun, and pipe smoking is equated with AIDS – it fucks up the air conditioning. But I battle on. Cockroaches come out all night in my immaculate tiled floor, and mosquitoes bite at dusk, but the library is terrific. I've discovered Jean Rhys and don't much care for your Mr Kazin [Alfred Kazin, American critic DS had recommended] – he's an academic! I can't use the computer reference section in the library so I go around like an old lady in Boots – have you got anything American? But psychiatrists and justices ask me out and boredom prevails. Won't be here long unless I find opals. Poor old Tripp. What did he get out of it all? The autobiog should be with you soon – I wish I'd put in a bit about Nifty, but it would be too self-conscious. Later. Really appreciated your letter. Meanwhile nothing happens.

Ever

Al

Sunday

Dear Ron,

I've just arrived back from Australia [1986] after months of prospecting for very small nuggets to find your letter amongst a pile of worthless bumf. I'm so glad you liked the autobiog – I've been at it off and on for about 3 years and then came home from Japan to rewrite it all – a real slog and, alas, no reviews to speak of, a flop in the box office which is hard because I was sweating on a commission to do Vol II. Never mind, you liked it, and a few more, and it's off my chest.

I was only thinking the other day, I haven't seen you since before I went to Japan and that was all of 1984 – I've been running around frenetically wherever there's a buck but I'm home for a long spell now, if not for good, to do God knows what as the markets for everything have practically dried up, but I mustn't moan to you – you've been through it all. I'm chesty at the moment, some good Ponty phlegm re-generated by 36 hours on an aircraft and then a bit of a holiday with Helen. The house is empty now. I want to flog it but Helen won't. She gets stronger while I potter and I'm a leaner now – leaning on an invisible stick.

In the meantime, I gob along. I don't know if your old car will make it down here but if so, it would be great to see you. If we have a fine spell, I'll try and get up in a

231

week or so. This is just to thank you for your letter. I really appreciated it – and to mourn the fact that we haven't seen each other for ages. It's been too long.

Ever

Al

326 Mumbles Road
West Cross
Swansea

23/10/87

Dear Ron,

Thanks for your letter. I've written to Downing Street [recommending a Civil List pension for Ron Berry] and to Wyn Roberts [Conservative Secretary of State for Wales] enclose copies – for your eyes only as they stamp confidential and warnings on anything – do not disclose!

I hope it comes off. We've done our best but you know what they're like. Fingers crossed!

As soon as the leaves are off the roads and the rain stops, I'll flash up one Thursday, unless you can think of a place to meet *that I can find*. I finish about 12-30pm.

I'm getting ga-ga on the bike.

All the best

Al

1990s

1, Ael-y-Bryn
Treherbert
Rhondda
Mid Glam

10th April '90

Dear Dai,

Thanks for the copy of 'Focal Heroes'. The names, some of the names took me back to my boyhood, and less distant to two old-timers (now gone) who boxed 'exhibition' bouts with Jimmy Wilde. And once I sat next to Wilde in the press box at Ninian Park. He was elderly, jowly, rather indifferent to the match. I was covering the game for the *Observer* – a spasm in quality journalism. A year or so later Wilde was attacked by young thugs on Cardiff Station. Once too, I had some correspondence with Tommy Farr, hoping to do his biography. He said the record was already down on paper, kept in a safe place pending the right time. Know what? Farr fought 13 fifteen-round bouts in 1933.

Anyhow, I went on to make *Hector Bebb*.

Admirable research and the way you've put 'Focal Heroes' together. It's a gift. The shape of Dai Smith's mind.

I heard your talk with John Ormond [on Radio Wales for *First Hand*], quite by accident in the first instance, and it came across as damn good radio. Never heard John so enthused other than in late night give and take.

But listen, I do not regard myself as orally entertaining except in spurts between doldrums. Howsomever, if you think it'll be all right, fair to middling, worthy, more nascent than jogtrot, then maybe we should do it here in this house.

For sharing bond,

Yours,

Ron

1, Ael-y-Bryn
Treherbert
Rhondda
Mid Glam

27th June '90

Dear Dai,

I'm inclined to think our chat [on Radio Wales] went a bit awry, stuff unsaid, fluff enhanced, but no matter. Posterity stares at its navel.

Heard a nice redemption story yesterday. One of my daughters works for the Citizens' Advice Bureau. Called to a big house in Porth, she met Miss Gardener, one-time Rhondda librarian, who banned *The Full-time Amateur* for a few years. Now she's utterly ga-ga, talking all day to her dead mother, half starved, isolate. Alone as vacuum. Once she strode Amazonian, long thighed and dominant. The pity is she had none. And too far gone to feel desolate(d). In a damp house. Neighbours phoned the CAB regarding the leaking roof.

Yet oddly enough, I've just been reading Glyn's *The Dragon Has Two Tongues* [1968], where he opines I'm scrawling Ichabod on Wales – this after saying some nice things, which I appreciate.

So there for you.

Yours,

Ron

Ael-y-Bryn

Treherbert

Rhondda

Tuesday

Dear Dai,

It's a swarm of a book [*Aneurin Bevan and the World of South Wales*, 1993]. Comprehensive. I can't read quickly on and on. From stirred memories and/or backtracking the text I'm trying to learn the size of what you're in charge. *Leaders and Led* flung lots of bygones into my head, personally gospel, marginal as history unless freaked to universal. The Gwyn chapter twanged chords. Another proof of Gwyn was in the nagging resentment of Welsh people who saw him on the box. My mother quite despised Gwyn's TV persona. Howsomever, my Swansea Valley old lady pronounced 'Ach y fi' (repeated whimsically by old Glyn Jones) on one of my novels. My father took umbrage at second-hand.

Although I ploughed forgetfully through Ch. 1, your/ our *World* recharges ducts of social conscience. Cracks

light on oddments of my times, too. The time I inter-
viewed Will Mainwaring off camera, for Aled Vaughan.
Beforehand I had grilled the blind, retired librarian of
Tynewydd Labour Club. Regarding Bevan and *The Miners'
Next Step*, Mainwaring reckoned Bevan stole ideas from
the men who crafted the manifesto. Aye, smoothie old
Mainwaring, like a white Inca, a dessicated quim of
power.

But there, I lack respect.

Difficult to imagine this turning world bringing thus
here and now from *Bevan and the World of South Wales*.
How it *was*, laid down in your book. Of course I feel
incapable of learning what history *means*. Condition
common as grass. Grass verbalised sometimes. Gwyn sang
this pasture. I wasn't aware of his allegiance to a *Cause*
until after he dies.

I'm on p 276. So-long for now. I'll get back to you
again.

Yours
Ron

Dear Dai,
    To continue.
    By now feeling severely ill-educated from following my
nose, the straight-forwardness of Raymond Williams
prevents me reading him. Scant regard for Alun Lewis too,
this too good to be true syndrome wrought from infancy.
I worked in Margam (1947) with his platoon sergeant,
Owen (?) from Port Talbot. We were chippies on shuttering.
While Chalfont [Alun Gwynne Jones, later Lord Chalfont]
reported Lewis died in a jeep accident, Owen said Lewis
shot himself in a jungle latrine. But I have read most of
Alun Lewis' work. As for Chandler, I was scouring *Partisan
Review*. Odd for a boy from Blaenycwm. Hemingway and
Miller (H) and Faulkner, Caldwell and Scott Fitzgerald,
Kenneth Patchen and Giono. Recently re-discovered
Nelson Algren short story: The captain was a card.
    But you've scoured deeper and wider. The definitive
hallmark of '*Focal Heroes*', unlike all the other stuff before,
in time and place, of which the fag-card is my inheritance.
The Farr-Louis fight on wireless, men and boys squatting
backs to the wall below a Bakelite set perched on a window-
sill. Shon Price (who fought Jimmy Wilde, 'exhibition' bout)
reckoned Louis' left leads were 'Swansea loaf', i.e. open
glove. Then watching the fight on film in the Palace, we
saw the lumpy rawness of Farr's face after the fight. The

same Farr, neither beaten nor hangdog. Strangely enough, in old age the Brighton gent sounded like a bit of a bopa.

You'll realise I can't review your book dispassionately. Always harking back or sideways to myself. This effective affect of it all. Memories and shitty unforgiveable hurts from dog cat dog poverty. Helplessness, the mind-bending manna of Rhondda between world wars.

Never mind.

Thanks for the book.

See you sometime

Ron

1 Ael-y-Bryn
Treherbert

3rd November 1993

Dear Al

I finally finished Dai's book. Had to tell him some parts I failed to read, the Raymond Williams stuff, the rugby, chunks of Chandler. Obviously others will take what they expect and want from Dai's book, relegating to dreck the material, the hoard which he brain-handled to make 358½ pages. So much has gone already into dust. The silence of oral culture.

Dai says his job is *buzzy*, he's hoping to have more 'literature' on air. Dai's ouvrage: culture hunter extraordinaire. Forget epic history.

See you sometime,

Ron

West Cross
Swansea

4/1/94

Dear Ron,

Thanks for your letter. I am in between GP and consultant with my ears full of drops and penicillin. I've been having problems for about a year – couldn't hear in meetings – and difficulty in crowded bars – I see myself as an elderly flasher, saying 'Pardon?' So will know the worst in a couple of weeks. 10 years ago the ENT specialist said, 'the natural deterioration due to age' and now it's come. I think I must have caught an infection over Xmas and have been putting it off until pain forced me into the surgery, also teeth – dentist tomorrow. You've probably had a gutsful with various things but I've been lucky since TB days and now it's my turn. I remember being very unsympathetic to poor old John Ormond, who used to come down here 'to the best man in Swansea' and you had always to sit on his 'good' side. Now I'm paying for it, in the ears!

Yes, I remember Henry Miller – I bought 'Cosmological Eye' and never forgot the short story *Max* and the run in with the Customs Office. I'd like to borrow the letters when I see you next. I've been reading anything I can get my hands on, sitting on top of the gas fire and yesterday I started back on the book which I can't see myself finishing. I write a page a day and then spend the rest of the day criticising it – can't get going properly yet, but plod on like a snail.

I get books from the University Library but can't

239

understand the reference systems, all computerised and I'm too frightened to ask – they're so bloody impatient so I make a trawl by geography, certain shelves only. Nothing but rubbish on the TV. Helen's going back to work two days a week for a term so I shall have the dog with his cataracts – he's deaf too. He can't quite jump into the car and she screams at him – I see myself being treated the same!

But thank Christ I don't have to go anywhere on time. I'm enjoying that and plod on. Your editor in Gomer sounds terrific. I'll keep my fingers crossed for the Arts Council Grant. I should write to John Lewis and ask for a dozen copies at discounted rates and when you've got rid of those, do the same again. I haven't seen him for years but I always found him OK. I agree with you about Seren – they're an Arts Council creation with minimal staff, in thrall with the academics on the Literature Committee. They could disappear any minute and probably will eventually. Problem is London publishers are in a perilous state too and won't touch anything unless it's got the smack of immediate money. It's a time for boxing clever and subsidised publishers. I've always had a strong suspicion that the Anglo-Welsh scene only exists as a sop to huge sums of money spent on the Welsh language – jobs, organisations like the Welsh Books Council – and the hard fact is that you don't get through to Welsh people except in London, W.H. Smith and Co. Etc. – the rest is a little cloud hovering about Park Place – magazines for contributors, not subscribers or a readership of any size. It's very sad, but there it is, incestuous and pallid. All you can do is find an outlet somewhere if you can.

Your brother's circular letter is v. commonplace with a certain type. I've stopped writing to all the people who do

240

it – it's usually to the in-laws and they end up with spare copies they don't know what to do with! 'Last summer we went to Mexico and Clarence cut his foot!' – things like that. As for tracing the origins I bet it's looking for *English* antecedents, rather than Welsh. John Osborne was delighted to find that his Welsh father was really from the West country – he traced that prodigiously. It's like servant girls saying they're descended from royalty – anything not to make me as ordinary as I am.

I mustn't go on. Will be in touch. My pal Dai Burgess [the distinguished Welsh architect] left Ponty for good yesterday. Moved to France and I haven't got a bed there anymore – that's the end of something.

Will be in touch.

All the best

Al

                                                    1, Ael-y-Bryn
                                                    Treherbert
                                                    Rhondda
                                                    Mid Glam

                                                    5th Jan '94

Dear Al

I sent you a letter just before New Year's Day. Unremarked during your Happy New Year phone call, so I assume it's missing. The letter dealt with a Family Tree from my brother Odwyn (he's been at it for years). No contact with Odwyn since my father died in 1981. Also, my reactions to reading the Miller/Durrell letters – a Xmas present from Simone [his daughter]. Surges of nostalgia, lost hankerings, pub and bracchi shop nights with Mathias, Chunks, Bob Thomas, Charlie Burton and broody longshanks Ernie Zobole on the fringe. The cheating short cuts, banana bravado. And now this windy beavering, this scaramouche wheeling and dealing between Miller and Durrell. Old Mathias gone forever. Chunks housebound in Southall, angina plus 'complications'. Bob's urgent righteousness in lieu of see-sawing in a straight jacket, spent out as lifeless sculptures. Charlie and Ernie retired from their life-time's teaching Art. Two cul de sacs harbouring detritus. And Berry, gouting ancient magma in spasms.

Also mentioned small royalties from Gomer on my skin-thin peregrine book. 400 copies still in stock, and I wondered how I might acquire a few dozen, essentially to sell. No bookshops in Rhondda. Reticent inquisitives keep asking where, how they can buy a copy. What d'you think?

Sent a short story to N.W. Review last week. What a shower they are, hop-scotching Welsh Arts Council loot. Like Gas, Electric and BT, like Banks and *Readers' Digest* they sent out a comprehensive questionnaire, sampling likes, dislikes, culture's LCD, indifferent as budgies to 'sweat of the spirit', 'art for art's sake', 'make it new'. It's called *How to raise phlegm from the man in the street*.

But as I was saying, I've been steeped in the past since Xmas – the past I re-created in *This Bygone* is wholly different, keyed to work, sex, streets, booze, samplers of the great unregenerative horde in time, in place. Although too, Odwyn stirred childhood and family memories with the Family Tree. Cousins and grannies and great aunts and times and places from my own particular age of innocence. Gamut of genes, of unfathomable coincidences, roots like Whitman's *Grass* making the wilful plunder of Being. That last phrase is just wrapping.

Before I inquire in Treorchy post office, please let me know whether you had my last letter.

All the best,

Ron

1, Ael-y-Bryn
Treherbert
Rhondda
Mid Glam

29th March '94

Dear Al,

The days pour away like abattoir blood, except everything kill't or stunned is mute. It's been sad visiting a man in Rhondda Nursing Home, Ystrad. We started work together as collier boys in 1934. Bachelor chap, lived in Cheltenham (worked in Gloucester) since the end of the war. Stroke hit him when he was 70. Long time in intensive care, in Cheltenham Hospital, brought to Rhondda some months ago. He's one of 9 children. Some dead now. No one ready to take him in, so he'll end his days among dozing or sedated geriatrics. Bernard Lisle, he's half-Jew. His father went to the 14-18 war with my old man, but Abie Lisle was taken prisoner, spent three years in the 'salt mines'. One of Rene's brothers married Bernard's Auntie – Muriel Lisle, who lived next door when I was a boy. Muriel's mother spent more than half her life in Bridgend Asylum.

Look after yourself.

Ron

326 Mumbles Road
West Cross
Swansea

18 April 94

Dear Ron,

Good to get your letter. I came back from the States on a trolley/wheelchair! The legs have packed up – some artery problem at the base of the spine – lumbar canal stenosis – I'm waiting to see a consultant to find out what's what. I can't walk more than 100 yards without chronic pain in the calf muscles. It goes when I stop. So I'm dieting like mad and waiting for the phone to ring. It hasn't happened to me for years but now I've got to revive the old Sully skills.

I sat by a swimming pool in Florida in the lovely heat – but it made no difference to the legs. Went out to eat occasionally and found a marvellous 2nd hand bookshop – couldn't ask for more. So I liked your Faulkner account – the lies and the dressing up. By a strange coincidence, I read a biography of John O'Hara – aged 55, a millionaire, he had some friends of his wife's in for a meal in his house in Princeton. As they were leaving, he said 'Got a minute?'

Then disappeared for 10 minutes and came back dressed as a cowboy together with pearl-handled six-shooters! No one knew about the outfit, not even his wife – he'd kept it hidden upstairs. Also, when I was in Tokyo I knew this writer Nicols, born in Neath, but emigrated to Canada. I called on him unexpectedly – he was dressed from head to toe in a Scottish outfit, complete with dirk in his stocking. He told the Japs, it was his evening dress! It's called being someone else if only for a moment. So I can understand Chunk's pilot's wings.

Yes, I'd like to read the Faulkner book when I can get up to see you. I've got a novel for you to borrow too – Cormac McCarthy – *All the Pretty Horses*. Have you read it?

Your account of your old pal coming home from Cheltenham is fascinating – you ought to keep a diary – the length of time you're connected from 1914 is extraordinary. People don't know each other for that long any more – they don't have neighbours/workmates, nor much of a life, I suspect.

I find it very strange not being mobile beyond a few hundred yards. It's not just the feeling of mortality, but the thought of all the things I'm not going to be doing that I planned to do, and the horror of handing myself over to doctors once more, waiting and hanging about in corridors, the usual thing. I steeled myself to it once and will have to do it again. So it's a question of waiting.

Dai Smith is going to Chicago next week to interview Howard Marks [a friend of DS' from Balliol], the Kenfig Hill drug smuggler doing life in Terre Haute, Indiana, then Studs Terkel and some old mate of Gwyn Thomas [the poet, Norman Rosten]. I told him to have a ball on expenses – the most intelligent use of BBC Wales' expenses since I went to Dublin to research a programme on Irish rivers. It'll be more interesting too.

I've got a piece about Keidrych Rhys [who had published AR in *Wales* in late 1950s] in this month's *Planet*. A debt paid but it's somehow not as good as it ought to be. I feel that about everything these days, but there we are.

Good to hear from you. I'll be in touch as soon as I hear anything and can move!

All the best

Al

1, Ael-y-Bryn
Treherbert
Rhondda
Mid Glam

Saturday

Dear Al,

Your letter and the card from Florida [April] landed on the mat together. Shocked to hear about your circulation problem. Bloody hell. I hope they can remedy 'lumbar canal stenosis'. From standard ignorance, I don't know what else to say, though I can almost visualise the bloody circumstance without understanding *why*, apart from the obvious reason(s) of wear and tear, i.e. usage, as the same applies to myself, namely arthritis (neck and shoulders) which makes pins and needles in my hands. I don't mind growing old at all. It's the accretions which debunk common sense and the innocence of so-called conscience.

Regarding John O'Hara, I can't recall much about his

work. Picture him rushing into his cowboy outfit! How the Christ did he regard his wife! We've seen actors and actresses changing identities. Very determined too. Forsaking all else. Not humbly. From besotted necessity. I don't understand the *stake*. Cheating I can fathom as ends and means, with often puerile limitations, I mean the ends are rubbishy. Old One-Eye Lewis [the painter, 'Chunks'] he stitched wings on his uniform because he's a phantasist seeking kudos. Of course they're older than Genesis. Faulkner too, he had a shallow, sometimes inane awareness of *himself*. Hemingway had a tersely brutal opinion of *Count no-count* Willie. As a man, that is, another American on his pasture. But Hemingway also reviled some of Faulkner's work, in particular *The Mansion* (I haven't read it). After reading the biography, despite knowing so little about William Faulkner, I now have scant appreciation for the man. Sometimes genius writer, ludicrous in most other ways. Rather like (not the *same*) Waugh. Brilliant stuff from oddballs, who, above all, have to be forgiven. Faulkner's historical South is slightly reminiscent of my maternal hill-farming forebears, when Welsh was the tongue of Swansea and Caradoc Evans' guile and skrimshanking ruled the hinterland. The ancient eke of Cymru souls. Rather less insane than the Cardi through-put perhaps, but of this ilk. A thrive of pimples on the globe, eulogised by the *New Welsh Review*.

Look forward to reading Cormac McCarthy in due course.

Thought Studs Terkel was dead. Didn't he project the great rabble emancipated by Roosevelt's New Deal during the Depression?

By God, Dai's a forager.

So long for now,

Ron

1, Ael-y-Bryn
Treherbert
Rhondda
Mid Glam

Dear Al

Cormac McCarthy is the best I've read for too long
[summer 1994]. Reminds me of time [Mervyn] Mathias
introduced me to Joyce, Giono, Lawrence, Eliot, Faulkner
et al. He'd be dropping relished items from these (and
buying beer out of Polikoff's union fund – always
replaced), then I'd scour bookshops and libraries and
Mathias would buy and I'd borrow. But at the end, to
whit one of the boat-burning episodes in my life, I gave
old Mervyn mint Faber and Faber copies of *Ulysses* and
Finnegan's Wake. Much later he sold a letter from
Henry Miller to a London dealer. This came about via
Graham Ackroyd, a RAF cobber of Mathias', who was
corresponding with Miller. Ackroyd crops up in the
Miller-Durrell letters, Durrell very critical and thereafter
Ackroyd became a speck of history. Actually, in truth,
Mathias regarded Ackroyd in the same light, i.e. a sincere
enough ponce dreaming in Sticklepath, Devon.

Aye, Cormac makes legends. He makes unbelievable
heroes, laconic to the point of subtle treachery. Cormac's
disguised simplicity, the all-out American style could
never come from Europe. Two-way brains serving eyes
and ears, unlike the descriptive narrative of country which
flowers to a different aesthetic.

D'you remember when you were 16, 17, aware of
peers, private and social behaviour, and the big space
between yourself and authority? Almost any kind of adult

248

authority. Instead though, young John Grady has the nous and physical expertise of a 21 year old. But it's Cormac's story. Shades of Hemingway of course, hints of the Beats, Kerouac's mystic seeing/conclusions, the *world*. Frequent references to the world. Philosphical exactitudes, made for real by Cormac, more so than the moil and blink and envy of academe. You can taste it, the instant action prose, glamorous to bookmen, officemen, time-cloaked men and women. Repulsive to clerics, alien to politicians, bankers, trade union leaders.

Words. About halfway through *All the Pretty Horses*, began jotting words I didn't know. Filled the back of a foolscap envelope. Several are Spanish/Mexican. But I like the context wherein they are used, especially of country, of moods and places.

I want to read the book again before sending it back to you.

Hope you hear good news from the tests. Appreciate you can't settle to anything. Me likewise. Just (last week) made a glossary for the NWR. A short story Christ, they're thick as greenheart... 'in the light of the closure of Tower...' said Robin Reeves [the Editor]. *Light?*

Cheerio then,

Ron

Swansea

2nd June 1994

Dear Ron,

Thanks for your phone call. I haven't felt like writing.
I'm having problems adjusting to my minor disability, as
they say – moving slowly and the strange feeling of the
pumps not working properly like an old and faltering
diesel engine. I'm trying manfully to get the boat ready to
put in the water – I can sit down in that – but it's hard
going. The joke was being on this X ray table for an hour
with colouring liquid being dripped into my veins and the
radiologist holding me in his arms and turning me to show
me small veins in my leg that weren't working – practically
disappearing – hence peripheral vascular disease – and the
first thing he said was 'You can drink but take plenty of
water with it,' and then: 'If you smoke you'll probably
lose a leg!' So, that's that. I'm trying to lose weight and
exercise but every walk is a gunman's crawl. So there.
Don't tell me, you've had it for years – it's the fly up my
nose, that ages. When I went to see the consultant in
Singleton, I saw some terrible sights, people half my age
so I'll settle for my minor disability – no badge for the
motor bike though! I'll try and get up sometime – not
quite confident enough yet.

A 92-year-old woman now moved into a home in
Henley on Thames sent her son with a gift of an oil
painting of the Gt. Western Colliery done in 1947 by a
chap [the painter, Glyn Morgan] who was in school with
me. I knew her as a boy and pinched a Turkish cigarette
from her house! I once went on holiday with the son and

family to St David's in 1940 – the three older relatives were all badly affected by the war, Russian convoys, Tobruk etc and the son's visit – his grandfather was a friend of my grandfather's – brought back things I'd forgotten. She wanted me to have the painting because my gt. grandfather started work as a boy with Gt. Western and ended up a Deputy Manager! Glanffrwrd's [Eisteddfodic bard and AR's fabled relation] brother. It's a view of Ponty from the Rhondda and you can see the smoke curling in 1947. All gone now. I have the old man's pit lamp on the mantel piece. History!

I'll be in touch with more McCarthy books – see you soon.

Ever,

Al

1, Acl-y-Bryn
Treherbert
Rhondda 5HD

Thursday

Dear Al

As for Cormac M, he leaves most of us like drop-outs from *Beano* and *Dandy*. Christ, he can write. Not to be believed, but Christ he puts down some magic. Some lines ring pure as William Blake the Cockney journeyman genius. Blessed stuff like bygone and forever weather. I kept hunting for the storyline. Found treachery and betrayal and deathly loyalty/ies. Some paragraphs sing above the work in *All the Pretty Horses*. Can't fathom the humans he makes. His restyled patch of USA history [in *Blood Meridian*]. Same man, same sayer as *All the Pretty Horses*. Same release from lit. baggage. Same refuting dismissal of wounds, injuries, disasters anti-Ten Commandments. The biblical bits of précis for each new chapter, foretelling what to *know*.

Recognised a sense of editorial management (his editor for 20 years). Definable placings of continuity. These among phases originated as Genesis, less the evolutionary gavel of faith. Faith beginning to fragment after a couple, likelier a few millennia. Similar mystical structures (and strictures) of destiny, like Genesis, less Hell and Heaven. Cormac relishes fortitude and bedlam. The withering of such as R. S. Thomas. Cormac would make his own plane to drop hydrogen bombs to finish a continent. A single-seater back-yard bomber. A mythical place, like the judge – who from Ch. 1 then reappears in Ch. 6. Perhaps the kid is Cormac's bomb, obliterated by the judge. Cormac is Jehovah. Perhaps. Therefore Judge Holden is subsumed as obliterator, as omni-potent, under old Cormac the maker's bloody Jawa. Sort of.

There's nobody like Mr McCarthy in all the weal and circumstance of our (?) AngloWelsh. I have another page of words... for deciphering from *Blood Meridian*. And if I was half my age I'd be afraid to meet him. For instance, what would he have to say to men like John Ormond and Aled Vaughan? Or old Herbert D? Or the guy who did a (for me) damn good life of Djuna Barnes? Who does the bastard relate to anywhere? Easy to drop names, Faulkner, Melville. Henry Miller would love him. Would have.

Following your *Memoir*, reluctantly sent a short story to *Planet*. Quit taking it a few years ago. John Barnie [Editor] 'enjoyed' *Comrades in Arms*. Offered £40 per 1,000 words. Next Spring. So I'll collect something over a hundred quid. The story concerns two collier boys who joined the South Wales Borderers in 1926. Returned in 1938 to labouring by night in the pit. Despite India, Egypt, Afghanistan, they're back where they started. Redeemed only by booze and sex. After sharing a wilful young girl, scandal. Then frenzied do-lally in the village pub, until felled by a copper. From jail back into the army. One is killed, lost in the retreat to Dunkirk. The other wins the M.M. Against Rommel. Finally brings home a Polish refugee wife, heavyweight like himself. To complete the cameo of existence, as senior citizen, the M.M. and his wife stroll past the bungalow where lives the wilful girl, now married to a head forester, incomes fitting the times. And they share peculiar greetings. As a throwaway final crunch, the girl is now too old to have children by her BA (Forestry) Bangor, husband. So I've collapsed history around two blokes.

I doubt if John Barnie sees it thus.

See you, Al,

Ron

Treherbert
Rhondda

Dear Al

My MS came back [1995] from Seren, '...must be something about your style which I can't admire' says [Mick] Felton, who 'respects what you have done in chronicling the lives of ordinary South Walians in such authentic fashion. Would that some of Wales' younger writers could follow your lead'. Like a few unknown insider experts, he rejected *This Bygone*. So, like P. Pilate, I must wash my hands – not that Felton has posterity on his side, other than manurial.

Take care

Ron

Swansea

17 July 1995

Dear Ron,

Did you see the obituaries of Glyn Jones in the *New Welsh Review*? He was a nice man and the acolytes all needed him – now all they have is each other! – a very poor swap! Then all the stuff on Goronwy Rees – he was great company – nobody said that. I don't know. Sometimes I think it would be better if all this Anglo-Welsh stuff finished tomorrow. The magazines are virtually trade journals for training college lecturers and the like. I am going to cease trading!

I miss not coming up to the Lamb and Flag – it gets me out of Mumbles and I have no connections in Ponty now – strange after all these years to keep thinking of 'home' – I suppose it's like the salmon!

I've been looking over all the false starts I've made on novels in the last 10 years. Not one of them is worth going on with and I don't feel like doing any more short stories and I really can't get started on anything. Hence the bituminous paint sitting gleaming in the can outside. I just sit up here looking through drawers – a bad sign, but the only statement I want to make to the world is, 'Fuck off!'

Bad news about Chunks. Mind, funerals get worse, I reckon, as you get older. Maybe he was a bit creased at his last surviving relative. I've rung him a few times – no reply.

If I get any large amounts of fish next week, I'll give you a ring, maybe get Helen to drive up. We'll see. It's all dead now. We need a good blow. Don't worry about the books.

Keep in touch.

All the best

Al

Treherbert

July 1995

Dear Al,

As you say, what import the words of Norris, Pritchard Jones and Pikoulis on old Glyn? Old Glyn, who enjoyed the Celtic limelight after all, more so than most, who felt he belonged like a partial albino in a flock of starlings. And because he was blessed, they suckered to him like leeches, advertising themselves as disciples, the first and last bastardy, destiny of obsequious holier than thou since Adam blamed Eve for fucking up his allotment.

I don't know either, or which comes *first* ['the radiation

from public to family veneration'], or why. Perhaps it's a Welshness of which we are ignorant, though I suspect there are shades of similar snakes and ladders in my maternal origin. They were Davieses, prone to respect, adulate social success in particular. One of my sisters, poor dab, has worked in Polikoff's factory all her life, yet they call her *Duchess* behind her back.

I reckon Welsh and Anglo-Welsh have always been bull-shitting and parochial, underspread by roots persistent as buttercup. Precious too, bible-precious, even 'ordinary south walians'. Quite spewy.

My car's off the road and due for MOT and tax. I'm dithering what to do.

All the best,

Ron

1, Ael-y-Bryn
Treherbert
Rhondda Cynon Taff

Saturday

Dear Al,

Signs of the times, butty, your lost boat and the quick nerves from your molars. We are presumed not to have regrets, to adapt graciously, to adjust oneself to zombiedom hereafter, but too often reflection hinges on rigor mortis. And grandfatherly serenity can be cheapjack, less earned than imposed.

I'm meeting the surgeon next Monday morning.

Pleurisy has gone now; breathlessness comes from the aneurysm, so I'm hoping to have an early date for this operation. As far as I know my kidneys are all right. Lungs, kidneys and circulation (and age no doubt) have to be healthy. Healthy enough anyway.

I feel a bit like Michaelangelo doddering about in his nightshirt, saying, wailing, 'It is not enough, it is not enough.' I think Cyril Connolly predicted cultural darkness in 1940, a clever sentence, pithy, untrue. But he cut a swathe with *Horizon* for years, shone light on Europe, and made some rungs for Alun Lewis. I've read a couple of reviews of *Connolly's Life* by Jeremy Lewis, one in today's *Western Mail* by Lewis Davies. A scrupulously careful review. I haven't read Lewis Davies' novels.

I haven't been to the Club since early February, or the local pubs.

Have a good time with Henry [AR's friend and doctor, Henry Burgess] in South Africa [the Lions rugby tour of 1995].

All the best

Ron

1 Ael-y-Bryn
Treherbert
Rhondda
Mid Glam

Thursday

Dear Al

On the 1st of Dec [1995] I had the green light from Gomer Press. They want to send the MS of my little epic to the Arts Council for a publication grant. But I have to mend some of the insular jargon relating to pre-war coalmining. They sent me a Reader's report 'from outside'. He compares *This Bygone* favourable against D H Lawrence and Alan Sillitoe because the work isn't 'sordid' and without 'class agony'. Funny rationale. Perhaps he's showing off his catholic taste.

I'm very pleased though, because four or five publishers rejected it. Even suspected nobody wants to know about the stuff, bygone and esoteric stuff that only I can do – my bloody criterion from the start. Namely I'm the only man alive who can put this down with candour and good faith. I mean after all the romanticised crap that's been done and swallowed as authentic by millions. Even brave historians like Dai. But it's always the case of writers who fuck up reality/ies. Also sculptors like Bob, of course.

Anyway, Al, my first novel for 23 years. Only now I'm too knackered to go fishing. Can't hunt peregrines. Can't get wet or cold. Rigour on ebb. Hardly any work done since last winter.

All the best
Yours
Ron

Wednesday

Dear Al,

I've been wondering about you. Assumed you were meshed in work, the olde treadmill. Sorry to learn about your afflictions. It's a bugger when the corpus starts creaking.

Gomer's Mairwen Prys Jones gushed over my re-worked climax for *This Bygone*. I made the heroine pregnant. The first heroine died, killed by a metal splinter in her throat – from a wayward, downed German bomber. Mairwen asked how I came to know about grief. Good Christ, Llandysul felt like the Sahara.

Arts Council verdict comes next month. [1996]

What I'm most satisfied about, and intentional from the beginning, there are no characters who belong elsewhere. They exist in time and place (place invented – Moel Exchange – shaped from images stuck in my brain cells), time of my time as real as I can make it. Moreover the narrative doesn't romanticise what's real, as friend Dai is partial to in his historical biopics of South Wales. As last night, no, *Monday* night when I came home from the Con, depicting heroism, idealism, protests, murders, with Dementia Griffith [Ken Griffith] enacting the ping-pong stuff of Idris Davies [A *Wales! Wales?* film from 1984]. Sure, it was like that on the surface, in throw-away pub banter, in cosy kitchens and pigeon-cots and in witful reflection. So Gwyn Thomas remains brilliant but untrue. And escaped reality like a scalded cat. To make another. Of course. What I've tried to do is reveal the innate acceptance of men (and women) to their world, the pedigree of birthright.

And now it's all gone. Gone forever when today's memories cease, become reliquiae for mongrelising by academics.

Well, I'm tired and my gut's been queasy for some days, despite tablets, so

Look after yourself

Ron

1 Ael-y-Bryn
Treherbert
Rhondda

Saturday

Dear Dai,

With Al for one of our Glynneath meets last Wednesday afternoon. Statutory drivers' intake along with some nosh in the Lamb and Flag. Latter day whole hoggers aware of our aches and pains and unagonised about Anglo-Welsh, cindering the lot, almost, from alpha to omega. Sharing mutual bugger-mugger, familiars knowing when to enjoy, laugh, revile, curse beyond redemption, each to each weighted on balance by separate chemistries in time and place.

Early on he told me about your phone call on New Year's

day [1996], confirming your halleluiah for *This Bygone*, for which I've been reluctant to frankly thank you due to reserve, a privately humble feeling, regard for custom and practice. Anyhow, now and in all truth, warm thanks.

Gomer's Mairwen Prys Jones listed the critique: *Third Welsh Arts Council reader*. She urged me to frame it. One of my daughters made some photo copies. So Al had one, but he's a disgruntled old bugger, sick of the Welsh scene in particular. It is a fucking ludicrous scene sometimes. Shiny reliquiae of maggots in aspic.

Unable to heed siren songs in this Land of our Fathers, I have, of course, long been aware and learned to live with antipathy from self-elected arbiters of taste. And because I belong I have things to say. To put down. Perhaps there's not much left either, but I'll put down whatever I have and disregard the consequences.

Al is set to 'go away'. He's taking a holiday with Helen shortly, then he's off on a last fling to Australia before peripheral vascular keeps him in Mumbles environs thereof. That's his campaign, and he's ultra conscious, worried about his incapacity to handle luggage – this a recent confidence from Al.

On my home front, Rene's still recovering from surgery last Spring, plus osteoporosis and arthritis.

Time past and present is a hawk tipping myriads of blank dice.

Greetings to Norette

All good wishes

Ron

326 Mumbles Rd

Swansea

5/10/96

Dear Ron,

I saw the programme [the BBC Wales documentary about Ron Berry] – glad you liked it – very good except for some mumbling – I thought the postman was Polish! – and could hardly understand Bob Thomas – I guess it's my hearing – and I'm going for more tests next week. I can't distinguish things now if there's music on top. The specialist said it was sinus problems and I have to do exercises, blowing and gobbing and stuffing menthol up my nose. I could have got that advice on Ponty market. So we go on.

They're putting Capt. Colenso [AR's BBC Wales play with T.P. McKenna and Gerald James] together in the rooms in Cardiff today. Haven't made a bad job of it but they cocked up the casting of O'Toole who would have made it a sensation, infuriating as he wanted to do it. Still, it looks good and hopefully, it will lead to another run.

I thought the sound from your Radio play [of 1967] with David Davies was terrific – some very clever filming. It's disgraceful that you've never done anything else for radio as it still stands out as a gem. I remember the singing room in a pub above Senghenydd where we used to get a pint of scrumpy for 7d. And just before stop-tap they brought out an eighty-year-old woman who could sing 'God bless the Prince of Wales' in Welsh – a freak. All gone now – 'one voice, one singer if you please!'

I'll be tied up next week – let's hope for a meet the week after.

All the best

Al

1, Ael-y-Bryn
Treherbert
Rhondda

3rd Nov '96

Dear Al,

Note from Robin Reeves last week. He's taken two short stories. Seems I'm in for the time being. Truthfully it's bloody weird, and devious. Off and on for years he's been saying NWR is overloaded, really prescriptive. Can't take any more stories until next year, next summer or winter.

John Pikoulis sent me a paperback [of Emyr Humphrey's 1965 novel], *Outside The House of Baal*. I made a few attempts to read it (Emyr's tidy sticking plaster bygone), then I had to leave it. I'm sure my mother and Auntie May would appreciate Emyr. We are the same age. One of his sons was cameraman when they filmed *Where Darts the Gar, Where Floats the Wrack* [a television play for HTV]. Long ago. Another life. Met Emyr in his office once, glasses on a lanyard. Very tidy.

I don't know what the weather's like in Mumbles, but I've been housebound for days. Rain and wind. Last summer's labour (ditch down to the blue clay and breezeblocks laid a yard up the porch wall) utterly futile. The pond remains saturated. More weatherproofing in a binder. I'm wondering what to do next. Bitumen perhaps. Jet black wall bubbling in heatwaves.

Rene screamed from the bottom of the stairs, 'The compost bin has gone!'

It's ribbed plastic, 4' diam, yard high, circular lid

nailed to a centre post (which snapped) and meagre wire ties around the circumference. Blown across the garden. I've been trying to keep the compost dry. Shovelled the stuff into bin bags, renewed the centre post, hammered it down to last my days, got soaked, wet legs, chest, rump; left it in situ until yesterday. And humped the compost back into the bin, guaranteed to stay wet until the end of next summer.

Remember *Beulah land, sweet Beulah land*? Aye, oh Beulah land...

All the best

Ron

326 Mumbles Rd

Swansea

6/11/96

Dear Ron,

I am very glad you are 'in'. It is very confusing, however. Those who are 'in' should be required to wear a white bandana around the forehead with a red sun in the centre, like the Japanese suicide pilots, then everybody will know. You are definitely in when the arts council rises to you and people can get grants etc/magazine articles (approved by the Prof) to further their academic careers, and – wait for it! – someone will ask to see your unpublished autobiography so that they can use it to write their own Arts Council-sponsored booklet. Myself, I should prefer *RONALDO BERRI, whistler-extraordinaire*, or something like that, but, very soon, I predict an approach. The important thing is to cash in on it and, for example, send something to *Planet* – chapter of autobiog, or a story.

It goes in cycles sometimes. I have been OUT of TV for years, now, thanks to Dai, I am IN again, but it seems, OUT in everything else. It doesn't matter much now, but there is a terrible fate awaiting Anglo-Welsh critics – we're running out of writers and in about five years there'll be precious little to write about. The terrible thing is that they have such easy lives whereas writers on the whole, do not.

We lost a small hawthorn tree in the gales and a monster fir tree down next door, but the roof held. All my damp problems have been publicly aired by cement and paint – nothing else works except plastic under the cement – sheets of which stopped small fountains in the garage. The weather now is lousy and I don't go far either although Helen is out every morning with the dog – I don't go, I can't keep up with her. She's also going back to school for 3 days a week next term – a fella who took her job got promoted so they asked her to fill in – she's flattered to be asked but the driving is a bit of a strain, I reckon, although she doesn't think so and will do what she wants to do, as ever.

I can't anyway seem to find anything to read that interests me for long and I've only just seen the finished film of Capt. Colenso – they didn't do a bad job, and now I'm soon to do the little half-hour radio play about the baker's wife for TV – (I've got my bandana on until Xmas!) After that, I don't know what next. I sit at the desk every morning and pother away but can't seem to get involved these days.

I got soaked coming home from the Lamb and Flag and still have a few ear problems after swimming – nothing serious though. I can swim but walking is painful after a bit – weight, everybody reckons. So we go on.

Wear your bandana with pride!

All the best

Al

1 Ael-y-Bryn
Treherbert
Rhondda

Thursday [December 1996]

Dear Al,

Having mentioned 'in' I didn't mean hormones flooding like a peacock. Only fashionable Anglo-Welsh gurus tongue the bastard gospel. But you also remarked something I haven't been aware of, or even considered – dearth of Welsh writers. Over the years names come and go, flutter their seasons like mayflies. Normal, too, I thought, past flirtations with the Muse, dalliance with aesthetics whatever the form it takes. So if the provincial novel/drama/poem is on the wane, tiddlers thrive in their absence. Honestly though, I'm not concerned. When Pikoulis nags about London publishers, the next band-wagon might be loaded with shit.

Anyhow, in role like yourself, most days I sit at this table, Cwmsaebren Basin across the valley like Swansea Bay from your room. If I know the material in hand, the head and gut of it, I leave my cells to conjure original prose. Whatever stuff I don't know, the prose result runs jogtrot or banal. Always though, bits of self-elected merit are threatened by sludge.

Bryan Forbes [actor, director, novelist] calls writing the other arrow to his bow. He's without bitterness and he loves people, especially performers. Old, old stars living in isolate splendour (or dereliction) make me wonder about our species. When I ate with Forbes in Pinewood Studios [in the 1960s], within minutes he said, 'You have the same rhetoric as Dick Burton'. Which stopped me in my tracks. Later I watched him directing Edith Evans in *The Whisperers*. Very quiet, gentle, patient. Brief undertone talks with Edith on the camera crew. And afterwards back to the Old Bath Road by bus with a freelance advertising photographer who'd been taking stills on the set. Casual braggadocio about his trade. I was spending a month in Chunk's flat, tapping out forgotten (forgettable) grist on a rickety, bamboo-legged card table. Ten bob second-hand from a junk shop.

Meanwhile, Chunks can't paint or even draw. His damaged heart won't let him and he's preparing to die. Often it's impossible to believe what he says because his time sequences are jumbled. He was mugged (not robbed) walking the cul-de-sac road to his flat. Passer-by helped him home. In bed for three days without calling his doctor or the police. But I cannot trace *when* it actually happened. His refusals to seek help are deeper than sea or sky. In a way I understand. His character (that blanket garbage) reflects his life. Very alone. Of course we all are, every man-jack and jill. Ignite, burn, gutter, out.

This morning I had letter from Edna Mathias – we

exchange Xmas cards since I located Mervyn's RAF friend Graham Ackroyd, who has a small, small publishing firm. Edna's alone in Tooting. Her mother in Pontypridd died last June. *93*. And she says '...thank you for remembering me' – I sent her a photocopy of the NWR article. She referred to a Chunks' story. He was boxing. A punch dislodged his false eye and his opponent's foot crushed it. He might have invented this one. He didn't have a false eye before he joined the RAF. As a youth he did some boxing in a local Unemployed Club. So he did have a *fancy dan* self regard.

Pray heed, Al, gather ye rosebuds while ye may... it's in my OED.

All the best then

Ron

326 Mumbles Rd
Swansea

26/2/97

Dear Ron,

I've just sold a short story to *Planet* after God knows how long – since John Tripp left – it's fashionable, set in the south of France – and will be in June's issue, although I won't renew my subscription – fuck Basque nationalism! My 'one life' piece goes out next Tuesday on BBC2 Wales at 10 pm – I reckon I've had a brief resurgence thanks to Dai – it won't be repeated I reckon, but it was nice while it lasted. Time to get back to a novel if I can summon up an idea. Thinking of 'Saturday Night' – whatever happened to the long story you did about a bastard – or is my memory playing me false? Was it published or did I read it in typescript? You ought to cash in on it if it never went anywhere. I'm going through old boxes looking for pieces I began and abandoned – there are plenty of them. The problem will be getting a routine going again and finding the will!

I laugh like hell at the idea of the creative writing tutor – rather like phrenologists in 1914 – they put their hands on the heads of conscripts, felt the bumps and decided who was coming back from France! The laugh is, it's never been more difficult to get anything published especially short stories and most of the people have no chance – like my old lags beavering away when I took classes in the nick in Swansea. But it must be social like the WVS and it goes down on somebody's report in Cardiff Uni – good work in the valleys. I know the score – I've been the distance, as they say, and it's well paid too – but you've got to see the funny side of it.

I hope your ailments respond to warmth or whatever – I'm against hospital operations unless they guarantee improvement and are life and death – the dentist now wants to do a cosmetic job – fuck it – I'll settle for cloves in the whisky.

This is in response to yours pronto. We'll speak again.

All the best

Al

1, Ael-y-Bryn
Treherbert
Rhondda

Wed

Dear Al,

One Life [March 1997, AR's monologue play on BBC Wales] was utterly convincing last night. I was greatly moved by the awful private rage, the tangle of blame and heedless possessiveness. The intense social aspirations of a baker's wife, and always someone else's fault, mother-hood blind as grass, neurotic as 'family planning'. So you dredged human nature, borne through to a new reality, something to live with. Again, forever, as if forever, Loss and Life.

I hadn't realised this dangerous awareness of motherhood. Nurture and fangs. Cruelly civilised. And bloody Welsh too, physically over-ripe as Hebrew.

I suspect my mother had variations of neuroticism depicted in *One Life*, but of course they weren't co-ordinated, weren't manifested as in this mother of *One Life*. My old lady had vindictiveness and also the blanket balm of impenetrable sanction.

Was it your idea to present silent tableaux of the mother's instinctive enemies? Another lost son? The awful wrack of delusion/conviction. *One Life* and one world. Damn all else. Excuses instead of tolerance.

You made it good, Al.

Look forward to your story in *Planet*. Barnie returned mine the other day. He said '...we won't have published the backlog before Feb. '98. For this reason I'm having to

270

put a break on what we accept... Could you submit it again in October – or some other stories?' Nice conundrum making brake as break. Or whatever. He's wayward as Lot's wife.

Starting rain here. Another day indoors. Rene's walking the dog. She'll sleep until suppertime. It's all 'one day at a time, sweet Jesus'.

So long for now then

Ron

2000-2004

326 Mumbles Road
West Cross

21.3.01

Dear Dai,

Many thanks for the two pieces [essays on Rhys Davies and Shirley Bassey] – bubbling, marvellous, you should do a book of such reflections. The glimpse of lost bosky Celtica to counterpoint the mongrelled streets of his own Wales – alas, I am not going to Australia again to claim credit for such phrases – just the right amount of cutting edge. (They are still talking about my boxing lectures over there!) I loved the sentiment. Davies' mother, however, wasn't too far from Glanffrwd's Llanwynno, chapel country mores and the gentility of the farmhouse, I guess.

Politics: his parents surely would have felt Welsh-speaking chapel people and colliers wouldn't have struck on their own, that this was the work of immigrant firebrands (Forest of Dean) with nothing to lose. The family politics would be determined by the weight of debt – every night Mam turned over the pages of the ledger and thought, firebrands don't save and pay up. All grocers, even the humble went down to the warehouses in Cardiff on Thursdays – early closing and met at places like Spillers where they were given refreshment, forming a little liberal school, according to my grandfather, where ideas were exchanged. Sometimes, wearing straw hats they went on the paddler to Weston. John Griffiths, late Communist BBC producer whose father had a backstreet shop in Mountain Ash in the 20s confirmed this. The very act of becoming a shopkeeper separated them and formed a bond with others terrified of debts. They formed a bond, helping each other, my grandfather would send a whole cheese to the tiny shop above Heath Crescent where the owner was tubercular – this was because his credit was going, I suspect, but it was marked by his wife on the book to be repaid. I went up there once with a message, looked very rosy cheeked in a nice red jersey and the shopkeeper, Cyril, must have been having a bad day, because he looked at me and I saw tears. He must've thought he didn't have very long to go, and he didn't. Who would have thought I would be in a terminal ward in Tonteg with six colliers 18 years later, earning my 5% honorary dust as they all died before Xmas! My grandmother was always saying, if you give credit to one, where do you stop? But years later I met people who used to relate my grandfather's good deeds performed unknown to his wife! The great fear was of the workhouse, a phrase constantly on the lips of elderly people before the war. I have never seen historians make enough of this, especially Welsh speakers who had watched the immigrants succumb first.

But the crucial point you make is – Rhys' growing consciousness of his own sexuality as different from the public aspect of the Rhondda life... became his insightful window etc. This is a very acute observation exactly paralleled in the life of Thomas Mann – it's a point I want to develop somewhere. It's nothing to do with geography or being Welsh. What you say about his knowledge of the alleys and by-ways is also very pertinent and something we all share – we could never forget it and he is included because we had seen into hearths other than our own. This seems to be the unique valleys experience.

The dust diseases, of course, like the attitudes to them, lasted until well into the 50s and the miners who died in my ward blasted the coal board for the cruelty of the compo tests. Piece work and high wages for those who drove mechanical coal cutters and took risks by not wearing masks were another frequently discussed subject. I may be wrong, but I got the impression that commercial companies had a lot to do with operating or servicing these machines. Many men were offered jobs in S. Africa as drivers, but they suffered the fastest.

The Bassey piece is also sparkling. I missed teaching her in Splott but I knew the Portmanmoor Rd and another famous coloured family, the Innocents, a champion boxer and an architect who was one of Dave Burgess' partners. You've done everything except sing HONEY HONEY –

273

DON'T STOP in this, but you didn't mention hammer toes (hers!) Excellent though.

Now, lastly, a plea. You said on the phone, what I would like you to do for your lecture [Annual Rhys Davies Lecture, University of Glamorgan] is this... And I've quite forgotten and don't really know what to do yet. Would you be a pal and tell me what you think I should concentrate on? I don't want to concentrate entirely on the valleys but on all my Welsh favourites. The truth is, I'm not really confident outside my own experience and haven't found a theme yet. What could it be?

This will be my last lecture I'm sure and I want it to be a success but need to be guided onto the box until under starter's orders.

Ever

Al

326 Mumbles Road

West Cross

Swansea

26/3/01

Dear Dai,

As for the lecture – mine – I am still confused – I don't want to go outside my own experience and want to confine myself to short stories. Actual sources of my own short stories v. difficult, don't know really, except it's a bit of this one, a bit of that, a lot of me! No, what I really want to talk about are the birds that sung to me – If I can find a posh way of titling and saying that and talking about half a dozen writers, Rhys Davies, Alun Lewis, Geraint Goodwin and a few others and state at the outset where I am coming from, also the 2 wars. It sounds very C– at the moment – I want a theme and no doubt something will come over lunch when we can manage it. I'm relying on you to keep me out of trouble, squire! Incidentally re the conference on The Valleys – very few people in Merthyr/ Aberdare/Ponty would have thought of themselves as coming from The Valleys until the 1960s surely? The idea!

So let's have a yarn as soon as you can make it.

Yours in sport

Al

326 Mumbles Road

West Cross

Swansea

19/8/01

Dear Dai,

...your pamphlet ['Out of the People: A Century in Labour' The Welsh Political Archive Lecture for 2000, published well after the Assembly Election in 2001] greatly enjoyed and much food for thought. What you point out is v. important it seems to me. Bevan was quite right – the culture which flowed in and around labour activism – abstract ideas to which experience provides a reference. Hence Jack London and H.G. Wells' early novels like Kipps – Mr Polly were all identifiable heroes to which people could relate. I think this is underestimated also surely the whole climate even in the dark days was internationalist – not just the Marxists and politicians – but influence of popular mags/returned soldiers of the 1918, then film. My grandmother's favourite film – SHE MARRIED HER BOSS! It's a society that was miraculously given to ideas and British ideas were not thought malign – witness nationalist idiots now.

Also, quote from Gwynedd Jones [former Professor of Welsh History at Aberystwyth] – 'breath-taking confidence' absolutely right and taking over the role of the aristocracy. Point not made often is mingling of country-folk with townies – the absolutely marvellous skills of Victorian mechanics – gas, electric, water mains, machinery etc – all seem to make life better – all adding to confidence of minor traders. The men who sold bacon slicers or overhead wires leading to office tills were a new confident breed – there were so many excellent efficient *things*, none of them made originally in Wales so it was Sheffield, Manchester, London that the good *things* came from. All this helped dampen parochialism – how could you feel parochial wearing a straw hat on the paddler to Weston and coming back with a ton of clotted cream!

Your major point is people somehow becoming the audience – the passive audience.

Myself, I think the weariness after the war to be general and in Wales, no less than anywhere else, but by this time there was a huge drain to England surely – teachers etc, many of whom were to have a gutful of Labour council nepotism which was widespread and the resentments of newly returned ex-servicemen from '46-60 were common. No one has ever found figures for the brain drain – the number of people leaving Pontypridd County School to work elsewhere, massive in my experience, but wholly uncharted.

What happened next is well known to you, the emergence of a Welsh-speaking middle class employed by the state for the most part which ballooned – they were for the most part not opposed since their demands for Welsh language education not thought to be political and where they stood in elections they were often high quality candidates of integrity compared to cliché spouting log-rollers. There was a sentimental resistance to oppose them by those with some Welsh in the memory. The resentment felt against the BBC in Wales, for example, was mostly to do with TV although Sir David Llewellyn the Tory MP overstated his case, in allegation of bias. However, the recruitment for these institutions was biased, hence sons of the manse gibes and it was not until last 10 years that there suddenly seemed to be a wholesale movement which felt strong enough to openly flaunt its exclusivity and separateness. Devolution was tinder to it and the amount of exposure of Welsh nats unique.

You are quite right, bad history makes bad politics and Kinnock is right about loss of democratic contact – how else would poverty be somehow equated almost exclusively to drugs/delinquency and neighbourhood? Your para on bread and butter policies absolutely right but Labour is somehow equated with a tired past – we vote labour instead of – *not* for something anymore. The danger is the Welsh middle class will become still more effective super-scroungers and run things, more and more things. Culturally, this affects only a few but they are there. A South African communist once told me the first signs of the seriousness of apartheid and its followers were when they got the blacks out of the centre of the city, out of jobs like lift attendants so that the cities were secure! It's true now in broadcasting but not effective because of dullness!

I liked Des Barry's book [the novel *Chivalry of Crime* centres on the bandit guerrilla Jesse James] and learned about the effects of civil war which were new to me.

I don't know the painting 'Running Away with the Hairdresser' [Kevin Sinnott's painting in National Museum of Wales]. Not my bugger!

Ever

Al

326 Mumbles Road

West Cross

Swansea

8.10.01

Dear Dai

First of all, my thanks for all the chores you had to do with my lecture. I didn't mean you to bother yourself with the spelling, God forgive me, but all your comments are much appreciated and your enthusiasm revitalises me, as ever. I've touched it up a bit (as they say) and hope it will do on the night. I mentioned Leonora Brito but I've only really read one story of hers which I liked very much. I generally despair of the situation here as far as writers are concerned, the magazines are awful and I don't really have any conversations with anybody about anything, alas. However, this will probably be my last appearance, as Wee Georgie Wood used to say, thanks to you.

I wish I saw more of you, but I expect you are, as you say, bushed into committees, God help. I have been sleeping downstairs and pissing into a bucket for five weeks, and so fingers crossed. All the weight I lost I've now put back on again and I've missed half a summer on various people's boats. Still, everybody else is suffering with operations, cancers, tumours, being or not being joined up, and after-effects. Also deaths. A Ponty story knocked me cold this week. An ex-girl friend, a nurse who I remember being very worried about having to wear black stockings on her first time in uniform, despite me saying I'd help her on with them – rang up and said her daughter had written the commentary to a child's book on Joseph Herman's paintings, and there was to be a launch in the Glyn Vivian and would I go etc. Yes, I did, and there saw her friend, Jane the ex Stipendiary's daughter who occupied two houses on Tyfica. We had a really old chin wag, all seventy-two now, too fat for sardines as I pointed out, and when I got home I thought I would give John, a third neighbour, a ring. His mother left me the Ty Mawr painting, remember. His wife who is very County, played squash for Glam and virtually brought up by her Llandaff nanny etc, answered. I chatted and said I'd met two old neighbours (unknown to her) and then realising I wanted to speak to her husband, said, 'He's dead. Died in July, Alzheimer's, just like his mother who died last year.'

She said she couldn't have let me know, couldn't find my address etc, then went on to talk about the people who came to the funeral, really the remnants of the Hopkin

Morgans whose grandfather virtually ruled Pontypridd up to the First World War. That was the pattern, back-street bakehouse on the Graig, then the money made from land deals and pit investment, then Tyfica Road (!) (Bronwydd originally), then two daughters in Roedean, Trevor, the judge (County School) another Tb, then all left. She said the remaining Hopkin Morgans have all married coloureds! Nobody we know is left in Wales etc. Incredible, to sit down at home and think about them all, and their children, and John's public school friends, young subalterns in uniform both killed in Korea, and the end of a dynasty. It affected me for hours, made me feel I haven't written the half of it, and it's too late now. I suppose, if you knew, you could go the length of Tyfica Road, or any road and uncover similar histories but you only have very few personal starting points. Felt very mortal after all this.

I've been reading Ed Wilson's diaries again, he was the boy for family histories, his angina attacks coinciding with mine at the same age, except I don't seem to get the tempers with my third wife! But he is very good on his drinking.

All the best,

Al

Dear Dai,

Thanks for your letter and the District Commissioner's Report which I will come to presently. I'm on a diet – eleven bananas today! – because my blood pressure is all over the shop and I'm taking it regularly and have to report to the quack next month. Also, I've attended three funerals of close friends in the last seven weeks, all my drinking mates and the last funeral, a go-as-you-please Gershwin affair in the Crem got on my goat with Andrew Vicari, the mad Arab painter, failing to read his own notes and, in all, a modern shambles. I want Marines resting on arms reversed, shots fired, football hymns and women with big black hats and fishnet stockings, please. I suppose it's age that makes me look down my nose at so many people, but then your letter, even your bad news, has reminded me, we do have many things in common, including a revulsion of the attitudes and mumbo-jumbo in the Stephen Knight piece.

He has some good points but has a foreigner's lack of perception about Glamorgan, heavily influenced by the Nat point of view which must be current in the Uni of Wales English departments. They take a kind of Kikuyu witch doctor's perspective, rolling the bones and saying, 'This is where my people went wrong, B'wana!' And there's a kind of underlying arrogance that makes most of us coolies! They simply don't understand historical perspectives, even what happened at any given time. And the elitist language, God help us! He's right when he says Gwyn [Thomas] was a free spirit eluding the grasp of the deacons, that was a common phenomenon, there's also the brute fact of obtaining work. The Welsh language and Welsh speakers in the main never gave anybody work (until today!). Most change came from outside and with it skills, feats of engineering, confidence, profit etc. Etc. As you have described again and again, and Gwyn like Ron was born in the wrong end of it when everything went bust. Ron used to revel in the old photograph of his parents dressed to kill on a day out just before the First War. They had a boon time, his generation didn't. Then again, your man makes no reference to the devastation caused by the First War inside people's heads. It broke many people, especially those who had lost children. It wasn't just that they lost their reward for faith and propriety, but that confidence went. One historian I read said that many of the men who came home swore that they would never call anybody 'Sir' again, such was the shock and bitterness and everything else. And this permeated industrial Wales, I'm sure. When I say, obtaining work, it applies to writers too. Caradoc Evans was delighted to write for *Titbits*, could only find a publisher in London, as did Rhys Davies (whom Gwyn never met surely?). Gwyn had to go to London like us all, and while later they exploited him and he exploited himself for *Punch* and so on, it was the combined pressure of being an entertainer, a public personage (egged on by TV) and generally being removed from the source of his material, his own people, that caused the web to get thinner and thinner. Then there was Oxford. Gwyn told Ken Tynan that he bitterly regretted going there. Perhaps because it was too removed for him and he found himself lost as a consequence.

The piece is full of things you want to take issue with. Like, 'No one I know has written about fiction with a first person plural focaliser'... Bollucks. There were a host of people like Erich Maria Remarque in his first world war novel who took it upon themselves to represent a generation, a platoon etc. And then again Gwyn as a playwright – he had a very poor ear which was why he couldn't write dialogue for a variety of characters and his radio plays had a poor audience reaction for this reason, and a lack of tension, ie what happens next seldom matters. He would never have been the Arthur Miller of Wales nor would he have made 'peace with his Welsh language familial demons'. Christ, he knew a creep when he saw one. As for a 'modern critical language that is actually appropriate to his situation' what's wrong with common sense, a knowledge of history and a desire to enlighten, not show off? This is what annoys me most of all, the Knights of this world seek something new, some idea, some fad and reapply it in order to draw attention to themselves and their cleverness, not to enlighten or offer a new insight, the true function of scholarship. Not a word, notice, about Gwyn's compassion, not a single quotation, nor his eye for detail when he could discipline himself as in Oscar. I'm afraid if Prof Knight sent his piece to Dr Richards, he would have had a curt, 'See me' written on the bottom when I would adjourn to the Greyhound and not turn up!

I think I am going to stop taking these Anglo-Welsh magazines, I still have a few stories in them from time to time, but there's so much in them that irritates me. There seems to be an industry now and they almost exist for uncreative work really, rather than the real stuff. The short stories are usually dreadful. The critics don't seem to belong to the world anymore, only this invented Wales that they are re-creating (in Canton?) I dunno. I've just finished the third volume of Caro's trilogy on Johnson. I've read him for years including his book on the man who built the Verrazano Bridge in New York, and his great skill is his ability to make you see the persons involved, including the minor characters – Johnson's staff, page boys, driver etc. In the third volume he describes Johnson scratching his arse and pissing in the Senate car park – half of the people here grew up on farms, says Johnson! Then there's detail like Johnson lusting for bigger offices, better shirts and his stroke is described in the minutest detail as a novelist would. If he had to lose two stone, he would lose three, if he had to rest for an hour, he would rest for two, doubling up on the doctor's advice. He never took an action that would not advance his own career, even if that meant liberal stands – incredible. He's one of the few historians who make me want to read by torchlight under the bedclothes, as one did as a child. I can't wait for the Presidency, the last volume. Apparently, a new source for historians in the US are tax records when you can get detailed accounts of medication from bills with the result that in Hemingway's case they can itemise the tablets and somehow the drink as well. Have you read THE THIRSTY MUSE – Tom Dardis who does for Hemingway, who was munching everything. I tell you, I've learned more about heart attacks from reading Caro than the *Sunday Times* supplement.

Ever

Al

326 Mumbles Road
West Cross
Swansea

19.12.02

Dear Dai,

I send this in haste with the girl before the coach leaves – marvellous. I don't know why you've stopped doing it. I am an avid reader of biographies and the early years are always the most rewarding [AR had just read an early/abandoned draft of DS' work on Raymond Williams] and, I imagine, the most difficult if you have not experienced them yourself. You've placed him in context, geographical and historical which only you could do. You, I mean the reader, can see it, and I know the straightforward narrative is the most difficult to do – the easiest to read and yet the most difficult. I can see both schools and the relationship with the vicar, and the primary school headmaster, God bless him. They were tin gods, these people. I remember reading a log of one school which contained two entries of note.

'This a.m. a thunderbolt struck the main chimney brace and there was general confusion until I restored order!'

And the last:

'This a.m. at the conclusion of the school year, the Headmaster took his own life!'

That was in Carmarthen. Cap that. Well, you've got it all, their reading and everything but the sand tray.

The grammar school too is great, but best of all for me is the railway ethos, down to the colour of the carriages. The glamour that attached to them – like air hostesses.

285

I think you should resume immediately. If you can do the early years, the rest should be easier surely?

Some points. Harry's [Raymond Williams' father] attitude to the First War. If you had time, perhaps his experiences could be filled out from the regimental war diaries if you felt like doing it, ratio of casualties etc. Also his pacifism which must relate to this and maybe – I don't know – there was a strong pacifist movement in railway towns like Reading and Swindon, probably relating to Quakers there and there were a number of people affected by it in WW 2. I know because there were two in our chapel. There must be some info on this somewhere, perhaps the NUR.

But the best thing is that the reader can see things happening as they happen. For this reason I'm not enamoured of the preface or whatever you call it. It should be written into the text in my opinion. The thing is, nobody else could have done the first chapters like you have because you understand them so completely and that's why if it's slow, just remember, the clever buggers won't be able to get inside the place and the man. They're just manipulating ideas, not telling it as it was.

So get on, well done, and get on! I know what it is to abandon good things. I've done it for the last ten years, lacked confidence or incentive to carry on what I've started, and also, perhaps, the inability to distinguish between good and bad in my own false starts of which there are plenty. But this brings me to the deciding factor, you realise that only you can do it. Ron used to say this and he wasn't only talking about information. It's the feel of things which you do well, so well done. I've now gone back to something I abandoned years ago and I plug away at it daily and wish

I had more conviction. I hope to finish it early next year but fear I've left it too long which I don't want you to do. Honestly, it's splendid and you shouldn't hesitate.

Get on... Mush. Whatever.

Ever

Alun

326 Mumbles Road

West Cross

Swansea

Friday

Dear Dai,

I have just finished a novel I've been working on for nearly 40 years so there's hope for Raymond W. yet, and am feeling up, as they say.

Yes I know about Lloyd Davies, importantly, Wales were beating the Kiwis in the old Arms Park with bomb damage evident (I was there) when he kicked to clear the line, sliced it and a blond wing called Driver Sherratt caught it and scored, after going like the clappers. It was a memorable try and Carwyn told me that kids in W. Wales played 'Sherratt' in the playground. Davies was a talented player but very shaky all round. Hilariously, when I was researching Carwyn I spoke to his old sports master, one Gwynfil Rees, a devout Methodist. We chatted about Carwyn and he said he'd coached other internationals, namely Lloyd Davies but he was a complete rotter of a chap.

'Really?'

'Yes, I caught him with one of the maids in a cupboard behind the kitchens when I had given him the afternoon off for training. He was being intimate with her.'

'Good gracious...'

'Shagging her!'

'I see.'

'I had no time for him after that – ever.'

Bleddyn Williams told me he was his best man, and he was the only player he ever knew who was brilliant when pissed. You could never anticipate his game.

On this day I was entertained in Clifford Hopkin Morgan's house in Whitchurch and passed the bread with my fingers.

'I'm afraid that's not acceptable.'

Let's have a pint or two of weak shandy in that Llantrisant pub one night.

All the best

Al

326 Mumbles Road
SWANSEA
SA3 5AA

Friday

Dear Dai,

Many thanks for all the trouble you've taken. You've come to the same conclusion as me but in a much more flattering way! It's a strain of my writing that I always felt

I could do but never seemed to be able to manage and it has its origins in long ago. Originally, over forty years ago, I determined to write a novel by working for an hour a night, directly on to the typewriter and I made a promise with myself that there would be no going back, no revisions, and I would just go on and on until I stopped and finished. I had a stolen half ream of E. A. Arnold exam paper from Ely and I did the business for eight weeks writing every night nearly and it was hugely comic and autobiographical vaguely, except it had zany elements like the flyers and the dampers and later, a huge conspiracy to smuggle dead Chinese from a laundry in Cardiff and deposit the bodies in Lan Wood with the intention of ridiculing the police! It was all hilarious until about halfway through when after writing continuously, I got a commission to do something and ready money when we were broke. So I interrupted the flow and although I made myself go back on it, it wasn't quite the same. O'Toole read it and collapsed laughing, a film company got hold of it and there were plans which never came to anything. Then I was very successful at something else and it died the death as far as I was concerned. Then after about five years I read it again, and decided to use some of the characters like Waldo, the Stipe and Lucas Thomas' bull and got the bad idea of insuring the daughter's virginity. I wrote four chapters and then got successful again and left it. Then, last winter, I got hold of the first two chapters and after an interval of thirty years, forced myself to write every day and finish it. It went on and on and in the end, it was broken backed and I thought, I daren't do anything with this, previews reviews and a publisher on the make would get it published but it would do me harm as I was dissatisfied with it anyway. But at the back of my mind was the remote hope that something could be done with it and so I trespassed upon your time, but both Helen and I thought best to scrap it and that's the right conclusion, I'm sure. I know there are good things in it, there were better in the first book which I called CHINK A LITTLE CHINK, but that was also flawed. You can't pick up what you left long ago, partly because the humour comes from deep in the subconscious and the furniture is the furniture of youth. I remember two blokes from Ponty RFC kidding another they had bought a racehorse. They were challenged as to its racing colours and replied at once, 'Blue pin stripe'. This when a desirable suit was showing in the Fifty Shilling Tailors in the exact colours. It all goes together and it was etched in my mind and stayed there when I left and now, at my advanced age, I have to realise that I never quite brought it off when, if I hadn't written so much for the media, I might have. Still, I have no regrets really as we've survived.

Anyway, I'm really grateful to you and it's a salutary lesson as Shirley Bassey would say, 'Honey, honey, don't stop!' Well, I did, but there we are.

The other thing was, as the years went by, I began to see a little humanity in 'nephew socialism' and was aware of bizarre things like the Stipendiary, who I knew, who hated physical fitness and punished accordingly. Like us all, I feel I haven't done enough or dedicated myself enough in bleak moments when the material is so rich and the humanity so great and nothing as good has taken its place. What gets my goat with these people is, one, they don't do their homework, and two they never consider the possibility of other, preferable worlds. Worst of all, is a new strain which I think you detected in which the Welsh-speaking mafia would prefer to deal with their English middle class counterparts than us, i.e. H. Pritchard Jones and Co. Very shortly, not to be Welsh speaking will itself be vulgar as it was in the Czar's French court, and as I predicted, just as Laski [Harold Laski, intellectual guru to pre- and post-war Labour Party] defined the civil service in the Foreign Office as an aristocratic nest of singing birds, here, we have, a gymanfa of inadequates who form an elite. French was the in language in St Petersburg and it is inherent in a Welsh civil service that Welsh will have to be an essential qualification, I mean while we drift to the Steppes unless we fight our corner... [but] it is not politic to write about it in Anglo Welsh letters.

Did you read Leo Abse's account of Cardiff in *Planet* recently, very interesting re his Mother's valley loyalties and his dismissal of the Cardiff ship owners. I remember the phrase, 'Cardiff docksman' appearing in obituaries, and they were some of the meanest ship owners in creation, much of their starvation packets undocumented.

I was grateful for the O'Hara review [a John Updike piece in *New York Review of Books*]. I'll get the biog for Xmas. What Edmund Wilson says about the cruel side of social snobbery, O'Hara's preoccupation, is very pertinent I think in relation to his short stories. 'The people are all being shuffled about, hardly knowing what they are or where they are headed, but each is clutching some family tradition, some membership in a select organisation from which he tries to draw distinction...' I thought of our milkman Wyndham Mann who was very proud of being wine steward in the Merlin lodge in Ponty altho it cost him a few hundred a year. I agree with the review really, but these people don't really understand the pressures caused by population growth as in Chicago and environs, like Dreiser did, and O'Hara in Pottsville. They are very similar to our own, I think.

Well, this is turning into a lecture. But, I really want to say thanks. I shall put it to one side and think again. The dog has a weak heart, we discover, he is on diuretics as are Helen and I. The house will no doubt smell like a stable shortly.

I enclose latest *PLANET* piece. I've been too kind to the bastards once again, but more to follow. When can we meet? Will you come down, or shall I come to Cardiff?

Thanks again

Al

326 Mumbles Road
SWANSEA

19.3.04

Dear Dai,

Many thanks for asking me to unveil Ron's plaque [put up by the Rhys Davies Trust] – a pleasure. I suggest we come up to you in Barry on the morning of May 8 and leave our car there if that is OK? Then we can travel in one car.

Apropos John O'Hara. The children of the affluent middle class all went away to private schools, many out of the state altogether so that when they came home, they had the outlook of outsiders in a sense, exactly like, say,

Michael Heseltine or Geoffrey Howe whose father was the Borough coroner, later forced to resign because of some irregularity. Like Clem Thomas and Phylis Bowen's son, they went first, to prep schools at 8. There was one in Bridgend, Bryntirion, I think, with Clem throwing sheath knives around the dorm! Then they went to Blundells, or King's College, Bruton, Somerset. The interesting thing and parallel with O'Hara's observations is that when they came back they too had the patronising attitude to local events, councillors, etc. For the most part, only the Golf Club provided a home from home, and they learned to imitate the local dialect, grammatical mistakes etc, from the maids, just like toffs in London spoke, phoney cockney. They were really strangers at home, short of friends and tended to stick together, having adolescent parties when people from school came down to visit them, exactly as in O'Hara. Thus Hopkin Morgan, beginning as a baker on the Graig with a Welsh-speaking wife, sent his two daughters to Roedean and his dull son away, but his eldest went to Ponty County and became a judge. This one was much more rooted than the others, knew more people and joined in everything like amateur dramatics etc whereas the others were more isolated. It was a common phenomenon. The parents or the grandparents made their money but they wanted the children, especially the girls, removed and it was natural when Trevor Hopkin Morgan was commissioned in the first war, he had Hector Alderman, a renowned Pontypridd athlete and boxer, as his batman and later got him to give his nephew boxing lessons when home from public school. It's really all quite similar to O'Hara's terrain. The stipendiary's wife and sister, the dependants of butchers, spoke of London as

293

'Town' in the manner of Twenties flappers and the entire Welsh connection vanished. They lived in some affluence, tradesman's entrances had to be used and there were uniformed maids etc, and the Salvation Army Band played Christmas Carols outside their houses on Xmas morning, sending the bandmaster around with a book for contributions! There was a fair number of drunk doctors too, having affairs and concealed scandals. O'Hara's view of the Polish districts in the anthracite fields wasn't too far removed from many of the incomers here.

O'Hara is at his best in the short stories and one or two, early novels. There were a lot of SS but most of the novels after *A RAGE TO LIVE* are vast and sprawling and unedited, although bad as they are, compared to *SAMARRA*, I always found them interesting because, like Dreiser you could understand the forces at work in a new society. Books of Dreiser's like *SISTER CARRIE* and *JENNIE GERHARDT* could be about valley girls going to Cardiff in one way and you can see the old Protestant Lutheran values crumbling in the rapid development of society with all the immigrants etc, your field.

Listening to you on the phone, I remembered the other day talking to Kyffin Williams who was discharged from the Army with epilepsy. Goronwy Rees told him, 'Whatever you do, you must give up painting!' Kyffin never forgot that and produced to tell the tale!

The next time you see me, I'll probably be tap-dancing. Thanks again.

All the best

Al

The Tonypandy Kid

Boxing every Friday night [in the thirties] in Trealaw, the old Judge's Hall perched above Tonypandy station. Local pro, Nobby Baker fought regularly, a miniature Hercules with nonstop courage of a Pamplona bull. There were great fighters like Ginger Jones, Ammanford; Cuthbert Taylor, Merthyr; Mog Mason, Gilfach Goch; ringmaster Tommy Farr maturing through the divisions; iron man Charlie Bundy... Billy Jones Ducks from Cwmparc, Georgie Wall Williams, Hector Alderman from Pontypridd, Sammy Jones Sa-ara, Billy Nicholas, Frank and Glen Moody, the Norris brothers from Clydach Vale, Ivor Thomas, Billy Coleman, Young Dando, Ned Jones, Young Beckett, Johnny Jones, Phineas and Tommy John, Dixie Kid, Llew Edwards, Constable Ned Dixon, Ivor Haddrell, Sid Worgan, Percy Jones from Porth, Trevor Evans, Tommy Davies, Kid Jones, Shon Price, Will John Williams who turned evangelist, Joby Culverhouse, Snowy Edwards, Ivor Drew, Gypsy Daniels, Ivor Pickens, Jerry Daley, Trev Gregory. Natural fighters with the clout of Da Vinci drawings. Gladiators who furied for shillings, lusty days when every sizeable Rhondda pub had a stable of boxers. All passed into the dark.

Ron Berry, *History Is What You Live*, 1998

Tommy Farr died, aged 72, on St David's Day, 1 March 1986, timing the significant moment to the end. After 1937, the year of his legendary fight with Joe Louis in New York, it is not the case that the rest of his life was without moment or significance. There were further pre-war fights, successful in Britain, not so in America, and fame without end, along with a considerable fortune which, in the way of things with boxers, had a habit of disappearing. He had to make a comeback, after the war, in which he had been found medically unfit to serve, to combat bankruptcy and he worked, to some acclaim, as a big fight reporter for mass circulation papers. And Tommy had the deserved luck to enjoy the clichéd, but true, long and happy marriage, living out his years in Sussex. Nonetheless, his significant achievement, and his cultural locus in the history of Wales, does pivot on 1937 and on all that had led up to it.

This is the burden of all the books and articles about him. This is what the doyen of American boxing writers, A. J. Liebling, suddenly recalled when he found himself sitting next to a hefty stranger on a flight from London to Dublin to report a contest in 1955: '...the hand-stitched face, with the high cheekbones, narrow eyes and Rock of

Gibraltar chin came back to me out of the late thirties. He was Tommy Farr, the old Welsh heavyweight who went fifteen rounds with Joe Louis in 1937.' I was able to commission a full-length documentary about him by BBC Wales, sixty years after the fight in 1997. It is why, in the changing mythical Chronos of Rhondda's history, Gwyn Thomas (born 1913) wanted to write a biography of the miners' tribune, A. J. Cook from Porth, but Ron Berry (born 1920) contemplated a life of the people's tribune from Tonypandy, Tommy Farr. It would have been called 'Bred in the Bone'. No other boxer has had a musical play, Mal Pope's *The Contender* (2007), written about him and performed in New York. 1937 was the capital on which Tommy drew for the rest of his life.

And so did all of us who lived in Tonypandy in the fall-out from his fame. Tommy Farr, at a time of extreme deprivation, sucked the sweet lollipop that was Americana – crooning, swaggering and nightclubbing – but we, then and in the immediate post-war years, thereby tasted that sugar, even if at a distance. Earlier, Freddie Welsh had actively sought to create an 'American Wales'; he failed and became an American. Tommy Farr yearned to consume what was the flaunted popular culture of America; he succeeded but did not materially change, and so after 1945 he became hugely emblematic, for a generation and more, of the meaning South Wales had come to have for the wider world. And at home it was of Tommy Farr my grandfather, who had worked in Cambrian with him, mostly spoke to me, not of the riots which he had witnessed in 1910 or the communal marches of the sullenly defiant interwar years. It was Tommy Farr we pretended to be when we scrapped on the

297

coal tips above Tonypandy in the 1950s. He had never left us in spirit and never could in reality after 1937. And then one day in 1986, shortly before he died, I was the last person to interview him on radio. Before the tape began, having mentioned Tonypandy and my grandfather, I said, 'Mr Farr, when we begin, may I call you Tommy,' and he half-smiled and half-snarled down the line from Brighton: 'Call me Tommy! If you don't I'll come down the line and knock you on your arse.'

*

Tonypandy is one of those sites where public and private memories intersect. The industrial struggle around the Cambrian Combine strike, which fanned out from Clydach Vale to spawn the social rebellion encapsulated by the destruction of the town's shops in late 1910, also tied the name of Winston Churchill irrevocably to Tonypandy. The then Home Secretary did send hussars and Metropolitan police to quell the revolt in mid-Rhondda. It was remembered in Labour's crushing victory over the Churchill-led Conservatives in 1945 and nurtured as memory of its infamy in the subsequent elections of 1950 and 1951. But by then such public and collective notoriety for Tonypandy also mingled with an individual fame that was collectively cradled with a different kind of inextinguishable pride and which, with sweet irony, linked another Churchill to the township. That was the one-legged saddler from Penygraig. Job Churchill was mentor in and out of the ring to the boy who first fought for money at the age of 12 as The Tonypandy Kid and who, aged just 24, fought for the Heavyweight Championship of the world in New York City as Tommy Farr. From 1937 Tonypandy entered the public memory with a different kind of violent éclat.

The historical question is why a defeat could have such a resounding echo. The cultural answer lies deep in the connection between Thomas George Farr, born into the large family of an immigrant miner from Cork in 1913, and the industrial urban complex made up of switchback streets and stone-strewn alleys that was Penygraig to the south, Clydach Vale and Llwynypia to the north, with Tonypandy itself bisected by the coal-fouled river Rhondda, and defined, despite its thrown-together appearance, by the perpendicular and broad-shouldered bluff that was Trealaw mountain to the east. All this, and its pubs and music halls, and the gambling, street fighting escapades of its workforce of over twelve thousand miners employed in its still beckoning pits – the Cambrian Combine in Clydach Vale, the Naval and the Anthony in Penygraig, the Glamorgan and Scotch collieries at Llwynypia – were the daily sights that young Tommy would take in as he stepped out from his first home, Railway Terrace in Clydach Vale, to walk the couple of hundred yards to Tonypandy Square from where the riots had exploded down Dunraven Street in November 1910. Then favourites among the ransacked items of clothing were caps and mufflers – the uniform of the Edwardian working class – but when their Working Class Hero returned from his transatlantic expedition in 1937, the outfitters of Tonypandy displayed trilbies and ties – appurtenances of a Hollywood-enchanted generation – under the sales legend 'As worn by Tommy Farr'. Even the poverty which had entered the DNA of mid-Rhondda in the interwar years could not entirely close down the dream which he had brought back by breaking out. And none had tasted the bitterness of real poverty more than Kid Farr.

The crisis in the coal industry, which spiralled away in the immediate post-war years via national strikes and local lock-outs into full-blown economic depression, was compounded for the Farr family of four girls and four boys by the early death of their mother in 1922 and, soon thereafter, the permanent physical and psychological incapacity of their once-mighty father. Tommy was ten years old. At home the older children cooked, cleaned and mended and were dependent on the charity of their increasingly impoverished neighbours. On the streets Tommy pushed a hand-made cart selling bits and pieces from buttons and cotton to vinegar and white lime and soap. He doubled up as a delivery boy. School was soon left behind. His face and his fate were well known on the streets of Tonypandy. His destiny was inevitably seen as the pits and the brute apprenticeship of being a collier boy. He went underground in the Cambrian pit at the head of Clydach Vale, a cul-de-sac of a cwm shooting off for a few hill-entrenched miles at a right angle from Tonypandy Square.

It was the spring of 1927 and the season was the only hopeful thing in the sullen aftermath of the General Strike and lock-out of 1926. He worked at the coalface, apprenticed with a curling box to gather up the coal prised from the seams by skilled colliers, on call, up to his knees in icy water, to fill the drams with lump coal and help clear away the clod and stone, all to a price list for piecemeal labour whose inadequacy had sparked the strike of 1910-11. The talk would have still been of that, and of the betrayals of 1921 and 1926, and the selective recall of men to work at the management's whim. Since 1923 until his victimisation in 1929, the checkweigher, essentially the men's workplace representative at the colliery, had been Lewis Jones, Communist activist from Clydach Vale and, before his untimely death in 1939, author of those two sprawling epics of Rhondda life, the novels *Cwmardy* and *We Live*. From mid-Rhondda alone, twenty-two miners would within a decade volunteer as International Brigaders to fight in Spain. Three of them were from Clydach Vale, one of whom, Harry Dobson, was killed at the Ebro offensive in 1938. Arthur Horner, Communist President of the South Wales Miners' Federation since 1936, had visited the volunteers, in July 1937, in Spain. He reported back to his Executive that they quizzed him 'about the development in China, whether unemployment benefit had increased to accord with the cost of living, and many... wanted to know whether Tommy Farr would beat Joe Louis'. Neither they, nor the subject of their enquiry, would have found anything incongruous in the connected query. The Penygraig Labour Club where Farr trained and fought from the late 1920s was refurbished and officially re-opened in 1929 by Councillor Mark Harcombe of Tonypandy, the Tsar of the Rhondda Labour Party for decades to come.

When Farr trained and fought out of Slough in the mid-1930s he did so conscious that he was part of a surge of migration from the Rhondda to that light industry area, and one whose connections were still on a two-way street. He wrote openly to the Editor of the *South Wales Echo* to protest at the way his removal to Slough had apparently also removed him from the radar of Welsh journalists and promoters who claimed he had become, by the autumn of 1935, a mere try-out for better fighters:

> Just a line re your remarks in last Saturday's article... You call me a punch bag. Ask [anyone who has fought him] if I'm a punch bag. I am unlucky if anything but still undaunted. I haven't a scratch on me since I've been up in Slough. If I had the press behind me like Petersen... I would be having just as much money for my fights as they do, and fighting a lot more often. I am being pulled down, and you by making those remarks are not giving me a fair crack of the whip which is all I want. If anyone deserves to get on, it's me. I lead a clean life and do good by everybody... since I have been in Slough I have found work for sixty-three Welsh unemployed, and if you would like me to write and confirm it let me know. Would any of the big noises do it?

He may have had no scratches since he arrived in salubrious Slough but he already carried enough of them on his body, and the attendant memories to mull over, before he got there. Most of them came from the colliery not the boxing ring. There had been a minor explosion underground almost as soon as he had begun work and shards of diamond-hard coal had splintered and pitted his face and body. It was these scars and the blue indentations of coal particles below the skin which caused Joe Louis to gasp, and perhaps for the first time to wonder how easy this Welsh miner would actually be, when they stripped for the weigh-in before their own epic began. Tommy Farr had no choice but to carry Tonypandy with him wherever he went. He always regarded fighting as child's play to anyone who had had to work underground and readily said so. Exhausted and angry at a foreman's chivvying he threw his shovel down for the last time when barely sixteen and, despite the desperate need for money to help support his siblings, he never went back. And he never forgot.

He left, of course, to fight in the itinerant boxing booths of Joe Gess and with mind-numbing regularity, often three and more times a month, on the undercard of the fight-nights which were stitched into the moth-eaten fabric of coalfield life. It was 1933 before he had his first fight outside the coalfield, very unsuccessfully at Crystal Palace. He fled home to the known comfort of the scuffed and smoky small halls and pub gyms of South Wales. On flyblown handbills and in the small newsprint of challenges issued and boasts strutted, his name flickers with a legion of others scrambling to make a mark in what Gwyn Thomas, born in Porth the same year as the fighter, would soon call the 'Slaughterhouse of South Wales'. The phrase was a shorthand for mass unemployment, mass migration and the euphemistically entitled 'material deprivation' which caused rickets in the womb. From twelve years old he fought, just out of the womb of any semblance of a protective society, as Young Tommy Farr or 'Kid' Farr or Battling 'Kid' Farr or Young 'Kid' Farr, against a host of other Young Battlers and Kid Scrappers going head-to-toe for six rounds and side bets. But Tommy, no immaculate natural genius of the canvas by any means, had two advantages the others never quite had: a genetic disinclination to take a backward step and the opportunity to learn when and how to do exactly that.

The pits had given him a daily work ethic and, more brutally, in its below-ground shadowing of the bloody spots that had once framed the slugfests of such as his father, a stage to frame his ferocity. Pit fighting was often between matched pairs of colliers or their boys, the latter cajoled or more likely bullied into contests for amusement and bets when the miners gathered for their cold tea and cold snap breaks in the roadways off the coal headings. The sport was as brutally direct in name as in its nature. It was called 'in the holes', where holes about a foot or so apart were dug to the depth of a fighter's waist. The chosen contestants, maybe as many as four pairs facing off, climbed in and punched each other until one or other bloodied fighter was knocked senseless whilst still on their feet in their enclosing hole. They hit each other, Tommy Farr recalled, 'until they were virtually unconscious. I have never forgotten it.' He was, of course, good at it too:

> Those were fights [in the holes] amongst the hardest I ever had. It taught you to parry, to duck, and above all to take it. It may not have been a proper school but it did establish your courage. If you were good in the holes, you were good anywhere.

It was that 'anywhere' that he now ardently sought. He persuaded Jobey Churchill, after endless nagging and persistence, to take his 'in the holes' courage to a level of ring knowledge where he could counter-attack after he had 'taken' it. He grew in height to just over six foot and in boxing size from cruiserweight to light heavyweight by 1933, when he beat Randy Jones on points in Tonypandy to become champion of Wales at the age of twenty. Jobey Churchill could see he would never be a dynamite puncher or one able to dominate by sheer speed or intimidating bulk. His game would be to wear opponents down. To be first to engage and last to retreat.

The classic Tommy Farr performance was a non-stop left jab and right hand counters delivered from a hard-to-hit crouch as inelegant as it was effective. He learned his trade piece by piece until in 1934, emerging again from the valleys where he was chalking up victories on points in too-familiar places with all-too-familiar faces, he hit the rails once more and stumbled when he tried to move up the rankings.

Londoner Eddie Phillips beat him in Holborn and in Wandsworth. That Farr was a hard-working and determined professional was clear but his bitterness and his chippy surliness now grew, as he saw his career stall in the doldrums and older, more popular and more media-friendly boxers of good looks and fluid style, like the formerly amateur Cardiffian Jack Petersen, take the paper pounds and seemingly leave him with the penny coins. In the early winter of 1934 Tommy Farr fought in Llanelli for nothing, only his expenses. He gave the fee to the disaster fund set up for the 262 men and boys who had been killed in the Gresford mining disaster of September 1934.

1934 ended with another bang as he knocked out his opponent in Trealaw in two rounds and he opened 1935 with a one-round KO in the same place, but it would prove to be another frustrating year. In February he was defeated over 15 rounds on points by his three times nemesis Eddie Phillips, even though they fought at the Pavilion in Mountain Ash. There were reasons – notably an injured right hand – but no excuses and he had to return to the task of building a solid, though scarcely dazzling, reputation. Meanwhile, to his intense frustration he had to watch Petersen hog the limelight even though the lumbering German tank, Walter Neusel, put Jack on his backside twice. No justice for Tommy, thought and loudly protested Farr, who desperately wanted some, any, big pay nights. Then, after five straight wins from October, his fortunes perceptibly changed.

First, in January 1936, he impressively outpointed former American light-heavyweight great Tommy Loughran at the Albert Hall. Then, undefeated that year, he took the Welsh heavyweight title in an eliminator for the British title when he knocked out Jim Wilde in Swansea in September. In every sense imaginable, though by no means foreseeable as the year ended, 1937 would be Tommy Farr's year of a lifetime.

He may have sensed it coming, however slowly, just as his own formative society had patently been on a cusp of advance after a decade of defeats. In 1934 there had been a slight upswing in the coal export trade and the first small wage increase for over a decade. The struggle against company unionism in certain pits reached a new dimension that heralded the fight back to dominance of the SWMF across the coalfield and in 1935 dramatic stay-down strikes in South Wales made headline news across Britain, as did the truly total demonstrations of these stricken valleys, weekend after weekend in January and February 1935, when entire communities came out onto the streets against the Government's proposed and vindictive Unemployment Assistance regulations. They were put on hold in the face of such gargantuan protests and subsequently withdrawn. A common people's victory and the first effective popular action since 1926.

On the evening of 16 December 1935, Tommy, as a late substitute, fought and beat Rhenus de Boer in Bristol before a crowd of supporters who had travelled from Wales. They were with him again on the night of the twenty-first, five days later in Cardiff, where a Welsh XV had that afternoon signalled the re-emergence of the national game by beating the All Blacks by 13 points to 12. Tommy duly knocked out, in round four, his very own former great hero, the Pontypridd veteran Frank Moody, who had in the 1920s singlehandedly carried Welsh boxing's formerly strong reputation in the United States. That, too, had suffered. For a generation it was becoming time to move on. Tommy's own time was coming. His luck changed. And then he made his own.

The ever-evasive Jack Petersen, intermittent British heavyweight champion since 1932, had been unexpectedly beaten by the ponderous South African Ben Foord for the British and Empire title in August 1936. Although Farr was still kept out in the cold by the promoters, with Petersen refusing to meet him before he had himself been re-matched with Foord – even if in a non-title bout – fate intervened. Foord went down with influenza. Petersen took Neusel on instead, for the third and final time, and was, again, soundly beaten. He promptly retired. That was in February with Farr at ringside. In March, also at Harringay, Tommy would be inside the ring with Foord to fight for the crown. It was the beginning of the six months that defined his life and established his legend. Like South Wales itself in the late 1930s, he would come through battered but intact.

He trained this time with Job Churchill back in Penygraig, running the mountains in the morning and ending up at the Cambrian pit when night shifts ended and talk could begin. His nights were spent yarning in pubs and workingmen's clubs. Under the informal tutelage of older miners Tommy Farr had been led to music and literature. Now that he could afford a gramophone and records, he had built up his collection of Verdi and the favoured Handel. His afternoons vibrated with their music. It was, anywhere other than in this Rhondda at this time, an odd concatenation of cultures, but then, as Tommy frequently told puzzled newspapermen, he was just a faithful Sancho Panza to Jobey Churchill's Don Quixote. When it came to tilting at windmills, though, quixotic is not the ready epithet. He was readied at his athletic peak of 14 stone 7 pounds and he was meticulously prepared with a pragmatic fight plan. If necessary he would bore Foord to death. This was to be no blood and glory effort. It was a calculated retreat, maul and accumulate performance. At its end he was, at last, the Champion. Pay day beckoned.

There was, before that, the obligatory return to Tonypandy, to a civic reception: crowds in the streets, banners between houses in Clydach Vale – 'Welcome to our own hero' – and on the Square a word for the reporters which he crafted with only one audience in mind, his own. 'These people know me for what I am and what I have been... quite rightly, they expect me to be the same Tommy Farr in the sunshine as the one they helped in the shadows. There's a friendship here more priceless than a dozen championship belts.' He stopped his open-top car outside a corner sweet shop in Clydach Vale and, brandishing a white five-pound note, itself a rare sighting in those streets, he entered like a latter-day Pied Piper, surrounded by an army of children. One of them, the future actor Glyn Houston, whose brother Donald would vie with Richard Burton and Stanley Baker for post-war fame, remembers him shouting over their heads· 'The sweets are on the Champ!' as he slapped the note on the counter. After he had beaten the dangerous and glamorous Max Baer the next month, he told these same Tonypandy kids: 'Call me Tommy and we shall be pals. Call me mister and we are going to have a few rounds.'

He had needed twelve to win on points in April against a bemused Baer. It only took him three to knock out, sensationally and in front of the Nazi ambassador Von Ribbentrop, the conqueror of Petersen, Walter Neusel, in June. It had only taken him three months, and eleven years of preparation, to become an overnight star. He revelled in the attention of newspapers and newsreels. Tonypandy was coupled with his name. In Britain in the late 1930s there was no doubt what that place name signified from its past. Or what it had struggled to bring about for the future. Tommy Farr was an early harbinger of the confident post-war Welfare State culture, with a Labour Cabinet and Government positively bristling with ex-miners from South Wales: Nye Bevan, Jim Griffiths, Ness Edwards, George Hall, Arthur Jenkins, and from 1947 Rhondda's Arthur Horner himself as General Secretary of the Federal National Union of Mineworkers.

Tommy Farr knew this script, implicitly, and by heart. It is precisely, therefore, what he meant when he talked across the Atlantic directly to his own deep supporters, first and immediately so, after his defeat by Joe Louis over fifteen unforgettable rounds in New York in the August of that turning point year, 1937. They had sent him a cablegram to read as he entered the ring: 'We trust you Tommy. Win or lose our faith in you remains unshaken.' Trust. Faith. Not the words normally used to drive a fighter on. But then neither was the newspaper-reported statement from a mid-Rhondda woman: 'Tommy has the spirit; we have hope.' His ring performance was, of course, his most profound and solo part in this act of communication between the fighter and his community. His crackling words were just an affirmative afterthought to that two-fisted soliloquy:

> Hello Tonypandy... I done my best... we, I, showed 'em I got plenty of guts. You know, the old Tommy Farr of old.

We, I, – as indeed they knew and exulted – had been given the unexpected chance to fight Joe Louis, the Brown Bomber from Detroit out of Alabama, only because the champion was advised by his canny handlers to avoid the former champion from 1932, the German Max Schmeling. Louis had won his world title earlier in 1937 from the Cinderella Man James Braddock, who had devastatingly beaten Max Baer in 1935. Schmeling had already knocked Louis out in a 1936 non-title bout that had derailed his seemingly unstoppable run to the top, and would have to wait until 1938 for a shot at the title, when he became yet

310

another K.O. statistic victim in Louis' unbeaten twelve-year reign as World Heavyweight Champion. In 1937 Tommy Farr was considered easier pickings and, in turn, was easily persuaded to pull out of his own next arranged fight with Max Schmeling. As it turned out they would never meet, as the Second World War interrupted all such careers. Instead, Tommy Farr travelled in style aboard the Queen Mary to New York, the place Tonypandy itself only ever saw on the screens of its four cinemas.

Newsreel film of the encounter was showing across Britain within two weeks of the night of 30 August at Yankee Stadium. It was heavily and selectively edited to show the best of Farr. It seemed to confirm the sense of radio listeners that he had been robbed of the decision after carrying the fight to Louis. That was the impression of countless thousands, and especially those gathered around the radio transmission relayed in the early hours of the morning to homes, public halls and pubs in the Rhondda. The Canadian commentator Bob Bowman raised his orgasmic speech levels in the fifteenth round to gasp how Tommy Farr was putting on a 'wonderful show'.

Indeed he was and indeed there were moments in the fight when his body punching troubled Louis but over the course of the fight there was only one winner and Farr knew it. He never claimed that he had beaten one of the greatest, the greatest Tommy always claimed, champions the sport had ever produced. Nor, consummate showman as he became, did he ever disclaim it when others raised the issue. Nor was the brave non-stop rally by Farr in the very last round the vital three minutes, though, as the last and most thrilling round, it naturally lingered in the collective memory. The crucial and revelatory round, if we wish to read the fight closely as its narrative text unfolded, was the seventh, and its established context was entirely the individual story of the Welsh fighting underdog.

For this life-defining bout Tommy Farr oozed confidence. On his dressing gown of yellow silk had been stitched the fiery red Welsh dragon which Freddie Welsh had worn on his trunks in 1914 when he became the world's lightweight champion. Now, at the end of a first round in which Tommy Farr had beaten Joe Louis to the punch and moved his left jab in and out of the champion's face, he had turned to Job Churchill and said 'Job, I can box better than Louis, and I'll take him places he's not been before.'

Halfway through the contest it was Tommy Farr who was forced back to the places he had been before – the holes. Joe Louis opened the seventh with straight jabs and then unleashed his trademark left hooks, three in a row, to spin the Welshman around. The attack on a blood-spattered Farr, to face and body, big right hand pile-drivers clustering in behind classic hooks, left the Kid from Tonypandy clutching the ropes to stop his legs buckling under him. When he ducked he was only ducking into more trouble.

This is how Joe Louis' opponents invariably ended – bewildered, shell shocked, toppling and then prostrate. Only Tommy Farr, squinting through cut-to-ribbon eyelids, did not fall. He found his corner. He had been in the holes again. And he came out, fast and grinning and aggressive, for the eighth. It had been decided. He would not go down. And, in the only sense that now matters, he never has.

*

His ashes were placed in his parents' grave in Trealaw
cemetery. It faces back across the valley to Tonypandy.
Abidingly so, as in the collective memory of Tommy Farr
the Tonypandy Kid.

Crossing Borders

The late summer of 1986 seemed such an anticlimax after the heat and misconceived passion of 1984 and then the slow after-burn of 1985, with the Miners' Strike, ended in a cold March that year, a distant historical ember. Whatever the rights and wrongs of both the tactics and the strategy of the strike, once it had lurched into the inexorable grip of a community struggle there was nothing to do but support its bravery on the ground whilst deploring its leadership at almost all levels of engagement. That had been my private view, expressed in the face of some hostile comment, even from friends, from the beginning. At its end the need to build again on the moral and value systems on which those communities, especially in South Wales, had drawn in the struggle, almost as an act of self-justification to shore up political and union bankruptcy, now seemed to be an overwhelming necessity as we confronted inevitable and long-term economic depredation, and an allied social destruction. For what was clear to those coming together hesitantly again in the ruins of a working-class society that had once created and was now quite bereft of meaningful institutions, was that a tempered intelligence after the heat of this fever was crucial. An intelligence, too, that left no doubt of its stance on one side of the continuing class divide. One such voice belonged, as had long been sensed, to Raymond Williams. And he belonged to us.

He had retired as Professor of Drama from Cambridge in 1983 and had come to spend more and more time in Wales radiating out from his base in Craswall, a remote hamlet settlement in a narrow valley below the Hay Bluff. His stone-walled cottage, an old dwelling opened up with picture windows and simply but effectively refurbished inside, was his writerly bolt-hole situated halfway between Pandy, his boyhood home, and Hay-on-Wye. Technically, it was in England. Emotionally, it was, for him, Wales, but borderland for all that. I had seen quite a lot of him since the mid-1970s, conversation and trust growing deeper each time, though the famous cogitation on his part was all too necessarily there to calm down the whippersnapper enthusiasm with which I tended to shower each meeting.

As my eventual biography of 2008, *Raymond Williams: A Warrior's Tale*, would reveal, to the surprise of most and the consternation of many, his most abiding effort, passion, and self-directed ambition, had been for the writing of fiction throughout his working life. In 1986, there were only five published novels to note but in the 1950s he had written several more complete and unpublished ones, with fragments and plot lines scattered about his papers. It was an unwelcome combination of

316

imaginative writing and Welsh subject matter which never, for this side of him, won many admirers east of the Offa's Dyke which literally marched through his home village. Yet here it was towards the last as it had been in his beginning. In 1984 he had broken off from longer time-scaled projects to write a novel that was impelled, in the immediate sense, by the contemporary Miners' Strike but whose origins and rhythms lay further back in the dubious personal morality he had observed, and detested, amongst sections of the British Left. It was, and remains, a book whose schematic narrative flow deliberately masks the slower currents of dubiety and complexity it is intended to convey.

At Raymond's request *Loyalties* was launched in Wales. I had helped him with some research for it and now acted as chair/interlocutor for him in packed meetings in Cardiff and Swansea. After its moment he returned to the historical novel sequence upon which he, with Joy Williams as researcher, had been engaged and which Joy would publish after his death in 1988 as the two volume *People of the Black Mountains* in 1989 and 1990. These were his obsessions; place, people and generational experience and how to represent all these in fictive writing that did not distance them by abstraction from their conjoined individual and collective existence. I think he had long felt the same way about how he himself was 'read' and perceived, so that when his former student and colleague, Terry Eagleton, proposed a book of essays – the traditional farewell Festschrift – in the departed Professor's honour, he had asked that his own 'Welsh dimension' was neither forgotten nor marginalised, and had suggested that I be invited to write a new essay for the book. Terry had subsequently contacted me, and so it was in August 1986 that, accompanied by Kim Howells, the NUM's prominent press officer in South Wales during the Strike, whom Raymond had known when Kim was resident in Cambridge, I made my way to Craswall for an afternoon of structured interview, beer, cheese and political free-for-all.

Kim took notes and I wrote my essay that autumn as 'Relating to Wales'. *Raymond Williams: Critical Perspectives*, edited by Terry Eagleton, with his own nuanced Introduction, and a further ten essays by other hands, duly appeared, but only in 1989, a year after Raymond's death. By then I had been invited by Joy Williams to become her husband's biographer. She was invariably helpful to me in that task which, I regret, her own death in 1998 did not allow her to see completed. There had been many revelations and pitfalls along the way as I wrote, in the last analysis, a biographical study whose weight of material led me to structure a book on the making of Raymond Williams to 1961 and the start of his greater fame as a public figure, in a way that, in my view and by evidenced argument, showed how his relationship to his own society of upbringing underlay his later meaning or significance.

Writing a biography imposes professional obligations. They should override personal attachments or dislike and, certainly, the otherwise unfounded speculation of what is ill-informed or misconceived without evidential material. Much of the latter had come Raymond's way both in his life and in some biographical work quickly thrown together after his death. In particular Fred Inglis had managed, in his *Raymond Williams* (1995), to mangle factual information, distort actual evidence, invent at will, misname and misplace, whilst pronouncing, ever so humbly as he claimed in a clotted prose, that his subject was spattered with the mud of bad faith in personal matters and, horror of horrors, insufficiently grateful for his formative Cambridge education; and worse, foolishly sentimental about his overstated and overrated Welsh roots. Oh, and the fiction wasn't up to much either. I am more than content to let my own published treatment be measured against such a fanciful gallimaufry but perhaps where I could have said more, critically and analytically, in a book that was purposefully biography-driven, is in the detail of the manner in which his writing of fiction and his sense of being Welsh were so intertwined, disentangled and then tied together again. Further, that it was fiction about Wales by himself, but also from Wales by others, around which much of his wider thinking and writing spun.

There remains, it seems, a need to translate Raymond Williams for those who still think they can read his imaginative prose in English as if it was indeed English in its content and reach.

*

On 5 May 1957, Raymond Williams, then a Staff Tutor for the Oxford Extra Mural Delegacy, who had been based in east Sussex since 1946, received a handwritten postcard from F.W. Bateson, Fellow of Corpus Christi, Oxford, and founder editor of *Essays in Criticism*, the

'Quarterly Journal of Literary Criticism', which had consciously replaced the gap left by F.R. Leavis' *Scrutiny* after its demise in 1953. It was a very Oxonian moment. First the praise and the mock-horror: 'You have done Hoggart – and *EIC* – proud. It's sad that my three best reviewers (D. Davie, F. Kermode, R. Williams – order alphabetical, not on merit) are all non-Oxford!' And then, via a few editorial quibbles, an avuncular editorial put-down: 'Your final conclusion – back to the realistic novel! – I'm not touching at the end of a barge pole. Tut, tut. Yours Freddy.'

Yet, when Raymond Williams' long review of Richard Hoggart's *The Uses of Literacy* appeared in October 1957, the 'conclusion' was still there. In fact, it was for Williams the most telling point of his review and an implicit justification of the work he had been undertaking for over a decade. That work would appear to the wider world to be, on its triumphant publication in 1958, the critical and cultural study he had finished in 1956 as *Culture and Society*.

That was, however, only one facet of an intellectual endeavour which he consistently saw as integrated work. To make it whole required the imaginative fiction he had been writing, and failing to publish, since the Second World War's end. In his review, gently chiding Hoggart for a 'confusion of forms' (sociological analysis allied to anecdotal evidence), Williams wished that his cultural doppelganger had written either an 'autobiography or a novel' which, 'even if unsuccessful would have been an offering in relevant terms... to the world he has experienced'. For Williams this meant the 'imaginative creation' of 'figures... set... in a theme'. His insistent

320

conclusion, one so puzzlingly outmoded to Bateson, was both disingenuous because it was what he had himself been attempting unseen and a cri-de-coeur because, in 1957, he was still a year and more away from the completion of the novel, *Border Country*, which, when published in 1960, would make his own imaginative and thematic linkage crystal clear. He wrote:

> I am not blaming Hoggart for this variety [of form], but since the condition is general, I am trying to insist on the distinctions we shall all have to make, if the voice of this generation is to come clear and true. We are suffering, obviously from the decay and disrepute of the realistic novel, which for our purposes (since we are, and know ourselves to be, individuals *within* a society) ought clearly to be revived. Sound critical work can be done; sound social observation and analysis of ideas. Yet I do not see how, in the end, this particular world of fact and feeling can be adequately mediated, except in these more traditionally imaginative terms. Of course it cannot be George Eliot again, nor even Lawrence, though the roots are in both. But there, I think, is the direction, and there, under the fashionable lightness of parody and caricature, this solemn, earnest, heavy voice that one hears, at the crises, in Hoggart, is a voice to listen to and to welcome.

It was, of course, his own voice for which he was preparing his readers. A year before the publication of his first novel he had analysed what he considered to be the 'great tradition' of realism in the English novel – dating it precisely as a critical term from 1856 – and its contemporary lapse into the merely personal, the knowingly parodic and the deliberately sensational. The article, which he reprinted in *The Long Revolution* in 1961, came out as 'Realism and the Contemporary Novel' in the American *Partisan Review* in 1959. Williams, in accord with the view he expressed then that creativity was about change and the tensions it caused, refined and reworked over the decades his sense of what 'realism' in the novel was, but here, in 1959, he is explicit about what the 'highest realism' entails. He did not doubt its difficulty in practice. He had been working at it throughout the 1950s and its abstraction, for him, came after the event of 'creative discovery':

In the highest realism, society is seen in fundamentally personal terms, and persons, through relationships, in fundamentally social terms. The integration... is not to be achieved by an act of will. If it comes at all, it is a creative discovery... any new realism will be different from the tradition, and will comprehend the discoveries in personal realism which are the main twentieth-century achievement... When we thought we had only to open our eyes to see a common world, we could suppose that realism was a simple recording process, from which any deviation was voluntary. We know now that we literally create the world we see, and that this human creation – a discovery of how we can live in the material world we inhabit – is necessarily dynamic and active; the old static realism of the passive observer is merely a hardened convention. When it was first discovered that man lives through his perceptual world, which is a human interpretation of the material world outside him, this was thought to be a basis for the rejection of realism; only a personal vision was possible. But art is more than perception; it is a particular kind of active response, and a part of all human communication. Reality, in our terms, is that which human beings make common, by work or language... realism, in the sense that I am offering [is] this living tension, achieved in a communicable form. Whether this is seen as a problem of the individual in society, or as a problem of the offered description and the known description, the creative challenge is similar... a continual achievement of balance... It is certain that any effort to achieve a contemporary balance will be complex and difficult, but the effort is necessary, a new realism is necessary, if we are to remain creative.

Border Country will achieve that rounded maturity of perspective on which Raymond Williams based his 'realistic novel' by foregrounding the history of settlement which follows on the arrival of railway signalman Harry Price and his wife Ellen to the village of Glynmawr just after the First World War. The published novel will bring us the story of the upbringing and education of their son, Matthew, or 'Will', but most of the agonising of adolescence and a conjoined removal of the boy from his class and community – via Cambridge, marriage and the Second World War – will be ultimately edited out of the successive versions to which it had once been central. Instead readers will only ever encounter an adult Matthew who has only reluctantly accepted his own necessary physical and social removal by virtue of his steadfast personal and cultural attachment to the class and community still present in the life (and through the death) of his father. *Border Country* is an immense achievement in our fiction and as much for its formal properties as for its content of argument and life story. If the General Strike episode of 1926 is epiphanic so too are the insistent, yet subtle, references to red earth, black water and a whole palette of colours, of light and of shade, with which Williams picks out the mood of the times of his people. Williams' voyage towards that satisfying completion was, in part, one of trial and error as he emphasised one thing at the expense of another – a passage of time, his own generation against the preceding one – until he discovered he could not tell of the crisis that was a general condition until he stepped out of the frame to look back at the pre-origins of his own Odyssey. To discover that resource for his fictional work he had to find the sources, private and public, that would, though by no means straightforwardly, lead him to *Border Country*.

Raymond Williams' 'inquisitors' for that volume of interviews-cum-autobiography *Politics and Letters* in 1979 looked at the chronological date line with which he had supplied them and surmised from it the long gestation of *Border Country*. They put it to him that: 'Looking at your biographical dates, it seems that between 1947 and 1960 you wrote something like seven successive versions of *Border Country*.' Williams did not demur. Indeed in 1966 he had come to the same conclusion when writing an autobiographical sketch for an American volume on

Mid-Century Authors: 'In 1946 I started again on the unpublished novel, and it went through about seven re-writings until it was finally published, now in a wholly different form, as *Border Country* in 1960.' The Chronology in *Politics and Letters* appears to confirm this:

1947 Wrote *Brynllwyd* (first version of *Border Country*)
1949 Wrote second version of *Brynllwyd*
1951 Wrote *Village on the Border* (revision of *Brynllwyd*)
1952 Rewrote *Village on the Border*
1954 *Village on the Border* rewritten as *Border Village*
1957 *Border Village* rewritten as *Border Country*
1958 Rewrote *Border Country* (publ. 1960)

And that indeed makes seven versions. However, as we will see below, this was a compression of the actual process of writing and a titular simplification that was the post hoc explanation he chose to give. In one of the Notebooks he was keeping for himself from the late 1950s he wrote a sequence entitled *Dates* to cover the sections of his life, in one-liners of births, deaths and events since '1921 Born 31 August'. The versions of the novel annotated in this earlier recall are not as clear cut:

46-47 Writing *Brynllwyd*
52/3 Writing *A Map of Treason*
54 Writing *Brynllwyd*
[*Between Two Worlds* is crossed out here]
55 Writing *Between Two Worlds*
Jan 57 Writing *Border Village*
Aut/Win 58 Finish writing of *Border Country*
Dec 60 *Border Country* published

In the private Notebook, then, though the trajectory is somewhat curtailed, the named stations to his final destination were more accurately remembered. Nonetheless this is still an author's teleological direction finder. Where Williams had actually stopped and started is bypassed. The detailed why and tortuous wherefore of the composition was, after 1960 and the universal acclaim for *Border Country*, subsumed by him into general reflections on the difficulties of form with which he had been confronted as he attempted to move both beyond the realism of novels 'shaped within a bourgeois world' and away from 'the separated novel about the working-class community, which became a kind of regional form':

> The early versions of *Border Country* were continuous with these kinds of writing... Then I gradually realised that with the degree of change after 1945 the problem was to find a fictional form that would allow the description both of the internally seen working-class community and of a movement of people, still feeling their family and political connections, out of it... The new forms of the fifties, to which many writers quickly turned, were usually versions of the novel of escape, which one part of Lawrence had prepared... They lacked any sense of the continuity of working-class life, which does not cease just because one individual moves out of it, but which also itself changes internally... what interested me most... was a continuing tension, with very complicated emotions and relationships running through it, between two different worlds that needed to be rejoined.

The resolution of this technical problem of form actually followed on the sundering in life of what remained of a close tangible connection. Straightforwardly, Raymond Williams finally completed his novel when his father died in March 1958. Even then there would be revision, editing and rewriting before that novel's blend of narrative, flashback, memory and consciousness would deliver the form which allowed Raymond Williams to imagine his 'figures... set in a theme'. The penultimate title of the novel, as late as 1958, was indeed *A Common Theme* and the process of writing since 1946 had been less sequential and more sectoral as Williams bound and unravelled and rebound the successive threads of the whole. The date lines he had later devised merely glossed over the pain of the life experience and the struggle of the imaginative writing.

It had begun, as he said, in 1946 when, graduated from both Army service and his Cambridge degree, he set out to write fiction about a working-class boy educated out of the social class into which he had born in the Welsh *border country*. This is the story of David West from the village of Bwlch in the 'foothills of the Black Range' and of his life immediately before and after the Second World War. The emotional pulse of the tale centres on his return with his English-born, middle-class wife, Mary, and the impossibility of securing again all the roots of his life. What remains extant is an intense prose narrative in which figures of family and friends flit across the shadows thrown by David West's psychological musings. It is the beginning of Williams' attempt to derive personal meaning from his located experience but it pays scant attention to that location's own preceding and ongoing meaning. He hacked away at physical description of that local world and spun out dialogue between David West and his wife or his pre-war friends that might serve to explain the social condition that was here being personalised. But in these beginnings there could not yet be the endings that would explain the journey to himself.

The early attempt is more in line with the short stories he had been writing since the end of the 1930s and into his undergraduate years. These were low key, and occasionally low comedy, tales of village life mostly written in a deadpan naturalistic style. His other stories, from the 1940s, were more complex and emotionally charged accounts of ordinary lives teetering on the edge of nervous instability.

He had two volumes in mind, one of which he envisaged as a Welsh volume. It was to this proposed collection that he had appended the longer piece of writing from 1946 though it was not, as yet, called *Brynllwyd*. These lengthy fragments, three of them dating from late 1945 into 1946, pirouetted around the emotional adjustment required for their protagonist, David West, whose disarray has been triggered by his cultural and hence psychological dislocation. Williams grouped them together, still with a long short story rather than a novel in mind, as 'Black Water', set to be the 20,000 word opening sequence of the Welsh volume of stories he thought of as *Mother Chapel*. But his ambition for the opening or ongoing work – sandwiched as it was by a number of other writing forays, both critical and fictive – grew insistently, as the work papers for 1948 reveal.

He kept, as he would consistently, the physical setting

and the strains of generational tension exaggerated to the point of crisis by educational removal but the panorama now widened. The surviving work papers are difficult to interpret in their fragmented state as pencil and ink drafts, notepaper scraps of thoughts and schemes, of lists of names and places, alongside extended narrative passages some of which are crossed out in his hand, some making it to typescript, others scrawled over with sequences of numbered episodes, diagrammatically and blocked-out transpositions from the times of day to his characters' actions and motives. Nor are they dated, though the use of pencil, green ink corrections and the paper used – sometimes flimsy, sometimes the back of Oxford University Delegacy sheets – can be tied in, from comparison with other extant manuscript, to the years 1946 to 1949 with some accuracy.

We can see, too, as he moves towards the first significant forerunner of *Border Country* – his *Brynllwyd* of 1950 – what he chooses, or is forced, to abandon. The most extraordinary projection can be found on a sheet that takes us furthest from his later insistence (or was it belief by then?) that all his early drafts were 'continuous' with an established 'regional form' of the working-class novel.

The one-page sketch of a novel to which he did not give a title but which he estimated at 90,000 words over four sequences is more emphatically, and explicitly in his outline, 'symbolic' in 'content' than it was doggedly 'realistic' in its eventual outcome. And we can date this page to the summer of 1946 because it is written on the back of a University of Cambridge Appointments Board notice of advertisement for the posts of seven lecturers – including one in English – at the Gordon Memorial College in Khartoum with a closing date of 17 June 1946. Raymond Williams did not apply but on the back of the cyclostyled sheet he dreamed of:

The Valley: St. David (Chapel)
The Augustines (Abbey)
Father Ignatius (monastery)

and of them as

ruins: a continual history as religious sanctuaries.

The incompatibility of the ideal both with its practitioners (fleshly weakness) and with the inhabitants (social interference).

The references are to the actual religious settlements in and around what he would refer to in the completed *Brynllwyd* typescript as 'Priests' Valley'. The pointer is to the ruin of Llanthony, past which the Afon Honddu flows towards the plain, and to a more recent religious settlement which greatly intrigued him. This was the Abbey built further up the valley at Capel-y-Ffin by Father Ignatius, a former Victorian businessman from Birmingham who felt he was called by God to establish a new monastic order. That, too, was a ruin by the time of Williams' birth though briefly run as an artists' commune from 1924 to 1927 by the sculptor Eric Gill. The novel was to have been begun by the (failed) idealism of religion and ended by the failure of 'J and wife' who have returned in the post-war period to live and bring up a child in this remote isolation: 'The final conflict is resolved in the same

terms as those of David, the Augustinians, and Ignatius.'
All of which would have meant that the Valley was to be
flooded for a dam in whose rushing waters 'J' dreams that
his own body floats away.

If that was the symbolism which he felt there was much
'need to define', the realism lay in the 'same alignment of
forces, socially', before and after the War, as they grouped
around support for, or opposition to, the building of a dam
that would be bigger than the existing 'reservoir at the
head of the valley'. He was to have shown the clash of
interests between hill farmers, gentry and incoming
communities of settlers, religious and pacifist, against the
requirements of those of the plain who lived and worked
rather than merely resided. Bitterly, since this was taken
from his actual experience of water schemes for villages
like Pandy from the 1930s to the 1950s, on his plan he
jotted down the observation: 'All the water piped away to
a town. Countryside only used for such conveniences –
water, tourism. The scheme for a larger dam, below the
Abbey. Water for the villages of the plain '

It was a rumbling undercurrent of discontent
throughout his youth and a cause of considerable content
for the dying Harry Price in *Border Country* when
Glynmawr is finally put on a mains water supply. What
had happened before this was precisely as his projected
novel would have had it, though the actual geographical
location of the scheme of the Abertillery and District
Water Board had been a precipitous valley to the east,
Grwyne Fawr, after which he would name *Brynllwyd*'s
fictional town, Abergrwyne, until it finally metamorph-
osed into *Border Country*'s Gwenton. The great dam
constructed in Grwyne Fawr, with its stone quarried

locally, between 1911 and 1928, piped the water away from its source in the Black Mountains to the populous districts in the eastern mining valleys around Abertillery – some 70,000 people. A smaller covered reservoir supplied Abergavenny's population of some 10,000 people from 1932. Outlying Pandy and the cluster of satellite villages made do with the wells and springs dug on and piped for communal use from higher agricultural land. Readers of Raymond Williams will know the use and vital importance of the freshly tarred water butts outside his characters' homes.

The symbolic continuum across all his versions of *Border Country* lies in water more than anything else. It is through a close fine rain that Matthew Price begins to trudge, 'as a stranger', when he sets out to walk home from Gwenton station to Glynmawr on his father's final illness until Morgan Rosser picks him up. It is into the river Honddu that the young Matthew, Will as he is known, inexplicably throws the book he has won as a prize in Sunday School and which, with no reprimand, his father Harry retrieves by wading into the stream. And it is to the measurable precision of ice cubes that Matthew forlornly compares his research into the actual fluidity of population movement into the industrial valleys of the nineteenth century: 'But it is a temperature I can't really maintain... it's a change of substance, as it must also have been for them when they left their villages.'

Water is a marker of boundaries: between life and death, exile and return: Wales and England. It does not have the same properties – encompassing and circular – of air. So it does not signify for *Border Country* in the same fashion as the bees that swarm and are gathered in by the entire Price family beating on tins or in the manner in which Harry can, at the novel's end, observe homing pigeons scatter and wheel above the signal box as he says goodbye to the Cambridge-bound son who will also need to find his own way home. But we are born from water into air and it is water not air that can carry all, including human life, away. It is literally how he will start and end the next version when, in 1949, he turned again, after writing fiction in different genres, to the issue of his own story.

This time, in 1949, the structure he plots is more akin to scaffolding than to sketching individuated ladders. The single summarising sheet is succinct, confident of its own hinterland. He headed it:

Marches
a novel by
R.W. Ridyear

and gave it seven chapters:

1. Brynllwyd
2. Tributary
3. The Valley
4. Tribute
5. Watershed
6. Cottages
7. Three Encounters

The final typescript would be more than 700 pages long and only two things had changed from the original scheme: Chapter 1 was now to be 'George and Ellen' and the whole had become *Brynllwyd*. It moves forward relentlessly and chronologically from the birth of Martin Price who is Jim at home, as was Raymond Williams himself, to Martin's departure to university and the subsequent crises, familial and emotive, which crowd in on him in the early war years. Familiar territory subsequently but here mapped in a different fashion. There are no flashbacks, of course, since neither the passing of time nor the growing consciousness of the writer had yet arrived at their deep source of potency. Nor is there anything other than fleeting reference to the ultimately defining General Strike. It is on Martin that we concentrate – his growth, his friendships, his love affairs, his anger towards both George and Ellen – until the novel stops abruptly at its most enigmatic moment. It is indeed an ending prefigured by the novel's opening pages:

From the gray ridge the storm beat, high wind in the darkness, lashing the valley with violent rain. The bare mountain trees, bent habitually to the winds, were driven yet closer to the dripping bracken and the glistening items of the burned heather. The sheep ponds filled, and in every hollow new pools were forming. Already, after eight hours of storm, new streams oozed through the bracken to find a course through the close trees of the hillside. In the small, westward valley, where the Blackwater ran impetuously over the loose stone bed, water ran from all sides to swell the river to flood, while above its tree-lined course the great curtain of rain drove headlong through the steep valley sides. In the main valley the Blackwater was already in flood, and the mill-wheel groaned above the race of water. Above the mill, in a loose fold of the hills, the unnamed brook, that ran through the group of houses which took its name from the gray ridge, swelled in a curdle of brown and white water towards flood point.

Out of this storm and flood comes the birth that night of the Martin Price who in the novel's closing pages, dressed in the uniform of the Home Guard in uncanny resemblance to the shape of his father, immerses himself in the black water:

He stepped slowly forward, and released his weight. His body fell stiffly, his face striking the water and submerging. He strove to keep his body still, to drift face downward in the water. He was carried, slowly, by the slow current, towards the vault of the bridge.

He extended his fingers, slowly, deliberately. His clothes hung heavy on his body; he could feel the water over his skin.

He waited, on the slow current. With the water over his body, he struck forward, as he had intended. He kicked out hard, and reached his hands forward to the bank. The fingers touched earth, and grass. He felt forward, drawing his body from the water. He lay, at last, face downward on the bank, his arms still extended above him.

...He shivered, slightly, in the cold air, and, at the involuntary movement, stood again, and looked out over the dark valley. He could see the screened lights of the station, and the line of the hill above Llanvetherine. He could see the line of peak and rockfall of the Holy Mountain, and westward, the dark scarp of Black Darren. He looked lower, over the road from Priests' Valley, over the darkness where the culvert stood, over the faint line of trees at the mouth of the lane. His eyes moved up from the line of trees, following the lane. There were early lights in the Brynllwyd houses, under the silence of the gray ridge.

The novel, along with all other offerings under the name of R.W. Ridyear down to 1951, was rejected. Raymond Williams reformulated it, over 1952 and 1953, as the story of Paul Ramsay who shared almost the same origins and outline story as Martin/Jim but who, after Cambridge and War, took the conflict Williams still felt within himself – the path of a directed life from an alienated starting point – into a different realm. This time, in *Map of Treason*, Ramsay becomes Paul Bergel, drawing on his mother's Austrian origins, and leads a double-life as an agent intent on uncovering truth about himself and his circle. It is a labyrinthine pathway into pre-war Communist attachment and post-war disaffection and the thread is held by the semi-detached working-class intellectual, Ramsay. In the light of *Border Country* this Ramsay prequel, firmly located in the recognisable environs Williams kept in his head as Brynllwyd, was an imagined world too far. It imposed a pattern of meaning readily understood in early 1950s Britain but one too brittle in its formulaic drawing together of character and event to convince. He was still searching for a meaning to emerge from a life, his own, which he felt, as the mid-1950s smothered the wider aspirations of his generation of progressive intellectuals, increasingly to be patternless.

If *Brynllwyd* was for two-thirds of its length, before it slipped away into a febrile psychodrama, the triumphant narrative of realism about his own life's direction for which he was reaching, its shift over 1954 into 1955 was towards a perspective that lost its solipsism as it looked steadily at the historical framework whose generalities had been made specific in the lives of his parents' generation. In particular, in 1954, he quizzed his father for memories of the 1926 dispute occasioned by the lock-out of the British mining workforce. He was, at this time, also loosely associated with leading members of the Communist Party Historians' Group, such future luminaries as Christopher Hill, John Saville, E.P. Thompson and Eric Hobsbawm, who had founded the pioneering journal *Past and Present* in 1952 and who would spearhead the intellectual break out from Communist Party orthodoxy after 1956. Some of the flavour of the thinking discernible about the coming scholarly discipline of 'Labour History' now seeps into his fiction in long passages of dialogue in the novel of 400 typescript pages he will finish, in the spring of 1955, as *Between Two Worlds*.

This completed typescript is the missing link between *Brynllwyd* and *Border Village*, the re-write of 1957, and, in its own terms, a hitherto unknown masterpiece in the canon of English language fiction from Wales. The locus is virtually the same – Glynmawr appears for the first time as an extended village below the 'gray ridge' of Brynllwyd and within which there is a cluster of houses known as Bwlch – and so are the main protagonists, a railway signalman and his wife and child: this time Arthur

337

Meredith, Ellen and John. The shift of focus, however, is significant enough to bring in a brother-in-law, Alec Lewis, who is from the Rhymney Valley and so into whose territory, the South Wales Valleys on strike, the novelist can enter directly. We also have David Mortimer, of Arthur's age and a sensitive member of the gentry class whose adult but distanced overview of the general struggle allows Raymond Williams the perspective which the exiled Matthew Price can finally bring to bear in *Border Country*.

This, then, is a novel exclusively devoted to the momentous events that divided a nation and united a class between May and December 1926. As a result the adult characters are involved more centre stage and the inner turmoils of a boy growing from 1926 to 1939 simply do not figure. Observation or even memory is no help to the novelist here and the imagined world cannot be restricted to the grander symbolism of distant societies or universals of birth and death. Details and the relationships called into human shape by such specifics become the stuff of that fictional imagining. More graphically than before, therefore, Williams creates a series of interlocking acquaintances, with subsequent tensions, across the class border because it is a way of introducing the 'other' – which he had by education become – into the contemporary situation by way of a Lawrentian device of cross-class friendship. To move directly inside that adult working-class post-war world at the active peak of its consciousness required, however, more than the localised memory of his father, important as that was for framing the actual class solidarity shown by the Pandy stationmaster and reflected here in this fiction and subsequently in *Border Country*.

'Imagination', Williams said in 1978 'has a history', and he went on to recall how:

'I could not get *Border Country* right until it was more than the past – the period of my childhood. I had to make that past present in the fully independent and contemporary figure of a father: in fact, as it turned out, two fathers, to make an inherited choice of directions actual. But then this was eventually accessible because it was a lived past. For the sequence during the General Strike I could go to my father's memories and to the documents he had kept.'

Now it is feasible that his father had kept a cache of ephemera – newspapers, leaflets, posters, union telegrams – which could have formed the basis of the various communications between the National Union of Railwaymen and the branches, instructions from the Great Western Railway to their employees and to some associated newspaper articles, all of which are quoted verbatim and at length in the General Strike sequences of his fiction. But if this is so, none survived as extant material in his papers. Nor would he have found ready expositions of 1926 available to him in 1954/55: in particular Julian Symons' able survey *The General Strike* did not appear until 1956 and contains no relevant documentary material. What Raymond Williams seems to have done, perhaps on the advice of his historian friends, is to have traced and read a remarkable compendium on the ideas and the actuality of a 'General' or revolutionary strike from Chartism in the 1840s in Britain through to

1930, and across the world. This was the American historian W.H. Crook's *The General Strike: A Study of Labour's Tragic Weapon in Theory and Practice*, published in 1931 and never reprinted.

Confirmation of Williams' use of Crook is entirely textual but, nonetheless, convincing. The telegrams from the NUR General Secretary C.T. Cramp to union members and the GWR appeals and instructions to their employees as they appear in slightly edited form in *Border Country* are all in Crook in their entirety and appear in the same sequential order. In addition the harsh terms and conditions laid down by the employers for re-engaged railwaymen are taken from one of the appendices to Crook's volume. These are the actual material things which allowed him 'to invent episodes which activated the sequence', not least the driven leadership of union activist Morgan Rosser who, in defiance of the turn of events as the nine days wind down, pins his own notice on the signal box:

> Railwaymen's response magnificent. Take no notice of lying wireless propaganda. All grades have acted well. But, apart from white collar men, signalmen have worst record. Though out of 4,843 on the GWR, only 384 still at work. Keep this up and we shall win.
>   Morgan Rosser
>   Branch Sec, Glynmawr

Such an exact figure is precisely that, an exact number taken from Crook though, for the novel's purpose and Rosser's characterisation, given a crucially different interpretation from that of the historian, who had concluded:

> Among the most vital men on the railroads the signalmen were, perhaps, the weakest in their strike showing. On the Great Western road [sic], as early as May 5, 384 signalmen were available, this number increasing to 584 on the 12th of the month, out of a total force of 4,843.

The novel ends with a discussion between Arthur Meredith and David Mortimer about what the latter has learned from his deep reading in labour history during the months of the miners' defiance to their defeat in December 1926 and how, patchily it seems but with another kind of defiance, this relates to the direct experience from life of the still resolute Meredith. It was a kind of signing off of the historical record of the fictional father by the novelist son. The sources were now squarely his own, acknowledged and ingested. He proposed other fiction for publication at this stage, especially the radically different *The Grasshoppers*, but he let *Between Two Worlds* wait in its place until he could see how it fitted into the longer scheme, or multi-layered saga, he had been plotting, and part writing, since 1946. This concept was a dead end but one which was still enticing him in late 1956 when *Culture and Society* was virtually completed.

In fact, under the generic title of *Between Two Worlds* he was contemplating three or possibly four novels that would unify his variegated spate of fiction and much more widely so than the first newly intended novel of the projected sequence. The first volume was to be an amalgamation of *Brynllwyd* and *Between Two Worlds* itself. It was now to be entitled *Border Marches*, a novel which would have kept the chapters from *Brynllwyd* that took us to 1939 but with the General Strike episode from *Between Two Worlds* spliced in.

Crucially, the forays to Cambridge and marriage into a gentry family were to be cut from the very early work, as was the empathy with the David Mortimer story in the later one. In a nutshell, dealings in fiction with people from the 'Big House' were being rejected as the story about his own people had grown in size and in confidence of its own significance in its own terms. This, in turn, meant that it did not have to derive importance from a fictional connection with the actual location of the struggle's epicentre in the mining valleys. That would now be understood rather than underlined.

It remained, then, to open his story afresh with the signalman and his wife, Harry and Ellen, coming to settle and work in Brynllwyd in the Glynmawr valley in order for the narrative to lead into 1926 and on out to the boy's training for departure. The inter-war years complete and QED. Or so he thought when he completed *Border Village* in April 1957 and, this time, showed it, as it was, to his publisher.

Border Village, though again not published, certainly works more fluently than either of the blockbusters from which it was quarried. He had found his central text. But it was only at the expense of tidying up the individual anguish he had not resolved in *Brynllwyd* and the social power of 'close living', even in a general crisis, which is so profoundly realised in *Between Two Worlds*. He had, in effect, written both his own later experience and his matured consciousness of that life's journey completely out of the odyssey of his text. To this stage in the novel's evolution most of its transformative periods had been about additions, of idea and of story, even if they were subsequently shortened. In 1958, however, it was an actual loss, the death of his father, which acted to clear the way to the resolution that had evaded him for so long.

He toyed with, and then rejected, the thought of writing a 'final' novel in the proposed sequence as *End of Exile*. The interrogative mark he sometimes placed at the title's end signalled his unease at the very concept. He settled instead for *A Common Theme* and planned it over 75,000 words as the return of Matthew Price, an academic historian married to but separated from Sheila/Susan, to visit his father who is in the throes of his last illness. The hinterland of the son here swells to be equal to the tale of the father which dominates the first of the novels which he is still envisaging as late as spring 1958 as:

Border Village:	1920-1938
Our Lords the Moon and the Sun:	1938-1945
The Grasshoppers:	1945-1955
A Common Theme:	1957-1958

By the time the writing of this last was under way his father had died. Its completion in the summer of 1958 is one that accepts the separation of lives and the impossibility of reuniting destinies. Then, in the autumn and winter of 1958, he made a last effort to undo this by interleaving the texts of his bookend novels so that the text begins, as did all the drafts of *A Common Theme*, with

Matthew's return journey across the border by train and moves on through this late recapture of home to Harry and Ellen's story as in *Border Village*, before concluding with Matthew's departure to London and his apparently still broken, emotional and intellectual settlement. It was a kind of balance though one that seemed to prefigure a further dimension of Matthew's life – how could it not? – after the rupture which Harry's death underlined.

If his publisher, Chatto and Windus, had not quibbled further, the first novel to be published by their hot young cultural critic, Raymond Williams, would have been known as *A Common Theme*. It would, in the detailed stories of its own final form, have guarded Williams somewhat against the later accusations he faced about neglect of or lack of interest in conditions of sexuality and emotional damage within the social framework of the lives of his characters. It would, too, have made the sense of community he invokes elsewhere as a transferable value less open to charges of romanticism. The Matthew Price of *A Common Theme* is a divided and remains a divisive character. He is dislocated. He is deracinated. He is separated from his wife. The title of the novel yearns for a link that is shown to be, at best, bruised or, at worst, snapped. The publisher thought it all too redolent of autobiography and, in detail, too overbalanced in its long, but late, introduction into the novel of the story of Matthew's family of London wife and sons. Whether he agreed with the critique or not, Williams was anxious above all now for publication. In 1959 he revised once more.

Perhaps it is significant that at this time a chart, in Williams' own hand, showing the genealogy of his characters as named in the published novel, now indicates the birth of 'Matthew (Will) Price' in 1920 but has no ongoing lines to marriage and other births. The Matthew Price who runs for a bus in the opening pages of *Border Country* and returns home to his suburban London home at the novel's end shares scarcely a dozen pages with his wife and their two boys. The novel, set before us at last in December 1960, as *Border Country*, is a novel about living through change and about the consciousness of that change being absorbed in order to allow lives to continue without diminution either of past realities or of future growth. It is a novel, as its author would say, about the 'record of this actual growth'. It has, in its pared-down form, a unity of place no matter which lines – of rail, road, telephonic, educational – run in and out of it. It holds fast to the human necessity of community. But it makes that contentious word as vital through its lived and revealed complexity as the terminology of Culture itself with which Williams had been simultaneously engaged over the decade. He had found what he meant by 'realism' in fiction and he scarcely moved away from it, showing generational change in and through location over and across lives and minds, in the novels that he wrote right up to his death in 1988. He was still returning to the themes and echoes common to 'Black Water' and *Brynllwyd*, and on, through *The Fight for Manod* to the unpublished fragment called *Manod* and the projected *The Brothers*, to the epic of historical time and close experience published posthumously as *People of the Black Mountains*: a title and a theme redolent with what was, early and late, the obsession of his imagination.

*

He had discovered then, a voice appropriate to both his critical and imaginative writing in the late 1950s. He handed his final version of *Culture and Society* to his publisher Chatto and Windus in 1956, and within less than a year he followed it up with a loosely bound typescript of the novel he was calling, in June 1957, *Border Village*. His letter of explanation said:

> With this I return to what I have always wanted to do in fiction, back into my own mainstream. It's about people and a way of life I know intimately, where the living is and always must be more important than any ideas about it.
>
> ...I've had a good many tries at this and really think at last I have got this first stage right.

Except, of course, it was not at all the 'first stage' – more, as we have noted, like the fifth or sixth since he had begun trying to write of the intersection of his own 'life experience' and those buffeting, swirling, shaping wider forces – of education, social change, economic disruption, cultural imperatives – that he felt, certainly from 1945, left him as both a typical product of such forces, and a tongue-tied one at that. The last epithet, given the wordy Williams of fact *and* myth, may sound odd until we reflect how the orthodoxies of late 1940s academicism stifled the kind of connections – in ideas, thoughts, research, *style* – that he would eventually need to voice in order to end the dreary Rankean history and timid scholasticism that let the baubles of social history and the insights of imaginative writing glitter and play but *not* influence academic work. That is, of course, why the

346

contrarian Leavis excited him. Why he tried in the 1940s for an activism – crazy and romantic – between textual criticism and political activism, and why, in my view, he sank into an almost catatonic despair (at least in a public sense) by the mid-1950s before the breakthrough we now celebrate as *Culture and Society* (1958) and *The Long Revolution* (1961).

He had come to understand, or perhaps to believe is a better sense of it, that his personal condition of intellectual debility after 1945 was indeed the outcome of a more general condition. The fiction since it was a personal projection was being written, in one form or another, anyway but, by the mid-1950s, he kept stubbing his mind against the realisation that to somehow tell his individuated story as an individual's life (almost all the early attempts, from *Blackwater* to *Brynllwyd* and on to the early 1950s do this) was to reduce rather than augment the story. The problem, in the orthodox canon of English Fiction, was that he had few ready models to follow or learn from – Lawrence and Hardy, yes, but with a fatalism and/or escapism he could not share; 1930s proletarian writing, too blunt and too cheer-leading or too doomladen to address his felt complexities – and so the resolution of his struggles of form and style, in successive unpublished novels, became, from the early 1950s when the first fiction stalled, also a search for a general grasp or description of the issues attendant upon Britain's emergence as the first industrial or massively urbanised society. If he could forge the links of Industry and Democracy and Class into the chain of Culture he might, just might, see the latter as, to quote from *Culture and Society*, 'a process, not a conclusion [since] the arguments which can be grouped under its heading do not point to any inevitable action or affiliation... They define... approaches... It is left for us to decide which, if any, we shall take up, that will not turn in our hands.'

The argument, then, is that *Culture and Society*, not as he put it in 1986 a book he any longer entirely recognised as his own, was a work-out, a training, an experimental laboratory with dead tissues and extracted cerebrums for the active serum he wanted to vaccinate into contemporary society – something that would indeed not 'turn in our hands'. And so fall from human grasp and social control.

His strange fate, as writer and intellectual, is the one that has haunted his overall reputation ever since. Namely that he succeeds, in his numerous critical and analytical works from *Culture and Society* onwards, in setting out the proper agenda and, in some instances, in laying down templates for such scholarly work to endure, but that his fevered 'Conclusion' to *Culture and Society* is just that, all too personal and upfront, whilst his measured fiction is, again, all too precisely that: wooden and worthy rather than spirited and expressively replete with subjective individual possibilities. He achieved renown, fame even, by splitting his own amoeba at precisely the time he was arguing for wholeness. Ever since it has been relatively easy to compartmentalise him, at least in his achievements, in a manner that downgrades or even denigrates the fiction. In *Border Country* he triumphantly deals with the splits in his father's actions and aims by creating the slow-living profundity of Harry Price and the quicksilver entrepreneurial, socialist-spouting Morgan Prosser. In his own life he was forced to see the formal intellectual splits he had effected as only a means to grasp two things together, so that it didn't 'turn in our hands', as a *permanent* description of himself as on the one hand a critic who had indeed grasped it, and on the other, an imaginative writer who had let it slip. Anyway, or so others have lamented, it is just not sensible or possible to do both. But what if, not only for him but for an articulation of a common experience of living, it was not a passing intellectual fancy but a forced march to a necessary articulation of a lived history?

I think I have shown in my biography of him how the writing of fiction was indisputably at the core of his desire, his effort, and ultimately his meaning, all his adult life. Clearly, differences of judgement can remain as to the relative success of those efforts and to the ultimate value of his novels, and that will require a detailed critique – already sketched by some admirers such as Tony Pinkney and some European scholars to date – which may yet see his reputation as a novelist rise. But what is not to be gainsaid is the concomitant position of such works as *Culture and Society* and *Border Country* in *his* life and in *his* intention. If we seek to understand the one we must indeed grasp the other. As is well known, in 1979 he grew frustrated at the distinctions so readily made and told his quizzers in *Politics and Letters*, where he first calls himself a 'Welsh European', that:

> ...Welsh intellectuals offer recognition of the whole range of my work... which literally none of my English... colleagues has seen a chance of making sense of...

The recognition, such as it was, need not detain us long: it was itself a cultural manifestation of the identity shifts of the 1970s within Wales which he found so refreshing in their apparent capacity to offer the possibility of change. 1979 saw the Devolution debate temporarily closed down and, via Thatcher and the destruction of 1984-85, he was dead before it limped back onto the agenda in 1997. What is really apt is the insistence he makes on putting the whole range of his work within an extended Welsh cultural continuum. And, to put it bluntly and sadly, neither that history nor its literary articulation has ever really, with the political exception of the two Thomases (R.S. and Dylan) they love to doubt, ever penetrated the English carapace of indifference. Why not? Because, and I refer to English language writing about Wales here, it is *indeed* poor stuff? Or because it is stuff about stuff that is itself a deviation of considerable proportions from the norm of English fiction? Even when the latter deals with the trials and tribulations of a class-divided society, and the individual trauma so caused, there is rarely, beyond the stasis of Class, the idea of a dynamic alternative that can be seen to have had an actual life whose existence can indeed be observed, documented and imagined.

Williams' groundbreaking book on the ideas and concepts that gathered around the greatest cultural wound in British industrial society was, of course, about *English* thinking – with a little Irish and Scottish mixed in – but his roaring chapter on the creativity, the culture if you will, behind voluntary societies and trades unions and co-operative movements and even political parties, was inspired directly by the catch-up society of industrialised Wales. By 1950, the end date of *Culture and Society*, this had become a central pillar of collectivism-in-action in British history from Robert Owen through to Keir Hardie, and 1926, and the Labour Government of 1945 with its Bevans and Griffiths and Edwards, and in the unions, its Cooks and Horners. Here, in sum, I can only assert the case for the exceptional nature of that world, particularly that of South Wales, across the broader British spectrum. It was the world in which Williams' railway-signalman father, geographically marginal but occupationally central, worked, and where the Williams family found its particular forming shape *against* other directive forces, and even individual educational exits.

Exceptionalism had been the norm when Wales, from the 1870s to the 1920s, was a forcing house for growth of all kinds. The population – unlike anywhere else in the British Isles – doubled and doubled again in the 50 years before 1914. It was a migrant *and* an immigrant society. To put it in a novel way: by 1911 there were both more English speakers *and* more Welsh speakers in Wales than ever before. And in the case of the latter, ever since. Wales created, in the space of 20 years before the First World War, the civic institutions of a National University, a National Library, the idea of a National Museum, and a National Anthem for both its National Eisteddfod and its new National Sporting Teams. Exceptionalism. By 1920 – Williams was born in 1921 – four out of five people in a population of just under three million lived in the industrial South Wales belt from the Eastern Monmouthshire Valleys to Llanelli in the west, and despite tinplate and steel, two of out three males of a workforce in excess of 250,000 worked in or on the coal mines which had bred the cross-hatch of railway lines carrying that coal which Raymond's father, in his outpost in Pandy, signalled through to England.

In short, it had become a concentrated collective society very quickly and one not flanked by influential and older gentry or infiltrated in a societal manner by the high bourgeois families of Nottinghamshire or Yorkshire or even County Durham. Its cultural DNA was a product of Welsh nonconformity and Victorian liberalism but, in its new mass guise, it moved with volatile speed into the direct action of union endeavours and independent Labour politics whilst secular voluntarism everywhere was imbricated in its self-empowerment tactics. Crucially, those tactics – strikes, riots, demonstrations, or reactive communal acts if you like – became a common strategy whose ideology was flexible but one where consciousness of the need for collective solidarity in a working-class world, one soon plunged into economic disarray, was readily apparent and, from the 1920s to the 1950s, long lasting.

Any expression of this dynamic and then depressed Wales in art, whether in literature in either language or in fine art, was, at best, etiolated and, generally, imitative of other inappropriate models of form *and* content; until, that is, a generation rooted in this society and released by education to reflect upon it emerged. Of course its lineaments can be traced through the variation of genre – melodrama, romance, epic, docu-naturalism and the like – and, warmed up in the little magazines, can still be palatably savoured, so long as it is dressed for academic dinner in the bland sauces of post-modernism and post-colonialism. I prefer the piquancy of original authorial intent – however misjudged – and the sourced ingredients of home and place.

So, we had the dogs' dinners of, say, by the late 1930s, *Cwmardy*, *We Live* and *How Green Was My Valley*. At the heart of both Lewis Jones and Richard Llewellyn is the tug and struggle of class identities within clearly defined communities. In Jones' novels, individuals, notably Len and Mary, save their communities from further depredations by personifying the leadership the community requires through the class-consciousness of the Communist Party. His novels, replete with blood martyrdom in Spain, are Salvation Novels. Richard Llewellyn, at exactly the same time, presents the angry counterclaim of the outsider, and of some insiders, to the arrogant exceptionalist claims of a specific South Wales, by universalising and mythologising his novel into the Story of the Fall. In this story individuals – Huw Morgan and his family, representing the best of the community, which is moderation and consensus – are betrayed by the worst of the community, which is the class divisiveness with which immigrants especially have infected a Welsh world. In this Betrayal Novel individual life is denied or suffocated by the tribe, and exit is the only possibility.

Which takes one startlingly enough, to Gwyn Thomas' 1949 hybrid work *All Things Betray Thee*. Now here we have a novel, much admired in 1940s America, which both generalises or universalises its names, locations and plot but which also particularises individual dilemmas concerning the possibility or efficacy or indeed morality, of leading or participating in any revolt (*aka* revolution) which cannot historically, and therefore in the novel's timeframe of the 1830s, possibly succeed. Thomas' answer here, and in different darkly comic mood elsewhere, was to counterpose both individual narration and third person objectivity with a plural voice that can only be said to be more akin to a wailing, but witty, Greek Chorus, or a Verdi blast from the Welsh National Opera which was, not entirely coincidentally perhaps, founded just as the choric novel appeared.

Raymond Williams not only knew of and read these works – Lewis Jones indeed from the 1930s – he was especially fascinated, in the late 1940s, by Gwyn Thomas, and quickly by that play for voices in a different but also plural mode, Dylan Thomas' *Under Milk Wood*. He wrote extremely sympathetically – making comparison with Joyce – about *Under Milk Wood*'s experimentation. He ended his inaugural Gwyn Jones Lecture in 1978, *The Welsh Industrial Novel*, with a paean of praise for Gwyn Thomas' novel of 1949 and he followed closely Thomas' early bravura prose and his later interventions in non-naturalistic drama with great interest. So much so that he readily agreed when I asked him to find the time to write a foreword to a reprint of *All Things Betray Thee* in 1986. This was two years before his own death and, of course, a year after the defeat of the miners' strike in 1985, to which he plangently refers in a disquisition on the trap of revolt and the inevitability of springing it. But, here, I want to quote his more panoramic view of Welsh fiction, and this from a writer, we should remember, who only wrote, in his own fiction, of the Welsh experience and who thought of himself, absolutely, as a Welsh novelist. He had signed off his challenging introduction to *All Things Betray Thee* as 'Craswall, 1986':

It is a remarkable experiment, which needs to be set not only within Gwyn Thomas' development as a writer but within the broader course of Welsh writing from the 1930s. Many forces worked to make Welsh writers of this period adopt different perspectives from most contemporary English writers whose language they now both shared and used for themselves.

First, in an unusually large number of cases – and certainly by comparison with what was most publicly happening in England – these writers were by family or upbringing or direct participation exposed to the full social crisis of poverty, depression and the disintegration of communities: exposed also to the movements that responded to these events: the positive movements of self-organisation, protest and political militancy; and those other movements, of emigration for a change of work or the different ground gained through the openings of higher education.

Secondly, in both their received tradition and their local contemporary stance, they were not persuaded by that dominant English pressure, now crude, now subtle, to leave the pain and anger and intricacy of this crisis to politicians, economists, sociologists, historians, keeping literature to what was said to be its true deep concern with private lives and private feelings. In every year since that stance was gained, Welsh writers emboldened by what their colleagues were doing have encountered the indifference or the anxious correction of the English literary establishment, and some of them, since a good harpist can play many tunes, have found ways of going round about and offering new, often consciously comic, alternatives. If the wisdom of attachment to a people was not acceptable, the wit of a lyrical semi-detachment might be, though the rhythms of other songs still hammered in the mind.

All Things Betray Thee is a monument of transition in Gwyn Thomas' writing, but it is best now seen, in wider terms, as a moment of unusual achievement. As such, if the composition of its voices is heard, it is an irreplaceable instance of a deep underlying problem in thought and feeling but also specifically in writing. The point to grasp is that shift of convention from observer to participant – the underlying movement of the story itself – which makes the harpist's history of the history at once a recognition of what that history truly is and an intricate construction of the often unforeseen and unwanted but finally inevitable connections with it, in the depths of the mind.

This is why, in this tradition, Welsh writers cannot accept the English pressure towards a fiction of private lives: not because they do not know privacy, or fail to value the flow of life at those levels that are called individual, but because they know these individuals at what is always the real level: a matter of inevitable human involvement, often disconcerting, which is at once the mode and the release of the deepest humanity of the self. This is a lesson painfully administered by the history of their own people; a lesson not to be forgotten if the most explicit pressures are distanced or temporarily removed, or while the music calls to a kind of life which everyone would prefer.

*

Collective aggregations of people for the purposes of work – essentially the bare bones of modern Wales to 1914 – *could* become communities of purpose and these commun ities *could* empower their own individual members *or* they could, via the agency of class consciousness, seek to imbue their ethical values, based on collectivities, into a wider sphere over and above individual or familial or even localised gratification. Williams' socialism, long and lasting, pirouetted around such beliefs and such contradictions even whilst the actualities of that charged, dangerous history were diminishing. For him its values would still constitute the validity of its example as experience. His theory of Culture was based on observation *and* participation. His conclusion to *Culture and Society* was a manifesto not just for the cultural studies that would come but for the practice of the novel he was finally to see published in 1960 as *Border Country*.

He was explicit in *Politics and Letters* that he did not want *his* Welsh voice, in fiction I mean, to be caricatured or pigeonholed as yet another adjective-laden blast from windy Cymru. His imaginative prose would consequently be spare in its imagery and its epithets. Some have found this too blanched of colour, though consistently in his lacquered work there is an enamelled lyricism with which he depicts natural landscape and there is, too, the subtle re-laying of metaphorical effect if we require the signs of one who does pass the usual test of being a 'natural' novelist. Further, what some critics have seen as stiff and stilted dialogue is to other ears a well-tuned rendition of how his cautious, word-wary and actual border country people did, and do, really speak, neither Welsh or English as they say, 'just us'. The pertinent point is that *Border Country* went through a number of shifts in its vocal range, notably from the individual sentimental-education narrative of *Brynllwyd* (1949-51) to the cross-class dialectic between Father and Liberal Gentry in the astonishing *Between Two Worlds* of 1955, and on to the wrestlings between generations in *Border Village* (1957), *A Common Theme* and *End of Exile* in 1957-58, before the final settlement achieved in *Border Country*.

What is constant is the need for individual liberation *into* a meaningful life. What changes as the work progressed is acceptance of the life of others and crucially of other generations. Comprehension moves beyond the framing of the Self as central. Limitations are not chafed against as boundaries which, in turn, become not fences but horizons. Resentment of village tomfoolery in the earlier drafts and a fascinated horror at the communal narcolepsy induced by eisteddfodic chanting thus give way to a feeling for choral involvement through music for which I know of no Anglo-Saxon equivalent. This is from *Between Two Worlds* in 1955:

And now it was again the turn of the choir, and the emphatic intentness returned to performers and audience, but with an obvious heightening of feeling.

The sense of commitment to the singing, even above its actual emotional power, was irresistible in its effect, while it lasted, and even beyond. To David, wholly and almost humbly attentive, it seemed less a musical than a social experience; although the singing was the form in which the living relationships expressed themselves. It was not the excitement, edged by hysteria, of a crowd; nor was it merely the exaltation, in a shared feeling, of a simple art. It seemed, in the end, to be more of an answering than an ordinary means of expression; yet an answering to something which could not be separately defined: a sense underlying the familiar categories of thinking; yet not thinking replaced by feeling, as if by an opposite; rather, in the intent and yet delighted commitment to the shared singing, an answering, not solely of pleasure, nor yet of seriousness and conscious responsibility, but an answering to the known singleness of men, in the actual terms of what it was like to live in a community. Because it was so positive, it needed no separable definition; it was less the consciousness of community than its willing, habitual and sustaining practice.

When at last the whole audience stood, with the choir, to sing their own anthem, David, standing among them, and not knowing the Welsh words yet lost, while the singing lasted, his own consciousness of the questions in which he habitually lived; lost it, however with a sudden accession of shared feeling which seemed wholly positive and reliable: the positiveness of extension into a partly unfamiliar, yet general, kind of living, which he had also felt, at times, in his meetings with Arthur Meredith. The singing excited him, physically, but he felt also that his mind was being changed, the whole basis of his thinking being extended and altered: not, however, with the discovery of new ideas, but with the discovery of the embodiment of ideas and their conversions or reconversion into practice and assent, in the way of common living.

*

Not everyday fictive fare to be sure but, for him, an emphasis on the choir because this was a reality, known and felt, that he and others experienced before they were abstracted from it by education and removal. For him a level of abstraction was required if he was to enter, in some measure, honestly back into it. In *Border Country* individuals are constrained, by their own necessary individual growth, to betray the people and places from which they came. There is no cyclical return. There is only the effort towards consciousness of the whole cultural conspectus that allows a restoration of individual balance by cherishing and championing the values of that original, nurturing community.

Border Country is a profoundly honest novel. Plain in its appearance and plain in its action. Yet with a corkscrew twist that has nothing to do with plot and everything to do with the revelation of consciousness. Matthew has to accept his exile from an unfolded history as well as a located life if the history is to be completed. Lives are released through consciousness of the connections between time and space as being the irreducible nature of human experience. Only the connections grow ever more attenuated if their complexity is not understood and shared. And the alternative is the literal diminution of all human growth.

In *Border Country* Raymond Williams strove to find fictional expression for how the silent denizens, who were mulled over as only the recipients of social change by the thinkers examined in *Culture and Society*, not only lived their own other-directed lives but also dreamed their own controlling dream, and so created their own cultural response. It is a novel that is unapologetic in its unremitting focus on working-class life in its own terms, *and* clear that these terms, in their outcomes and ramifications, are not reducible to lament, rebellion or know-nothing tribalism. It is, assuredly, today a back-lit projection more than a digitalised future but that does not compromise its centrality in the increasingly acknowledged corpus of Welsh fiction as one of its essential works. A work that will stand in one whole piece when the architectural ruins of *Culture and Society* are packed into boxes and labelled by the vultures of a profession still unwilling, or merely not able, to make the connection Williams achieved in his life and work.

At his death he left an unpublished manuscript fragment titled *Manod* but which, I believe, he intended working into a novel he intermittently called *Brothers*, and of which he wrote in a notebook:

First definition 11/86 some relation to drafts of 'The Brothers' years back but now coming up irresistibly; I haven't looked back at the earlier papers.

361

He planned and plotted time sequences and genealogies spanning the twentieth century and uniting (or dividing) families from Aberdare in the old coalfield to Gwenton (or Abergavenny) on the border. That border, between Wales and England, past and future, possibilities and hopefulness, and misunderstanding, was, as ever in his work, to be crossed and re-crossed. He put in the tentative date for completion or publication as 1990. On 26 January 1988, he died. What follows here is an extract from Chapter One of *Manod* which, he scrawled in his work book, would be 'For The Brothers'. Here Dewi Probert and his English wife Claire are driving into Wales but, lost in incessant rain on minor roads, they cross and re-cross the Severn until:

He sounded the horn suddenly.
    'There it is then.'
    'What?'
    'Wales.'
    She stared around, through the rain-misted windows.
    'I can't see any difference.'
    'Yes, but that was the border.'
    'And I didn't even notice it.'
    'You should have. It said *Croeso*. Welcome to Wales.'
    'That's only a notice.'
    'It is. It is only a notice.'
    He braked at the crossroads and then swung quickly left. She checked the name on a sign.
    'Pontafren?'
    'Yes.'

'Should I look at the map?'

'Not now, for God's sake. This is almost home country.'

'Well it isn't to me.'

He again took no notice. He was still driving fast.

'Will they signpost Manod?'

'Not until we're in it.'

'That's helpful.'

'They won't put *Croeso* up either. That's only for tourists.'

It was the place, the name, that seemed to start it. Manod. But still it was only a place, where he had once grown up, where his mother still lived. And if it was only that, why this strangeness to her; this edge of hostility, widening the ordinary distance between them? He was whistling now under his breath. His hands were moving, excitedly, on the wheel. All his earlier tiredness seemed to have dropped quite away. But he was there on his own. She was a passenger, even a stranger. She stared ahead, along the lights, at the steep high banks, covered with hazel and bracken and foxglove, all dripping with rain.

'This is real border now.'

'Real?'

'This country. This border country. Not the political line or the legal arrangements but this change in the ground.'

'Yes. I can see that.'

'You'll see the holly getting thicker as you get nearer the mountains. There, that hedge, look, did you see?'

'The road, David.'

'No, in a mile or two you'll look back to *this* like a freeway. When you get really in.'

'What happens if you meet something?'

'What do you think happens?'

'l don't think I want to think. Not going like this.'

'There's no problem. You stop. And then one of you goes back.'

'I can see you liking that.'

'No, we just learn to take turns.'

Full Circle:
Tonypandy 1910

In the late afternoon of Monday, 17 May 1965, I walked with a jaunty step out from a stone staircase that gave onto teaching rooms and accommodation for dons, onto and diagonally across Balliol's handkerchief-sized inner quad towards the lodge gates that opened up to the outside world. I was still reeling, heady with the excitement of discovery, after a particularly rumbustious tutorial on the subject of de-Christianisation – the murder of priests, the sacking of churches, the pillage of sacred property – which had marked the early years of the French Revolution. The tutorial, with a weekly essay read by one of two tutees and then discussed, but never with anything so vulgar as a mark assigned, had been scheduled, as usual, for an hour. It had rattled on for more than two, unusual even for the rather special tutor who was the forty-eight-year-old Richard Charles Cobb. His reputation, at that time, was for an unrivalled knowledge and close reading of the provincial archives of the 1790s in France.

His two-volume account of the revolution's zealous spread and social ramifications had been published in French between 1961 and 1963 as *Les Armées Révolutionnaires*. Later works in English, translucent text trailing a flamboyance of footnotes, would establish him as the transcendent French historian of his generation, hailed as such even amongst some of the notoriously coterie-ridden French. Later still, in increasingly fragmented shards of scholarship that delved obsessively into the private lives or inner torments of those caught up in events, Cobb made style and form agents of explanation and representation. He turned, naturally enough, to memoirs of places and biographical vignettes of people, from the magnificent *Second Identity* in 1969 to the elegiac collection *The End of the Line* which he completed just before his death in 1996. It would have greatly amused and somehow deeply pleased Richard that I once saw it on the shelves of a second-hand bookshop in Hay-on-Wye under the section for Steam Railways.

Richard Cobb, a wild child let loose amongst the staid and scholarly, had a unique ability to convey his obsessive enthusiasm for his brand of historical study whilst avoiding, despite his reservoir of almost unattainable knowledge, any condescension towards his pupils – as he delighted in calling us – whom he treated as equals in every human respect that mattered. That day he had exceeded even his habitual disregard of convention. After I had read my essay its judge, pacing up and down as always, and sucking on a Gauloise with slurpy gasps, thanked me as usual and turned to grin at my fellow tutee, the amiable Yorkshireman John Rhodes, who had been expected to 'do the reading' if not, this time, the writing. 'I wonder,' he said, inviting a reply, 'how then we should assess the revenge motives – personal slights, class hatred, humiliation of sons and daughters, family lore, spite, pure and impure, and so on – of these individual cases of rape and arson and killing of nuns and curés, alongside a perhaps more collective impulse, hidden and unforeseen until it erupted, then self-directed and unstoppable, of crowd behaviour. I wonder, indeed, what Rudé would say to that, eh?'

The reference was to George Rudé, the English historian whose 1959 book *The Crowd in the French Revolution* had debunked the notion that it was a Dickensian Mob, mindless and incoherent in their animal fury, which had stormed the Bastille on 14 July 1789. Instead, by employing a sophisticated analysis of trades and through individual biographies, Rudé had re-created an artisan world in which, composite as well as singular, the Crowd was shown to have both the motive and intent which suggested the dynamics of their activity together. John and I looked at each other. We knew of the book and its argument. We knew that Professor Rudé had been a close friend of Richard Cobb in the 1950s when both had worked in Paris on the 'revolution from below' with their contemporary, the stern communist Albert Soboul; all three under the magisterial aura of the legendary pater-familias Georges Lefebvre. We would learn that Cobb (b. 1917) and the older Rudé (b. 1910) had both been at Shrewsbury School and that both, though only Rudé as a committed member of the British party until 1959, had been closely involved at a personal level with the

Communist Party in France. They reeked, in person and in outlook, of the Popular Frontism of the 1930s. The Cold War had kept Rudé out of academic employment in Britain. On the wave of the success of his 1959 book George Rudé had gone to Australia to lead a highly successful career as a university teacher. In the silence that followed Cobb's post-essay question his eyes, magnified behind the thick glass of his Michael Caine spectacles, bulged in a face that seemed to be glowing with a red flush and straining above the loose collar of a white shirt pulled together by a striped and egg-stained tie, the whole sartorial effect sealed by a faded brown velvet jacket which was also too big for his pipe-cleaner frame. His face, all planed surface, from wide forehead to stretched mouth and hollowed-out cheeks, was positively twitching with anticipation. He had a habit when too excited, or maybe a little drunk, of patting down with some vigour his combed and parted lank, golden-brown hair. We sank further back into his wicker-framed armchairs and their downy blue, shot-silk cushions as he whirled about in a peculiar, hopping dance in the middle of the floor. 'What, eh, what?' he squawked in that clipped and nasal thirties public-school accent he no doubt shared with the Australian exile. We remained transfixed, and mute. But he could bear the suspense of his joke no longer and lunged across the room to a white-painted four-panelled door that led off his sitting room. He grabbed the Victorian brass knob, turned it, and with the shriek of a mischievous adolescent at a party where no responsible adults were present, he said: 'Well, let's ask the man himself, shall we?'

And out fell, almost literally so, from behind the door,

the body of fifty-five-year-old George Rudé, clutching two glasses and a bottle of Scotch to which some damage had already been done. Richard's friend George had flown in to London from Sydney that morning and arrived by train in Oxford in time for lunch, and for whatever was thereafter. Our tutor, chortling with pleasure anticipated and now created, found two more glasses and we settled back to drink whisky, discuss crowds, hear gossip about their old comrades (Rudé had told a delighted Cobb that the more structured and intentionally serious Eric Hobsbawm had proclaimed Cobb's empathetic, wilfully personal history to be 'dangerous'), denounce villains (chiefly Robespierre) and extol the eye for detail of novelists (mainly Simenon). It was all a wonder. One of many, though not all as dramatically staged, which I would experience with 'l'étonnant Cobb'.

I left elated and in need of a lungful or two of riparian Oxford's soft air. At the lodge gates I turned right past the chained ranks of bicycles outside the college's forbidding Victorian grime, all lower windows iron-barred in the ugliest façade in Oxford, then sauntered, still in my flapping signal of an Exhibitioner's gown, across the Broad to glance in the window of Blackwell's paperback shop before making my scholarly way amongst the parade of the privileged to the corner where Ellison's Department Store gave onto the Cornmarket. I was, in my second year, an Oggsford man from my Beatle crown to my inky fingertips. And as phoney as the Gatsby I had already read and was yet to understand. Around the corner then, and up towards the junction with the High with, at this time of day, more properly Oxonian people and accents amongst the strollers and shoppers. My cigarettes of affectation at the time were Sweet Afton, for their name, their Irish manufacture, and the light ochre yellow of their push-up packet. On the front was a medallion-round head and shoulders of Robbie Burns in grey-black tints, with an encircling sketch of bridge, river and trees to make the fags as pastoral as could be. They were untipped and carried no warning, only the enticement of Burns' quoted lyric.

Flow gently, Sweet Afton,
Among thy green braes
Flow gently, I'll sing thee
A song in thy praise

They had become an irresistible street prop when, with a very close school friend, Christopher Reynolds from Barry who was reading History at St John's and whose considerable literary promise would be cruelly snuffed out by his death in a car crash in 1972, I had gone, one dilatory afternoon, to the Scala to see a Louis Malle film, *Le Feu Follet*.

The 1963 Malle movie, from a 1931 novel by the right-wing fanaticist Dreiu La Rochelle who migrated to full-blown fascism before his suicide in 1945, was a loopy reverie perfect for youthful angst and existentialist melancholia. Its seductive charm, however, lay in the contemporary setting of a Paris revealed scene by meandering scene in an artful documentary style. The 'hero' is a recovering alcoholic, soon to be a suicide, who mooches around his old haunts and visits former acquaintances who once, but now no longer, held some meaning for him. Incredibly, for us, he even ignores the salvation offered by the downturned mouth and forsaken eyes of Jeanne Moreau. The suitable hangdog male lead was bleary-eyed Maurice Ronet who at one point calls in at a tabac and asks, as if it is the Holy Grail, which might be denied to him, '*Avez vous de* Sweet Afton?'

Chris had his sudden enthusiasms, then and later – once in Lancaster, watching *Casablanca* for the first time on a clapped-out, twelve-inch Bush TV set, we had to eat market-bought quail's eggs and drink Bollinger to do justice to his father's wartime memory of it; once in Swansea he left me talking to the air on the top deck of a bus puttering along as he skittered off the open platform in pursuit of a girl with whom, seen through the upstairs window, he had instantly fallen in love; once, in Morecambe, at a tatterdemalion Variety throwback Show which had only drawn us since the rubber-necked Nat Jackley and the lugubrious genius that was Max Wall somehow haunted it with their bygone presence, he refused the last bus home in order to lay siege to the dressing-room door because of a high-kicking, short-beamed dancer with a hole in her fishnets that was revealed every time she raised her right leg in the ragged chorus; once in Oxford he took a bike, not his own, that was leaning against a college wall just to ride into a glimpsed sunset and later pleaded, and was found, guilty in court of borrowing transport for the purpose of Fantasy – and so after that trip into the illuminated dark of the Scala, our drink of choice would become Pernod and our smokes, Sweet Afton.

Back on the not-so-mean streets of Oxford, Chris and I scoured the city for a tobacconist who stocked them. They

371

did not exactly fly off the shelves in the early 1960s but we finally found a specialist in a side alley and, thereafter, we lit them to the combined and addictive pungency of struck flint, smouldering cotton wick and the sharp tang of lighter fluid encased by rubber and mephitic brass. The loose-leafed tobacco in the saliva-wettened cigarette paper stuck to the lower lip and the spirals of smoke stung our eyes into Ronet-like slits. We were serious poseurs, avid to give the world our full attention. I do not recall, as we scanned backward horizons oblivious of the futuristic decade about to break – even though one of its attendant impresarios, the unlikely Physics student Howard Marks from Kenfig Hill, would soon enter Balliol as a cross between Candide and Casanova – ever discussing the future lives we might lead, creatively and intellectually, in any terms that were bound by the history of Wales. We were far too profound and prophetic for that.

The future was retro. The future was verso. The future was magic. The future was Gallic. I, for one, had no doubt as I stopped in an Oxford shop doorway that May afternoon to burn an Irish cigarette market-branded by the verse of a Scottish poet into firefly life courtesy of a Nouvelle Vague film. I walked on, abuzz with the headiness of inhaled smoke, my mind still adazzle with the mirror-bright glitter of French history into whose looking-glass world I was more than eager to step. I walked on and up the High to my destiny. Only it was not France that was waiting. It was Nemesis.

In the near distance I could see the news vendor's metal stand with the black scrawl of the day's news on the attached white paper sheet. I never bought the *Oxford Mail*, unless I wanted to see what films were on in one or other of the city's three cinemas. Local happenings were nothing to me or to the rest of a student population ingesting the University's protein for the lives-to-come. I did no more than glance, a disinterested and aloof passer-through, at the latest declaration of the inhabitants' trivia. Then I stopped, and read the sheet's headline again. It had said: Colliery Disaster South Wales – Explosion Underground. I bought a copy of the paper. I read it swiftly, shaking and alone on the crowded, indifferent street. There had been an explosion underground in the Cambrian Colliery in Clydach Vale. Thirty-one men would later be confirmed as dead. The latest tragedy in the Rhondda was a dramatic newspaper story in Oxford, and, though I would not know it for a while, a fingerpost in the direction of the historian I would have to become.

Three weeks later I stood at the open grave in Trealaw Cemetery as we buried my grandfather alongside his wife in the family grave. He had died in Llandough Hospital, Cardiff, where he had travelled for years for tests and analysis for pneumoconiosis, the lung disease of colliers, the breathlessness that led to inhalers and oxygen as the victims struggled to fill their lungs with the air that could not enter the coal-dust ravaged organs. They had finally given in and, like an abandoned colliery heading, flooded, so that he died. My mother gave permission for the lungs, what remained of them, to be dissected for any medical clues that might assist with research. I had had a telegram on the afternoon of 9 June – we still had no telephone at home – pinned to the pigeonhole marked with an S in the lodge. I ripped it open. It was written in the black capital-lettered, ticker-tape style then used, and I knew as I opened it that there would be bad news for such were the only telegrams working-class people ever sent or received: DADDAD DIED TODAY IN HOSPITAL. LOVE MAM. I had not even known he had been taken into hospital. He was seventy-seven years old. No more songs then.

The funeral was scarcely a state occasion but there was wry kitchen talk that he had, at least, lived to see the interment of Churchill in late January of that year. For us the semaphore of historical connection, however faint and personally remote, was clear. The great wartime leader could never, for us, shrug off the cloak of shame that the name Tonypandy draped over his shoulders. We wept in June. We had not mourned in January. Of course it was all too easy, given Churchill's later fame, to be transfixed by that reputational glamour as a double act with Tonypandy's fleeting notoriety in 1910. It had, after all, stuck. When Churchill's wife, Clementine, had had Graham Sutherland's 1955 portrait destroyed because it so angered the family with its disturbing slurry of oils, the speculation of some was that the painter had not so much gotten beneath the skin, as made the depicted flesh a career outcome. In post-war Britain Churchill had not, in his lifetime, sloughed off the tell-tale actions of a belligerent for whom there had, indeed, been an enemy within. Us.

At the funeral I told my cousin Robin of the only time I had been constrained to think of any of this local lore at Oxford. It had been the previous year, in 1964, when I had piped up as a chippy defender of the firm Pandy belief that Churchill had deliberately sent troops as an instrumental weapon to foil the Cambrian Combine strikers. This had happened when I attended a Balliol student society addressed by the Warden of St Antony's, an Oxford research college for International Relations and Politics. The Warden had been in post since 1948. He was to be given a knighthood in 1975 as Sir William and he was already, aged 51 in 1964, a very distinguished historian of the Balkans, of wartime politics and the Axis between Hitler and Mussolini. But before all that F.W. Deakin had been one of Churchill's pre-war research assistants, freshly drawn from the aristocratic well of Christ Church, Oxford, to work on the becalmed politician's life of his ancestor, Marlborough, and the wider *History of the English Speaking Peoples*. After the Second World War, Bill Deakin returned to help the defeated Prime Minister with his *History of the Second World War* but it was what Deakin had done in the war which had made him quickly celebrated and marked out his own scholarly contributions thereafter. He had been parachuted into Yugoslavia in 1943 to make contact, as the first leader of a British mission, with Tito's Communist Partisans, who were engaged in a ferocious life-and-death struggle with the occupying German forces. Deakin concluded that the Partisans were more numerous and more reliable than their own countrymen, the royalist-inspired Chetniks, as an ally, and against all the odds had persuaded Churchill the same. It was, and had remained, a worrisome call for many close to Churchill as Tito, with a further British mission of greater strength assisting him in the war, emerged after 1945 as head of a Communist, albeit quickly maverick, state. Deakin, a lifelong friend and summer guest of Tito in the vein of Aneurin Bevan, was fascinating on all of this, in an urbane and witty

375

manner that allowed undergraduates to think themselves privy to the intricacies of tortuous public events and personal relationships.

Naturally, Churchill's name had flitted across the canvas of his talk as both intensely human as well as epically heroic. Perhaps it was trying to emphasise the former before an audience whose broad sympathy he must have sensed that caused him, out of nowhere it had seemed, to refer to the calumnies that had occasionally been visited upon the Great Man's name even when, as at 'Tonee Pandee' as he elongated it, the Liberal and reform-minded Home Secretary, friend of the radical Welshman, David Lloyd George, had attempted to calm an unnecessarily inflamed local situation by sending in unarmed Metropolitan Police. From that day to this, Deakin intoned, slander had followed.

In the discussion that followed I put aside my nineteen-year-old nervousness to offer the testimony I had learned at home and now took for granted. I had no facts to hand of course, only the reiterated mantra of Troops, Troops, Troops. F.W. Deakin was good manners personified. My own historical claims might have had the proletarian thrust of my grandfather's version, given with the force of my accent behind it – I had summoned up every ounce of syllabic contempt to pronounce Tonypandy properly – but it was easily deflected by the patrician parry of intent and context. Honour sort of satisfied I could put it aside, a relic with which to remind others that there were resentments to be nurtured, though scarcely to be examined. And definitely not by me for whom the road from Tonypandy had widened out into an arc of

376

intellectual aspiration that had literature, its study and its writing, pulling me further and further away from historical work.

That trajectory could have led me anywhere. Only my marks were always set to radiate, out and in, from a fixed position. I certainly went to New York and Columbia University in 1966 both to study with the subtle moral genius of the incomparable Lionel Trilling, whom I had encountered in Balliol in 1964 when he was that year's visiting Eastman Professor, and to escape the grappling hooks of historical scholarship. In all that Wales was, for me, neither here nor there. Trouble was, it was deep in everything else I was, socially in terms of a convinced politics based around class, and morally in a more diffuse and diverse unease about how that 'politics' truly expressed that 'class'. For me the answer had become in the course of that year a sense of literature, study or practice, which had an historical well of evidence on which to draw. I did not. So I abandoned the political novels of Joseph Conrad which appeared to show me how, in exchange for the garnering of what I might show. Work on a doctoral thesis at Swansea University was a mere, but funded, excuse. In 1967 I returned home to find a way out. In fact I had taken a path that would lead me further and further in.

Osmosis can act on the bones of any historical researcher, even one who did not know what he was looking for. Like me as I sat, in the days before digital reductionism, on a high stool before a sloping desk on whose black-leather, cracked surface lay the bound and open newspapers, small printed and yellowing with age, with which I held the past of interwar Wales like water droplets running off my palms. I was looking at industrial conflict, the immense coal strikes of the early 1920s and the political whirligig of a South Wales spinning from Lib-Lab consensus to Labour domination via the hallucinatory colours of Syndicalism and Communism; but neither my eye nor my hand was steady. In every day's newspaper – those Victorian heralds of Capitalist Wales, the *Western Mail* and the more attuned *South Wales Daily News* – there were stories and incidents that captivated me. A young professional man from Swansea, learning the coal trade in Barcelona, has killed his lover's husband, a Catalan bourgeois making pesetas in Wales. A gully has overflowed in a steep-sided cwm in the Rhondda and children are swept to their death in a spate of flood-water and builders' rubbish. An international rugby match at St Helen's has been invaded by thousands without tickets, but self-given post-war rights. It is a society of suicides, infant deaths and disorder, whether drunken or not, beneath the surface. Or maybe the surface is a misnomer for this inverted state of affairs. Anyway, the compendium laid out in haphazard fashion in the newspapers, and then in other sources, began to fascinate me. I began to seek connections between the phantas-magoria of detail and the contemporaneous struggle for control through the vehicles of religion or politics or culture or family. I valued the consciousness with which this dominant working-class society palpably yearned for a level of institutional domination.

And if there was a helpful swell of social and labour historiography elsewhere that could carry a Welsh endeavour – that of mine and of others – some way along, it was chastening that there was no historiography of modern Wales that had, as yet, strayed far from the orthodoxies of economic history and the well-lit by-ways of political electioneering. I cannot say I succeeded in fulfilling my rather inchoate intellectual ambition at this time. But, at least, when published work began to appear I confessed the sin: 'This is not the book we intended to write' is the first sentence of *The Fed*, written in the late 1970s with Hywel Francis, and the next was 'It is not the complete, rounded social history of South Wales we plotted and carried in our heads for years.' 'Plotted' and 'carried' now sound to me like the words a dreamy writer of fiction might cling to rather than the more structured and dictated work of academic scholars. Yet it was indeed the case that it was against much of what the latter passed off as 'history' that I was instinctively and intellectually rebelling.

In this sense I should have chosen earlier to be an historian of the sprawling and immeasurable sea-change in peoples' lives that were the revolutionary years in France. At Balliol I had quickly sloughed off the repeat of sixth form drilling that would have been, for me anyway, entailed in further study of the Tudors and Stuarts, even under the Marxist doyen of those centuries, the genial Christopher Hill who became Master of the college in 1965. Instead I went down the disreputable route of studying American history – pre-Civil War society and politics – outside the college where the tutors were as ineffably dull as the historiography was enticing, and the revolutionary European period which I took inside Balliol with the single most important historical influence on my

379

work, Richard Cobb. There were several things that I had loved about Richard. The first was that he had called me 'Dai' when I had gone up to sit the entrance scholarship in 1962, and persisted with it ever since as if we were not just equals but friends. Secondly, to a prickly working-class boy from South Wales he was personally warm and endlessly supportive at one level and at another, like no one I had ever known, mischievously anarchic in all formal relationships and irresponsibly, wildly addicted to copious drink, malicious gossip and lust. In the company of this skeletally thin, goggle-eyed, socially inept and chaotically organised tutor, the sixties had arrived for me before they properly began (which is more like 1965 than 1960 itself when scarves, duffel coats and dimpled pints still marked out the student territory). There was a third, and most telling, thing of all, and that was that he wrote prose that was designed neither for belletrist effect nor for the clarity of reasonable argument and the edification of summary, but rather in the interest – adverbs and adjectives, plots and epiphanies – of vivifying, and thereby honouring, his often obscure subjects. Through the eyes and in the words of the pregnant, the murdered, the starved, the violent and the loved, dead or alive, he enacted what E.P. Thompson yearned for, and that is to refuse to take part, as historian-writer, in the 'enormous condescension of posterity' which so much history-writing has almost automatically implied.

But if I once wanted to follow him, and the generation of revolutionary historians he was influencing, to the archives in Marseille, into the *mairies* in Normandy and the great libraries of Paris, I was to be firmly rebuffed. I was Welsh. I should do this work in Wales. Richard was clear, and he had pointed me in the direction of David Williams in Aberystwyth with whom I shortly corresponded on a possible thesis on the Welsh '*philosophe*' Dr Richard Price, whose presence was felt, via Tom Paine, in both the American and French Revolutions; and he mentioned Gwyn A. Williams (not yet the 'Gwyn Alf' of popular embrace) with whom he had also taught during his own enjoyable and (in)glorious years in mid-1950s Aber. When I chose, even before my finals, to go to New York and dabble in more literary fields, he did not demur, though he remained convinced I would not stay there, nor return, despite the strong urgings of others who thought I was unnecessarily shunning a higher route in academe, to Oxford. In 1969 Richard came to my registry office wedding in Pontypridd. When he had taken his ocular fill of the beautiful women around him – at Aberystwyth he had admired Llanelli girls especially for their dark-eyed looks – he told me I had now 'married South Wales'. Whether he meant my wife or the place was not made clear. He was, I concede, right in both instances.

Either way, indemnifying me in my marginal intellectual pursuits as he generously claimed I had helped encourage him, he nailed me down, in a mutual pact of honour, for a further quarter century, when he wrote this head-turning praise in the Introduction to his marvellous book *Paris and its Provinces, 1792-1802* in 1975, and made me, in passing, a 'Dai' in print for the first time:

I have derived much encouragement, too, over the years, from my former pupil, Dai Smith, now a lecturer at the University College of Swansea, and a

381

leading member of a team carrying out research on the history of the South Wales Miners' Federation. Mr Smith is a man of most unusual gifts, combining acute literary awareness with deep insight into human behaviour and popular culture. He is an admirable historian of the communities of the valleys and the paper that he read to my seminar [Cobb had become Professor of Modern History at Oxford] on the subject of Arthur Horner and of other leaders was so full of life, so revealing of the assumptions of a closely integrated and very proud community that it served as an example both of research methods and of the sort of human questions to be asked on such subjects as the employment of leisure, clothing, status, furniture, appearances, community relationships and inter-village rivalries. I have also been heartened by Mr Smith's approval of my own methods of approach to my 'dead souls', as a recent reviewer... has described some of those whom I have attempted to rescue from total oblivion, not so much because of their contribution to events, great or small, but rather because they were so often bypassed by them. Mr Smith has the Welshman's peculiar capacity to describe people caught unawares, to puncture solemnity, and to blend an alert malice with gentle humour. Any historian has a great deal to learn from the Welsh and, at the same time, it has always seemed to me that only a Welshman can write Welsh history, because only a Welshman can perceive the multiple ties of 'cousinage' that so much dominate Welsh society.

So, I was caught, hooked and reeled in. Or rather framed and then returned to the waters in which, perforce, I was expected to swim through a skein of 'cousinage'.

That had been the burden of my work to the mid-1970s as I worked on the relationship between the South Wales Miners' Federation and its cradling society. The emphasis had been rather more institutional than a Cobb would have liked but then, as I saw it, this was not the eighteenth century, in either France or Wales, but a complex industrial world at the apex of early twentieth-century modernity. The problem was finding a means to reveal the inner mechanisms of those creative cultural achievements, the collective institutions of the working class, without making them the mechanistic agencies of a teleological trade-union chronology. Labour history, of the best kind, had this tension at the heart of its shape-shifting in the 1970s. Ironically the contemporary Labour 'movement', as we rather all-embracingly identified the chaos of action and ideology all around us, had long abandoned this chicken-and-egg dilemma to celebrate the battery production of what too many conceived of as the inevitability of a class-based history, namely continuing class politics. But what if, as there clearly once was, cultural and class divisions without the institutional markers of collective political and industrial action? I was increasingly intrigued by the world of South Wales before 1926 and, perhaps, before 1914 when outwardly the Lib-Lab consensus held a hegemonic grip on the culture and society of the coalfield as much as over its politics. What was also evident was that doctrines of Syndicalism or workers' control or even Industrial Unionism, however sharply defined by some from 1912, were not organisers of any collective mentality amongst those whom the ideologues worked to unite in a semblance of mass power through industrial action, including the misnomer of an eventual General Strike.

In other words, how did the so-called riots of Tonypandy in 1910 fit into this picture? The short, and prevailing, answer was that they did not. Orthodox trade-union histories, such as Robin Page Arnot's *South Wales Miners, 1898-1914* in 1967, subsumed the riots into a narrative of the more significant year-long Cambrian Combine strike. More subtle scholarship, such as L.J. Williams' article 'The Road to Tonypandy' in 1973, examined the underlying economic factors that had strained industrial relations to a breaking point, and hence the strike, by 1910. Only Lewis Jones (1897-1939), himself a youthful onlooker of the troubles, hinted in his thunderous novel *Cwmardy* in 1937 at some kind of symbiosis between the actuality of riot and the potential for more concerted rebellion, even of revolution. However, the novelist who was in the 1930s a dedicated Communist activist wish-fulfilled the riots into being a precursor to the politicisation of a people enraged by police aggression into violence. He threw in the fictional strike's eventual, and strictly a-historical, victory for good measure. In converse yet connected fashion, Richard Llewellyn's *How Green Was My Valley* in 1939 makes defeat follow on the aggression that has, in turn, been whipped up by political agitation.

What no one seemed to question was the immediate cause of the destruction of shops in November 1910. There were nuanced variations to be sure, but mob anger vented after the successful defence by police of the Glamorgan Colliery was, apparently, established fact. When I first read David Evans' detailed and contemporary account of 1911 in *Labour Strife in the South Wales Coalfield, 1910-1911*, I had seen no reason to do other than concur, especially, perhaps, because subliminally I, and everyone else, was actually reading a facsimile reprint of 1963 which had been paid for and published by the NUM in South Wales as part of its educational programme. The union had clearly not given any thought to its content or argument. Then, in 1978, Llafur's Annual Conference in Swansea, still buoyed by the swell of a general membership beyond historians and indeed beyond Wales and into Europe at that time, was to take as its theme 'Class and Community', and I was asked to give a lecture. For no particularly thought-out reason I offered to do something on Tonypandy in 1910. I would have been thinking of some historically more accurate rendition of Lewis Jones' linkage between action and politics, that bond between institutions and society which I felt had given South Wales its peculiar, distinctive resonance. So, in preparation, I read David Evans again, and this time it did not make sense.

To begin with it was a polemic against the strike which, when it dealt with the riots, became a diatribe. The cornerstone of his argument was that the men on strike were determined to invade and destroy the police-fortified Glamorgan Colliery in Llwynypia, and were beaten back. I could not explain, if this was so, why a relatively small group of officers could so thwart such a large 'mob'. Questions began to come at me from all sides: was it a drunken mob? Was it politically inspired? Were they

385

'strangers' out for trouble? How could any of this describe my grandfather and his friends? Were they, instead, a crowd in the Rudé meaning of the word? And if they were, how could their riot be explained if primary motivation fell away as its rationale? What had begun as a quick, sidelong piece of work for a conference became an obsession.

Sources were crucial. The official papers that seemed, now, a trifle ambiguous. The memoirs which were, even by the military, somewhat ambivalent. I retraced footsteps, of the rioters and those of my childhood self, to confirm that the spatial world of mid-Rhondda could not accommodate the mythical events Evans had described. In the Glamorgan record office there were nine bound volumes of newspaper cuttings on the strike. I read them for what they did not say. I quizzed them for what they revealed inadvertently. I looked for clues, signs, revelations indeed, of the lives of people taking such action within the very maw of their own community. In what sense was their surrounding society an actual community?

Around the act was a penumbra of meaning. I left the action of 1910 to research the names and hunches I had gathered together as they were before, and as they would be after that particular climax. The mystery unravelled so far as the issue of troops and of police was concerned. They were only incidental actors in all this. The mystery deepened to place the act at the centre of a more profound interplay between a class and its community. Insights, from epiphany to semiology, from novelists to social historians of less-industrialised societies, had taken my local feel for the matter, at last, to the condition of professional expertise. I could now argue that the events in Tonypandy were, in fact, a code whose commentary, on either side of their happening, lay within the formative and unfolding chronology of that rather special place in that decidedly vital time. Those who had acted then, and would recall their role in the years to come, were right to understand how crucial Churchill's decision over troops and police was to be, after the riot had occurred, in the context of the strike itself. That was why he was not to be excused or forgiven. They knew that it had only been, for them, the first explosive act of a drama they had to play out throughout the rest of their lives.

When I published my work in *Past and Present* in 1980, the first article on an aspect of modern Welsh history ever to appear in what was for me the most prestigious historical journal in the world, I felt I had tipped my dai cap, and paid my dues. I had certainly come full circle to home, and Tonypandy in 1910. It appears here in its original form and resplendent with that austerity of footnotes which its outrageousness of style and argument then required, to show the workings of a professional at the face.

*

'Tonypandy', Grant said... 'is a place in the South of Wales...

'If you go to South Wales you will hear that, in 1910, the Government used troops to shoot down Welsh miners who were striking for their rights. You'll probably hear that Winston Churchill, who was Home Secretary at the time, was responsible. South Wales, you will be told, will never forget Tonypandy!'

387

Carradine had dropped his flippant air.

'And it wasn't a bit like that?'

'The actual facts are these. The rougher section of the Rhondda valley crowd had got quite out of hand. Shops were being looted and property destroyed. The Chief Constable of Glamorgan sent a request to the Home Office for troops to protect the lieges... but Churchill was so horrified at the possibility of the troops coming face to face with a crowd of rioters and having to fire on them, that he stopped the movement of the troops and sent instead a body of plain, solid, Metropolitan Police, armed with nothing but their rolled-up mackintoshes. The troops were kept in reserve, and all contact with the rioters was made by unarmed London police. The only bloodshed in the whole affair was a bloody nose or two.... That was Tonypandy. That is the shooting-down by troops that Wales will never forget...

'It is a completely untrue story grown to legend while the men who knew it to be untrue looked on and said nothing'.

'Yes. That's very interesting; very. History as it is made.'

'Yes. History.'

'Give me research. After all, the truth of anything at all doesn't lie in someone's account of it. It lies in all the small facts of the time. An advertisement in a paper. The sale of a house. The price of a ring.'[1]

The two fictional characters who ruminated, inaccurately on most specific points but with some perception in general, on the meaning of Tonypandy, did so in the year that Winston Churchill became Prime Minister for the second time. By 1951 the purpose of the historical Tonypandy was that it could be waved as a flag of proletarian resistance or dismissed as a minor scuffle. The very name had come to symbolise subsequent militancy in the south Wales coalfield, to provide an easy reference sign for poets, to stand as dramatic focus for epic novels.[2] Tonypandy had entered into history too soon to escape the burden of its usable myth. There are understandable reasons, for it seemed to stand at the centre of so many other events: it indicted a Churchill whose liberalism, as Home Secretary in 1910, could be seen as a smoke-screen for the domestic bellicosity he demonstrated in 1926; it heralded the great wave of industrial unrest in pre-1914 Britain; its ten-month strike, though ending in defeat, paved the way for an airing of the issues that resulted in the national strike of 1912 with its minimum-wage provisions; around this local struggle gathered militant leaders and various brands of socialist ideology which, winning wider acceptance, threatened both the entrenched dominance of Lib-Labism and the long haul of parliamentary reformism. There was sufficient validity in these, and other, factual conglomerates to allow Tonypandy to be representative for historians, too, of economic trends or frames of mind, which this place and time appeared to sum up.[3]

However, what attracted attention at the time was not this reverberating significance but the violent outburst on Tuesday, 8 November 1910, when the town's commercial high street was wrecked. 'This was the event which, at a time of high Industrial tension elsewhere in the coalfield',[4] marked Tonypandy out and brought the troops in.

The question of whether or not Churchill was responsible for the use of troops and even whether troops ever saw the place at all[5] has bedevilled the historiography of the riot. Churchill's biographers have been too intent on translating his reluctance to become 'Tonypandy' Churchill – as another Liberal Home Secretary had become 'Featherstone' Asquith, after troops had shot two men at the Yorkshire Disturbances of 1893 – into an absolute unwillingness to use the military.[6] It is indeed the case that the troops requested by the local magistracy and sent by G.O.C. Southern Command after disturbances on 7 November were halted by Churchill in confirmation of Haldane's earlier decision as War Secretary (before they reached the area) but they were on their way again the following day. There were troops on patrol in Tonypandy, and neighbouring valleys, from the early hours of 9 November. The Riot Act was not read in mid-Rhondda nor were any shots fired. On the other hand the troops were in attendance, in diminishing numbers, until the defeat of the strike in October 1911 and, more importantly, played a vital role in support of the large numbers of police, especially the well-trained Metropolitans, sent by the government after the initial vacillation over the troops. Together they constituted a formidable force: in the vicinity were two squadrons of hussars and two infantry companies (with three further companies within a thirty-mile radius) as well as eventually over a thousand police, of whom a hundred and twenty were mounted. Infantry, using fixed bayonets, did assist the police in subsequent clashes but the only fatality that arose directly from confrontation between police and strikers was that of Samuel Rays, a miner, whose skull was fractured 'by some blunt instrument' on 8 November. The circumspect manner in which the military conducted themselves, along with Churchill's desire not to offend a predominantly Liberal electorate whose annual miners' gathering in 1908 he had personally attended, has obscured the fact that, in essence, the troops ensured that the miners' demands would be utterly rejected.[7]

It was the general scope of these grievances that gave the mid-Rhondda struggle its centrality and has led to the riots being seen as a mere appendage of the strike itself: an unfortunate psychological aberration or an understandable mistake but tied, umbilically, to the Cambrian Combine strike. Now, whereas the strike was a catalytic agent for the riots, the latter had other and deeper causes, which were expressive of a social crisis, heightened in mid-Rhondda but permeated throughout a South Wales whose history, in the last quarter of the nineteenth century, differed in a number of respects from that of the rest of Britain. Either compartmentalising that history on the assumption that its most crucial aspect is its effect on the past traditions of Wales or taking it, where there are common areas, as an appendage to the social history of England is to distort the chronological rhythm of the actual society which requires a Welsh history in which the noun's subtlety will automatically restore the epithet's genuine complexity. At the root of a great deal of twentieth-century Wales' intellectual contortion is a failure, almost self-willed, to investigate the social processes that led to the making of a 'modern' Wales.[8] Whatever indices of growth are taken – house-building, population increase, immigration, export commodities, production, individual wealth – South Wales proves to be on an upward, albeit fluctuating, curve and one that responds to an 'Atlantic' rhythm of growth rather than to the domestic British economy. It became, in fact, like Bristol and Glasgow before it, not so much a colonised fringe as one of those metropolitan nubs of empire from which British domination radiated. The Atlantic was its lake. For over two decades, more than one-third of all exported British coal came from a South Wales whose coalfield was a major supplier of industrialising France and Italy, of colonial Egypt, of developing Brazil and Argentina. In its south-west section 90 per cent of all British anthracite was mined, with over 55 per cent shipped out, mostly to new markets in Scandinavia and France.[9] On this rich economic mulch a dynamic middle class, heir to a culture of *Welsh* self-improvement which had marked the political and social drives of nineteenth-century Wales, now gloried in its radical tradition in nonconformity and liberalism, given due worth, at last, under the imperial umbrella. It regarded Wales, a nation reborn, as an organic community over which a natural leadership held sway.

The contradiction of metropolitan growth was not that an alien rule had been imposed upon the native population but that within the metropolis (even from the 'community') a distinct working class was being nurtured. This necessary working class was not a uniform proletariat conscious of its own class interests in an explicit sense. When it did express itself collectively, apart from momentary strife, it was still dependent upon its traditional focusing agencies, notably religion. Religion was *the* cultural mode of the emergent Welsh middle class too; it was the channel both of its social status and its political thrust. By the turn of the nineteenth century it was also, in its larger and more ornate temples, in its cultivated and highly trained clergy, a mirror image of a society, now in the second phase of industrialisation, that was increasingly professionalised, corporate and hierarchical. Although massively dependent upon youth, muscle and basic skills in its economy, it praised and rewarded, in its chapels, those who boasted letters after their name or who attained, through age and respectability, the position of elders. At work a combination of deference to this dominant cultural image allied to the more practical need for trade defence led to the boosting of the notion of the skilled, craftsman-like collier whereas, in fact, the rapid promotion of youths was effectively undercutting the reality of apprenticeship. When, in 1904 and 1905, Evan Roberts, the collier-blacksmith lay preacher from the geographical divide between rural and industrial Wales, led his Revival on its spectacular whirl through Welsh communities it was grace through individual salvation without benefit of clergy which proved most attractive to a population normally shepherded into social response even in their chapels. In particular it was those sidetracked groups, women and youths, given limited roles in the chapels, at home, in politics, attaining a false maturity through dress, which aped, and therefore respected, those older, who could only assert their total being in the releasing frenzy of a Revival which, for all its enthusiastic commitment, was the start of the death-rattle of Welsh Nonconformity in its hegemonic guise.[10] That totality speaks, when it does appear, of common, usually repressed, assumptions. The Tonypandy riots, too, should be seen as evidence of social fracture as much as of industrial dispute. The crisis occurred within the framework of conventional labour relations; the crowd's response, in both strike and riot, was strictly that of an already industrialised society; but they also chose targets symbolic of their discontent with a community which was supposedly their own natural focus of being. Forced, via the strike, to reassess their own status, they ended by commenting on their relationship to a community defined *for* them in a graphic coda of selective destruction that was incomprehensible to those whose *idea* of the community was now threatened by this ugly, intrusive reality. Churchill himself, writing to King George V on 10 November 1910, retailed the popular (police-inspired) explanation of the 'insensate action of the rioters in wrecking shops in the town of Tonypandy, against which they had not the slightest cause for animosity, when they had been foiled in their attacks upon the colliery'.[11] This brand of 'history as it is made', delivered complete with simple motives and moral judgements, cannot survive the revealing detail that comes from research into 'the small facts of the time'.[12]

*

The origins of the dispute lay in the refusal of men in the Ely pit to work a new seam at the price per ton offered by management.[13] The seam, experimentally worked for over a year, contained a lot of stone which, the men alleged, meant that they would be unable to earn a living wage if management did not increase the allowances for 'dead', or unproductive, work. Failure to agree led to the dismissal of not only the eighty men directly affected but also the locking out of all eight hundred men in the Ely pit from 1 September 1910. The Ely pit was a part of the Cambrian Combine which D. A. Thomas had put together on the basis of the Cambrian Collieries in Clydach Vale inherited from his father.[14] In 1906 he took control of the Glamorgan Coal Company Limited in Llwynypia (with three pits) and in 1908 of the Naval Colliery Company Limited (with four pits, including the Ely) in Penygraig and Tonypandy. By 1910 he had the Britannic Merthyr Coal Company, in Gilfach Goch over the mountain from the central township of Tonypandy and, altogether, the employ of some twelve thousand men in the mid-Rhondda area.[15] From 5 September the men in the other Naval Colliery pits struck unofficially and, on 1 November, after a coalfield-wide ballot that promised financial aid only, the rest of the Cambrian men, against the wishes both of the executive council of the South Wales Miners' Federation and the local Rhondda miners' agents, also came out in support of the Ely men.[16] The conduct of the dispute was to stay firmly in the hands of the Cambrian Combine Committee, made up of representatives from all the separate pit lodges.[17]

From the first few days the mood of the strikers was clear: the stoppage, if it were to be effective, would require a swift resolution that would be dependent on the non-importation of 'blackleg' labour and the prevention of colliery officials from attending to the pumping and ventilating machinery on the surface which would keep the pits free from flooding. Extra police, from outside the district, had been drafted into the area (142 of them) under the personal command of the chief constable, Captain Lionel Lindsay. They were concentrated at the

Glamorgan Colliery, Llwynypia, a quarter of a mile north of Tonypandy Square, so that when early on Monday, 7 November, bands of men proceeded from colliery to colliery, preventing all officials, engine-men and stokers from working, they met with little opposition from the otherwise thinly dispersed police. Fires were raked, boilers and ventilating fans stopped. At the Cambrian Colliery in Clydach Vale, a precipitous defile running up from the valley bottom at Tonypandy Square, officials were stoned out of the new electric powerhouse. Mounted police were subjected to foot rushes and pelting with various missiles as the crowd, holding blacklegs in white shirts with cards proclaiming 'Take a Warning' pinned to them, marched through high winds and drenching rain. At the end of the afternoon only the Glamorgan Colliery remained inviolate: here waited the police and between fifty and sixty officials and craftsmen under the guidance of the general manager of the Cambrian Combine, Leonard Llewellyn.[18] There were underground over three hundred horses brought in during the previous week from other pits. The pits to which the horses had been deliberately transferred were especially liable to flooding and the animals were to be the focus of much public and royal concern. To deal with the danger an electrically operated pumping plant, supplied by a large generator, had been installed in the yard. From 9.00 pm the strikers mounted a huge demonstration outside the colliery yard which, around 10.30 pm, turned more serious and finally erupted in a series of fierce clashes with the police that only petered out around 1.00 am.[19]

The following day, Tuesday, Lindsay's request for troops was blocked by Churchill, at least to the extent of halting them in Swindon and only sending seventy mounted police and two hundred Metropolitans. The men who had assembled on the Athletic Ground, Tonypandy, after being paid off by the combine, received this news, relayed by Daniel Lleufer Thomas,[20] the stipendiary magistrate, in silence and, shortly after, marched in force to the Glamorgan Colliery where, about 5.00 pm, a crowd remained behind to demonstrate. They were estimated at between seven and nine thousand strong. Stoning of the powerhouse led to a number of baton charges by the 120-strong police (18 of whom were mounted). Intense close-quarter fighting followed.[21] So much, in brief outline, is not in question but what now led to the riot is the point at issue, since there has been general acceptance, even by historians who have pointed to his bias as a pro-coal-owner reporter, of the account of David Evans in his contemporary volume[22] which attributes clear, if unworthy, motives to the strikers in their destruction of shops in Tonypandy.[23] Evans, in lurid prose, describes the repulse of the demonstrators by a gallant band of police, the consequent dispersal of the crowd, and how, frustrated and angry, they wreaked unjustified revenge upon the unprotected shopkeepers. This is the umbilical cord between the strike and its handicapped child, the riot.

Evans mixes description with imagination at will or convenience. His presumption that the strikers were intent on possessing the colliery physically, as opposed to stopping its working, is without direct evidence and in contradiction of their earlier resolutions and activities. On the contrary it was police-rushing of the crowd which led on 7 November to invasion of the premises, from which

397

the demonstrators, having driven the police back, then retreated voluntarily. The same pattern of events caused the serious fighting that began on the following night around 6.00 pm. A close reading of contemporary accounts, and later testimony from a policeman involved in the fracas, demolish the view that the crowd, though dispersed, was actually driven back the quarter of a mile from the Glamorgan Colliery to the crossroads, or square, at Tonypandy. It was the police who regrouped and returned to their base. Between about 8.00 and 10.00 pm there was no effective policing of the town. The magistrate's request for the troops was sent at 7.45 pm, before systematic attacks on the shops began. The inescapable conclusion is that it had been decided as early as the weekend, both for strategic and provocative purposes, to make the Glamorgan Colliery, near to Llewellyn's own house and bisected by the railway line, the citadel of the coal-owners' assertion, not so much of property itself, as of the rights of property-ownership.[24]

The aggressive assertion of these rights by the police was the immediate spur to the riot of 8 November, though the crowd was more angry than either fearful or frustrated. The attack, now, on other property-owners flowed down well-worn grooves. There were, in a sense, two riots. While the police were preparing to charge the crowd just after 7.00 pm two things, amid a confused welter of events, seem to have happened. The first is that fighting ceased outside the colliery at about 7.00 pm and 'thousands of strikers', scattering with their 'staves', rushed through Tonypandy to the station because 'the rumour had got abroad that cavalry would arrive' at about 8.00 pm. In this burst down the narrow, winding main street, shop-windows were smashed in and some goods taken.[25] Perhaps those who discovered no troops had arrived moved back through the half a mile from station to square where they found the victims of the last, and toughest, bout with the police milling about with the rest of the crowd who had been unable to proceed in a peaceful march up to the colliery. By 7.30 pm a number of shopkeepers had put up makeshift shutters. These were simply torn down as, after 8.00 pm, more intensive smashing of shop premises went on, in the wake of the struggle with the police, and continued virtually unabated until after 10.00 pm.[26]

When the riots were over analyses came thick and fast. What caused most disquiet was the apparently wanton attack on shopkeepers. It was this destruction of the social fabric of a new community that had to be explained away so that, in Lleufer Thomas's phrase, 'the good name of South Wales' should not be further besmirched.[27] An obvious explanation, one in considerable favour with General Macready and other moderating influences, was that 'the doctrine of extreme socialism preached by a small but energetic section... [was]... entirely responsible for the premeditated attempts to destroy property.[28] However, the miners' local leaders, though out of sympathy with their conciliatory officials, were not, primarily, those 'syndicalists' who came to prominence after 1912 and they went out of their way, in private and in public, both to dissuade the men from damaging property and to condemn the destruction of the shops.[29] Their unexceptionable sentiments were endorsed, in varying degrees, by the troupe of British socialists, of all persuasions, who trekked to the Rhondda after that

Tuesday night. The riot, whether justifiable or not as a retaliatory weapon, was not, they felt, a part either of union progress or socialist advance. They emphasised the necessity for future political organisation and joined in the chorus of miners' agents and sympathetic MPs who denied that there was any widespread damage at all. From all responsible quarters, with concerned clergymen, editors and even local tradesmen agreeing, came the concerted view that the shops had been smashed by 'a gang of about 150, chiefly youths and men let loose from the public houses' or was 'the work of... not one hundred... many... were strangers' and, combining both, 'half-drunken, irresponsible persons... from outside the... district... the mad outbreak of 150'.[30] This verbal diminution of a crowd of thousands as well as the shuffling aside of the violent events of the nights of 7 and 8 November outside the colliery itself is inextricably related to what was the apparently unacceptable thought that a very large number of people had been actively involved in the destruction of Tonypandy's commercial life. Instead a tirade of arraignment was directed against the outcast groups of youths, drunks and strangers. Youths there certainly were (around 14 per cent of the entire mining work-force in the coalfield was under sixteen years of age) but those same youths who stoned the Glamorgan Colliery were also rescued from the clutches of the police by 'young men of apparently from twenty to thirty years of age'.[31] Men in drink there were, too, though the fact that the magistrate had closed the pubs early (at dusk) might have kept some from being drunk, while the bulk of the crowd had been at a mass meeting in the afternoon or on the streets for hours. The accusation against 'strangers',

400

like that against youths, seems common to the aftermath of most riots as a way of pinning guilt to those with no real stake in what is considered the day-to-day reality of the local life, but the strangers can have been few at most, while of the meagre number of seventeen who were tried in 1911 for their part in the riots all were from mid-Rhondda and five were women.[32]

Women had been involved from the start. On 7 November they were out in the streets in Penygraig, Llwynypia and Clydach Vale as early as the men and led the cheering as action was taken against non-unionists and, later, the police.[33] That night, outside the Glamorgan Colliery, women by gathering up loose stones in aprons and buckets acted as ammunition carriers for the men whom they urged on.[34] Lleufer Thomas had pressed that women and children keep indoors when he relayed the Home Secretary's message to the strikers on the afternoon of 8 November, but they were certainly out in numbers again that night.[35] The crowd acted, too, with a measure of control and of local knowledge remarkable for so many drunken strangers. The action could be depicted as premeditated, if inspired by ideologies, or as frenzied, if sparked off by anger or drink. That it had a patterned logic of its own was insupportable, to be brushed aside even in a reporter's 'objective' description: 'it is curious to note how, in several cases, a row of half a dozen shops, though all around them had been damaged, had escaped. This must not be attributed to any discrimination on the part of the rioters...'[36]

They began by knocking in the shop window of T. Pascoe Jenkins, JP, the senior magistrate of the Rhondda valley and a resident of thirty-years standing;[37] amid scenes of widespread wreckage they scrupulously avoided one iota of damage to a particular chemist's shop, despite the fact that all other chemists were prime targets: this was the shop of the locally born Willie Llewellyn, former rugby international footballer who had played a large part in the success of Welsh rugby teams. He had opened his shop immediately after helping to defeat the otherwise invincible All Blacks of New Zealand in 1905. Other grievances were so direct that J. Owen Jones, a Tonypandy draper whose shop was gutted, inserted a notice dated 10 November in the local paper in which he offered £50 reward to the Cambrian Combine Committee to be given to any named charity 'if a certain statement attributed to me can be proven'.[38] An eyewitness who was a boy in 1910 described how he and a friend observed the start of the riot from a side-road above the square:

> They started smashing the windows... they smashed this shop here, J. O. Jones, a millinery shop that was on the other corner.... We saw that being smashed and then next door to the millinery J. O. Jones, there was a shop and they smashed the window there... on the other side here, there was Richards the Chemist... they smashed that. And they smashed the windows of these three small shops here, one was a greengrocer, the other one was fancy goods and the other one was a barber's shop, and I knew the name of the barber quite well, it was Salter, because we used to think it swanky to go to Salter's to have a haircut, you see. They smashed Richards the Chemist, then there was the boot shop next door to it... and next to that was Watkins the flannel merchant...

402

they smashed that and they stole the shoes out of the boots, flannel out of Watkins and greengrocery, well they only picked up there. Well next to that there was a few steps up and there was a dentist and one or two private houses. Well, they didn't smash. We didn't see anything that happened below the bridge because... we were afraid to go down there in front of the crowd... oh, there was a huge crowd.[39]

The crowd was not organised but it knew what to do in the euphoria of release that followed the catalytic police action. It shared both special grievances and communal assumptions about the direction and legitimacy of its action. For the editor of the Rhondda's newspaper the riots, instigated and carried out by thoughtless youths and women from further afield, 'the mania for loot strong upon them', meant that 'a national obloquy has come upon Wales through the roughness of the times. 'Tonypandy', he wailed, 'is no longer an unknown township.... The pity of it all is that Tonypandy has to bear the brunt of the defamation and for years the ill repute will stick to it.'[40] No such qualm disturbed the majority of the local population, who were more in tune with the brash topsy-turviness of their real world of false appearances. The music hall, so well patronised by coalfield society, was doing its unconscious best to offer ironic reflection. That Tuesday night the management of the Hippodrome closed the theatre because of the trouble, though not before customers were given tickets for later readmission to see the comedy pantomime, *Wrecked*. At the Theatre Royal close by, 'despite the tumult raging within almost a stone's throw', remarked a singularly oblique critic, the packed audience watched *The Still Alarm*, an American drama in which there was a 'Special Engine House Scene introducing the beautifully trained horses'. In a place addicted to the escapism of theatricality, the art of gesture could invade the streets, whether in the contemptuous spillage of foodstuffs and apparel on to the roads in place of theft, or by dressing up ('colliers paraded the streets wearing box hats and new overcoats'), or in the joy of disrespectful, self-glorying parody 'rendered heartily' by young men and women in the streets of Tonypandy a week or so after the riots to a well-known tune:

Every nice girl loves a collier
In the Rhondda valley war
Every nice girl loves a striker
And you know what strikers are
In Tonypandy they're very handy
With their sticks and their stones and boot
Walking down the street with Jane
Breaking every window pane
That's loot! Pom pom. That's loot![41]

The jubilant defiance which turned the riots into a festival of disorder had its roots in the nature of mid-Rhondda. Its development dates from the latter end of the nineteenth century when, in rapid succession, pits were sunk by the Naval Colliery Company and opened for production – the Pandy pit in 1879, the Ely and Nantgwyn in 1892, and the Anthony in 1910. The number of men at work rose from 800 in 1896 to 2,460 by 1908. At the other end of the raw village of

Tonypandy, with its straggle of wooden huts, stone cottages and a few shops, the Glamorgan Colliery Company were opening up pits No. 4 and No. 5 in 1873 at Llwynypia, with No. 6 to follow in 1876, while in Clydach Vale, branching off from the main valley bottom, Samuel Thomas, father of D. A. Thomas, had two pits working in the year of his death, 1879, and there were three by 1900.[42] The amalgamation of the pits in mid-Rhondda into the Cambrian Combine gave the group over 50 per cent of the total coal production in Rhondda by the outbreak of the First World War and made it, with its subsidiary shipping and patent-fuel interests in Britain, France and Scandinavia, one of the two 'most complete self-contained organisations in the coal trade of the world'.[43] In 1875 the main Tonypandy road running alongside the river, not yet an oil-silk black, was mostly bordered on its western side by small stone cottages, but as the area boomed after 1890 the street, given its position below the slopes that loomed over it, became the only likely area for a commercial high street in a ribbon development.[44] Undulating terraces of houses were now strung out on the steep hillsides above the main road of De Winton and Dunraven Streets where was built by 1900 an imposing grey-stone police station set slightly off the road and flanked by a double flight of steps like a sawn-off French chateau. Other required amenities followed – the Tonypandy and Trealaw Free Library established in 1899 by local businessmen, and the red-brick Judge's Hall which could hold fifteen hundred people and contained both library and billiard hall. It was opened in 1909 by HRH Princess Louise who, since it was situated conveniently near the railway station, could have avoided the mean drabness of the town itself, though this was now alleviated by the Empire Theatre of Varieties, itself opened in 1909. The following year the enterprising Will Stone's electric biograph was enlivening the Theatre Royal (erected in 1892), while at the Hippodrome the electric bioscope was projecting its flickering images twice nightly. Boxing booths, portable theatres, and travelling fairs on a field behind the square, all added to the raucous glitter of a spectating world which was undermining the more sober pursuits of nonconformist *Weltanschauung*.[45] For the more energetically inclined (brass bands, choral-singing and rugby apart), and for paying customers only, J. Owen Jones, draper, launched out in early 1910 when he formally opened, just above Tonypandy Square, the Pavilion, which housed the 'Express roller-skating rink'. Later that year Big Bill Haywood, the American syndicalist, would thunder at the mid-Rhondda miners from the stage of the Theatre Royal; police would be housed in J. Owen Jones' skating rink and Lleufer Thomas would, after a nervous request, issue a notice to the effect that the draper had no choice in the matter (in December gales the tin roof blew off and the police shifted to the Hippodrome); and in 1912 an intricate debate, at a highly sophisticated level, would proceed on the virtues of nationalisation versus workers' control before a full house in Judge's Hall.[46]

Between 1901 and 1911 the total population of Rhondda increased by 34.3 per cent from 113,735 to 152,781 (thrice the average increase for England and Wales). The 1911 figure was undoubtedly lower than it would have been in 1910, since the Cambrian strike had witnessed a temporary exodus from the mid-Rhondda district, whose estimated population in 1910 was 38,819 (there were 7,116 inhabited houses in the area in 1910). Housing needs had been met by private speculative building (in 1909 the number of houses in mid-Rhondda was 6,868) which did not, despite basic patterning and haste, adequately house a population whose birth rate was outstripping the death rate, whose colliers married in their early twenties at the peak of their earning capacity, and where many lived in single rooms or cellar dwellings. Houses were often too expensive or too large for some families; the Urban District Authority, in being since 1894, had not made any housing provision themselves. At a conservative estimate the number of inhabitants per house was circa 5.8 in the first decade of the twentieth century. Houses would vary from four-roomed cottages to more substantial three-up and three-down terraces. The pits had spawned a rash of houses, shops, chapels and pubs, whose only saving architectural grace was that they had to conform, in local materials of slate and pennant sandstone, with red and yellow brick for the recent construction, to the limiting physical configuration of a twisting valley whose bed was hemmed in by clumps of steep hillsides on which the orgy of house-building had to proceed.[47] Effluence poured into the river from works and houses, so that in the summer the high, rich smell of decayed matter and slaughtered meat was pungent indeed.[48] Nevertheless the prevailing grimness of the environment was countered, in turn, by the very social capital which had brought it into forced being. Here a whirligig of sounds, smells and sights caught up a population barely a generation (and often not that) away from the land. Packaged foods and ready-made goods were consumer luxuries that made shops seductive enticers to debt as well as welcome centres of social intercourse.[49]

Every Aladdin's cave had its statutory Uncle Ebenezer: from May 1909 the mid-Rhondda grocers decided, secretly and by a mutual indemnification pact, to operate a 'black list' system of credit for known customers. Nor did they prove more generous with their own employees, for they decided in the summer of 1908 to end the common practice of giving Christmas boxes.[50] These primary concerns over the security of profit margins apart, it was the tradesmen who were initially, and predominantly, concerned to instil a sense of community without whose social mediation their own role as citizens and shopkeepers, in a society pulled together only for profits and work from coal, would be barren. To this end T. P. Jenkins, magistrate, was insisting as early as 1896 that the direct payment of taxes and rates would alone bring the Rhondda's disorderly working class to 'full, responsible citizenship'.[51] It was the outward signification of a civilised respectability that, as cause for hope, they most valued. The playing of impromptu football in the streets was frowned upon and the police were urged to prosecute.[52] They reacted rather stiffly, through their chamber of trade, to 'young people wandering around and desecrating the Sunday' and 'thought the playing of gramophones on a Sunday was quite a disgrace to the locality',[53] with which the Free Church Council, itself worried about the 'prevalence of boxing contests' in Tonypandy, doubtless concurred. Other desired improvements were not quite so restrictive: they were to the fore in having a public drinking-fountain put up in the square, constantly urged better electric lighting in the main street (especially after the riots, when they requested it be kept on all night), suggested in the summer days that 'small boys be employed to collect manure from the roads during the day', and provided a deputation to the council to urge 'provision of Public Lavatories for both sexes in the district, more especially for ladies'.[54]

At the beginning of 1910 these midwives of modernity had cause to congratulate themselves on their past endeavours and future possibilities when the Mid-Rhondda Horse Show Association, formed in 1905 to assist the fire brigade, gave a banquet in honour of its retiring president, Leonard Llewellyn. The toast was 'The Trade of the District', to which its proposer said:

> that if they looked back upon the history of Tonypandy for the past 18 months, they could honestly say that no other district in the Rhondda could show such great development, and much of that was due to one of the most public-spirited bodies in the country – the Mid-Rhondda Chamber of Trade.... He hoped that the present movement for Incorporation would be successful, and that they would have the control of the police, reduce their rates, and place Tonypandy in the front of Rhondda townships.

Councillor D. C. Evans, in response, had no doubt that leaders on both sides of the coal industry would prove conciliatory in the current negotiations, while J. Owen Jones, the chairman of the Mid-Rhondda Chamber of Trade, declared, to great applause, that the tradesmen's earlier fears of loss of trade after the formation of the

Cambrian Combine had now been exchanged for 'hopes of a good time in store'. Unfortunately the president of the horse show for 1910, D. A. Thomas, was not present to praise his predecessor so Alderman Richard Lewis, JP, did it, extolling Leonard Llewellyn as a man who had:

> realised the claims and duties of true citizenship. Looking around him he saw the sons of men who had started in business with him at Tonypandy 40 years ago, and the sons were better than their fathers. The future of mid-Rhondda, socially, need not be in danger at all when they had such sons taking their part in the social welfare of the district. After touching upon the past managers of the Glamorgan Colliery, the speaker said that Mr. Llewellyn was a noble successor of that noble line.[55]

Leonard Llewellyn was generous, too, in his hospitality and the availability of his animals, even if the ingrate General Macready, who refused invitations to his officers and himself to dine, did describe him as 'a forceful, autocratic man... who, by his rough and ready methods, was apt to drive those working for him to a state of desperation'.[56] The chief constable, Lionel Lindsay, had no such qualms, sharing both dinners and horses with Llewellyn, who managed policemen, collieries and publicity with equal aplomb.[57] Public sympathy had from the start been directed to the plight of the hundreds of horses who were supposedly at risk in November 1910, and of whose safety Llewellyn had hastened to assure government and king after the arrival of the military.[58] Llewellyn had been photographed holding a black cat he had brought up from the mine and in an indictment of these anthropomorphic tendencies the strikers, whose offer to allow the horses to be brought up under their supervision he had refused, now devised a bitter language of their own – whenever Llewellyn's name was mentioned at meetings they set up a chorus of miaows; when they marched to Pontypridd in December to hear charges of intimidation against Gilfach miners they carried a white banner decorated with a lean black cat and inscribed with the legend 'Hungry as L...'; while in February 1911, when the first set of charges was brought against John Hopla, checkweigher at the Glamorgan Colliery, they followed a wooden hobby horse. Those charged, and sentenced or fined, wore their summonses in their caps during the march, while others shepherded a black and white retriever with a card that said 'Leonard's pet', or held notices asking 'What about the horses?'[59]

Llewellyn answered that question in March 1911 when he and his assistant manager were presented with medals at the annual dinner of the Polo and Riding Society at the Hotel Metropole, London, for their bravery in rescuing the horses from drowning. Llewellyn, referring to the 'temporary mental aberration of the men', said that 'as a Welshman he very much regretted that such a thing should have happened in Wales'. Then in May 1911 the countess of Bective gave out RSPCA medals for the same service of 'heroism in rescuing pit ponies' and Llewellyn presented his black cat to a London newspaperman.[60] It had been a rough, but hardly downward, journey from the day in January 1910 when he had been hailed as 'the pioneer of all the important movements that had tended to the better welfare of the Rhondda in general'.

411

That was the occasion when he was re-elected president, for the year of 1910, of the Mid-Rhondda Chamber of Trade. The speaker was the retiring chairman J. Owen Jones, draper, stockist for cotton, linen and woollen goods on Tonypandy Square. Drapers were the great hold-all emporia for everything, other than food and ironmongery, in places like the Rhondda. 1910 was not a good year for them in Tonypandy. J. Owen Jones had announced his winter clearance sale in late January as 'big purchases with a small purse'. He pleaded and warned in a judicious mix – 'owing to the absence of draper's weather during autumn and winter, his stock in all departments' was 'exceptionally heavy', while 'the serious condition of the cotton market' meant that, 'except for a few days in 1904, cotton has not been so dear for thirty-five years' so that customers should 'secure their wants in this sale'. Nonetheless J. Owen Jones, at his summer sale of all-round reductions, had to explain that his price cuts were 'much greater than usual, owing to my stock being considerably heavier, the death of His Majesty King Edward VII, and the exceptional weather [that is, prolonged rain] we have had for the greater part of the summer'.[61] On 8 November the people of mid-Rhondda finally took the hint.

The persistent rain, on the other hand, may have added to the trade of J. W. Richards, a dispenser of poor relief on the Pontypridd Board of Guardians who carved the meat in the Llwynypia workhouse on Christmas Day 1909, but usually a dispenser of spectacles and medicaments. On the side of his shop on Tonypandy Square was painted a large advertisement: 'Kurakold – Richards' Unrivalled Remedy at 1/- and 2/9 a Bottle –

A quick and permanent cure for all disorders of Chest and Lungs'.

Doctors were few, and attached to the collieries. Chemists were quicker, easier and cheaper. They were, with their bright displays of coloured bottles and chemicals, the equivalent of the nineteenth-century peasant's healers, charmers and travelling quacks. There was in Rhondda every aid to a full bionic life. By post could come 'Artificial Legs, Surgical Boots, Deformity Stock – Hands, Arms, Artificial Eyes from 7/6'. Less drastic cases could settle for 'vegetable pills to purify the blood', 'effervescent salts', 'Thompson's Electric Life Drops for the cure of Nervous Debility' which 'act so quickly on a weak and shattered condition that health is speedily restored', or the *sans pareil* Burdock's pills from Swansea, 'one of the oldest and best of Medicines having been more than 60 years before the public for purifying the foulest blood, and removing every disease of the stomach, liver and kidneys. Cures Scurvy and Scrofula, Sores, Eruption of the skin and all diseases arising from an impure state of the blood', while for the young, Worm Lozenges whose 'effect upon weak, delicate children (often given up as incurable) is like magic'.[62]

Such ardent advertising knew its potential consumers. In 1905, the year the new £25,000 electric powerhouse was installed at the Cambrian Collieries, Clydach Vale, 33 men and boys were blown up in the Cambrian No. 1 pit; two months later not five miles down the valley at Wattstown 119 were killed underground.[63] Clydach Vale and Llwynypia had in 1909 the highest birth rate in a Rhondda where illegitimacy was rocketing above the British average. There were in 1909 throughout the valley

413

only 130 deaths for every 1,000 live births of children under twelve months old, whereas the average for 1899 to 1908 had been 190 per 1,000, but this can have been scant consolation, even given a greater degree of resignation than now conceivable in industrial societies, for the parents of the 724 children from a 1909 total of 5,557. Colliers died of 'pulmonary consumption' or 'Phthisis' at eleven times the rate of any other occupation. The coroner's table of investigated deaths for the years 1897 to 1900 showed a low rate of death for those succumbing to alcoholism, strain (*sic*), hernias, homicide and injudicious feeding (*sic*) and rose through convulsions, heart disease, burns, drowning and being run over by carts, trains and trams, before revealing that between a third and a half of these deaths were from routine accidents in the pits.[64] Those colliers who greeted Dai Watts Morgan, the second miners' agent for Rhondda, in the summer of 1910 with shouts of 'What price are flowers, Mr Morgan?' had their equivalents on 8 November in those who threw Studley's fruit and vegetable produce all over the road in Tonypandy Square underneath two hand-painted signs that read, in tandem, 'Studleys – Fruit Merchant' and 'Wreaths to Order'.[65]

During the months that led up to the strike the repeated complaint of the men working for the combine was that management was endangering life in their drive for profits to feed their overcapitalised concerns. The chaotic bargaining system of payment for various work done underground (other than hewing), from setting up props to packing waste stone away in a difficult stall, was over-reliant on the verbal contract of collier and foreman, while the latter could find his allowances to the men squeezed by a margin-conscious management. Colliers doing similar work in different seams or pits often had an enormous discrepancy in wages.[66] At the Ely pit, before the dismissal of the men on the Bute seam in September, there had been some disquieting accidents, from the death of five men in a pit-cage crash in August 1909 to the crushing of a collier underneath the fall of an inadequately propped section of coal in 1910. Both cases for compensation brought to the courts were dismissed by the coroner as accidents caused by thoughtless workmen, though the Naval Colliery lodge committee alleged management's deliberate negligence.[67] The committee called for courts of inquiry composed of men 'who know the miner's life as it affects him from within' and claimed that South Wales coal-owners 'in order to create big dividends at the expense of the most cheapened labour are constantly employing men as colliers who are without knowledge or experience of any aspect or feature of the miner's life and work'.[68] D. A. Thomas had that same month stressed the independence that he gave to his managers and, exulting in the jibe that with the creation of the Cambrian Combine he had bought 'a few sucked oranges', countered that 'he did not mind if there were a few more sucked oranges about. With Mr Llewellyn to look after them, they were prepared to go on dealing in sucked oranges and Cambrian marmalade.'[69]

As the industrial crisis deepened in mid-Rhondda local clergy and tradesmen made representations to both sides in the industry. This alliance was not surprising since, apart from the fact that eleven Welsh clergymen held shares in the Cambrian Combine,[70] the Free Church Council's Welsh Federation had been active in September

1910 in agitating against the government's attempt to repeal the 1677 Sunday Observance Act. This would have opened certain shops legally, but closed down the large number of shops which were opening illegally, to the detriment of the leisure of shop assistants whose hours of work, from sixty to one hundred a week, were way beyond those of colliers, who now had some protection from the 1908 Eight Hours Act. It was argued that shop assistants in South Wales were particularly overworked through late opening on Saturdays and deliveries on Sunday mornings.[71]

Traders were centrally involved in these industrial troubles. At the end of October 1910 the Ely pit men had been out for two months and distress was already severe in the Penygraig area. The Mid-Rhondda Chamber of Trade publicly congratulated itself on having given £30 to the distress fund; the Penygraig local chamber of trade pledged financial and moral aid to the workmen in their struggle for improved conditions, and simultaneously sent a successful deputation to Glamorgan County Council to plead for a local police station since the one in Tonypandy was all of three-quarters of a mile away, allowing advantage to be taken 'by young powerful men of the disorderly class'. When the final offer, hatched between the South Wales Miners' Federation executive and the owners, was rejected unanimously by the local men in late October it was the plight of the traders that was the first concern of the community's 'glue-maker', the local newspaper:

We deplore the result of the vote because an industrial struggle of this magnitude brings in its train, not only complete disorganisation of the trade

416

of the district... but also because of the suffering...
[of] ...those who are no part to the dispute... But
apart from mere sentiment, a strike at this period of
the year, when trade is looking up and tradesmen
are laying in large stores in preparation for a brisk
demand, means the withdrawal of a huge sum of
money from active circulation in the district, with the
consequent paralysis of those trades and industries
which depend upon the coal trade for stability.[72]

Matters did not improve when a mass meeting of the
strikers greeted Leonard Llewellyn's offer on behalf of the
Cambrian Combine directors of £100 a week to the
distress fund so long as the strike lasted with cries of 'Let
him keep it' and 'Let his money perish with him'.[73] It was
the irrecoverable nature of profits lost that worried the
commercial elite of mid-Rhondda, and not only the profits
from trade. During 1909, spurred on by the Housing Act
of that year, the Mid-Rhondda Trades and Labour Council
had begun to collect evidence on the housing conditions of
their district. A conference was held with other areas in
upper Rhondda in early 1910 and representations
eventually made to the Urban District Council over
crowding, insanitary conditions, subletting, high rents and
the practice of some tradespeople in compelling tenants
to buy in their shops.[74] These allegations had been made
as early as 1905, when local miners' leaders warned of
'the drastic action to be taken by the men as a body' if
these 'evil practices' persisted.[75] The medical officer of
health was asked to investigate the complaints, which he
assessed in a special report presented in July 1911. This
accepted the general complaints of poor living conditions

and asserted that the worst situation, so far as sanitation and overcrowding were concerned, was to be found in Clydach Vale, Llwynypia, Tonypandy and upper Trealaw. Dr J. D. Jenkins agreed that 'key money', or the highest bidder having preference in obtaining tenancy, was common, as was the arbitrary raising of rent when one set of tenants moved out and another in. Moreover there were:

> cases in respect of whom the inspectors are informed that houses are only obtainable on certain conditions, such as an undertaking or promise on the part of the incoming tenant to purchase goods such as furniture or groceries from the owners. Some house-owners, again, object to tenants with many children, while some provision merchants are said to prefer tenants with large families, because every additional child helps to swell the bill for provisions.[76]

Consequently the summer of 1911 saw a degree of suffering among tradesmen: one who owned half a dozen houses had lost £40 in rent and his weekly shop takings were down from £90 to £25; another estimated losses at around £800, with a drop of £160 a week, while a 'gentleman who is in a big way of business and who owns a very large number of houses and shops estimated his loss at well over £1,000 since his receipts had dropped to about £30 a fortnight'.[77] Such monetary concerns were not the major worry of most of the strikers (the exceptions were the Naval Colliery workers), who had received their last wages prior to the week of the riots. They had, to that extent, money in their pockets yet none, of course, to spend on inessentials. That their deprivation was relative rather than absolute hardly diminished their sense of grievance. Out of reach now were those conspicuous goods whose consumption, in a high-wage society, went some way towards excusing that world's more brutal aspects. They ranged from Saturday-night shaves and barbered hair to women's hats and the white muffler scarves that no collier dandy could be without. The shops in Tonypandy were not looted for food. They were wrecked by men and women who knew closely the intricate and inseparable local factors that made up the skein of social and economic connections which enwrapped their community. They knew, further, who aspired to control everything through this basic lever. The riots were not planned in advance yet they were not merely the spontaneous response to the kaleidoscopic incidents of those two strife-torn nights, for they were structured both in the sense that the crowd acted together and also in that the damage they wreaked was a deliberate assault on the civil order of a world that had been made for them.

From early on the Tuesday thousands of men had strolled or paraded, in groups large and small, through the packed face-to-face streets that stood in tiers above the river bed, criss-crossed by the sheer hill roads covered with loose stones, that debouched on to the main road below. They discussed the fighting of the Monday night; they sang popular music-hall ditties or strode along behind amateur fife bands to the engaging sound of concertinas. During the morning a tailor's dummy had been commandeered from a shop and was now held aloft in his finery as a mascot. A baker's van which stopped on a call in a back street lost all its bread, perhaps in reprisal for the firm's prominent announcement earlier in the week that it had reduced the size of its farmhouse family loaf to meet the requirements of strikers' families.[78] When the riots broke out that night those who had anticipated a simple industrial struggle misread the signs. The correspondent of the *Western Mail* wrote in disbelief: 'Even drapers' establishments were smashed open and wearing apparel, as well as drapers' goods of all descriptions, was looted unceremoniously.'

The crowd which stoned windows after 8.00 pm did so to a 'stop and start' pattern of whistling, so that 'the absence of the police and other important events' were 'notified by members of the apparently inoffensive crowd to the aggressors'.[79] Dummies and finery, silks and top hats, were thrown on to the road in contempt or worn in mockery. Jars of sweets, cigarettes, pans of ice cream and packets of tobacco were scattered around and raided by children. Sixty-three shops were damaged. Some were completely ransacked – J. W. Richards, chemist; J. Owen Jones, draper and milliner; J. Haydn Jones, gents' outfitter. T. P. Jenkins, draper; M. A. Phillips, gents' clothier; J. R. Evans, draper; and four refreshment houses, including two owned by the Bracchi Bros whose name became eponymous for all Italian cafes in South Wales. Butchers, grocers, furniture shops and others suffered less or minor damage.[80] T. P. Jenkins, the magistrate whose shop was the first to go, said that the crowd made 'wild threats both in Welsh and English and then went on their work of destruction'.[81] The windows of the twinned draper shops of Mr and Mrs Phillips were knocked in at 7.45 pm. The crowd returned at 9.15 pm and systematically broke all the windows as they tore apart the shop, which they had illuminated by lighting the gas jets. Mrs Phillips told an outraged reporter for the drapers' profession:

> People were seen inside the counter handing goods out. They were afterwards walking on the Square wearing various articles of clothing which had been stolen and asking each other how they looked. They were not a bit ashamed, and they actually had the audacity to see how things fitted them in the shop itself. They were in the shop somewhere about three hours and women were as bad as men... Everything was done openly and the din was something horrible.[82]

One outfitters was completely denuded of its extensive stock of mufflers. At 10.00 pm, and although the recently-arrived Metropolitan police were housed in the skating rink only one hundred yards away, Haydn Jones' drapery, already 'smashed to atoms', was now further reduced as 'collars, straw hats, braces and caps were passed from hand to hand openly in the street and exchanges were indulged in between the looters'.[83] These were revolutionary acts, albeit without a play to frame them, nor was Lionel James of *The Times*, who arrived two weeks after this world-turned-upside-down had reverted to the stability of a war of attrition, so far wrong when he despatched the news that though the place was quiet:

> knots of sullen men are parading the streets, and the mouth of every alley way is blocked with idle

miners. It is just the same oppressive atmosphere that one experienced in the streets of Odessa and Sevastopol during the unrest in Russia in the winter of 1904. It is extraordinary to find it here in the British Isles.[84]

The riots were not a momentary aberration. Similar incidents, though smaller in scale, are peppered through late 1910 and into 1911. The conventions of social behaviour continued to be flouted, to the dismay of more responsible society. Thus in April 1911 when renegotiated terms were again put to the men (and massively rejected) those who voted by secret ballot walked about with the unused portion of the ballot paper stuck in their coat, 'publicising to the world at large how they voted' and rendering 'the ballot nothing short of a travesty'.[85] There were shifts at ballot-box level, too. Leonard Llewellyn had resigned his seat for Clydach Vale for 'business reasons' in September 1910;[86] by 1912 all three local councillors for the ward were Labour representatives; William Abraham, MP, Rhondda's member since 1885 and the Lib-Lab president of the South Wales Miners' Federation, was re-elected as usual in December 1910, though in a poll whose reduction coincided with his own loss of votes; more significantly he, and the Welsh national anthem he customarily invoked, were both booed at an eve of poll meeting. The four ILP and two SDP branches in the Rhondda had contemplated running a candidate against him and, despite the fact that finances forced their withdrawal, urged all socialists to 'abstain from voting and working in this mock election for Mabon [Abraham's bardic name] as a protest against his industrial and political action'.[87] From 1911 onwards there was an independent labour organisation established and the unofficial reform movement in the South Wales Miners' Federation found itself a solid base in a mid-Rhondda from where in 1912 *The Miners' Next Step* trumpeted recall of MPs, reorganisation and reform as the platform for wider action. The Mid-Rhondda Trades and Labour Council had pressed for local Labour councillors to give an account of their stewardship twice a year at public meetings, 'with the aim of nursing the electors in the importance of having Labour men in our Councils',[88] two years before the articulation of ideologies and plans of action in that famous pamphlet tilted, from a real strength, at the amorphous hegemony of a society whose public face had been more vulgarly marked on the night of the riots.

The riots laid bare the underlying shape of the mid-Rhondda community Structural alterations would prove a longer process. On the 1911 Rhondda Urban District Council, out of a total of thirty seats, nine were held by Labour men, four by nominees of the coal-owners, four by representatives of the building trade, three by shopkeepers, two by doctors, two by clergy, two by publicans and brewers, and two by independents. At the 1912 elections Labour representation increased to thirteen, but only nine of these were avowed socialists.[89] Those who were brought before the courts for intimidating non-unionists or for theft were imprisoned or fined and treated to the magistrate's line in moral homilies: he told Thomas Richards, fined £1 because he had stolen coal from a truck in the Glamorgan Colliery yard to light a fire for his wife and three children, that strikers had been warned of 'the gravity of such offences'; William Morgan, who stole clothes from an outfitters to pawn and was given three weeks in gaol for his pains, was informed that his theft was 'an extremely mean one'; and a fifteen-year-old caught pawning goods taken from J. R. Evans, draper, on the night of 8 November was fined £2, bound over for a year and made to attend regularly the Sunday school which had not seen him since the strike began. Will John and John Hopla, who had spearheaded the combine strike, were given twelve-month sentences (later reduced to eight) for their part in the last disturbances of 1911.[90] With blame apportioned as far as leaders could be singled out and the strikers back in work on the price-list they had spurned in October 1910, the management applied salt to smarting wounds. They issued strict orders that the men, out for almost a year, should handle most carefully all horses since the latter's long lay-off would have softened them. A haulier, who was dismissed for alleged disobedience and for hitting a farrier in the course of this, was summonsed for assault. Lleufer Thomas, extending his all-encompassing brief, remarked that 'it was absolutely essential that discipline should be maintained at the colliery by the officials'. The haulier was gaoled for six weeks.[91] At the Cambrian Colliery offices current rent and back rent for houses not owned by the company itself were deducted from pay without the employees' consent.[92] These were the bitter fruits of defeat, while for those policemen who had distinguished themselves in action came the rewards of promotion: three inspectors became superintendents and seven sergeants made inspector. They put something into the district, too – a paternity case brought by a Clydach Vale waitress, deprived of her wedding-ring and delivered of a male child born on 29 August 1911, and Inspector (formerly Sergeant) James Davies of Mumbles near Swansea, who 'stands 6' 2" in height and has a physique of commanding appearance', now to be utilised in Tonypandy.[93]

The sum total of these stabilisers had a swift outcome, for just before Christmas 1911 those traders whose advertisements had noticeably diminished in the course of the year now severally announced 'Tonypandy's Great Shopping Week'. For fathers and mothers, they pronounced, 'Santa Claus is undoubtedly the shopkeeper and Tonypandy tradesmen are doing their best to attract them' – 'young men looking at the windows of Messrs Jones and Evans, outfitters, Tonypandy, cannot fail to notice something to their taste... Their range of mufflers is claimed to be the finest in the Valley'; 'The chemists generally seem to have almost forgotten that they ever were chemists and have apparently entered into a league with Santa Claus with the idea of supplying everyone with a present of some description.'[94]

The echoes of 8 November did not however die away easily. In early 1913 the Glamorgan Colliery doctors, who were being pushed unwillingly into a new local medical scheme in the wake of Lloyd George's National Health Insurance Act, clashed publicly with the local lodge committee, which withdrew repayment of debts incurred since November 1910, because the doctors would not reveal their accounts nor allow a medical committee elected by the men any direct control of their payments.[95] The question of control could no longer be divorced from the issue of ownership or the nature of community. It was the apparent disintegration of the latter, depicted as the loss of moderation through the decline of religion and of

'Welshness', that underlies the more detailed probings and recommendations of the government's commissioners into industrial strife in 1917:

> the Rhondda has an abundance of cinemas and music halls, but not a single theatre. Owing to the absence of municipal centres and centralised institutions, the development of the civic spirit and the sense of social solidarity – what we may in short call the community sense – is seriously retarded.[96]

The Miners' Next Step (1912) with its 'No-leadership' proposals had been a conscious attempt to find an organisational framework in which the collectivity of action and sacrifice expressed in 1910 and 1911 would not be either controlled, other than by its own volition, or dissipated. The working class of mid-Rhondda in 1910 did not, could not, own its own self as yet, but it was, as it demonstrated through industrial struggle and social crisis, its own self. And with this self-knowledge new definitions of community could come.[97]

Notes

1. Josephine Tey, *The Daughter of Time* (London, 1976), pp. 94-5. This was originally published in 1951.

2. See David Smith, 'Myth and Meaning in the Literature of the South Wales Coalfield: The 1930s', *Anglo-Welsh Review*, xxv (1976), pp. 21-42.

3. For the role of Tonypandy in, respectively, the economic and political development of South Wales, see L. J. Williams, 'The Road to Tonypandy', *Llafur*, i (1973), pp. 3-14; K. O. Morgan, 'The New Liberalism and the Challenge of Labour: The Welsh Experience, 1885-1929', Welsh Hist Rev, vi (1973), pp. 288-312.

4. Martin Barclay, '"Slaves of the Lamp": The Aberdare Miners' Strike, 1910', *Llafur*, ii (1978), pp. 24-42.

5. The confusion has lingered on. See *The Times*, 21 Sept, 3, 10 Oct, 1978; *The Guardian*, 15 Oct, 1978.

6. Randolph S. Churchill, *Winston S. Churchill: Young Statesman, 1901-1914*, 5 vols. (London, 1966-76), ii, pp. 373-8, 386; Henry Pelling, *Winston Churchill* (London, 1974), pp. 136-7.

7. *Colliery Strike Disturbances in South Wales: Correspondence and Report, November 1910*, Parliamentary Papers (hereafter PP), 1911 [5568], lxiv, pp. 7-10; K. O. Fox, 'The Tonypandy Riots', *Army Quart and Defence Jl*, civ (1973), pp. 72-8; J. M. McEwen, 'Tonypandy: Churchill's Albatross', *Queens Quart*, lxxviii (1971), pp. 83-94.

8. Eugen Weber, *Peasants into Frenchmen: The Modernisation of Rural France, 1870-1914* (London, 1977), is a salutary, though less comforting, corrective to the sociological pattern-making of M. G. Hechter, *Internal Colonialism: The Celtic Fringe in British National Development, 1536-1966* (London, 1975).

9.   See Brinley Thomas, 'The Migration of Labour into the Glamorganshire Coalfield, 1861-1911', and J. Hamish Richards and J. Parry Lewis, 'Housebuilding in the South Wales Coalfield, 1851-1913', in W. E. Minchinton (ed), *Industrial South Wales*, 1750 1914 (London, 1969), pp. 37-56, 235-48; G. M. Holmes, 'The South Wales Coal Industry, 1850-1914', *Trans Hon Soc Cymmrodorion* (1976), pp. 162-207; W. D. Rubinstein, 'Wealth, Elites and the Class Structure of Modern Britain', *Past and Present*, no 76 (Aug 1977), pp. 99-126, points out that for South Wales there were two millionaires in the period 1809-58 but five for 1858-1914 (Table 2, p. 105); for Wales and the Atlantic economy, see Brinley Thomas, *Migration and Economic Growth: A Study of Great Britain and the Atlantic Economy* (Cambridge, 1954); Brinley Thomas, Migration and Urban Growth (London, 1972), pp. 170-81; H. Stanley Jevons, *The British Coal Trade* (London, 1915), pp. 660-93.

10.   There is still no complete account of the Revival. My own characterisation is based on Henri Bois, *Le reveil en Pays de Galles* (Toulouse, 1907); J. Rogues de Fursac, *Un mouvement mystique contemporain: le reveil religieux en Pays de Galles* (Paris, 1907); David Jenkins, *The Agricultural Community of South-West Wales at the Turn of the Twentieth Century* (Cardiff, 1971), ch. 9. A general review is offered by Basil Hall, 'The Welsh Revival of 1904-05: A Critique', in G. J. Cuming and Derek Baker (eds), *Popular Belief and Practice* (Cambridge, 1972), pp. 291-301.

11.   Quoted in Churchill, *op cit*, ii, p. 375.

12.   For different, but confirmatory, perspectives on the semiology of riot, see William M. Reddy, 'The Textile Trade and the Language of the Crowd at Rouen, 1752-1871', *Past and Present*, no. 74 (Feb 1977), pp. 62-89; Richard J. Evans, '"Red Wednesday" in Hamburg: Social

Democrats, Police and Lumpenproletariat in the Suffrage Disturbances of 17 January 1906', *Social Hist*, iv (1979), pp. 1-31.

13. Detail on 'abnormal places', the minimum-wage issue and falling productivity can be found in Williams, 'The Road to Tonypandy'; Rhodri Walters, 'Labour Productivity in the South Wales Steam-Coal Industry, 1870-1914', *Econ Hist Rev*, 2nd ser, xxviii (1975), pp. 280-303; accounts of the Cambrian Combine strike are in Ness Edwards, *History of the South Wales Miners' Federation* (London, 1938), pp. 33-49; R. Page Arnot, *South Wales Miners*, 1898-1914 (London, 1967), pp. 174-273.

14. On D. A. Thomas (1856-1918), Liberal MP, coal-owner and future Lord Rhondda, see K. O. Morgan, 'D. A. Thomas: The Industrialist as Politician', in Stewart Williams (ed), *Glamorgan Historian*, 11 vols (Cowbridge, 1963-75), iii, pp. 33-51.

15. E. D. Lewis, *The Rhondda Valleys* (London, 1959), pp. 89-91; Jevons, *op cit*, pp. 320-2. The numbers employed at the collieries were Cambrian (4,054), Glamorgan (4,142), Naval (2,144), Britannic Merthyr (790): *Rhondda Leader*, 5 Nov, 1910.

16. Arnot, *op cit*, pp. 181-3.

17. The history of the joint committee is sketched in *The Rhondda Socialist Newspaper: Being the Bomb of the Rhondda Workers*, no. 1 (19 Aug, 1911).

18. Leonard Llewellyn (born 1874) was from a coal-owning family in the neighbouring Cynon valley. He had studied 'industrial methods' in Europe, Asia and America: Arthur Mee (ed), *Who's Who in Wales* (Cardiff, 1921), p. 290.

19. This summary has been assembled from *Rhondda Leader*, 12 Nov, 1910; *Western Mail*, 8 Nov, 1910; *South Wales Daily News*, 8 Nov, 1910. Subsequent newspaper references are to the nine volumes of newspaper cuttings

that relate to the Cambrian Combine strike in the Glamorgan Record Office (hereafter Glam RO). D/D NCB.

20.   Daniel Lleufer Thornas (born 1863) was the epitome of that socially-aware class of functionaries which nineteenth-century Wales bred to service its new society. He was secretary to the Welsh Land Commission of 1893, stipendiary magistrate for Pontypridd and Rhondda from 1909, president of the School of Social Service and of the WEA in Wales, and a leading member of the 1917 Commission into Industrial Unrest. See the entry by David Williams in *Dictionary of Welsh Biography* (London, 1959), pp. 939-40.

21.   *Western Mail*, 9 Nov, 1910; *South Wales Daily News*, 9 Nov, 1910; *Rhondda Leader*, 12 Nov, 1910.

22.   David Evans, *Labour Strife in the South Wales Coalfield, 1910-1911* (Cardiff, 1911; repr Cardiff, 1963). Evans was the industrial correspondent of the *Western Mail* and the future biographer of D. A. Thomas.

23.   There is the exception of Bob Holton, *British Syndicalism, 1900-1914* (London, 1976), who states 'it is clear that the looting of shops was more than the random violence of the rampaging mob' (p. 82), though he follows Evans in the view that 'Strikers, beaten back from the colliery by police, expressed their bitterness and frustration by looting shops' (p. 81).

24.   Evans, op. cit., pp. 40-9; *Rhondda Leader*, 5, 12 Nov, 1910; *Western Mail*, 8, 9 Nov, 1910; *South Wales Daily News*, 9 Nov, 1910; transcript of an interview with ex-PC W. Knipe, 1973: Oral History Collection, South Wales Miners' Lib, Swansea (hereafter SWML).

25.   *Western Mail*, 9 Nov, 1910. According to David Evans, of course, such events could not have taken place until after the crowd had been 'repulsed'.

26.   *Rhondda Leader*, 12 Nov, 1910; *Western Mail*, 9 Nov, 1910.

27. *Rhondda Leader*, 12 Nov, 1910.

28. *Colliery Strike Disturbances in South Wales*, 1910, p. 49.

29. The leading 'syndicalists' in Rhondda were Noah Ablett and Noah Rees, both of whom had been at Ruskin College, Oxford, before helping to establish the Marxist Central Labour College in 1909. They motivated the writing of *The Miners' Next Step* in 1912. However, Ablett was not directly involved in the Cambrian Combine while Rees and W. H. Mainwaring (both influenced by Ablett at the time), though active members and officials of the Cambrian Colliery lodge and the joint committee, did not dominate the conduct of the strike, whose principal leaders were Will John, John Hopla and Tom Smith. John was secretary of the Glamorgan Colliery and of the Mid-Rhondda Trades and Labour Council as well as being chairman of the joint Cambrian Combine committee. He was a prominent Welsh-speaking Baptist. After imprisonment in 1911 he was elected miners' agent and then Labour MP for Rhondda West in 1922. Hopla, chairman of the Glamorgan Colliery lodge and also imprisoned, was elected to the executive of the South Wales Miners' Federation in 1911. Tom Smith, check-weigher of the Naval Colliery lodge, too, became an executive council member as did, in turn, Rees, Ablett and Mainwaring (MP for Rhondda East, 1933-59). All these men, with the exception of Ablett, were, or became, closely associated with representative politics at local and parliamentary level. See *South Wales Daily News*, 24 Apr, 1911; for Ablett and John, see Joyce Bellamy and John Saville (eds), *Dictionary of Labour Biography*, 5 vols (London, 1972-9), i, p. 195, and ii, pp. 1-3. More background information that illuminates the complex nature of 'Welsh syndicalism' is in Richard Lewis, 'South Wales Miners and the Ruskin College Strike of 1909', *Llafur*, ii (1976), pp. 57-72; David Egan, 'The Unofficial

Reform Committee and *The Miners' Next Step'*, *Llafur*, ii (1978), pp. 64-80.

30. Cambrian Colliery lodge minutes, 21 Nov, 1910: SWML; *Rhondda Leader*, 26 Nov, 1910; *Justice*, 18 Nov, 1910; *The 'Plebs' Mag*, Dec, 1910; *Western Mail*, 14 Nov, 1910; *Labour Leader*, 18 Nov, 1910; *South Wales Daily News*, 17 Nov, 1910. The minutes are of the colliery and not the Cambrian Combine Committee whose deliberations, along with those of the other individual collieries concerned, have not been traced.

31. *Rhondda Leader*, 12 Nov, 1910.

32. *Western Mail*, 13 June, 1911.

33. *Rhondda Leader*, 12 Nov, 1910.

34. *Western Mail*, 8 Nov, 1910; *Globe*, 8 Nov, 1910.

35. *Rhondda Leader*, 12 Nov, 1910.

36. *South Wales Daily News*, 10 Nov, 1910.

37. *Ibid*, 12 Nov, 1910; *Western Mail*, 9 Nov, 1910.

38. *Rhondda Leader*, 12 Nov, 1910. For the social significance of Welsh rugby, see David Smith and Gareth Williams, *Fields of Praise* (Cardiff, 1980).

39. Transcript of interview with Bryn Lewis, 1973: SWML.

40. *Rhondda Leader*, 19 Nov, 1910.

41. *South Wales Daily News*, 10, 24 Nov, 1910.

42. Lewis, *The Rhondda Valleys*, pp. 81-3.

43. *Commission of Enquiry into Industrial Unrest... Report of the Commissioners for Wales including Monmouthshire*, PP, 1917 [8668], xv, p. 6.

44. Harold Carter, *The Towns of Wales* (Cardiff, 1966), pp. 326-31.

45. Lewis, *The Rhondda Valleys*, pp. 224-7; *Kelly's Directory of Monmouthshire and South Wales* (London, 1914).

46. *Rhondda Leader*, 15 Jan, 26 Nov, 24 Dec, 1910; 'Socialism and Syndicalism: The Welsh Miners' Debate', ed K. O. Morgan, *Bull Soc Study of Labour Hist*, no. 30 (1975), pp. 22-37.

47. Reports of the medical officer of health to Rhondda Urban District Council, 1910-11: Rhondda Borough Council Offices; Lewis, *The Rhondda Valleys*, pp. 229-33; John B. Hilling, *Cardiff and the Valleys* (London, 1973), pp. 100-2; Reynolds Newspaper, 27 Nov, 1910.

48. Mid-Rhondda Trades and Labour Council minutes, 27 July 1910: National Lib of Wales (hereafter NLW).

49. See Rhys Davies' evocative autobiography, *Print of a Hare's Foot* (London, 1969), pp. 8-12.

50. Mid-Rhondda Grocers' Association minutes, 5 May, 9, 30 June 1909: NLW.

51. *South Wales Daily News*, 6 Feb, 1896.

52. *Ibid*, 7 Feb. 1896.

53. *Rhondda Leader*, 7 May 1910. Meetings of the Mid-Rhondda Chamber of Trade were reported regularly but I have been unable to find any extant minute-books.

54. Rhondda UDC minutes, 24 May, 22 July, 9 Sept, 1910, 10 Feb, 10 Mar, 9 June 1911: Rhondda Borough Council Offices.

55. *Rhondda Leader*, 15 Jan, 1910.

56. Nevil Macready, *Annals of an Active Life*, 2 vols (London, 1924), i, p. 140. For a withering look at the excessive prandial tendencies of Rhondda's bourgeoisie, see Sir Wyndham Childs (then a captain under Macready), *Episodes and Reflections* (London, 1930), pp. 79-80.

57. Diary books of Lionel Lindsay: Glam RO. These are not a complete run, though they stretch from 1889 to 1941; the one for 1910 is missing.

58. *Rhondda Leader*, 12 Nov, 1910.

59. *Ibid*, 17, 24 Dec, 1910; *Western Mail*, 15, 17 Dec. 1910.

60. *South Wales Daily News*, 11 Mar, 1911; *South Wales Echo*, 19 May, 1911.

61. *Rhondda Leader*, 15 Jan, 16 July, 1910.

62. See *Rhondda Leader*, 1 Jan, 1910, and weekly throughout 1910 and 1911; Cyril Batstone, *Old Rhondda in Photographs* (Barry, 1974).

63. Lewis, *The Rhondda Valleys*, p. 280.

64. Reports of the medical officer of health to Rhondda Urban District Council, 1900-9.

65. *Rhondda Leader*, 9 July, 12 Nov, 1910; Batstone, *op cit*, plate 88.

66. This was argued forcibly by H. S. Jevons (resident in South Wales, 1904-14) in *South Wales Daily News*, 12 Nov, 1910.

67. *Rhondda Leader*, 26 Mar, 30 July 1910.

68. *Ibid*, 13 Aug. 1910.

69. *Ibid*, 9 July 1910. He was addressing the National Association of Colliery Managers in Cardiff.

70. *Rhondda Socialist Newspaper*, no. 3 (Oct. 1911).

71. *Rhondda Leader*, 10, 17 Sept, 1910; Mid-Rhondda Grocers' Association minutes, 6 Apr, 1910.

72. *Rhondda Leader*, 17 Sept, 29 Oct, 1910. The Mid-Rhondda Chamber of Trade was anxious to dispel the rumours circulating to the effect that tradespeople, in the event of a strike, would 'stop shop'.

73. *Ibid*, 5 Nov, 1910.

74. Mid-Rhondda Trades and Labour Council minutes, 1 Dec, 1909, 9 Feb, 1910, 25 Oct, 1911; Rhondda UDC minutes, 11 Nov, 15, 29 Dec, 1910.

75. *Rhondda Leader*, 9 Dec, 1905.

76. Special Report of the Health Committee re the Housing Accommodation of the District, and upon the Housing, Town Planning Act 1909, nd, in Rhondda UDC minutes.

77. *Rhondda Leader*, 24 June, 1911. Rate books for Rhondda do not survive for the years before 1968. There is considerable corroborating evidence of this multi-house ownership (for example, J. R. Evans, draper, leased twelve houses; Emrys Richards, chemist, leased six) in

the lease rentals for 1909, Dunraven Estate Papers 184: NLW.

78. *South Wales Daily News*, 9 Nov, 1910.

79. *Western Mail*, 9 Nov, 1910.

80. *Rhondda Leader*, 12 Nov, 1910; *Western Mail*, 9 Nov, 1910; *South Wales Daily News*, 9 Nov, 1910. Subsequently ninety-six claims for damages were assessed: *Rhondda Leader*, 11 Mar. 1911.

81. *Sunday Times*, 13 Nov, 1910.

82. *Drapers' Records*, 19 Nov, 1910. Eight drapers suffered extensive damage.

83. *Rhondda Leader*, 12 Nov, 1910.

84. *The Times*, 23 Nov, 1910.

85. *Rhondda Leader*, 1 Apr, 1911.

86. Rhondda UDC minutes, 9 Sept, 1910.

87. *Rhondda Leader*, 17 Dec, 1910.

88. Mid-Rhondda Trades and Labour Council minutes, 23 Feb, 1910.

89. *Rhondda Socialist Newspaper*, no. 10 (30 Mar, 1912). The Urban District Council had banned the use of public halls for secular meetings in late 1910 to the fury of the socialists, who protested at this restriction. See *Rhondda Leader*, 21 Jan, 1911; Mid-Rhondda Trades and Labour Council minutes, 20 Dec, 1910.

90. *Rhondda Leader*, 31 Dec, 1910, 6 May, 3 June, 11 Nov, 1911; *South Wales Echo*, 10 Mar, 1911.

91. *South Wales Daily News*, 17, 20 Oct, 1911.

92. *Western Mail*, 24, 27 Oct, 1911.

93. *Ibid*, 20 Oct. 1911; *Rhondda Leader*, 29 Dec, 1911.

94. *Rhondda Leader*, 16 Dec, 1911.

95. *Ibid*, 8 Jan, 1913.

96. Commission of Enquiry into Industrial Unrest, 1917, p. 12. Lleufer Thomas, who headed the commission in Wales, was not concerned only with the effect of 'alien' ideologies on 'retarded' Rhondda intellects – in 1913 he

rejected the defence, on aesthetic grounds, of a barber prosecuted for exhibiting 'indecent postcards' because 'what would appeal to the artistic mind in Paris would not have the same influence in Tonypandy': *South Wales Daily News*, 22 Jan, 1913.

97.   For an analysis and account of the actual 'solidarity' and community sense that enveloped south Wales after 1918, see Hywel Francis and David Smith, *The Fed: A History of the South Wales Miners in the Twentieth Century* (London, 1980).

Framers

At the end of a book as insistently personal as this one, doubts about the accuracy of intermeshing a public world with a life story readily occur. So, it was with some consternation that I followed up a reference, in David Kynaston's chronicle of 1950s' life, *Family Britain 1951–57* (2009), to an article by the great journalist, Geoffrey Goodman, in *The New Statesman* of 26 April 1952. It was entitled 'The Rhondda: 1952'. How would it tally with the native memories of a seven-year-old boy? Would its perspective from an adult contemporary world simply contradict my sense of growing up as lines of force intersected? I read it more than half-a-century later with a relief that gave way to delight. It had tapped into the resource of that place and time in such a fresh way as to become another source for memory-in-society:

> Pumping life back into these blackened valleys has
> not been easy. The planners have had to deal with

437

more than finance and blueprints. A fresh soul had to be built. They have had to build it up as a foundation of memories which would come bursting back from the past...

Yet prosperity – in the relative sense of course – has crept on the valleys almost unnoticed: it has grown like the mass over the slag heaps until the young ones accept it as if it had always been there and the older ones – still the majority – regard it with a certain ironical scepticism. They are the legatees of desolation.

[But if] you go to the Rhondda [today] in search of fear, doubts, a morbid preoccupation with the ghosts of the Thirties... you will in fact be quite out of step. Of course the miners I spoke to at the big Lewis Merthyr pit [which became the site of the Rhondda Heritage park in 1989] wonder what the Tories will do, and Tonypandy still shows you, with that harsh bitter pride, the scars of 1911 – and the equally tangible scars of the Thirties. But now there is a present as well as a past. Life is different today.... Businesses in Pontypridd, which nestles in the hollow where three valley converge is... a remarkable testimony to a revolution in social standards and social tastes.... New clothing shops, food stores, electrical and radio shops have all elbowed their way into the cramped hub of the town.... Glass and chrome bars have come to the valleys' market town and over rough cobbled streets run high-heeled shoes, nylons and West End Drapes. It is a far cry from 1933.

When we sat in the colliery manager's room at

the famous Naval pit and discussed the changed times – the lodge chairman and secretary, a collier, a Coal Board official and the manager, chatting away like old colleagues – this seemed in itself proof of the long road from Tonypandy.... But you must not think that the job is even half finished. The surface has been scratched and we have found a healthy race of humans. Now they must build, without fear. But, as Edward Evans said, while we sat in the canteen at the Lewis Merthyr pit, 'The Tories, what do you think they will do? Anxious? Yes I suppose it's in the stomach, it lies deep, you know.' For what politicians have done can be undone.

*

My sources have been oral, visual, written, pictorial, spatial, olfactory, auditory and memorial. They colour the text throughout. For those who want to dive and delve further and deeper, here is a thematic guide to those who helped frame the whole and where more detailed references can be found.

On photography and photographers I have made direct use of Eugene Smith's notepad entries which I consulted in the National Archive for Creative Photography at the University of Arizona in Tucson. I derived information and insights, in equal measure, from Ben Maddow, *Let Truth Be the Prejudice, W. Eugene Smith: His Life and Photographs* (An Aperture Book, 1985) and Jim Hughes, *W. Eugene Smith: Shadow and Substance* (McGraw Hill, New York 1989). I interviewed John G. Morris, the picture editor for *Life* in London in the Second World War, for my

BBC4 film *The Lost Pictures of Eugene Smith* in 2005, and consulted his truly illuminating memoir *Get the Picture: A Personal History of Photojournalism* (University of Chicago, 2002). For Robert Frank I found Philip Brookman's essay, and quotes, in the volume *Robert Frank: London/Wales, 1951-53* (Corcoron Gallery of Art, Washington DC, 2003), which he edited, as invaluable as seeing the pictures on display in the Tate Modern in 2004. There were insightful essays, too, in *Robert Frank: Moving Out* (National Gallery of Art, Washington DC, 1994), edited by Brookman and Sarah Greenough. The quote from Glyn Morgan's letter of 1950 can be found in Peter Lord's *Winifred Coombe Tennant: A Life Through Art* (National Library of Wales, 2007). Dr Paul Cabutt, photographer and historian, re-constructed for his PhD research the possible photographic essay Eugene Smith might have envisaged for Coedely, and kindly allowed me to see it.

On actors and acting, there was Robert Shail's *Stanley Baker: A Life in Film* (University of Wales Press, 2008) and Peter Stead's *Acting Wales* (University of Wales, 2002). On historians and Merthyr, we have Mario Basini's enchanting *Real Merthyr* (Seren, 2009), *Degrees of Influence: Glanmor Williams*, edited by Geraint H. Jenkins and Gareth Elwyn Jones (UWP, 2008) and, as memoirs, by, respectively, Glan and Gwyn A. Williams, *Glanmor Williams: A Life* (UWP, 2002) and *Fishers of Men: Stories Towards an Autobiography* (Gomer, 1996). On boxing and boxers, there is the chapter 'Focal Heroes' in my *Aneurin Bevan and the World of South Wales* (UWP, 1994) and *Wales and Its Boxers: The Fighting Tradition*, (UWP, 2009), edited by Peter Stead and Gareth Williams, in which earlier versions of 'Boxing with Life' and 'The

Tonypandy Kid' first appeared. Rhys Evans' *Gwynfor Evans: A Portrait of a Patriot* (Y Lolfa, 2008) was illuminating on the relationship between the politician and his home town, Barry. On Bevan and Bevanism, the foundation of my article on Nye in the *New Oxford DNB* (OUP 2006) can be supplemented by the blind-side barbs of Woodrow Wyatt as quoted in 'Nye: The Beloved Patrician' by David Llewellyn (*Western Mail* publication, 1960) and of Hugh Trevor-Roper in *Letters from Oxford: Hugh Trevor-Roper to Bernard Berenson*, edited by Richard Davenport-Hines (Phoenix, 2007). Finally, on South Wales, value systems and Native Americans, see Charles Taylor, 'A Different Kind of Courage' in *New York Review of Books*, Vol.iv, No. 7, 26 April 2007 and the wonderful book he therein reviewed, Jonathan Lear, *Radical Hope: Ethics in the Face of Cultural Devastation* (Harvard University Press, 2006).

And there is one last hurrah to make. I had sent Vernon Harding, whose face and pose is now forever immortalised in Eugene Smith's photograph of three generations of miners, a draft of my first chapter, 'No Through Route'. After nodding a recognition, and more, of the names and places I had written about, Vernon told me what he thought I was trying to do. He was right about the intent and I can only hope he, and now other readers of this book, think I did not mistake entirely 'those stories [which] live on in the memory and... play a part in shaping... life':

> If I understand the chapter correctly you are saying that these painters and photographers are making images, in their separate mediums, of scenes existing

in the Valleys at that time, the terraced streets cut into the hillsides, the railways and collieries, the flat-capped men gathered at street corners, the women scrubbing the front doorstep or washing the windows, the young children playing in the back alleys, the black slag heaps perched on the mountainsides. As you say it's a mirror image; if the mirror is dirty, or cracked, or hanging askew, they can only reproduce what is seen on the face.

But this is where the Writer, and the Historian, come into their own. They can look behind the mirror.

In the back gardens of those terraced houses, those same men planting and tending their rows of beans and lettuce, the rose bushes and dahlia blooms, against the back wall. In the evening dressed in blue serge, making their way to choir practice or maybe silver and brass band recitals. At Christmas time, making the rounds of those terraced streets, and standing, with their fingers bare to the cold, going through their repertoire while the coins chink merrily into the tin cup placed on the pavement. Those same women, in their flowered dresses, floppy hats and white gloves, accompanied by children with shiny faces... on their way to the local church or chapel.

The young men, members of the local teams, heading off for rugby or football training, or maybe catching the bus to attend evening classes at Treforest School of Mines, Ponty Market on a Saturday, the crowds thronging around the busy stalls, the friendly greetings, faggots and peas in the little café, or a cup of coffee in the nearby Bracchi's, the social life enriched by the families from Bardi. Walking the mountains, the noise and grime of the colliery left behind, quiet, the air fresh and clean, the mountain streams running clear and cold, the hawk and kite wheeling in the clear blue sky. There was a life behind the mirror, and it was a good life, peopled by men and women with values and aims that are too rarely seen today.

Acknowledgements

Principally to Helen Richards and to Lesley, Simone and the Berry family for permission to quote the letters and works of Alun Richards and Ron Berry. Similarly to Jeffrey Robinson for permission to quote the works of Gwyn Thomas and to Merryn Hemp, Ederyn Williams and Madawc Williams for permission to quote from the published and unpublished work of Raymond Williams. I am grateful to *Past and Present: A Journal of Historical Studies* in which 'Tonypandy 1910: Definitions of Community', first appeared in No. 87, May 1980. It resurfaces here as an inevitable centenary and personal capstone.

Once again Gwyneth Speller has proved indispensable in producing draft after word-processed draft, and her speed, care and attention have been critical. Penny Thomas has proved to be an editor sympathetic to intent and rigorously insistent on its lucid delivery. My thanks to my publisher, Richard Davies at Parthian, is a heartfelt salute to one of Wales' brightest cultural stars. Every network needs its informers and, amongst others, I need to thank my friends, old and new, in Charlie Burton and Vernon Harding. Professor Chris Williams, another old friend by now though he was just seventeen when we first met in 1981, commented on some earlier drafts. In many ways his work, especially his important *Democratic Rhondda* (1996), is taking our needed memory-in-society forward, and I am delighted he is doing it from my first, and last, university base in Wales, at Swansea. Finally, though I dedicate this book to our grandchildren, in the hope of their connected future to our past, the last word, though thanks here are inadequate of course, is to my Mam, Enid Wyn Smith neé Owen, who is, for me at least, the surviving link.

SERIES EDITOR: DAI SMITH

1	Ron Berry	So Long, Hector Bebb
2	Raymond Williams	Border Country
3	Gwyn Thomas	The Dark Philosophers
4	Lewis Jones	Cwmardy & We Live
5	Margiad Evans	Country Dance
6	Emyr Humphreys	A Man's Estate
7	Alun Richards	Home to an Empty House
8	Alun Lewis	In the Green Tree
9	Dannie Abse	Ash on a Young Man's Sleeve
10	Ed. Meic Stephens	Poetry 1900-2000
11	Ed. Gareth Williams	Sport: an anthology
12	Rhys Davies	The Withered Root
13	Dorothy Edwards	Rhapsody
14	Jeremy Brooks	Jampot Smith
15	George Ewart Evans	The Voices of the Children
16	Bernice Rubens	I Sent a Letter to My Love
17	Howell Davies	Congratulate the Devil
18	Geraint Goodwin	The Heyday in the Blood
19	Gwyn Thomas	The Alone to the Alone
20	Stuart Evans	The Caves of Alienation
21	Brenda Chamberlain	A Rope of Vines
22	Jack Jones	Black Parade
23	Alun Richards	Dai Country
24	Glyn Jones	The Valley, the City, the Village
25	Arthur Machen	The Great God Pan
26	Arthur Machen	The Hill of Dreams
27	Hilda Vaughan	The Battle to the Weak
28	Margiad Evans	Turf or Stone

WWW.LIBRARYOFWALES.ORG

LIBRARY OF WALES
titles are available to buy online at: